DATE DUE

Resht

Abbas

of Oman

cat

Rub al
(Empty qua

Muscat

Sana

Yemen

Taiz
Mokha

Aden

South Arabian Fed.

Gulf of Aden

Arabian Sea

Socotra

The United States and the Arab World

The American Foreign Policy Library

THE
UNITED STATES
AND THE
Arab World

REVISED EDITION

William R. Polk

HARVARD UNIVERSITY PRESS

Cambridge, Massachusetts

1969

For Ann—

There lies Syria

Foreword

BY CRANE BRINTON

This Foreword was written for the first edition in 1964, when Mr. Brinton was editor of the American Foreign Policy Library. He died on September 7, 1968. The new editor of the series is Edwin O. Reischauer.

The American Foreign Policy Library was founded in 1945 by Sumner Welles, then undersecretary of state, and Donald McKay, professor of history at Harvard, then on leave with the Office of Strategic Services in its Research and Analysis branch. Both men had had direct experience of the relative unpreparedness of the United States for the grave responsibilities in international politics thrust on her by the war. They designed the Library primarily as a series of handbooks directed toward the formation and guidance of an enlightened public opinion on important and difficult problems of American relations with specific countries or areas. One of the first volumes issued was *The United States and the Near East* (1947) by E. A. Speiser of the University of Pennsylvania, then a colleague of Professor McKay's with Research and Analysis in the OSS. Professor Speiser, a distinguished historian of the ancient Near East, had excavated and traveled widely in the region. During the war he had concentrated on the study of the area's modern and contemporary aspects. His book, which very successfully achieved the compromise between the scholarly monograph and the broad popularization of journalism that the Library aims at, has long been out of print. Moreover, it dealt with an area in which fundamental changes in the last two decades have been at least as significant as those in any other part of the world. The essentially contemporary character of the Library required that our treatment of the Near East be brought up to date.

The present editor, with the kind consent of Professor Speiser, who has returned to his studies of ancient history, decided to divide the materials of the original study into two books, one on the United States and Israel and another on the United States and

the rest of the old Arab World. The first, written by Nadav
Safran of Harvard, appeared in 1963. The second, by William R.
Polk of the Policy Planning Council of the State Department,* is
now before the reader.

Dr. Polk has lived in the region he writes about, and has gone
successfully through a long apprenticeship in Arabic and Islamic
studies. He has that intimate personal knowledge of what he
writes about that the founders of the Library regarded as essential
in their writers. He has also something even more important than
technical mastery of language and history and personal experience
of the lands and peoples he deals with; in discussing this very
important region, divided by the moral dilemmas set by the
establishment of Israel as an independent nation in the heart of
the Arab World, Dr. Polk maintains the detachment of the
scholar, the fairness of the judge. Such an attitude is not easy to
achieve toward the basic problem of Israel and the Arabs, a
problem in one sense like that of the Spanish Civil War in the
1930's, a *cas de conscience* for many Westerners of our time.
Dr. Polk's is not an attitude of indifference, let alone one of "a
plague o' both your houses." He likes and understands the people
he writes about, but his sentiments do not stand in the way of his
judgment. For the United States, involved directly ever since
the war in the manifold problems of the Arab World, of which,
as the reader will see, that of Israel is only one, the importance
of the region has increased rather than diminished since Dr.
Speiser's book appeared in 1947. It is a pleasure to welcome to
the Library Dr. Polk's fine book.

---

* In 1965, Mr. Polk left the State Department to become Professor of History and Director of the Center of Middle Eastern Studies at the University
of Chicago and Director of the Adlai Stevenson Institute.

Preface to the Revised Edition

BY WILLIAM R. POLK

October 1968

This is the second edition of a book first published in 1965. Differences between the two versions reflect changes on various fronts in the last four years.

When the first edition was being prepared, I was a member of the Policy Planning Council of the State Department. In that post, I was necessarily restrained from speaking with complete candor about the policies of the United States government and of other governments. That restraint no longer exists. In 1965 I resigned from the State Department to become Professor of History and Director of the Center of Middle Eastern Studies at the University of Chicago. Within the frame of scholarship, therefore, I can now speak openly and, in a special sense, "irresponsibly" about government policies.

In the period since the first edition appeared, radical changes have occurred in the shape of world politics—though, paradoxically, not in the Middle East itself. It has remained a volatile, crisis-haunted place. It has been convulsed by the Arab-Israeli war. But its basic pattern was not overturned by the impact of the new events. To explain the nature of this paradox, as well as to gauge how far the Middle East has in fact changed, a new appraisal of the area is in order.

Such an appraisal is doubly necessary because changing events force students of international affairs to correct their angle of vision on the Middle East specifically and on the dynamics of world politics generally. The case will be amplified later in this book when I take up the concept of "national interest." A short-hand statement of the matter is all that is being offered here.

Some scholars still tend to analyze other nations' international affairs without reference to domestic political constraints. They assume that the foreign policy actions of a given nation necessarily

draw their motive force from a rational grasp of "national interests." If Nation A, for example, has an interest in the territory,
passage, production capabilities, or potential hostility of Nation B,
these objects of interest are assumed to control the foreign policy
of Nation A. Since the "geo-political" interests of Nation A can
be plotted and evaluated—as they are in the simulated conditions
of "war-gaming"—then if its politicians fail to act in the light of
those interests, they are either stupid or perverse.

Events of the last four years command students of foreign
affairs to see and draw a distinction between two countervailing
forces in the foreign policy field. One force is comprised of the
interests of *nations*. The other force is comprised of the interests
of *governments*. The interests of nations are generally compelling,
though they may be inarticulate, vague, or even blind in their
specific expression. The interests of governments, for their part,
are seldom made explicit when a grand strategy in foreign policy
is being enunciated, yet they often determine the specific actions a
government can or will take and those a government will avoid.
Such actions and inactions often run counter to the more abstract
interests of the nation.

Egypt is an appropriate illustration. Egypt may have a *national*
interest in making peace with Israel as a general proposition. Yet
the Egyptian *government* may be unable in a specific circumstance
to guide its action by that national interest for fear that the government itself may not be able to survive the domestic popular
reaction. The case here (and many other illustrations from other
countries can be cited), adds force to the following simple proposition: while factors of national interest are the general preconditions for international relations, the form the relations actually
take is primarily determined by the domestic face of intergovernmental *political* relationships.

The essentially artificial distinction between domestic and foreign affairs gives rise to another consideration. I feel that many
students of international relations need to align the quality of their
perceptions about international affairs with the higher quality of
their perceptions about their own domestic affairs.

Take our own case as Americans. We know or think we know

why and how people act in Chicago. We have refined this knowledge into a quasi-science of political prediction. In the practice of that science we respect the complex factors which enter in our own political decisions. We identify not only classes, ethnic groups, and religious affiliations, but pressure groups, personal preferences, and individual experiences. These are "inside" views. But when we shift our gaze to the political dynamics of a second nation, we often fail to see how the nuances of individual action and opinion within its decision-making process shape its decisions. We blur these nuances and present the decisions of the second nation as though they stemmed from robot-like mechanistic forces.

Similarly, when we stand within our own culture and look at its decisions, we know that they often proceed on irrational grounds or at least on grounds that are left unstated or which are only vaguely related to the point at issue. We know that the decisive factors in the management of our practical affairs often tend to be considerations of an immediate and personal nature rather than grand value concepts of politics. We know, for example, that Mr. Jones can vote Democratic not because he believes in the philosophy of the Democratic party, but rather because he lives in the fifth ward or has a brother who works in the post office. But we rarely make the same allowances when we look at the play of politics in a second nation. We rarely assign a proper importance to the minutiae of this nation's politics. Rather, we envision its issues and events in condensed and abstracted forms.

We can hope to correct this kind of distortion only by accumulating a greater amount of detailed information about the second nation in view. Yet in doing this, we face a danger from another side. If, in accumulating added information, we fail to ask the right questions about the second nation, the results of our added information can prove to be worse than useless. Wrong questions coupled with correct answers can set in train a movement toward bad decisions. For example, if we view the process of national development solely in economic terms, we ask economics-oriented questions. The answers we get may be correct. But in failing to give due weight to many other elements that are or must be part of the developmental process, we can embark on policies which actually impede or derail a nation's development.

Iraq in the 1950's is a case in point. The avenue of approach to this country's national development was almost exclusively economic in nature. While correct economic measures were forthcoming, the neglect of a host of other matters led to grave social and political troubles. Events culminated in the 1958 bloody revolution, which virtually destroyed the development program.

Another kind of faulty perception commonly found among students of international relations can be called a "folks is folks" or non-cultural approach to foreign affairs. Secure within our own culture, directed and conditioned by its imperatives, we assume a "norm" for behavior—the norm being our own culture—within which we ask our political questions. However, when we view a second nation with a culture of its own, our perceptions can be disordered in two ways. We can neglect the cultural context entirely and thereby fail to understand the specific political demands it makes. Or, alternatively, we can become so absorbed in grasping and appreciating the exotic elements of the alien culture *as* a culture, that we fail to see the importance of cultural factors for the internal political relationships of the nation in question.

A reviewer, for example, criticized the first edition of this book on the ground that it dwelled too long on the cultural context in which Arab political affairs unfold. I remain unmoved by this line of criticism. On the contrary, experiences of the last four years have strengthened my initial conviction that unless the cultural context for politics is understood, nothing significant can be said about Arab political affairs or about the relations between the United States and the Arab world. I assert with added conviction that if we are to understand how and why people act as they do, we must first pose and answer *intra*-cultural and *intra*-system questions and only then proceed to pose and answer *inter*-cultural and *inter*-system questions. The sequence, as stated, is the one followed in this book.

Even if an observer accepts a dual view of culture—the "them and us" view of the world—his view of a second culture may be distorted by the difference in the angle of vision he brings to it and the one he brings to his own culture. Unless his perception is sharpened by studies of diverse cultures, the observer will almost inevitably tend to compare the alien cultural system towards which he is an aloof outsider, with the system where he is an inside participant. When he looks at the alien system, he sees things in a more self-aware way, and in a form which he has consciously organized for his own understanding. When he looks at his own system, his understanding of forces on the move around him tends to be loosely organized, subjective, with but a limited degree of intellectual self-awareness. We see this most clearly in a comparison of his learning processes; the alien culture requires years of conscious application whereas his own is absorbed through his pores. The difference between the two experiences poses real but perhaps unperceived problems of measurement.

To get at the nature of these problems, we can look closely at an American observer. Since he comes from a culture in which personal dignity, for example, is generally assumed, he will tend to be as little aware of its active force as he is of the air he breathes. On the other hand, he will find it curious or "oriental" that a value like "face" should play a strong part in the culture of another people he has objectively studied. His standards of comparison rather obviously need to be overhauled so that he will be able to "look in from the outside" on his own culture. If the overhaul is successful, he may come to see that at different times and in different situations, Americans—as well as the Japanese, the French, the Russians, and so on—act as if dignity were the most important of all human quests.

In the American case, of course, it is only when dignity appears to be threatened that it comes to the focus of political attention; otherwise, because it is taken for granted, it is not part of the vocabulary of day-to-day politics—that is, not for white, middle-class Americans. But for the submerged American Negro? He now sounds with quite a different political vocabulary. Indeed, there is much about contemporary American Negro politics which is no more and no less exotic than Arab politics. Dignity is as central an object of the Black Power movement as it is the object of any so-called oriental politics.

In a symmetrical way, the foregoing applies to the issue of violence. In the relatively peaceful and complacent years of the 1950's in America, we tended to deprecate the violent and transitory nature of African, Middle Eastern, and Latin American politics. Yet from the painful perspective of America's own experiences in the late 1960's, we are aware that violence is not so exotic as we thought or wished. We are thus being forced against our will to acknowledge that there is a community of politics—a community of human responses to the needs of a shared life with other men—which seems to transcend the differences among communities of shared perception which we call "cultures."

To acknowledge this is not to argue against the study of detailed differences within and between various cultures. To the contrary, if we are to transcend the apparent differences we must firmly grasp the ways in which different men articulate their responses to the challenge of life with their fellow human beings. The unity of world history arises from the diversity of these responses.

A further matter falls in place at this point. To what degree does an outsider's deep and prolonged saturation in the culture of another people become an equivalent for sympathy or identification with it? In the Department of State, one of the most telling criticisms of an ambassador was that he had "localitis"—meaning, that he had identified himself too closely with the people to whom he had been sent as an ambassador.

In their encounter with an alien culture, most students pass through several stages of emotional commitment. In the first stage, it is perhaps necessary, if not inevitable, that they should identify themselves with the people whom they are trying to understand. Students who fail to make this identification are likely to attain little more than a superficial appreciation of the motive forces that run deep in the culture under study. In fact, a psychic identification with the culture is required if only to sustain the extraordinary effort required to master its language thoroughly. Then, comes a second stage in which students are repelled by the manifest shortcomings in the practices of the people under study, or even by the very essence of the culture. The simple fact of physical weariness from the demands of careful study may heighten the repulsion and the inclination toward rejection.

When the first and second stages are passed through, however, one strives to reach a third stage. Here the individual student achieves a personal, artistic interpretation of the other culture—an interpretation whose quality depends on the student's personal aptitudes. At that third stage, he is in a position to say: "This I approve, and that I dislike, but both I understand."

The student who reaches this stage must be reconciled to the likelihood that he will satisfy neither the opponents nor the proponents of the political system under study. I realized this fact after the appearance of the first edition of this book. In Israel the book was severely criticized. In Egypt it was banned outright. By some it was regarded as an exercise in pro-Arab sentimentalism, by others it was regarded as clever Zionist propaganda. In my own view, the only sensible criteria for evaluating a book on politics is to be found in the extent to which the book helps in the task of predicting the future and guiding men toward rational goals. That was my purpose in the first edition. It remains my purpose in the second.

If a reader is interested in the forces at work in world history instead of in current propaganda, he will be rewarded if he makes the effort to understand the Arabs for themselves instead of viewing them narrowly through the lens of the tragic Arab-Israeli competition for a corner of the Middle East. This kind of understanding has an essential and direct bearing both on the long view of trends in world history and on the more immediate attempt to achieve peace in the Middle East. To fail to see that the Arabs in themselves are a people worthy of sympathy and understanding is not only to betray a certain poverty of human spirit, but also to declare one's indifference to the needs of world peace. It is my own object in this book to portray a major component of the world population and to perceive in all of its dimensions a culture which must be understood for its own sake, and also for its bearing on the quest for world peace.

A final word as an American writing about the Middle East: I am disturbed by a concern consistently absent in works of Arab scholarship undertaken by Arabs themselves. It is true that we have had a number of specific descriptions by Arabs of recent political and military events in the environmental setting of the Middle East. But as far as I can judge, no Arab writer in Arabic or in any other language has made a particularly noteworthy or detailed analysis of the problems *within* Arab society and of how these problems impinge on two particular matters: the achievement by Arabs of a respectable rate of progress toward modernity and the attainment by Arabs of a cardinal object like the respect of other nations. A start in this direction was made in a recent article entitled "Moment of Truth," by Mr. Cecil Hourani. The tenor of the article itself, however, made it clear to an outsider that Arab thinkers must still make a quantum jump away from contemporary bombastic propaganda and internal witch-hunts until they reach the plateau where they can get on with the work of constructive scholarly endeavor. We can only hope that Arab writers will increasingly assume the hard but indispensable task of analyzing Arab affairs from within and, further, will themselves produce the mirror image of this book, *The Arab World and the United States.*

Preface to the First Edition

December 1964

When Professor Crane Brinton asked me to write this volume of the American Foreign Policy Library, I was teaching at Harvard University with a year's leave seemingly just ahead. In my mind's eye I saw myself ensconced on the lovely island of Rhodes, alternating a diving lung and a typewriter, as I leisurely prepared this book.

Now, four years later, I sit in my snow-bound study in Washington, D.C., never having been closer to Rhodes than a 35,000-foot-high seat in a jet. If less relaxed, I am nevertheless the richer by experience. For in January 1961 I was asked to join the Policy Planning Council to assist in planning American policy toward the Middle East.

Obviously, in many ways, some perhaps not clear even to me, my work in the council has altered my perspective, broadened my knowledge, and, perhaps for the better, chastened my thoughts. Additionally, of course, my appointment has imposed a degree of restraint on my pen. This will not, I believe, prevent me from accomplishing the task I set out to do in this volume, but it is fair to the reader to record the disability. Naturally the views expressed here are my own and do not necessarily reflect official opinion.

My work on the Policy Planning Council on all major aspects of American relations with the Middle East has posed the question to which this book is directed: what are the essential facts, ideas, emotions, and guesses which one needs to understand the relations between the United States and the Arab World?

A few words on the organization of the book may be of assistance to the reader. Part I sets out the basic human and natural factors of the Arab World. Part II is an episodic history of the

Arabs. No attempt is made, nor could it be made in this short space, to treat exhaustively the whole of Arab history. What I have done is to show the development of four pertinent factors of the modern scene, the social code, the religion, the heritage of a golden age, and the deep gulf between society and the state. Part III illustrates the impact of the West during which the traditional ways of life have been altered, thus moving the Arabs from a medieval into a modern period. Part IV documents, in more detail, the development of the Arab states as we know them. The mandate period was a school in statehood in Iraq, Transjordan, Syria, and Lebanon. The Arabian Peninsula stood apart in splendid isolation for which its people paid by relative lack of modernization. Egypt, the most modern of the Arab states, on the contrary, paid for its modernization by political subordination. Palestine, a special problem, has left deep imprints on several aspects of Arab thought. Formal independence has brought radical political changes. Part V gives the matrix of current social revolution in the Arab lands, the rise of new elements in society, changes in the economy, and the development of thought on the place of the Arabs in the world. Part VI discusses the new relationship between the Arabs and the United States and analyzes United States interests, offering some projections for the near future. It is followed by suggested reading. In each chapter I have made every effort to cut out all that I thought not essential to the reader in understanding the present.

My own work on the Middle East goes back to 1946 when I first visited the Arab World. It owes more than I can record to numbers of friends, colleagues, teachers, supporters, and students. Without sharing responsibility for my words I want to mention with gratitude John Badeau, Gabriel Baer, Leonard Binder, Charles Cremeans, Nabih Faris, Sir Hamilton Gibb, Manfred Halpern, Albert Hourani, J. C. Hurewitz, Adib al-Jader, John Marshall, Emrys Peters, Chaim Rabin, Walt Rostow, Herbert Salzman, and James Spain. I also wish to thank the John Simon Guggenheim Foundation, the Rockefeller Foundation, and the Ford Foundation.

The western or North African part of the Arab World is covered in a companion volume by Charles Gallagher, and Israel is discussed in another by Nadav Safran. Therefore, except where essential to the development of the discussion here, all issues relating to these topics are omitted from this volume.

CONTENTS

Contents

The United States and the Arab World

THE ARAB WORLD AT A GLANCE

UAR (Egypt) has a population of 31 million of whom 30 percent are literate, an area of 386,000 square miles of which 3 percent is arable, and a Gross National Product (GNP) of $5 billion or $168 per capita.

SAR (Syria) has a population of 5.6 million of whom 30–35 percent are literate, an area of 71,200 square miles of which 32 percent is arable, and a GNP of $1.1 billion or $204 per capita.

Jordan has a population of 2 million of whom 30 percent are literate, an area of 37,300 square miles of which 10 percent is arable, and a GNP of $512 million or $262 per capita.

Lebanon has a population of 2.7 million of whom 80 percent are literate, an area of 4000 square miles of which 25 percent is cultivated, and a GNP of $1.25 billion or $475 per capita.

Iraq has a population of 8.6 million of whom 20 percent are literate, an area of 172,000 square miles of which 13 percent is cultivated, and a GNP of $2.2 billion or $268 per capita.

Kuwait has a population of 600,000 of whom 30 percent are literate, an area of 6000 square miles of which 1 percent is cultivated, and a GNP of $1.7 billion or $3208 per capita.

Saudi Arabia has a population of 3–6 million of whom 10 percent are literate, an area of 620,000 square miles of which 0.1 percent is arable, and a GNP of $1.7 billion.

Yemen has a population of 4–5 million of whom 25 percent are literate, an area of 50–75,000 square miles of which about 4000 is cultivated, and a GNP of $515 million.

Qatar has a population of 60,000 of whom about 10 percent are literate, an area of 4000 square miles of which virtually none is arable, and a GNP of $80 million or $1335 per capita.

PART ONE INTRODUCTION

I. The People on the Land

The Middle Eastern Arab World—encompassing Egypt, the Arabian peninsula, Jordan, Lebanon, Syria, and Iraq—is a vast stretch of mostly barren land joining northeastern Africa to western Asia. Roughly half the size of the United States, the Arab World has a climate similar to that of the Great Plains. The summers are intensely hot and dry; the winters are often bitterly cold. From the point of view of the inhabitants, perhaps the most significant physical feature is the lack of sufficient rainfall to support agriculture in most of the area. This fact has had and today continues to have a profound impact on every aspect of life. From the perspective of outsiders even more significant is the fact that the Arab World is the junction between Africa and Asia and Europe. The linchpin is Egypt, through whose land, sea, and air routes pass much of the world's commerce. Taken together the area constitutes a great highway—or a roadblock.

These two factors, the internal poverty and the strategic importance of the area, have from the dawn of history brought invading armies to the Middle Eastern shores and today make the Arab World a scene of the Cold War. These same factors have also driven the people to occasional bursts of energy and inventive genius to which the world's civilization owes a vast debt. Indeed, civilization began in the valleys of the Nile and the Tigris and Euphrates. Occasionally, too, the people of the area, frustrated by their harsh environment, have lunged outward to conquer vast empires or create far-flung commercial links.

Every American school child is familiar with the Phoenicians, the Babylonians, and the ancient Egyptians, but the Arabs came upon the stage of history at a time when our historical focus had shifted westward. It is difficult, therefore, for Americans to speak with precision of the Arabs, their history, and their culture. But it is also difficult for the Arabs themselves to formulate a commonly accepted definition of Arab, Arabism, and Arabdom.

The Arabs, wrote one of their early poets, are "parasites of the camel." The true Arab was a nomad. Only in his veins coursed the pure Arab blood and only on his tongue the pure Arabic language. Corruption and weakness are the vices of settled life. When the plow crosses the threshold, said an Arab proverb, manhood departs. Thus, "nobility" could be measured by the distance of penetration into the great sand seas of western Asia.

Actually, however, the great majority of the people who speak Arabic are peasants and city dwellers. The bedouin nomads are today, as they probably always have been, a minority of the population. About as few Arabs today can trace their origins to the Arabian Peninsula as Americans can to England. Arabs, like Americans, are a mixed lot. The overwhelming proportion of those who are today called Arab are descendants of the native populations, once called Babylonians, Phoenicians, or Egyptians, who have adopted the Arabic language during the last fourteen centuries since the coming of Islam. Yet so deeply have the Arabs impressed their image upon those with whom they came in contact that the drawing of distinctions on ethnic or linguistic grounds is pointless. The Iraqi is, in a political and cultural sense, no less an Arab than is the Saudi Arabian. To understand the modern Arab world an appreciation of the impact of what has come to be called Arabism is essential.

It was not the desert which was the matrix of Islamic civilization. Islam was always an urban culture. To call a Muslim of the Islamic middle ages an Arab would have been an insult. His was a different order of culture, a different mode of life, and he held the nomad in a contempt tempered by fear. Some of his values he derived from the nomad, whose marvelous poetry, that thread on which Arabic civilization has been strung and in which are embodied the values of Arabic society, he relished. But the city man found in the Islamic order of society, in brotherhoods and guilds, and in fixity of dwelling new norms of life alien to those of the nomad.

Between these two, as wheat between grindstones, was the peasant. Taxed and exploited by the one, he was bled or evicted by the other. Lacking the organization and resources of the one, he was weaker and less warlike than the other. Never was he able fully to participate in the culture of either. Both despised him. Yet he literally furnished the wheat of Middle Eastern life. Upon his labor was built urban civilization and upon his resources the bedouin drew in the frequent lean years of drought.

These three, the bedouin, the peasant, and the city man, are the Arabs. Between them are wide and deep cultural, economic, and political schisms. Yet between them are also important bridges of mutual dependence. And across these bridges, throughout history, a steady stream of men have moved.

Impelled as they were by the harsh and unpredictable conditions of their environment and aided by the fierce qualities they possessed as warriors, the bedouin constantly encroached upon their settled cousins. The clash of the desert and the sown, the parable of Abel and Cain, is a persistent theme in Arabic history. Usually the bedouin were content to levy a tribute and retire when the coming of the rains and the absence of more powerful foes made the desert again safe, but periodically groups spilled into the settled lands and remained. Throughout recorded history there has been a tendency toward what has been called sedentarization. In the last century, sedentarization has increased, but only the scale not the fact of sedentarization is new.

Indeed, the gradations from a purely nomadic to a purely settled way of life are imprecise. Practically all bedouin plow some land. Even in the midst of the vast deserts, one encounters plots where water seepage, flash floods, or occasional rainfall periodically make agriculture possible. There men sow seed, move on with their herds, and return to harvest a crop. On the belt of steppe lands between the desert and the true agricultural lands the villages are semi-nomadic. Their populations fluctuate with the seasons. During the winter rains part of the village will move off to pasture the flocks, returning in the late spring to work the land and harvest the crops. Even in the "black lands," the irrigated plains, the villagers are in part herdsmen.

Yet in general terms the "frontier" between the desert and the sown land can be drawn with considerable precision on a map. In order to stay in one place to cultivate the land, a farmer must have the equivalent of at least eight inches of rainfall yearly. Where this much water is available from rain, oases, or rivers, men have settled. Where the water amounts to less than eight inches or is unreliable, men have had to move. In the Arab World the frontier between these two ways of life has been called the "Fertile Crescent" as it is a great arc running from Jerusalem northward to Aleppo, eastward to Mosul, and south to Basra. Inside the arc only by irrigation can men settle to farm.

Let us examine the area to see how the physical facts have shaped society and culture.

The vast majority of the Arab World is today, and has been throughout history, desert. In Egypt, for example, the total land area is the size of Texas and New Mexico but 97 percent of this is waterless sand and rock. More richly endowed are Iraq, about two-thirds the size of Texas, which is 70 percent steppe and desert, and Syria which is about half desert. Jordan is about 80 percent desert while Saudi Arabia and Kuwait, comprising about 630,000 square miles or an area one fifth the size of the United States, have an agricultural area only about twice the size of Long Island or one tenth of one percent of the total.

Scattered in the vast empty areas are "islands." Some are large oases where an outpouring of spring water makes settled agricultural life possible; others are merely cisterns where rain water is collected and stored for men and animals. Normally these cisterns and some of the oases are meeting places for nomads when the intense heat of the summer desiccates the desert's plant life. Then, as the winter rains come, the nomads and their flocks move out into the suddenly, and briefly, lush pasture.

The rainy season is short, normally about two months, and the summer is long, about six months, but the bedouin manage to stay in the desert or the fringes of the desert upwards of eight months. Only by living in small groups and by moving about can men and animals live there.

Many, including settled Arabs, have thought of the bedouin as aimlessly wandering gypsies who, to avoid the hard physical labor of settled life, follow their animals around the deserts, stealing a bit now and then from their hard-working cousins, the peasants, and contributing nothing to the well-being of their fellow men.

The reality is quite different. The bedouin way of life, like that of the Eskimo, is a highly sophisticated adaptation to an extraordinarily difficult environment. It takes great skill, daring, and perseverence to live in the desert. And unless one is constantly supplied from outside, as armies and explorers are, he must move

LEBANON
LAND UTILIZATION

Crops predominant
Small areas of natural
vegetation

Forest and scrub. Small
areas of crops and valleys,
on slopes and terraces

Sparse vegetation or
barren ground

MEDITERRANEAN SEA

Tripoli

Harmal

Batrun

Jubayl

Juniyah

Baalbek

BEIRUT

Zahlah

Alayh

SYRIA

Sidon

Rashiya

DAMASCUS

Marjuyun

Tyre

ISRAEL

to live. The resources of the desert can be exploited only by
the bedouin through his animals. The animals which can stand
desert life are the camel, the sheep, and the goat. Others, even
the horse, are, like man, ill-fitted for desert life. But, though the
desert is harsh and poor in any particular area during most of

the year, the resources of the desert taken in the large are immense. Winter rains create vast and lush pastures for short periods and fill water tanks and cisterns. Chance thunderstorms, with their telltale flickers of lightning, are watched as eagerly by the water-hungry bedouin as guides to green valleys as are thunderheads by the Polynesian sailors of the western Pacific as guides to unseen islands. When rain falls, the patches of desert

which receive it burst into meadow lands to which the bedouin and their herds must hurry before sun and wind destroy the grass and flowers. The Arabs, whose whole artistic powers have been channeled through their language, even have a particular verb, *shāma*, which means "to watch for flashes of lightning to see where the rain will fall." Few scenes in Arabic literature are treated with more care, sensitivity, and delight than the coming of a rain storm.

Apart from movement to take advantage of a chance rainfall, the bedouin must move for two other reasons. The animals quickly exhaust the pasture and both men and animals quickly drink up the water in wells and cisterns. If the season is cool and the vegetation wet, the animals drink little water and men live on their milk. But even camels need some water. The change of

seasons provides another reason for migration. In the summer the desert is the literal hell described in the Koran. Scorching heat, suffocating sand storms, and raging winds bring unquenched and maddening thirst and are murderous to plants, animals, and men. The plants that grow in the desert survive underground but men and animals must move to the cooler areas of the hill country where they can find water holes and some grazing. Even there the water may be so brackish and undrinkable that men must live on camel milk. (It is not without reason that the bedouin has been called the parasite of the camel.) With the coming of cold and rainy weather biting, icy winds drive them back to the lowlands, for the camel needs warm areas to breed. With rain the desert once again becomes the "Garden of Allah."

A true tribal map of the Arab nomadic areas would be unlike any other land map. What it would show is the route of march with an area of approximate winter pasture at one end and summer pasture at the other. Perhaps the best analogy would be a map of the sea showing fishing areas: one could trace the route of the boats and their general location but could not predict exactly where they would be, for this would depend on where the men found fish. So, for the Arabs, little or nothing is fixed and their civilization traditionally has lacked the concepts, so strong in our civilization, of home, homeland, and patriotism. The sentiment which we find in place of birth, home, and death exists for the nomad, of course, but it attaches to people not to land. It is the family, the clan, and the tribe which capture loyalty and devotion. In the classical literature, the pre-Islamic poetry, the nomad is usually pictured as he happens upon an abandoned campsite, but for him the place means nothing—on it he lavishes no brilliant description—it only serves to remind him of a loved one. It is to scenes of desert life as a prelude to the glorification of his folk that the poet addresses himself. Land per se has little meaning for him, and the Arabic word which comes closest to meaning "homeland" has none of the emotional overtones of *patria*.

In other ways, as well, the material conditions of bedouin life are reflected in his social organization and thought. In the desert no man can live alone. The bedouin is required by his harsh environment to be a social animal. Resources are too scattered for large numbers of people to live together, but efficient utilization of those resources requires team effort. Under normal conditions the "team" appropriate to the task is what the Arabs call the *qawm* or the clan. The "tribe," of hundreds or thousands of men, based on genealogy and on grazing areas and water rights, can have effective existence only when enough water and fodder is available—and that can only be sporadically. It is the clan that lives, herds animals, and fights as a corporate group. It normally is composed of several generations of children of a single man but often absorbs clients whom it agrees to protect and others who, in the Arabic expression, "put on its skin."

To the qawm the individual owes total loyalty and from his membership in it he derives social identity and legal standing. Since the primary function of the qawm is to enable the individual to live in a hostile environment, every cultural and social pressure is brought to bear on the individual to do his part in making the qawm cohesive, strong, and effective. Within the qawm property distinctions are minimal.

In a society without external institutions or means of coercion, a man's safety depends upon the ability and willingness of the clan to protect him. But, since the mode of life of the bedouin demands that he spend much of his time alone and far from his fellows, the notion of vengeance came to be substituted for protection. Failure to take vengeance, of course, would reduce the credibility of the threat and so undermine the safety of everyone. However, unlimited warfare and the taking of vengeance would destroy that minimum element of security which makes life in the desert possible. So, as we shall see in the next chapter, various other sorts of safeguards were created to give men a degree of tranquility.

Bedouin society has always been a pulsating organism, subject to rapid coagulation and to equally rapid disintegration. As one clan grows rich and numerous, other clans will ally themselves to it and it will absorb numbers of clients. When it outruns its resources or becomes politically unwieldy, the clan subdivides.

There never have been large numbers of bedouin and today their numbers are decreasing. Reliable statistics do not exist, but there are probably not more than a million bedouin in all of the Arab countries. Always, the lure of city comforts attracted and the unpredictability of the desert climate expelled some nomads. Now, with the tractor reaching out to plow the steppe lands and the pump bringing more areas under regular cultivation, with property rights of the settled peoples enforced by governments whose weapons are carried on airplanes, tanks, and trucks and who are guided by radios, the bedouin are held in check. As the market for camels has declined, with the coming of the airplane, railroad, and truck for transport and beef cattle for meat, the bedouin have ceased to command markets and perform services which once gave them an assured place in the economy. Moreover in the last century it has been the policy of governments to force the bedouin to settle so that they can be controlled, conscripted, and taxed. As a result the frontier of settlement has moved out into the desert areas further each generation, and by the 1930's a French sociologist could accurately say, "the contemporary Arab East is a vast peasant farm." About two thirds of the Egyptians, Syrians, Iraqis, and Jordanians today derive their living from agriculture.

Like the nomadic encampment the village is predicated upon the proximity of water; but unlike it the village is relatively fixed. There has been distinct and constant change in the location of villages. The frontier of settlement of Syria and Iraq as well as, but more dramatically than, Egypt has varied a great deal in the last century, and old tax registers of even such relatively stable areas as Lebanon show great changes over the centuries. Yet village life presents perhaps the most stable element in the area.

There is no "typical" village in the Middle East, but certain characteristics are sufficiently widespread to give an idea of peasant life. Most villages define themselves in terms of kinship, locality, livelihood, and religion.

Villages are small worlds unto themselves. Today, with the advance of the motor car and the radio, this is less the case than formerly, but it is still pronounced. Villagers tend to marry within their villages. Of the nearly 400 marriages contracted over the last century in one Lebanese village, for example, only 40 were with "foreigners" from neighboring towns. The vast majority were with cousins inside the large extended families or clans. Thus, the village and its component families achieve a high degree of homogeneity and control over people and resources which might otherwise have been alienated. Real or ascribed kinship becomes a conceptual scheme by which all contemporary relationships are explained and codified.

Subdivisions within a larger kindred among villagers, as among the nomads, re-enforce their kinship with neighborhood. In many mountain and hill villages in the Levant the neighborhood of a clan is a miniature fort whose houses present a windowless wall to the outside and front on a courtyard in which a well or cistern is shared by all. Within the court the women go about their daily chores unveiled and the children play as members of one family. Often the rules of inheritance will result in a graphic portrayal of the family tree on the ground. For example, one can observe in a Lebanese village the sort of "geography of kinship" illustrated in the accompanying diagram.

The geography of kinship in a Lebanese village

Other parts of the village may be held in common. In Jordan and parts of Syria and Iraq a sort of village commune has existed. In this system land is reapportioned among inhabitants from time to time. In other villages, where the custom of individual holdings is stronger, the village might hold grazing lands and a market place in common. Resources, such as access to a spring or cistern, would be carefully regulated by custom or even by a written "treaty" between the major clans of the village.

The fact of life most central to all is the community of the village: any threat to the stability or economic well-being of a part of the village is necessarily a threat to all. As in the nomadic life the rights of the individual are severely subordinated to those of the group; above all, the system is conservative. Major dislocations by migration, death, or impoverishment have to be righted by social means, so the village brings in or excludes outsiders as it sees fit, protects village rights to water or land, and endows shrines and religious organizations.

Whereas the bedouin can protect himself, his fellows, and his animals by moving, the villager, tied to his plot of land, his house, and his access to water, can not leave except in dire emergency and at high price. In times of unrest or anarchy villagers did become partly or wholly nomadic. The perceptive Swiss traveler John Lewis Burckhardt noted in 1810—a time of anarchy—that few Syrian peasants died in the same village in which they were born, so oppressed were they by the government tax collectors and the rapacious bedouin raiders. Even today and even on irrigated lands, the Iraqi peasant is at least semi-nomadic, partly out of the habits of insecurity and partly because for nearly a thousand years the central government has failed to regulate irrigation and drainage. But for most of the peasants in the Middle East, kinship has been replaced by geography and the central function of all organization is to protect one's little world from outside encroachment.

Among settled people, as among the nomads, those are most safe who are least easy to reach. And so the inhabitants of the remote mountain villages of Yemen, Hadhramaut, Oman, Iraq, Syria, and Lebanon have been able to preserve, through the changing times of many centuries, their culture and their independence, while the peasants of the open plains of Syria and the river deltas of Egypt and Iraq could not. It is not surprising, therefore, that the minority communities and religious sects are often to be found in the mountains while there is more homogeneity in the plains.

The large-scale, irrigated agriculture of the Middle East has, historically, given the area its wealth. Indeed, it is probable that the "birth" of civilization as we know it, in the sense of human organization on a large scale, is intimately associated with the need to control the mighty rivers of the Middle East. This problem, it has been suggested, is at the base of oriental despotism. It is certainly clear that the settled agricultural areas have always lived under highly centralized, autocratic governments which have closely regulated not only the commerce but also the details of agricultural production. In fact, so intimately have the governments, from ancient Egyptian and Babylonian times, intervened in the lives of the people that they represented the whole spectrum of organized life from economic, military, bureaucratic, and legal power to matters of personal status and religion. But the people fear and resent this interference and usually resist by withdrawal, having as little to do with government as possible while submitting to its outward power. As Father Ayrout observed in *The Peasant*, "They have changed their masters, their religion, their language and their crops, but not their way of life. From the beginnings of the Old Kingdom to the climax of the Ptolemaic period the Egyptian people preserved and maintained themselves. Possessed in turn by Persians, Greeks, Romans, Byzantines, Arabs, Turks, French and English, they remained unchanged . . . A receptive people, yet unyielding; patient, yet resistant." So accustomed are they to living apart from government and yet so pliant are they before government as to make both the development programs of today and the attempts at representative government of recent years extremely difficult.

The peasant is deeply suspicious of any move the government may make—even if, on the surface, it appears to be to his benefit.

When the governments tried to get him to register his lands, he often did so in someone else's name, fearing taxes and conscription. When modern governments have sought to get him to use better methods and seed, he has been reluctant, since the old ways, though perhaps not the best, were known, trusted, and reliable. The peasant can ill afford to gamble and is little disposed, in any case, to trust any government. And indeed governments of the last century, even when occasionally proclaimed in his name, nearly always were or became centers of power for the landlords to oppose all measures designed to help the peasant. It was, after all, the elected Iraqi parliament which in 1932, upon achieving independence, passed a law to convert free tribesmen into serfs, bound to the land and policed by machinery of the state. It was the elected Egyptian parliament which stoutly resisted to the bitter end any moves to enforce equitable taxation, introduce better and cheaper fertilizers, or to give the peasant a share in the land.

The city, as personified by the government, always has lived leechlike on the countryside and often gave little in return. Between the way of life in the cities and that in the countryside there has been always a vast gulf, unbridged even by a common culture, for the peasant actively partook little of the Islamic culture of the urban areas or the Arabic culture of the bedouin, although he was the passive recipient of both.

Like the bedouin, who was attracted to settled life, the peasant was constantly lured by the city. In times of rural anarchy and chaos men huddled in walled towns for protection. As economic opportunity or political considerations led them, they moved to cities or garrisons or palaces and, by encamping around them, created new urban areas. At several times in the Islamic period such movements have been particularly pronounced. During the Islamic conquests the early caliphate, to keep the hastily assembled tribal armies from fading into the countryside, encouraged them to settle around the garrison-administrative centers which gradually grew into such cities as Basra, Kufa, and old Cairo. When Baghdad was laid out in 762, its founder, the Abbasid Caliph Mansur, planned only a palace and an administrative center but founded, in fact, the core of a city. And, finally, in the period of rapidly expanding commerce that has extended over the last century the cities have grown considerably in size and, like magnets drawing together iron filings, have clustered around themselves concentric rings of shanty towns.

But, of course, rings of shanty towns are not cities. And the Middle East has had an unbroken urban tradition from the earliest historic times. This is particularly evident in Egypt and Mesopotamia but Damascus, Palmyra, Petra, Tripoli, Sidon, Tyre, Jerusalem, Medina, and Mecca have their roots deep in the past. Jerusalem and Damascus were well enough known, but Mecca, even before the birth of Muhammad in A.D. 570, was a great international entrepôt, controlling through diplomatic and military ties with the "nations" of Arabia, the bedouin tribes, and a caravan trade covering thousands of miles. This center had a sophisticated oligarchy dealing with intricate problems of commercial law, money, and banking, and an urban pride and sense of identity celebrated in the pantheon, the Kaaba, which long before Islam was a focal point of Arabian religion and commerce.

The coming of Islam provided a powerful stimulus to urban life. Muhammad was a city man who thought in urban terms. His "Constitution of Medina" was, among other things, an attempt to transcend the limits of kinship and neighborhood of the tribe and village by creating a sense of community which would embrace rival groups of kindred, men of different hamlets, and even men separated by the frontiers of religion. Inherent in the structure Muhammad created in Medina is the intricate social pattern of the medieval Islamic city, interlaced as it became with religious and craft guilds and neighborhoods centering on mosque schools, with its markets patrolled and organized by inspectors of weights and measures, police, and law courts. The civic pride of the medieval cities was often further expressed in great popular religious festivals while wealth, learning, and power were institutionalized in foundations, libraries, and schools.

To a tragic degree this aspect of the Arab cultural heritage was destroyed by the invasions of the Mongols and the Turks, in which such great urban centers as Baghdad, Aleppo, and Damascus were virtually obliterated and by the centuries of waste and neglect which brought floods, famine, and pestilence in their wake. Baghdad, which in the twelfth century had a population of nearly a million—or five times that which Paris was to achieve two centuries later—was sacked and massacred in 1258. When this happened, culture, which in Iraq in Islamic times was always an urban phenomenon, withered like a plant in the scorching blast of a desert summer. Unlike the plant, the culture was not deeply rooted in the soil and little survived for the refreshing nourishment of subsequent, peaceful centuries. Moreover, when centralized control over the vast and complex irrigation system was ended, great tracts of land were ruined. Irrigation and drainage ditches were allowed to fill with silt, the desert broke in to the black lands, and much of the best land turned into a swamp. With its rural base sapped, the urban structure of Iraq did not again reach the scale of its medieval days until this century.

Yet, by the end of the eighteenth century urban life was beginning to recover, and some cities, such as Aleppo and Damascus, though small by modern terms, had again developed relatively high standards of cultural and commercial life. Damascus was described by a French visitor in 1833 as "a vast factory town comparable to Lyon." And the merchants of even such small seaports as Jiddah were able to buy and sell shiploads of merchandise from Zanzibar, India, and the Red Sea ports. Little towns like Gaza derived their importance in part from the fact that the caravan routes passed through them and they were trading centers for the bedouin.

The point is that a real urban society existed. It offered both an urban government and a satisfying community life, based upon villagelike neighborhoods and laced together by religious foundations, brotherhoods, and guilds. Life was sufficiently organized to encourage cultural and educational development, and so to keep alive the forms of Islamic culture.

The three levels of Arab society, the nomadic, the village, and the city, though separated in important ways culturally, politically, and geographically, historically have been in other ways dependent upon one another. The bedouin furnished meat, wool, and transportation to the villagers who raised the grain that sustained the bedouin in bad years and the urban people always as well as the cotton and silk which were fashioned in the cities and sent out again on the backs of bedouin camels. These patterns of life interacted and for all their differences were accepted. As we shall see, it was in part the dislocation of this pattern which has been a prominent feature of society in our times. For today, in the Arab countries as in most society, the urban areas are growing rapidly in numbers and in power at the expense of both the steppe and the sown cultures. Cairo today has a larger population than all of Egypt had in 1800 and Beirut has grown from about 10,000 in 1830 to half a million in 1963. As industry develops relative to agriculture this trend will continue.

The "frontier" between desert and sown land, as we have seen, is a highly determining factor in the structure of the Arab world. Another of the "frontiers" of Middle Eastern Arab society is religion. Before the advent of Islam some Arabs had become Christians and Jews, but most of the nomads were pagans with rudimentary cults of gods and goddesses often symbolized by stones. As we shall see, Islam became a great codifier of society, giving not only law but also highly specific rules and mores, and a unifier of society in that it set forth principles that transcended the boundaries of clan, tribal, village, and regional strife. Islam also tried to transcend religious differences by marking out the rights and duties not only of its own citizens, the Muslims, but also of the members of other religions. More than other great religions, notably medieval Christianity, Islam was highly successful in extending the perimeters of tolerance. One measure of this fact is that for many centuries after the conquest the peoples of the new empire of Islam retained their separate languages and religions. Conversion to Islam is still far from complete in the Arab lands and as late as the last century many whose descendants now regard themselves as Arabs spoke other languages.

In the Arabic community are many who are not today Muslim while among the Muslim community are several sects and many non-Arabs. Historically these differences were abetted by the Muslim rulers who allowed each community, as distinguished by religion, to rule itself in matters of personal status, taxation, and internal security. Western powers have often been associated with these minority groups. The Italians and Greeks had their own nationals in several of the Arab countries; the French protected the Catholic community; and tsarist Russia aided the Orthodox community. Great Britain traditionally aided the Druze and the Jews, and private American groups helped to create and then foster Protestants. So the existence of minority communities has import both in domestic and international terms.

Egypt has nearly four million Copts. The word Copt is a corruption of the Greek word for Egyptian; the Copts are the remnant of Hellenized ancient Egypt. Today, they share with other Egyptians the Arabic language but remain monophysite Christians under an unbroken line of 116 patriarchs since the Council of Chalcedon in A.D. 451. Like minorities elsewhere, the sect was often used by, and lent themselves to use by, alien rulers who knew that the Copts, while having detailed knowledge of the country, could never threaten their rule. Thus, the Copts tended to become identified as a clerical class, although many are peasants, and to be tarred with the brush of governmental tyranny and alien privilege. As late as the end of World War I almost half of the Egyptian civil service was Coptic.

Egypt also has had large communities of Jews, Greeks, and Italians, although all three have declined greatly in recent years. They benefited to such an extent from alien patronage that hardly any members of these communities could be brought to an Egyptian court for any offense and virtually all were able to escape taxes and other obligations. Quite naturally they were resented, often bitterly, by the less fortunate natives. As a British satirical writer once said, in every wave of nationalist violence it was the Greek grocers who laid down their lives for Britian. The Greek grocer was the usurer of the typical Egyptian village. Alexandria was largely a Greek city until quite recently. The Italians aroused less public ire but have suffered in the generally antiforeign feelings which followed the coming of independence.

The Jews have suffered proportionally as violence and hatred between Egypt and Israel have increased. As early as the 1930's, when Zionism became strong in the Palestine Mandate, there were anti-Jewish demonstrations, and when Israel defeated Egypt in 1948–49, public feeling increased in violence. The Egyptian government took various steps to control the animosity but when, in 1956, Israel attacked Egypt, it openly encouraged emigration.

Lebanon, on the contrary, as a vast natural fortress of steep valley sides and rocky crags, has been historically a refuge of minorities. Indeed, Lebanon has no true majority. In a population of about 2.4 million about 6 percent are Armenian, and 0.5 percent are Jews. Of the rest, the Arabs, the latest estimates give this breakdown: 7 percent Druze, members of a heretical offshoot of Islam, 18 percent Shii or non-Orthodox Muslim, 20 percent Sunni or Orthodox Muslim, 38 percent Uniate Christian, 16 percent Orthodox Christian and 1 percent Protestant. These subdivisions are so woven into the "confessional" system of Lebanese political and administrative life as to enable each community effectively to defend itself today as, behind the walls of villages and the rocks of steep mountain sides, it did traditionally.

In Jordan (including the West Bank of the Jordan under Israeli occupation) about 2 percent of the population of two million are Circassians whose ancestors in the last century migrated from the Caucasus to escape the Russians, and 1 percent are Armenians who came for similar reasons. Nine percent of the people are Christian, mostly living in what used to be the mandate of Palestine on the west bank of the Jordan River, and all the rest are Orthodox Muslims.

Of the roughly 8.6 million Iraqis over 75 percent are Arabic speaking and about 20 percent Kurdish and Turkoman. The Arabs are divided into the Sunnis and the somewhat more numerous Shiis while the Kurds and Turkomans are mostly Sunnis. Iraq, like Lebanon, has no true majority: religiously, the Sunnis are preponderant but are divided ethnically and linguistically between Arabs and Kurds while ethnically and linguistically the Arabs form the majority but are divided religiously and culturally between Sunnis and Shiis. Other minorities include the Chaldeans, Armenians, Jews, Yezidis (popularly called "Devil Worshipers"), and Assyrians, each in small numbers.

IRAQI MINORITIES

Syria, with a population of 5.6 million, is basically Sunni Muslim but contains 13 percent Christian, 11 percent Alawi, 3 percent Druze, and 1 percent Ismaili minorities.

Alone among the Arab areas, the Arabian Peninsula is comparatively devoid of minorities. North and south Arabic differ somewhat, but they are in their written form the same language, and almost everyone who now lives in the peninsula is today Muslim. Yemen did have a large Jewish minority and was once ruled by Jewish kings; but in recent centuries it has been ruled by an imam who represented the Zaidi branch of Shii Islam. Otherwise, the people of the peninsula are primarily Sunni Muslims.

The total population of the Arab Middle East has exploded in the last century. The birth rate, apparently, has always been high but it was canceled in large part by a very high rate of infant mortality and by famine and plague. Centuries ago the Arabs of the desert, aware that the settled areas were sources of disease, strove to remain in the cleaner air of the desert, but drought and famine drove them in tidal pulsations toward the urban centers. Hunger accounts for some of the most graphic and tragic pieces of Arabic literature. The peasants usually managed to eat but their economy hovered barely above mere subsistence. It was partly for this reason that they resisted growing nonfood crops like cotton. For the food they grew they paid a heavy toll in their exposure to malaria, bilharzia—the snail-borne disease associated with irrigation—and dysentary.

There are no accurate population statistics even now for most of the Arab countries—figures for Saudi Arabia over the last decade have varied from two to ten million—but reasonable estimates in the third decade of the nineteenth century give the basis for an informed guess that there were then about six million Arabs in the Middle East of whom half lived in Egypt. Today, Egypt's population is more than 30 million and, increasing at 3 percent yearly, will double in a quarter of a century. It is clear that this extremely rapid rate of growth places the most serious pressure on the economies of the Arab countries which will require enormous investment of capital and skill to enable them to feed their people. But not only are the actual numbers of people increasing, the minimum scale of living for which they are prepared to settle is also rising. Thus, in political and economic terms the difference between 1830 and 1965 is not just six million compared to roughly sixty million but six million at a certain living standard and sixty million at a living standard several times as high. Today, economies must not only feed and clothe but furnish medical care, education, consumer goods, industrial plants, roads, dams, and, unfortunately, highly sophisticated and highly expensive weapons for large armies.

In most natural resources other than oil the Middle East is poor. Even where minerals exist, they either are difficult of access or are not present in usable combinations. For example, Egypt has iron deposits but no coal; Jordan has phosphate rock but no power with which to process it. The whole area is deficient in timber. Therefore, most industry is still primarily engaged in processing agricultural products.

Oil is the great exception to generalizations about the Middle East. Here, Middle Eastern Arab resources are tremendous. Kuwait, the golden land of the Middle East, with an area of 6000 square miles or roughly the size of Connecticut and a population of a third of a million of whom only about half are native, has about a quarter of the world's oil reserves. Saudi Arabia has roughly 16 percent and Iraq 8 percent. Other parts of the Arab Middle East account for an additional roughly 3 percent of proved reserves.

As Europe has recovered from World War II and the whole world has taken to wheels and wings, the oil industry and the oil-producing countries have prospered. The Arabs now draw nearly two billion dollars yearly from royalties on their oil. But, tragically for the economic impact of this flow of capital, oil is primarily to be found in those areas of the Middle East least suited for human habitation and where nature has provided little else in which men could invest. It is only recently that the Arabs have found ways in which the income from petroleum could be put to work effectively in the Arab area rather than causing a boom in the real estate markets of Cairo, Beirut, and Lausanne.

From the point of view of outsiders, the Arab Middle East contains assets of great world importance. The Suez Canal, now closed, which yielded about $250 million yearly to Egypt, is of enormous value to international commerce and industry. In 1966, 246.7 million tons of cargo in some 20,289 ships passed through the canal. But even before the canal was dug, Egypt was a transit point in international commerce and communication. In the Middle Ages Egypt waxed rich on this trade. Its later poverty was in part a consequence of one of the great blockades of all time, the seizure of control over the mouth of the Red Sea, to close off Venetian-Egyptian commerce, which was the consequence of the Portuguese sailor Vasco da Gama's great feat in rounding the Cape of Good Hope in 1498. For both Napoleon and the British,

Egypt seemed a key to Europe's control over India. Finally, the existence of the canal was a major causative factor in the Anglo-French invasion of Egypt in November 1956.

And, in this age of air travel, the airspace over and the landing and transit facilities in the several Arab countries, but most importantly in Lebanon and Egypt, are of the greatest importance in international relations.

In their own terms, the Arabs face the problems of poverty, backwardness, and ambition shared by the "developing" nations of Africa and Asia. But, as Arabs, as Middle Easterners, and as heirs to a particular historical experience, they face the common problems in a highly individual way. To discern the particular in the communality and the communality in the particular is, perhaps, the supreme challenge in international understanding. Thus, for themselves, for their assets, and for their very weaknesses, the Arabs will command the attention of the great powers in our time.

PART TWO FOUR LEGACIES FROM THE ARAB PAST

II. The Ancient Arabs: The Code of Honor

Like most peoples, the Arabs cherish a memory of times of glory, halcyon days when the world paused to allow men to aspire to the fullness of their bravery, strength, and refinement, and which, ever after, set a banner on the pinnacle of their achievement and a seal on their aspirations. Ancient song and story; in its content and form of expression, forms the core of a classical tradition, the quarry of artistic endeavor, and the repository of national ethic. The Arabs call these *Aiyamu'l-Arab* or "the Days of the Arabs." For all those who speak and relish the richness of the Arabic language and who call themselves Arab, the Days of the Arabs are an ideal past.

Such a period in Western civilization was the Age of Pericles, or, in a slightly different form, the England of the Arthurian Legends. Americans, even with our short history and varigated backgrounds, have already begun to make of the early years of the Republic—or of the Wild West—an idealized past in which men stood straighter, strove more nobly, and reached more surely for glory.

An idealized past, even one with which a person can identify only by great stretch of imagination, is a mirror for the present. However dimly it may be related to a real past, it provides a clear and bright picture of the aspirations and values of the present. What then has come down to modern Arabs from this dim, distant, and wild past?

The traditions and values of the ancient Arabs are not simply of antiquarian interest. Ancient Arabic poetry is today the syllabus of linguistic and literary study in every Arab school. Poetry to the Arabs is what folk stories, drama, legend, and epic are to the West. Few indeed are the Arabs, even those who are illiterate, who have not memorized hundreds of lines of poetry, and few are the political discussions, social gatherings, or entertainments in which poetry does not figure prominently. On its poetry Arabic civilization has lavished all of the inventive genius which in other cultures has been spread over the whole range of the arts. Study, memorization, and repetition of ancient Arabic poetry tie the modern age to previous ages and on this string is hung that sense of continuity which makes those who live in the modern Middle Eastern Arab states think of themselves as Arab. It is not only a living tradition, it is the essence of tradition.

By their British and French rulers and by many Western visitors, the modern bedouin nomads, and so by extension ancient Arabs, were regarded as the "good Arabs," a wild, childlike people, indolent perhaps and unproductive of social well-being, but whose courage and simplicity one could admire in contrast to the superficially Westernized, devious, difficult "town Arabs." Others, including their Turkish governors under the Ottoman Empire, have thought of the bedouin as gypsies, a people wandering aimlessly through the deserts, or pirates who, living in the vast inner sand sea of the Middle East, raided and plundered the coast and then retired, out of reach, to their distant "islands" and "fishing grounds." Arab philosophers have thought of the bedouin in terms similar to the eighteenth century European philosophers' "Natural Man"—the bedouin were the simple, pristine, children of God, uncorrupted and untamed by civilization, a bloodbank of new vigor for jaded urban society.

These attitudes have led, of course, to different policies. The British attempted to police the bedouin while protecting them from the city Arabs. Transjordan was to be their state, and in Iraq they were to have a strong voice in parliament. The French were less protective but, if anything, more appreciative of *la civilisation du désert*. The Turks generally sought to destroy the bedouin as others have sought to destroy pirates. Punitive expeditions were tried repeatedly but succeeded only against the settled or semi-nomadic tribes, who, having invested in lands and houses, could be caught. The true nomads vanished before the slow Turkish infantry only to reappear before isolated garrisons. Few were those governors wise enough to lure the bedouin to settle so that they might be controlled.

The attitude of the urban Arabs themselves was and still is ambivalent. The Arabs glory in the traditions and art of the bedouin as ancient Arabs, and nobility is claimed by descent from the bedouin. Historically to say of a student of Arabic that he studied with the bedouin was to accord him the best of credentials. Classical Arabic was the language of the bedouin of the Arabian highlands. Yet, the bedouin are feared and even hated, for if they have infused new vigor into society they have also drained off the old life and have overthrown existing orders of society. Today in the Arab World there is no government which can be said to be sympathetic with the bedouin. All seek to convert him into a settled peasant and all have upset the administrative arrangements which set him apart from other citizens.

Actually, nomadism has been in decline for at least a half a century. Settled peoples have not needed the meat and wool of the bedouin camels, for they could get them elsewhere cheaper. They have found cheaper and faster means of transport. And, with the use of the airplane and the truck with a machine gun mounted on top, they could prevent the nomads from raiding one another and the settled lands as never before. As the high commissioner of Iraq wrote in 1924 in his report to the League of Nations, "now, almost before the would-be rebel has formulated his plans, the droning of the aeroplanes is heard overhead." Always bedouin life has been fragile; now the delicate balance of conditions which sustained it have been upset. The bedouin, like the knight and the cowboy, is rapidly passing from the scene, but like all heroic figures he leaves behind a legend which dwarfs reality.

As we have seen, the harsh realities of desert life shaped bedouin society and thought. The bedouin never lived under government, and even their own tribes were loose federations in which every man was an equal. The shaikh was little more than a respected arbiter and generous host, never a ruler to his people. Burckhardt, one of the great observers of bedouin life, wrote in *Notes on Bedouins and Wahabys*, "the shaikh has no actual authority over the individuals of his tribe; he may, however, by his personal qualities obtain considerable influence. His commands would be treated with contempt; but deference is paid to his advice . . . thus the Bedouin truly says that he acknowledges no master . . . and in fact, the most powerful chief dares not inflict a trifling punishment on the poorest man of his tribe."

But, if the desert gives scope for such democracy, it also puts a heavy premium on social cohesion. Life in the desert is and must be a team effort. The clan or qawm is the group of kindred which lives, herds animals, fights, and makes peace together. The qawm was the effective social unit—it was, in reality, the nation-state of the bedouin. No larger or more elaborate social gathering had more than transitory existence and none had real authority over the clan. Since there was no "international" law and no supraclan institutions, the identity and protection of the individual were derived from membership in a clan. It was the certainty that a man's clan would protect him where possible and exact retaliation when he was harmed that gave him security of property and person.

Pride in folk and boasting of their qualities is one of the common features of the Arabic poem. The poet, the propagandist of his day, finds many ways to enhance the reputation of his folk, detailing their bravery, their wisdom, their generosity. As an-Nabighah sang,

. . . a people are they whose might in battle shall never fail

When goes forth their host to war, above them in circles wheel battalions of eagles, pointing the path to battalions more:

Their friendship is old and tried—fast comrades in foray, bred to look unafraid on blood, as hounds to the chase well trained . . .

Of steeds in the spear-play skilled, with lips for the fight drawn back, their bodies with wounds all scarred, some bleeding and some half-healed.

And down leap the riders where the battle is strait and stern and spring in the face of Death like stallions amid the herd;

Between them they give and take deep draughts of the wine of Doom as their hands ply the white swords, thin and keen in the smiting-edge.

In them no defect is found, save only that in their swords are notches a many, gained from smiting of host on host.

(translated by Lyall)

Behind the boast of his folk is the poet's implied and, at the end of the poem, explicit boast of his own virtues.

Most of the poet's virtues could be shown in performance of the duties of the tribe but the ultimate in personal bravery was to pit oneself against all mankind and all nature. If a man were expelled by his qawm he was literally an outlaw against whom the hand of every man was turned, living as Hobbes said in "continuall feare and danger of violent death." Since the ideal of rugged individualism always clashed with that of corporate subordination, some Arabs, including some of the greatest of the poets, were expelled from their clans and tried to "go it alone" by feats of almost superhuman endurance. As the greatest of these outlaw poets, Shanfara, sang,

By your life, the earth is not so narrow that a man cannot find elbow room,

As long as he uses his wits and by desire or fear travels in night's black gloom.

In supreme irony, the poet expels his own folk, choosing wolves for his qawm, since wolves do not break confidence and live by a sterner code than fickle men. He fears nothing as, accompanied by his three companions—a stout heart, a glistening sword, and a long singing bow—he moves through deserts so awesome that before them even riding camels panic and in weather so hellish in the "dog days" of summer that the very mirages melt and vipers writhe on the stones, "prolonging my hunger so long that it is the *hunger* I kill and I become unmindful of it." But the outlaw-poet wants his audience to know that he does not punish himself for masochistic reasons. "Were it not to avoid a shameful action, no drinking bout or feast would be found without my being there."

But a proud and bitter soul will not uphold me in the face of wrong, except as I plot my vengeance.

I am the master of patience draping its gown over the heart of a wolf and tenacity I wear for sandals.

Such stark and unbending glorification of egotism, violence, and hatred led to lives that were often, as Hobbes put it of *his* man in nature, "solitary, poore, nasty, brutish and short."

The centrifugal forces of individualism limited the centripetal forces of clan cohesion. In the last resort, at terrifying personal sacrifice, the individual could save his own honor even at the expense of loss of his folk. In this direction lay heroism and poetic ennoblement. In more normal circumstances a family quarrel could be ended by a split of the qawm into two parts, each of which could live normally, or by grafting the weaker group onto another clan in the same tribe much as one might migrate and become naturalized in another nation. In this direction lay salvation.

Westerners—and most Arabs—may find the content of this poetry of bravery, as the Arabs called it, objectionable, but its grand gesture, its eloquence, the flow of its language, cannot but sway men's emotions. No one who has watched an Arabic audience can fail to have noted the extent to which linguistic virtuosity hypnotizes the people. It is this which has given to the radio station in our own time such extraordinary influence throughout the Arab World and which allows even vitriolic and vile propaganda, if well said, to be accepted.

Ironically, even in the poems which express hatred of one man for others or one folk for another, and which are, therefore, divisive propaganda at its most effective, there is a force for cultural unity. Over the years, as names and events were forgotten, the poems lost their political sting and came to be a common heritage of all Arabs. It was, indeed, the sharing of the classical literature which provided the common cultural experience of the ancient Arabs.

The contrary sentiment to a rugged individualism bordering on suicide is the intense emotional attachment to one's clansmen, right or wrong, and the personal acceptance of responsibility for any and all of their acts. The Arabic word for the sentiment which bound together the clan is the same as the modern word for nationalism, *qawmiyah*. In one of the most widely quoted poems in Arabic, this sentiment is summed up by a bedouin poet of the clan of Ghaziyah. The clansmen have been on a raid and foolishly stop their retreat before they are out of reach of their enemies. The poet Duraid bin Simma, having warned them and realizing their folly will probably cost him his life, stays to fight for, as he said,

When they spurned me, I was still with them, having seen their folly and my own imprudence

For what am I apart from Ghaziyah—if the clan goes astray, so I,

And if Ghaziyah is rightly guided, I too am rightly guided.

Then he fought the

Fight of a man who nurses his brother with his own person, knowing that man is not immortal.

Failure to protect one's kinsmen or, if they are killed or wronged, to retaliate against those who inflicted a wrong would destroy the meager protection the individual could find in desert tribal life. It was the categorical imperative of bedouin life and honor. To fail or shirk was a cowardly action which stained the individual and his kindred with the "stain of shame." Only the blood of the enemy could wash away this stain. And virtually every Arabic poem has some reference to the fear of blame for not acting as a man should.

This duty was incumbent upon a clan not only for its own members but also for those they undertook to protect. Annoyance at the "protected stranger" often showed through the lines of the poems. As Urwa bin Ward sang:

God curse the starving thief who concealed by the blackness of night steals behind the tents to suck the marrow bones in the refuse heap.

Who counts as the riches of his lot to be every night where he can demand hospitality from a luckier friend.

But each poet boasts of his folk's generosity and protectiveness toward the guests or dependents. And no more bitter reproach could be made of a qawm than that it had failed in this duty. In the earliest of all known Arabic poems, the Basus Cycle, the poetess taunts her protectors by warning a friend that she is in "the encampment of such a folk that even when a wolf attacks he always seizes *my* lamb." Her protector, insulted beyond all compare, prepared to take vengeance on those who have harmed her after begging mankind not to blame him for "My protected one, know you one and all, is of the closest of kin." And so, like the Trojan War, began, poetically at least, a war of honor. For the Arab, said one of the greatest of Arab poets, must be a "spring pasture to the protected strangers." This is one of the deepest of obligations which has been rooted in Arabic civilization and nurtured by the tradition embodied in Arabic poetry.

The wise man is not foolhardy. Patience, cunning, and reserve are so much the attributes of the perfect man that they even spill into Islamic thought, Indeed, in the Koran God is described as the "best of the Plotters" (iii.54). But the final and greatest quality of the perfect man is generosity. The arbitrator is "one above the fray, possessed of such a generosity as leads him to aid others to show their generosity."

Generosity is not a virtue among the weak. For them the proper road is retaliation which should lead to the status quo ante. Other ways, however, could create a new balance of power. If the wrongdoer offered to pay recompense, the wronged could, after a decent interval, accept, and peace could be made. The strong, on the other hand, could be generous and could make peace without loss of face. One of the seven "Golden Odes" of ancient Arabia celebrates the peacemaker, who by his personal generosity and wisdom manages to stop war between two clans.

. . . If we set our hands to Peace, base it broad and firm by the giving of gifts and fair words of friendship, all will be well.

"Yea, glory ye gained . . . the highest—God guide you right! who gains without blame a treasure of glory, how great is he!"

(Translated by Lyall)

Otherwise war to the knife was not only sanctioned but demanded by the social ethic. Even if it meant death, no man could with honor or pride shirk his duty of retaliating, goaded as he was by his womenfolk and the very ghost of the slain and wracked by a "burning fever"—"Hearts are cured of rancour-sickness, whether men against us war, or we carry death among them: dying, slaying, healing comes."

To Western tastes some of the value system embodied in classical Arabic poetry is not appealing. The boasts of the poets, the thirst for vengeance, the hunger for fame, and the fascination for the wounding of the foe, though not unfamiliar to readers of classical Greek literature, are not attractive. But to understand their impact on modern Arabic thought is vital to an understanding of politics in the Arab Middle East. For the imperative of preserving or achieving dignity, the fear of reproach as being unworthy or impotent people, and finally, the importance of the form of action and the word of communication as equal to or surpassing that of the content, greatly influences Arab political behavior. To outsiders who would understand, whether condoning or opposing, this is the beginning of knowledge.

III. Islam: The Regulation of Society

Islam never made peace with bedouin society. In the Koran the bedouin Arab is scorned as one who, failing to believe in the religion, merely submits to the outward power of the religious state. However, Islam was born in an Arabia deeply colored by the values, the presence, and the literature of the bedouin Arabs. And Islam defined itself in the framework of a corporate, tribal society. The wonder is not that Islam was so influenced by Arabian experience but rather that Muslims were able so to elaborate the structure they inherited as to form one of the great religious civilizations of human history.

The historical role of Muhammad, the society of early Islam, and the Islamic creed are here set forth in bare outline. But this bears to the civilization of Islam the relationship of a skeleton to a man: omitted are the nerves, brain, heart, and flesh, an account of which would fill more than this volume. In short compass, this chapter will attempt to show the structure of the skeleton and to suggest the richness of the whole body.

Muhammad, the Messenger, who delivered the Word of God to the Arabs in Arabic, as the Koran explains, was born in the commercial city of Mecca about A.D. 570. Around his life has grown an immense literature of fact and fiction, devotion and scorn, conjecture and artifice. But from the Koran and the Traditions related by his early followers we know that he was born into a poor branch of Mecca's ruling oligarchy and was an orphan from his early youth. When about twenty-five, he married a wealthy widow whose business agent he had become. With her capital he acquired some status in the community while engaging in the caravan trade with Yemen and the Levant.

Then, apparently quite suddenly, when he was about forty, Muhammad had a vision of the Angel Gabriel who ordered him to "Recite in the Name of the Lord." The stunned and frightened Muhammad is said to have stammered, "But what shall I recite?" After an interval in which he received no further visions, he transmitted to his people, in an unending stream until his death in 632, what has been collected by his followers as the Koran.

For his contemporaries as for later, non-Muslim writers, Muhammad has proved to be a difficult and complex figure. To some Western medieval writers he appeared as a satanic adventurer who sought to undermine Christendom or, to the more fanciful, a "fallen" cardinal who, having been passed over for the Papacy, set out to create his own religion. Modern writers have portrayed him as an epileptic, a sufferer from hysteria, a self-deceiving spiritualist, a madman, or a dupe of the Devil. The pagan oligarchs of his own city were unconcerned with precise labels. To them, he was a troublemaker who was upsetting the pagan religion on which was based the prosperity of Mecca.

For himself, Muhammad claimed no superhuman attributes except one: he was the messenger through whom God's Word—the same Word as that delivered by previous prophets, both Christian and Jewish, to their peoples in their languages in former times—was to be taken in Arabic to the Arabs. He admitted that he could perform no miracles although Jesus, with God's permission, had; though Islam specifically denies the divinity of Jesus, it does ascribe to him an exalted place in Creation. But God intended, the Muslims hold, that Muhammad, in his time and in his language and among his people, should be the leader of men to the Highroad of the Virtuous.

After some initial success in converting members of the community of Mecca, although few among the citizens of the oligarchy, Muhammad reached what appeared to be a dead end in his mission: with the popular support he had he was at once too weak to defend himself and win more converts to his faith and too strong to be tolerated by the defenders of the pagan cults which intertwined Meccan commercial practice and political structure. Meccan prosperity was conditional upon pan-Arab recognition of the city's special status as a sanctuary in which no fighting could take place and of the "Forbidden" months when men could trade freely throughout Arabia without fear of raid or vendetta. The fact that the new religion would upset this balance was apparent both to the rulers and the ruled—the one viewed it as sedition and the other as a rallying point for opposition to their oppressors. Probably it was not lost upon the oligarchs of Mecca either that to accept Islam meant accepting the primacy of its prophet.

The fact that Muhammad was tolerated at all was due to the requirement of Arab society that his clansmen protect him. Then in 619 the clan found a way to expel him as one who behaved disreputably toward his fellows. In that year in quick succession died Muhammad's first (then his only) wife and an uncle who though a pagan had been his main support. When Muhammad was asked if his uncle was in the Islamic Heaven as a virtuous man or in its Hell as a pagan, he replied "in Hell." He was immediately repudiated by his clan and became an outlaw, exposed to the fury of the Meccans. In desperation he fled from Mecca to find a safer haven.

First, Muhammad took his message to the nearby town of Taif which, like Mecca, was prosperous, well-organized, and conservative. Like Mecca it had a pagan pantheon intimately associated with its trade. Poor soil it was for the seed of Islam. As a Meccan, Muhammad was able to command an audience of Taif's chief men but, as the Victorian scholar Sir William Muir imagined, "the disproportion to the outward eye between the magnitude of the prophet's claims and his present solitary condition turned fear into contempt." The men of Taif set their slaves and street urchins against Muhammad, stoned him, and literally ran him out of town. Bloody, exhausted, and shaken, Muhammad returned to a hostile Mecca where he lived in seclusion for over a year, until, feeling that "his thorn had been cut," another Meccan gave him protection and succor.

But others had heard of his mission. To Mecca came men of many of the Arabian towns and tribes to trade, to experience the delights of a market town, to exchange information, and, to listen to the soothsayers, poets, and storytellers. Mecca was the intellectual and cultural, as well as the commercial, market of Arabia. Under the "peace" of the Meccan gods men who would have fought—would have *had* to have fought on sight—elsewhere were able to mingle freely. In such a situation Muhammad met some of the men of the northern Arabian town then called Yathrib and later (and now) called Medina.

Medina, unlike Taif and Mecca, was agricultural. Moreover it had no pantheon, and, inhabited by a Jewish or Judaized Arab community, it was familiar with monotheism. More important, Medina had no organized corporate life, being less a town than a collection of hamlets, midway between a bedouin encampment and a city. Like the former it lacked a government to settle differences and enforce security but like the town it so constricted its members that they could not escape from one another as could nomads. Hostility could be settled neither by official pressure as in Mecca nor by movement as in the desert. In Medina a perpetual civil war threatened the very life of the community. The situation, in fact, had so far degenerated a few years before Muhammad's mission that in an orgy of destruction the rival clans had hacked down one another's trees and almost ruined the economy.

In this circumstance it was natural that the town should seek a neutral arbitrator to settle their differences. This, it seems, was what they sought in Muhammad. The fact that Muhammad was a Meccan lent prestige to his name and that he was a man of religion gave him a moral stance above the partisan politics of Medina. Whereas both Mecca and Taif felt endangered by a new creed, Medina welcomed any solution to its war and agreed to obey Muhammad "in all that is right."

Muhammad, with the painful memory of his Taif adventure

fresh in mind, carefully negotiated for over a year on what his status would be and sent ahead, by small parties, about 150 of his followers to form, as it were, his qawm in Medina. It was as a prophet armed that he was to enter the city. Glad to be rid of him, the people of Mecca did nothing to halt this migration until the very end when they decided to take no chances on the future by assassinating him. At the last minute Muhammad slipped away and rode northward to his new home. This was the Hijra, the "Flight," from which the Islamic calendar is dated.

Upon entering Medina, Muhammad faced the initial problem of winning an immediate peace; then he had to settle his followers; and finally he had to secure his own power. All of these tasks he approached within the political traditions of Arabia. The pattern which emerged is expressed in a document called the "Constitution of Medina," dating from the second year after the Hijra.

With a flash of brilliance, Muhammad established his people as a part of the economy of Medina by arranging for each immigrant to be adopted as a "brother" by some member of the community. Like most things Muhammad did, this was to linger through Islamic history as a social ideal—all Muslims are supposed to be brothers and to assist one another in personal as well as institutional ways.

The central problem, however, was to get the warring clans of Medina to sink their differences in some larger social organization. The theoretical unit larger than the clan in Arabic society was the tribe, but among the nomads, due to the nature of the desert economy, the tribe rarely had actual existence. Its "chief" had no real power and was merely the most respected clan shaikh. But within the tribe it was possible to negotiate an end to hostilities, through the payment of "bloodmoney," whereas against foreigners the settling of hostilities was far more difficult. Therefore, it was both natural and reasonable that Muhammad should think of the city in terms analagous to a tribe. And, indeed, the community he set out to create in Medina was to have the same essential qualities.

Like the Arab tribe, the new community of Islam laid upon its members obligations for the defense of the whole. The "believers and adherents" were to struggle together and jointly to pay blood money or ransom. If an outsider harmed a member of the community, in a way parallel again to tribal society, the entire force of the community was brought to bear against him—"the Believers to a man will be against him." The community of believers was enjoined never to abandon one crushed by debts, and jointly to oppose those sowing sedition. Believers, the "clansmen of Islam," were ordered never to kill believers or to help others against believers. Like the tribe, the Islamic community could grant protection, for "the protection of God is one," and the weakest Muslim could impose this obligation upon all his brothers. As in the tribe, so in the Islamic community, foreigners could seek protection and succor. And as befit the new basis of society, religion, in a way parallel to the old basis, kinship, not only men of different kindred but also those of different religions could be so protected. The Jewish clans of Medina were confirmed in their customary rights, property, and practices, but, since they did not fight in the militia of the community, they were obliged to contribute to the defense of the whole through taxation. Lastly, the community was bound to act together; the clans were prevented from making a separate peace and had to accept responsibility for the acts of all.

Muhammad had profited from his one major failure by learning that in order to establish the religion of God in a moral society he needed political power. In a corporate society this could only be "tribal," and the tribe is the essence of the early Islamic community. The boundaries of Muhammad's tribe, however, were religious rather than genealogical.

It was the Koran which was to set the moral tone and the way, or sunna, of the community. This again was not an alien thought in Arabia. As the pre-Islamic poet Labid, in one of the *Golden Odes,* sang, "And we are of a clan whose forefathers laid down for them a sunna since each qawm has its sunna and its imams."

Whereas the tribe had no fixed abode, Islam, being based on

a town, did. Muhammad, borrowing from his native city, institutionalized Medina as a sanctuary in which no fighting could
take place. Theoretically, throughout Islamic history the *Daru'l-
Islam* or the abode of Islam has been a place of peace in distinction to other areas which were the abode of war. In this abode of
peace lived Muslims and men of other religions and men of many
clans.

When Muhammad died eleven years after the Hijra, in A.D. 632,
he had barely had time to draft the outlines of his conception of
the community. As we shall see, he appointed no successor—indeed, there could be no successor as the Messenger of God—to
govern the community. Few of his followers understood his concept. To the "adherents," those who formed the bulk of the new
"religious tribe," Muhammad had been a sort of paramount chief
to whom, as a person, they submitted, and whose death freed
them from all obligation. The true believers were few and, without Muhammad, without a guide. Consequently, it appeared that
like other empires based on a tribal structure, Islam would not survive the founder's death.

Islam started as a community and only much later became a system of thought. This sequence, markedly different from the history of Christianity, has deeply colored the system itself. Muslim
theologians and jurists have worked from precedent—the Traditions of the Prophet (*Hadith*)—as much as from the Book. From
the beginning they were as much concerned with the regulation
of man in earthly society as with the preparation of man for Divine Judgment.

The sunna, or "way," of Islam is based upon the society which
Muhammad created in Medina. In this code, men are separated
from one another by their religions. Each is entitled, within certain bounds, to practice his own faith, but Islam is recognized as
the proper religion for Arabs. And though all three of the then-
known monotheistic religions are theoretically the same, as the religion of Abraham, both the Jews and the Christians are said to
have corrupted what they received from God. Muslims hold that
the Jews have distorted their texts and altered various practices

(Islam is closer to the less Orthodox Jewish sects) and that the Christians have committed the sin of associating Jesus with God, who is Alone, One, and Unapproachable. To correct these mistakes and to guide a new people, the Arabs, God revealed again his one and unchanging message to Muhammad.

Concerned as Islam was with precise definitions and with the practical administration and moral tone of the Medina community, we should expect to find, and do find, explicit and full treatment in the Koran of such affairs as property rights, inheritance, marriage, divorce, punishment of theft and adultery, treatment of slaves and orphans, commercial practices, food, drink, games, and bribery.

Islam envisaged no division of Church and State. To be precise, it foresaw no Church at all. Society, if not a State per se, encompassed all aspects of man's proper life. Indeed, in early Islam those functions we call "religious" play a utilitarian part—in a new society fighting for its life against external enemies and beset by internal divisions, even the ceremonial of public prayer had a disciplinary quality not different from the drill of new recruits in an army. But Islam went beyond simply laying down the rules of society by addressing itself to the method of living the correct life in all of its detail.

Formally, the religion of Islam was extremely simple. To be a Muslim, a man must affirm the Unity of God and the Prophecy of Muhammad, saying, "there is no god but God and Muhammad is His messenger." Beyond that, the latitude of action or inaction is wide. Muslims are supposed to pray in a prescribed manner, give alms in a certain amount, fast during the daylight hours of the Holy Month, perform the pilgrimage at least once, and "strive in the way of God."

These are the "pillars" of the faith. To convert these into the elaborate, formal civilization of Islam, as the subsequent centuries were to know it, was the work of generations of scholars, theologians, and jurists who, mining the lodes of the Koran and the Traditions, fabricated from this simple ore an elaborate structure. Their task, difficult enough in a changing and growing society, was complicated by the gaps, alterations, and conflicts within the materials they worked. Since Islam, like Christianity, is divided into many sects, it is well to understand something of this early source of difference.

The 6000 verses which have come to us as the Koran were not written down in the lifetime of Muhammad. It was the fact that many of those who had memorized the verses were being killed in warfare that led Muhammad's successors to collect his messages. Naturally, there were different renditions. Several of the more famous were collected into "rival" Korans, which began to spread throughout the Islamic world. Individual versions tended to become associated with regional or tribal groupings. Ultimately this situation became so dangerous that a single authorized codex was prepared and all other copies were ordered destroyed.

However, Arabic writing at that period, like early notations in Western music, allowed considerable interpretation; the letters were, in fact, prompters for those who knew the text. Not only were vowels not written (so that, for example, the first part of this sentence would read "nt nl wr vwls nt wrttn") but no distinction was made between a number of consonants (for example between n, t, th, y, and b). Therefore, a single line could have more than one meaning. Thus, within the official text a number of different interpretations were equally orthodox. In fact, in a typical commentary on the Koran one finds after most verses, "but so-and-so reads it thus and another reads it thus."

Later, the issue was further complicated when various religious thinkers and, indeed, whole sects within the family of Islam suggested that the text of the Koran itself was subject to an inner meaning and required allegorical interpretation.

So complex was this problem to become, even early in Islam, that the religion developed not a priesthood but a legal profession who specialized in the application of Koranic law to social problems. This body of jurists and scholars of the Law has remained the cardinal organizational cadre of Islam to the present day.

The absence of a priesthood, holy men, and saints in Islam was felt early in its history. The religion, in the limited sense of man's relationship to the godhead, was in primitive, Orthodox Islam— as it is today in such puritanical sects as the Wahhabis of Arabia

—an austere, stark, and cold system. Between man and the all-powerful, unrelenting God-Judge was a vast gulf, across which no man could help another, since not even Muhammad was an intercessor. Nor was the religion satisfyingly visible. It began by destroying the visible signs of pagan cults and was even hostile to the sensual representation of religious subjects. A patch of desert was as "holy" or acceptable to God as a place of prayer as the most beautiful and elaborate mosque.

It is not surprising, therefore, that early in Islam men sought softer, warmer, and shorter ways to reach God. As Islam spread to areas which had known other religions, elements of sensualism, sainthood, and ecstasy were injected into it. The early followers of Muhammad were accorded a position not unlike that of the Apostles. Locally revered good men achieved locally recognized sainthood and their graves became places of pilgrimage—often, indeed, these places were associated with the gods of former religions. The intercession of such figures was devoutly sought despite the formal anathema of Islam. Ultimately, a religious art grew, although this never flourished among the Arabs, and great care in the design of religious buildings brought about an architecture comparable to Gothic Europe. Finally, the faith received a symbol in some ways akin to the Crucifixion when the grandson of Muhammad was killed on the battlefield against a government which many regarded as oppressive and secular. Those who opposed that government, who came to be called the Shiis or Partisans, seized upon the death of Husain, Muhammad's grandson, as the emotional nucleus of their political rebellion against the Orthodox State.

But the Shiis, like the Orthodox or Sunni Muslims, became deeply divided amongst themselves over points of dogma and interpretation. Some of the Shiis actually merge their imams with the godhead, ascribing to them, in inherited succession, the spirit of God. Others express in a religious medium their political, social, or economic differences from the rulers in a theocracy. Thus it is that many of the conquered people who were treated as second-class citizens in the new Islamic empire expressed their resentment against the Establishment by espousing unorthodox religious beliefs. Even Orthodox Islam, coping with the multifarious problems of a vastly expanded society and drawing on various sources, developed four distinct schools of law.

The greatest of the merits of Islam is that it has been able to retain the simplicity of its beginnings, so that to be or become a Muslim is easy, while being flexible enough to embrace a wide variety of practice, to accommodate dissent, and even to submit to total reinterpretation. For this flexibility a price has been paid. The religion has never made possible the weaving of the strands of society into a social fabric capable of clothing in one garment the whole Islamic world.

In Islam, as in tribal life, geographical division and separate historical experience gave additional scope for diversity. It is for this reason that the Arabs hark to language—the language of the Koran and of the poets—as the immutable base of their dream of nationhood.

IV. Conquests and the Caliphate: Glorious Yesterdays

When in A.D. 622 Muhammad moved his Meccan followers and fled himself from the hostility of the Meccans to Medina, he set the stage for the growth of the Islamic community. What distinguished the move to Medina from the abortive venture in Taif was that Muhammad went as a Prophet armed with the nucleus of a state. The fact that he had his own partisans raised him above the position of a neutral arbitrator and gave him the balance of power in the community. With his Book—and his sword—Muhammad was able to fuse the natives of Medina, who were composed of two Arab and several Jewish tribes, with his own followers to make a new and much larger tribe whose membership was defined not by kinship but by religion. Within the group no fighting was allowed and the hand of every man was turned against the common external enemy, but the enemy always had the option of joining the group, as believers in Islam or as adherents who accepted its suzerainty.

In this arrangement was a powerful stimulus to growth since the energies of the groups of members, formerly balanced one against another, were now turned outward. The community of Islam was spurred to action and given certainty of victory by the messianic force of God's favor to their leader. But the proof of divine grace was the conquest of Mecca. Muhammad realized that he must prevail over Mecca, the chief city of western Arabia, or fail in his mission.

To humble Mecca was not easy since the Meccans were rich, numerous, and experienced; but they were divided internally and lacked the fervor—and the lean hunger—of the new rival. Moreover, Mecca, depending as it did on the caravan trade, was vulnerable to blockade. As a former merchant himself, Muhammad began his "campaigns" with a thrust at Mecca's lifeline by attempting to intercept a caravan. The raid failed, however, when bedouin tribes allied to Mecca gave warning. It thus became evident that though the strategy was correct, its first tactical step must be to subdue and bring within the Islamic community the tribes who controlled the desert.

A normal tribal group, the clan, was small. When the groups it encountered were also small it could survive. Muhammad, however, had found a way to combine a number of clans into a large unit. Since no fighting was allowed within this unit, all its warlike energies were turned outward. Thus, it brought overwhelming force to bear on each clan it battled. The old balance of power had been upset. The tribe attacked was unable to combine with other tribes, since its only means of achieving a limited degree of political cohesion was based on real or imagined kinship, and alone it could not stand against the larger Islamic community while facing other, traditional tribal enemies. Only by submitting could it save itself, and, having submitted, it had to renounce the use of its force against other members of the Islamic Community and so its power was added to that directed outward against other tribes. In this way a large if ephemeral tribal "empire" was rapidly created. And, finally after several encounters, Mecca itself submitted to Muhammad in A.D. 630. The prestige thus gained and the addition of the most sophisticated and able men in Arabia in turn brought in to at least nominal submission tribes from all over the peninsula.

The tribes, however necessary as a force against external enemies, were always regarded with great suspicion by Muhammad and the early Muslims, who were, after all, urban Arabs. Tribesmen at best were lukewarm adherents rather than true believers (Koran xlix. 14) and had to be taught civilized manners toward the Messenger (Koran xlix. 1-5) and treated severely if

they got out of line. More economical than trying constantly to
suppress the tribes was to give them a target for their warlike
energies. Only in this way could they be made loyal members of
the Islamic community. Thus, shortly before his death in A.D. 632,
Muhammad had planned a foray into Palestine.

Muhammad's death presented the community with what might
have been a mortal crisis. So completely had his mission captured
the imagination of his inner group of followers, the true believers,
that some could not accept the fact of his death. Muhammad
himself had made no provision for his succession. He had established no formal organization of statehood or of religion; only in
his person was the state manifest to believers and adherents alike.
The only "office" held by anyone in the community was leadership of public prayer in the absence or sickness of Muhammad.
It was this office which was seized upon by Muhammad's inner
circle and imposed upon the rest of the community. And it is
from this humble beginning that the caliphate (caliph meaning
successor) derives.

To the tribes, however, this innovation was unacceptable; in
their eyes Muhammad's death dissolved all bonds of allegiance.
Throughout Arabia the empire, like a mirage, vanished, as the
tribes, in the religious terminology of later Muslims, "apostat-
ized." The caliph appeared to have inherited a memory. So strong
was the hold of Muhammad over his inner circle that the caliph
nevertheless honored Muhammad's last command by dispatching
the small remnant of the Muslim army into Palestine on a raid. It
was with great difficulty that Medina withstood attacking bedouin until the army returned with booty and boasts of successes
yet to come. The nearer bedouin once again leaped aboard the
bandwagon of success, wealth, and glory and as before were
turned against the other tribes in what became the bloodiest and
most repressive war in Arabian history. So successful were the
flying columns of cavalry scouring Arabia that they fused, almost
imperceptibly, into an army of conquest. Their leader, Khalid ibn
al-Walid, nicknamed the "Sword of God," was one of the great
generals of all time.

To understand what happened next, it is important to realize that the two great Middle Eastern empires of that era, Byzantium or Eastern Rome and Sassanian Iran, had fought one another to an exhausted standstill. In A.D. 611 the Persians had invaded Syria and Palestine and in 614 had captured Jerusalem. Returning to the attack, the Byzantine forces slowly won back their lost ground, took repressive measures against the pro-Sassanian Jewish community, and tried, vainly, to enforce the Orthodox faith among the monophysite Christians who prevailed in Syria and Palestine. Both empires were exhausted, faced financial crises, and were rent by internal schisms. To economize, the Byzantines stopped paying subsidies to the Christian Arab tribes who had guarded the steppe lands of Syria and Jordan. This may have been the crucial factor in the Muslim Arab success.

In 633 the caliph launched probes of tribal forces northward into Byzantine territory; in the following year his great general marched northward in Iraq and, turning westward, rode straight across the Great Syrian Desert for 500 miles, appearing suddenly outside the walls of Damascus. After looting Damascus this army and the other Arab tribal groups fought several brief battles with Byzantine forces, until in July of 636 on the Yarmuk River in what is now Jordan they met and destroyed the assembled Byzantine forces led by the emperor.

What had started as a punitive expedition became a raid, and the raid became a war of conquest. Spurred on by the very shock of their success and by the tales of glory and booty, a torrent of tribes poured out of Arabia. In the words of Sir William Muir, "It was the scent of war that now turned the sullen temper of the Arab tribes into eager loyalty: for thus the brigand spirit of the Bedawi was brought into unison with the newborn fire of Islam. The call to battle reverberated throughout the land, and was answered eagerly . . . warrior after warrior, column after column, whole tribes in endless succession with their women and children, issued forth to fight. And ever, at the marvellous tale of cities conquered; of rapine rich beyond compute; of maidens parted on the very field of battle 'to every man a damsel or two'; and at the sight of the royal fifth [the caliph's share] fresh tribes arose and went. Onward and still onward, like swarms from the hive, or flights of locusts darkening the land, tribe after tribe issued forth and hastening northward, spread in great masses to the East and to the West."*

The defeated Byzantine forces fell back upon the seacoast, abandoning the hinterland to the Arabs. The caliph himself came to Jerusalem in 637 to make peace and organize the new province. In the chronicles he is described as riding a white camel, dressed in worn and torn robes, as he came to pray at the place where Muhammad dreamed he had ascended to Heaven and to which the early Muslims had directed their prayers, as modern Arabs do to Mecca. As in Arabia, so in the new empire, the "People of the Book," the Christians and Jews, were given the status of protected clients and allowed to continue to practice their religions, to manage their internal community affairs, and to avoid military service by payment of a tax.

The Muslims, who regarded Islam as the religion of the Arabs and who wanted revenue more than soldiers, put little effort in an attempt to convert anyone to their religion. Meanwhile, a world was waiting to be won. In the same year as the caliph's visit to Jerusalem an Arab army defeated the forces of the Sassanian emperor and captured his capital of Ctesiphon near modern Baghdad. Now all Persia was open before them. Shortly thereafter, another Arab general convinced the caliph to let him conquer Egypt. He is related as saying "its people are playthings, its soil is gold and it belongs to those strong enough to take it." With a force of Yemenite cavalry the general defeated the first Byzantine garrison he met. Reinforced and aided by the local Coptic Christian community he then captured Babylon, near modern Cairo, and laid seige to Alexandria, which surrendered in 642. By 669 the Arabs had created a navy and had attacked Cyprus; six years later this force was able to destroy the bulk of the Byzantine fleet of 500 ships. Meanwhile, Arab armies were plunging deep into Anatolia to the north and eastward into Afghanistan.

The Caliph Omar, the second caliph, was assassinated by a Persian slave in 644. Once again the young Islamic state was left

* *The Caliphate, Its Rise, Decline and Fall* (Edinburgh, 1915), p. 43.

without a designated successor. This time the powerful Meccan oligarchy, which had chafed under the puritanical rule of the first two caliphs as it watched others reap the spoils of the conquests, managed to get one of its own number, Uthman of the Umayyad clan, elected caliph. Quick to profit from their new position, the old oligarchy reached out to gather the fruits of power and majesty from the vast new empire.

The empire itself was the jerry-built creation of expedience. The tribal armies, interested in loot rather than in rule, would have melted away had they not been gathered into cantonments or garrisons and paid a share of the booty. The garrisons, Kufa, Basra, Qum (in Iran), Old Cairo, and Qairawan (in Tunisia), rapidly grew into towns and cities as the local people flocked to them and settled to sell goods and services to the soldiers in the exchange for their newly won riches. But the gathering, conversion, and transportation of the caliph's fifth of the booty, the payment of the army, and the administration of taxes and governmental expenditures were vast new undertakings. The inner core of Muhammad's followers were not fitted by experience for these tasks; alone among the Arabs, the oligarchy of Mecca was. Eagerly they sought to reap this worldwide harvest. For their private gain, they were immensely aided by the fact that there were no universal laws or customary practices and little thought of ethics. In most parts of the new empire the old practice and often the old civil servants were maintained, with only such changes as were necessary to accommodate a different ruling group in the place of the Byzantine or Sassanian overlords. For men of wit, and the Meccans were certainly that, the interstices in the several conflicting tax systems opened onto enormous fortunes.

Resentment grew against the old Meccan oligarchy, the late comers to Islam, the men who had driven the Prophet from their city and who only submitted when they were beaten, and yet who now reaped the Muslim harvest. The resentment came to rest upon the third caliph who, though personally a good and pious man, was an "agent" of the Meccans. Not only Arabs grew resentful but also the conquered, who found in the rich and pompous Meccans a target for their hostility against the victors. So, while Islam rolled from one brilliant victory to another, internally it was wracked by dissension and corruption. Finally, in 656, after a campaign of extensive public criticism of his rule, the caliph was murdered by a group of Arabs from the mutinous army in Egypt.

Never again were the Arabs to be united. As universal as the discontent had been, it had no internal cohesion. Ali, son-in-law and cousin of Muhammad, was proclaimed caliph by those who had murdered Uthman, but he had to fight for his title, first against the other members of the "old guard" of Islam, including a widow of the Prophet, and next against the entrenched relatives of the slain caliph. Even his own followers were split into mutually hostile groups so that he could never direct his force against his major rivals. Finally after a sequence of pitched battles, truces, and conferences, Ali himself was murdered by a fellow Muslim in 661 in his new capital of Kufa. His reign was brief, but his name and memory linger on as the spiritual leader of the movement of dissent in Islam, the Shiis.

The provincial governor of Syria who defeated Ali and became caliph was the nephew of the Umayyad Caliph Uthman. With the forces of discontent against the Umayyads scattered and defeated, he set about unabashedly to found a dynasty which was little concerned with Islam. Under his successors this Arab kingdom held sway until 750 from Syria; after a brief hiatus it managed to re-establish itself in Spain where it lasted until 1030. The Umayyads were great patrons of the Arab poets and laid heavy emphasis on the bedouin virtues of hardihood, chivalry, and enjoyment of life within a code of honor. Little did they care for the spiritual life in Islam. Yet, their armies won for Islam its vast empire. They attacked Constantinople itself in 669, and blockaded it from 673 to 678. Their armies thrust eastward into Afghanistan, taking Kabul in 664, and northward across the Oxus to take Bukhara in 674 and Samarkand in 676. To the west they took Carthage, in modern Tunisia, in 698. From 708 to 715, Arab armies plunged deep into India and in 711 began the invasion of Spain. In 717 they tried again to seize Constantinople and in-

vaded France. By 733 they had conquered Georgia in the Caucasus and in 738 reached their highwater mark at the battle of
Tours or Poitiers in France. At that time their empire was probably the largest yet known in history.

But the Umayyads were never able to find an acceptable foundation for their empire. The real bases of their power were the
Arab tribes of Syria, but these were so scattered over the vast
empire that the government ultimately had to hire mercenary
armies of Armenians. The Arab forces, moreover, were split by
tribal and ultimately geographic interests. The conquered peoples,
attracted by Islam but repelled by the Arab government, were
drawn to movements of protest within Islam.

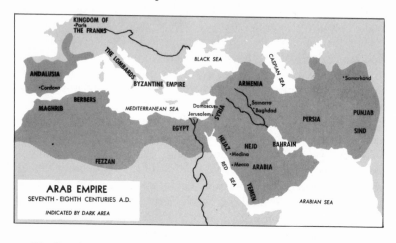

Finally, in 747 a revolt broke out in eastern Iran. Picking up
adherents, the insurgents turned it into a full-scale revolutionary
war in which they defeated the Umayyads and killed the caliph.
For a while it was not clear in whose name this revolt had been
fought, but after some months another branch of the Prophet's
family, called, after his uncle Abbas, the Abbasids, emerged as
leaders of the victorious forces of revolution.

The Abbasid revolution has often been portrayed as a Persian
reaction to Arab rule. There is much truth in this. The revolt
began in Khorasan, or eastern Iran, and many of its partisans

were Persian converts to Islam, but the new ruling house, the bulk of the army, the language, and the religion were Arab. What had changed was the political matrix: the new dynasty could not impose itself upon the empire as an Arab kingdom. The Abbasids had to find a new base of authority and build a new structure of power. The Arab warrior caste was deposed from its privileged position because it was no longer strong enough to justify that position. In an attempt to find a replacement for the cohesive force of the tribal confederations and the Meccan oligarchy, the rulers allowed a new class of scribes to become a bureaucracy. The easterners, both Arabs and Arabized Persians, infused into the government elements of Oriental magnificence and mystery. The armies became less and less Arab and more like those of the Sassanian Empire, comprised in large part of contingents of mercenaries and foreigners. Yet emphasis on Islam, in the ruling group still defined as Orthodox or Sunni Islam, was heightened, for it had acquired a new popularity among the citizens of the empire.

The vast size of the empire influenced its politics and economic life. The richness of its far-flung provinces and the relative peace and stability they enjoyed in early Abbasid times supplied ample wherewithal for a brilliant and cultured urban civilization in the new metropolis of Baghdad which became the capital of the empire in 762. Apparently the original idea had been to lay out a garrison and administrative center, but rapidly a city collected around these and in the ninth century Baghdad had become perhaps the largest city in the world outside of China.

The world of the "Good Caliph Harun ar-Rashid" as it has come to the West in the *Thousand and One Nights* is a part of the treasure of legends of both East and West. In many ways it does mark the height of Islamic pomp and circumstance. But precisely because history is here so incrusted by the jeweled glitter of legend and fancy, it has exercised a powerful attraction on later ages of Arabs. So hypnotic, indeed, has this become as to immobilize the many for whom its greatness, learning, and wealth could never be matched. Arabs have found an escape from subsequent weakness, ignorance, and poverty in daydreams of this past instead of galvanizing themselves for efforts in their own times. Even today, the typical Arabic history book is a "heroic harangue," as a prominent modern Arab-American historian has written, in which "modern historians have addressed themselves almost exclusively to the glorious aspects of Arab and Islamic history, depicting them in bright colors and skipping over the many dark spots and inglorious episodes [or] to a mere listing of personalities, theories, works which were translated into European languages, Western scholars who were influenced by them, and orientalists who sang their praises."* This makes it useful to know both the myth and the reality.

The myth is perhaps best spelled out in the dozens of stories in the *Thousand and One Nights* or in Hollywood movies—enjoying record-breaking runs in many Arab cinemas—which rightly depict the Arab Empire as the bright light of civilization during the European Dark Ages. The Arabic contribution to world culture was not solely associated with the Abbasid caliphate but even more with successor governments and with the rival caliphates in Egypt and Spain, but the nationalist myth of Arab grandeur makes few distinctions, so here it will be treated as a whole.

The major contribution made by the Arabs was in keeping alive, during the long period of European ignorance, the substance and some of the spirit of inquiry which had been the gift of classical civilization. Translations from Greek and other languages into Arabic were actually begun under the Umayyads but were officially encouraged by the Abbasid government. Moreover, the Islamic men of learning were able to draw upon other civilizations they encountered. From the Indians they got their system of numbers—an innovation which made possible mathematics as we know it—and from China that great tool of our civilization, paper. The concept of zero; basic work on optics, in which the classical notion of Euclid and Ptolemy that the eye emitted a beam of light was upset; advanced work in mathematics, including the development of algebra, geometry, and trigonometry; and significant contributions in astronomy came from the

* Nabih Amin Faris in *Middle East Journal*, 8 (1954) : 157–159.

members and clients of the Muslim-Arab Empire. The fact that many of the contributors were neither Arab nor Muslim is a great tribute to the tolerance and receptivity of that civilization. This great contribution was to be transmitted to and to stimulate Europe at a time in which, hungering for knowledge, it emerged into the beginnings of the Renaissance. Indeed, from the recapture by the Christians of Toledo in 1085 Muslim learning was available to all who wished to study it in Europe. The names of such of its philosophers, scientists, and doctors as ar-Razi (d. 925), Ibn Sina (d. 1037) and al-Biruni (d. 1048) fill medieval texts. But in the Islamic world itself from about the twelfth century onward the increasing power of the Orthodox religious leaders contributed to a gradual intellectual paralysis. As its scholarly lights dimmed, a Dark Age came to Islam, as it had to Europe.

At the time of Harun ar-Rashid the central administration of the state was in the capable hands of a family known as the Barmakids, who also figure prominently in the *Thousand and One Nights* as the boon companions of Harun. This family, to whom much of the stability and richness of the empire was owing, was descended from a Buddhist temple guardian in the city of Balkh. For reasons which are so obscure as themselves to be sources of many legends, after seventeen years Harun dismissed the Barmakids and confiscated their wealth. Thereafter, his reign was a disaster. Upon Harun's death in 829 the empire, at his instructions, was divided between his two sons. The result of this division—in which one got the army and the other the capital—was a civil war which so weakened the central authority as to accelerate the process of disintegration. Province after province peeled off from the central core.

Within itself the caliphate ever had great capabilities for growth and equal susceptibility to destruction; what it always lacked was a basis of stability. Never had it managed to integrate its rural base into its civilization; ever was it exploitive of its resources. Neglect and decay are fatal to a system of irrigation, which was the wealth of Iraq and Egypt, and ruinous taxation makes refugees of productive peasants. Both were features of Abbasid rule. One of the more quaint and yet horrifying records of the Abbasid caliphate is the *Tabletalk of a Mesopotamian Judge*, but it is by no means unique in retailing the frivolous way the ruling elite squandered the resources of the empire.

The very success of the empire in conquering so much of the known world undermined it in two ways. First, so vast were the expanses of territory to be covered and so slow the means of communication, that decentralization of power began almost from the inception of the empire. And second, the *élan* of the empire could not be sustained: neither the original quest for loot nor the opposition to rival world empires sufficed. Looting had to be stopped if the government was to function, and Byzantium, the other side in the "Cold War" of that era, was too distant to pose a threat credible and immediate enough to cause men to rally around their flag. Rather, politics was played on less grand stages as provincial governors, petty officials, and army commanders performed vivisection on the body politic.

Within the ruling group itself sufficient man power was lacking to staff the bureaucracy and the army. The bureaucracy, the virtual creation of the Barmakid family, improved and diffused by study of Persian court ritual, managed to develop a degree of a tradition of the service but not sufficient to survive in a basically hostile environment which lacked the public and governmental forces necessary both to sustain and to tame a bureaucracy. The army was always a problem. As the opportunities for conquests were dissipated in building an empire, other means had to be found to employ the army's energies. The Arabs increasingly withdrew from the military or were thrust away from it by suspicious caliphs, and were replaced by praetorians of many nations. As long as these contingents balanced and checked one another peace could be maintained, but outside of sheer force there were no balancing factors. So, as we shall see, those hired to act as the guardians of the state became its tyrants.

V. The Alien Empires: Arab Exclusion from Rule

The Arabs were always a small minority in their vast empire, as they are today in the world of Islam, and even this small minority was rent by schisms. Tribe opposed tribe, one geographical area contested another, and Arabs were attracted not only to different religions but also to different sects within Islam. Moreover, these various religions and political groups attracted non-Arabs as their adherents and partisans. Thus, the exercise of centralized authority became more and more difficult as the establishment of a principle of allegiance and identity, which most people today seek in nationality, became impossible. More immediately significant, lack of political consensus produced such turmoil as to induce the caliphs to seek politically neutral agents of power. It was thus that the last Umayyad caliph, Marwan II, came to rely upon Armenian mercenaries and the early Abbasids created separate guards regiments of "foreigners" from eastern Persia, Central Asia, and North Africa.

As they found their way to power in the military and civil bureaucracy blocked, the original elite, the Muslim Arabs, began a process of withdrawal. In some provinces, notably in north Syria, Arabs remained supreme, but this was the exception. Elsewhere, tribal groups returned to nomadism, and urban Arabs began to detach themselves from the politico-military functions of the state to specialize, almost as a caste, in the legal-religious aspects of Islamic society. These divisions—the politico-military and legal-religious—come the closest to matching the division of

Church and State in Western society. Thus, long before the fall of Baghdad the exercise of authority passed out of Arab hands and was not to return for many centuries.

The principal disadvantage of the alien bodyguards of the early Abbasids was that they tended to become Arabized too quickly and involved themselves in Baghdad politics. This was partly because among the "foreigners" of eastern Iran and North Africa were many Arabs. This "conflict of interest" made these regiments dangerous, or at least compromised, in a system in which the caliph sought to hold the balance of power between rival groups in his capital. It was the Caliph Mutasim (833–842) who took the fateful step of creating a praetorian guard of truly alien Turkomans from the lands beyond the Oxus River in Central Asia. Prior to Mutasim's time some Turkomans had been in the guard, but under him the guard as a whole, including its commanders, became Turkoman.

Troubles with the Baghdad mob and plots within the other regiments of the guard caused the Caliph Mutasim to move from Baghdad to Samarra where he established the new capital in 836. This city, a sort of Arab Versailles, was laid out on a vast scale with separate quarters for the divisions of the army. The caliph's hope was that there he would be safe from the Arab politics of Baghdad. His hope was realized but at the cost of upsetting the delicate balance of power on which his freedom of action was contingent. Isolated in the magnificence of Samarra, with its vast gardens, palaces, and a mosque three times the size of St. Peter's Cathedral, the caliph was at the mercy of his guardsmen. The outward magnificence contrasted violently, suddenly, and tragically with the near collapse of the caliphate. The Caliph Mutawakkil was murdered in 861. Then, in rapid succession came— and went—four caliphs, mere puppets of the Turkish generals, who inspired the satirical poem

> A caliph in a cage, between [Generals] Wasif and Bugha,
> > Who says what they say to him, just like a parrot echoes.
> Kha-li-fa-tun fi qa-fa-sin baina Wa-sif wa Bu-gha
> > Ya-qu-lu ma qa-la la-hu ka ma ta-qu-lu al-ba-ba-gha.

Mutawakkil's first successor was poisoned in six months, the second and the third were stabbed and the fourth was killed in battle against his guard. During this decade of chaos the outer provinces of the empire defected. In the south of Iraq, the home province, black slaves, originally from Zanzibar, who worked the salt deposits revolted and set up a revolutionary state. In Egypt the Turkish governor began to lay the foundations of what became an empire within the larger Abbasid empire, and in Iran the Saffarids carved out another kingdom. Meanwhile, the Arab tribes, who had even in the time of Harun been "bad neighbors" to the caliphate, espoused dissident religious movements under whose banners they were to sack Basra in 923, Kufa in 926, and Mecca in 930.

In Spain, at about the same time, a similar train of events had been set in motion. Abdur Rahman, a grandson of the tenth Umayyad caliph of Damascus, had established himself in Cordova in 755, and his descendants managed to recapture in Spain something of the grandeur of the Umayyads. Abdur Rahman III (912–961) carried Spanish Islam to its apogee and assumed the title of caliph in 929. Like the Abbasids, he brought in slaves and mercenaries to overawe his fellow countrymen; the main difference was that in Spain it was the *Saqalibah* or Slavs who were the praetorians.

In Egypt the governors since 858 had been Turks. The greatest of them, Ahmad ibn Tulun, who ruled Egypt from 868–884, best remembered for the great mosque he built in Cairo, was a sort of shogun, ruling Egypt, Syria, and much of Anatolia under the nominal suzerainty of the Abbasid caliph in Baghdad. Following him, Egypt was ruled by other Turks, an Abyssinian, and a motley crowd of rival bands of mercenaries, slave warriors, and bureaucrats who jostled one another for power and revenues. None was strong enough to win or establish a dynasty. But their rivalries so disrupted the life of the country as to attract the aggressive attention of the Arab-Berber dynasty of the Fatimids who had risen to power in North Africa.

After an initial failure in 914 the Fatimids conquered Egypt in 969. Laying out their capital under the guidance of the astrologers when Mars (al-Qahirah) was in the ascendant, they named it Cairo (al-Qahirah), and proclaimed a new era of Egyptian power and prestige. Legend has it that when the fourth Fatimid, the conqueror of Egypt, was questioned on his claim to be a descendant of Fatimah, the daughter of the Prophet Muhammad, he assembled the learned men and jurists of Egypt, unsheathed his sword, and said, "here is my pedigree."

Unlike the other Arab-Muslim dynasties, the Umayyads and the Abbasids, the Fatimids were bolstered by a religious movement, the Ismailis, an offshoot of Shii Islam. This gave them wide influence throughout the Middle East, and at one time they appeared on the point of absorbing the Abbasid caliphate, but it raised against them powerful counterforces of Orthodox Muslims. It was not the Fatimid religious mission but Egypt's rich Nile Valley and strategic central location in East-West trade that carried the new dynasty into a brief golden age. Their great mosque-university al-Azhar, founded in 970, still embellishes Cairo and stands today as the oldest university in the world.

But the Fatimids, however much they were favored by their location, the richness of Egypt, and their religious mission, were unable to consolidate a base of authority. Like the Spanish Umayyads and the Iraqi Abbasids they were forced to rely upon alien mercenary troops to whom they gradually lost power. By the time the fourteenth Fatimid caliph died in 1171 the Fatimid empire had lost its former grandeur.

In Baghdad, meanwhile, the caliphate had, after the bitter and tragic period of praetorian violence, managed to restore some of its former power. But, as in the later Roman Empire, the cost was great. From 870 to 908 the empire was reconquered, rebels destroyed, and tribute reassessed, but the effort virtually exhausted the dynasty and again the praetorian guard intervened, extorting and pillaging the citizenry, so that by the third decade of the tenth century the empire had virtually collapsed financially. Province after province broke away and refused to pay its tribute—it has been estimated that the revenue for the year 900 was about 3–4 percent of that of a century before. Men of influence in the bureaucracy and army commanders carved out estates for themselves even in the home province of Iraq and evaded all taxes. Smaller owners and men of little influence, on whom the remainder of the taxes had to fall, were ruined, abandoned their lands, or made over their titles to those rich enough to defend them. Lacking real power, the central government needed more, not less, revenue to buy allies and friends; moreover, it proved incapable of deflating the bloated administrative structure which had grown, sporelike, through all of the changes of Abbasid fortune. Even the imperial court, now ruling only a memory of an empire, continued to live on a lavish scale. It was as though the Abbasids could pretend to rule an empire only so long as they sat in an imperial court—even if it were supported only by a single, misgoverned, impoverished province.

In their desperation the Abbasids created yet new pieces of bureaucracy with the frank and honest names of the "Office of Bribes" and the "Office of Confiscations." Judging from the chronicles, these were staffed by the hardest-working bureaucrats in Baghdad. Increasingly, as money became difficult to get, officials came to be paid for their services in land or, if their assignments were of limited tenure, in rights to the revenue of certain estates for given periods of time. This, apparently, was the origin of the system of fiefs which was later to become common.

Finally, in 945, a Persian dynasty of Shiis, the Buwaihids, put an end to the pitiful pretense that was the caliphate. Under the new ruler, self-styled as *sultan* or holder of temporal power, the caliph became little more than a court functionary to be brought out on ceremonial occasions and discarded when troublesome or tiresome. At one point three former caliphs who had been blinded (and thus made legally unfit to hold office) by order of the sultan were alive in Baghdad, and one had to beg in the streets.

Only in Mosul (from 929–991) and Aleppo (944–1003) had an Arab dynasty, the Hamdanids, who were charged with guarding the Byzantine marches, managed to survive. But, ultimately, they too succumbed. As their great poet laureate al-Mutanabbi sang,

Men from their kings alone their worth derive
But Arabs ruled by aliens cannot thrive:
Boors without culture, without noble fame,
Who know not loyalty and honour's name.
Go where thou wilt, thou seest in every land
Folk driven like cattle by a servile band.*

In their turn the Buwaihids fought amongst themselves, and by the end of the eleventh century anarchy again prevailed throughout their empire.

Meanwhile, at the other side of the Asian land mass, in China, the Turkomans played a similar role in the affairs of the late Tang Dynasty. It was a Turkish general who ended the Tang Dynasty in 907 and Turkish officers who established the "Five Dynasties" which preceded the Sung. The re-establishment of a strong, centralized rule in China in 960 closed the northeastern frontier to further Turkish tribal incursions. Blocked by the Chinese and by a Mongol dynasty, the Liao or Ch'i-tan, bands of Turkoman tribesmen turned westward.

What distinguished the Turkish incursions of this period was that they came not as individuals to serve in the praetorian guards of Arab rulers, but in tribes, under their own leaders, knowing that they could not return. One of these groups, now known by the name of their chieftain Seljuk, was moving ever westward, bringing a new future to the Islamic Middle East. By 1040 the grandson of Seljuk had conquered eastern Iran, and in 1055 he captured Baghdad. Gathering Turkish bands as he went, the Seljuk Sultan Alp Arslan invaded Anatolia and in the battle of Manzikert in 1071 defeated and captured the Byzantine emperor. Anatolia was now open to Turkish migration and settlement. His successor, Sultan Malik Shah, and the famous vizier, Nizamu'l-Mulk, brought the Seljuk empire to the crest of its power and completed the conversion of what had been a money economy in the Middle East into one based on fiefs in land.

In Egypt at this time the Fatimid caliphate was dying out, and Syria was divided between several petty states. The Middle

* Translated by R. Nicholson in *Literary History of the Arabs* (Cambridge University Press, Cambridge and New York, 1953).

Eastern Islamic world was suffering, on the political level, from that sense of confusion and drift which is symptomatic of physical and emotional decay of civilizations. It was at this time, in 1096, that the First Crusade was launched against the Muslims in the Holy Land.

After a long march through the Balkans, the Crusaders were urged rapidly forward by anxious and mistrusting Byzantine officials. As they moved down the Levant coast, the Crusaders were relatively unopposed and were able to capture each town on their route. Finally, on the evening of June 7, 1099, they encamped before "Jerusalem the Golden."

The native Christians, perhaps having heard of the treatment of their cousins along the coast by these crude barbarians, who were interested in little but loot and cared not a whit for the religion of its former owner, were not pleased to see the Crusaders. But the Fatimid governor of Jerusalem took no chances on the enlightened self-interest of his Christian subjects or their loyalty to his empire and expelled them from the city. The Jews and Muslims resisted the invaders and after the Crusaders broke into the city were massacred. Most of the Jews were burned alive in their chief synagogue, in which they had taken refuge. Even those Jews and Muslims who surrendered were cut down in an orgy of blood, plunder, and religious ecstacy.

The state founded by the Crusaders, gradually tamed and softened by the balmy climate and easy ways of Palestine, lived, as it were, in the schisms of the Islamic world. With Syria divided between Aleppo and Damascus and Egypt under a weak and decayed regime, the Crusaders could survive. No sooner, however, were the Muslims to gain even a semblance of unity than the Crusaders were expelled. This was the work of the great Kurdish leader Saladin, who in 1171 put an end to the Fatimid caliphate, assumed all power, and set out to reunite Egypt and Syria. In 1187 he was able to muster just enough strength—and no more—to reconquer Jerusalem and most of Palestine. Upon his death in 1193, however, his state was shattered.

Again, the scene must shift far beyond the Arab lands to Central Asia where Genghis Khan (1155–1227) was putting together the most powerful military empire the world had ever seen. In 1215 the Mongol armies invaded China and took Yen-ching (modern Peiping), in 1219 they advanced into Korea, and in 1221 made their first raids into Russia and invaded Iran. The death of Genghis Khan temporarily slowed the Mongol advance, but soon Mongol armies were masters of most of Asia. In 1238 they took Moscow and two years later Kiev. A grandson of Genghis, Hulagu Khan, resumed the westward march in the Middle East and in 1258 captured Baghdad, killed the last, the thirty-seventh, Abbasid caliph, and abolished the caliphate. Pushing still westward, the Mongols reached Palestine where in 1260 they were finally stopped by forces of the Turkish "slave-rulers," the Mamluks, who had been established in Cairo after the death of the last of Saladin's heirs in 1260.

By this time the rapid turnover of masters had long since ceased to concern the subject Arab population. Deprived of their old military functions, excluded from authority, mere servants of those who exercised rule, the Arabs turned increasing to the preservation of the institutions of Islam. For Islam itself this was an era of external expansion. Muslim traders spread Islam deep into Africa and eastward into south and southeast Asia. Even the Mongols, who had wiped out the remains of the political power of the Arab Muslims, were converted in large numbers, so that Islam became in the full sense a world religion. But in the realm of Islamic learning, as in Europe during the Dark Ages, scholars devoted themselves to the task of preserving the pale glow of a great civilization with little hope of rekindling its fire or adding to the former blaze, never daring to experiment or tamper for fear of snuffing out what little remained.

Further devastation, pestilence, and flood followed the sack of Baghdad in 1285. The remnants of the city population shrank within its walls. The peasants tried desperately to avoid contact with all outside their villages. Only the bedouin, who had already withdrawn from the empire, remained virtually untouched. The dreary chronicle of this period would net us little. Men clung to niches as we have imagined some might in the aftermath of nuclear war, desperately trying to survive, not daring to hope to live as they or their fathers had in former times. Then, in 1400–01 Tamerlane led another invasion of the Arab Middle East in which he sacked Baghdad, Aleppo, and Damascus. As the English historian Stephen Longrigg has written, "If the scenes and losses were less dreadful than those of the ruin of the Khalifate, it was that Baghdad in 1401 had not the same pride to be humbled, the same materials for atrocity." Part of Tamerlane's spoils in Damascus were the learned men and artisans whom he took back to his Central Asian capital and so dealt yet another blow to the civilization of the Middle East.

In Anatolia the petty states left by the decay of the Seljuk Empire struggled with Byzantium and with one another; gradually one of them, the House of Osman, the Ottomans, prevailed over the others and began to grow. In 1361 the Ottomans seized Adrianople and then moved into the Balkans. Their plan to capture Constantinople in the last years of the fourteenth century was delayed as they tried to ward off the attacks of Tamerlane who in 1402 captured the Ottoman sultan. But this was only a temporary setback. Finally in 1453 the Ottomans had recovered and were able to take Constantinople. For half a century their attentions were turned to Europe, but in 1514 Sultan Salim took Tabriz in a war with the Persian Empire. The problem of securing his flanks led him to conquer Kurdistan in the next year, and the following year his forces clashed near Aleppo with the Turko-Circassian Mamluk forces of Egypt. The great victory of the Ottomans encouraged them to seize Cairo, which they did in 1517. Rapidly they spread over the whole Middle East. A Turkish fleet was in the Persian Gulf in 1529. And in 1533, having just failed in their second attempt to seize Vienna, Ottoman forces took Baghdad.

Initially, the Turks made few efforts to change what they found. Often they confirmed the governments, as they did in the Lebanon, or merely imposed a chief functionary over the existing structure as they did in Egypt. Even when they sought changes, the great distances and slow communications of the empire made for a large degree of local autonomy. By the end of the sixteenth century the empire was in its more central parts a kingdom but further afield more of a federation, as local chieftains, the "lords of the valleys," exercised the functions of government while paying allegiance to the sultan. The vast desert and steppe lands, of course, were never effectively a part of the empire. And frontier provinces were often under a state of seige. Baghdad, which had been reconquered by Persia, was again beseiged, sacked, and massacred in 1630. By 1704 Baghdad had recovered sufficiently to become the seat of a dynasty of pashas who were, for all practical purposes, independent. In Egypt, meanwhile, the Ottoman pasha had become little more than a figurehead; real power was in the hands of the landed Turkish aristocracy, the Mamluks. What is now Israel, Lebanon, Jordan, and part of Syria became in the middle of the eighteenth century an autonomous state, which in 1775 came under the rule of a Bosnian adventurer named Ahmad Jazzar, whose importance in Western history is that he was to give Napoleon one of his few defeats.

All over this vast expanse of empire the common people, tribesmen, peasants, and townsmen, lived their lives much as they always had. In religious brotherhoods, craft guilds, neighborhood associations, village councils, and tribal kinship, they found meaningful social life. Economically, they needed little as their standards of life and their expectations were minimal. Matters of their personal status, even transactions in land, taxes, and religious and civic expression, were governed by custom and legal codes which had little or no relationship to secular government. Their judges and religious leaders were not dependent upon their governors either for appointments to office or for salaries. Between the government and the people was a gulf defined not alone by language, culture, and temperament but in that the spheres of life were different. So total had this withdrawal become that it resembled a caste system: Turks were governors; Arabs were governed. Turks were warriors; Arabs were peasants or men of Islamic learning. In the colorful analogy to be drawn from Turkish terminology, the Turks were the shepherds and the Arabs the flocks.

PART THREE   THE IMPACT OF
THE WEST

VI. First Encounters: Point Counterpoint

Toward the end of the eighteenth century the Arab areas of the Middle East, although under the suzerainty of the Ottoman Empire, were in fact ruled by local dynasties or alien slave, military bureaucracies. The Arab population was not only small—with perhaps two million in Egypt and two million each in the Levant and the Arabian peninsula—but widely scattered and economically, administratively, and culturally isolated from all but near neighbors. Groups of towns, villages, and nearby clans of nomads or semi-nomads tended to cluster together as autarkic units. Few towns were large, but many which later became insignificant were in this period important trade centers. Even such widely scattered towns as Sidon, Kuwait, Jiddah, and Mokha carried on a wide-ranging and relatively prosperous trade. In some of the larger cities—Cairo, Aleppo, Damascus—as well as in a number of towns, medieval industrial crafts were practiced on a large scale.

Where men were favored by nature, as in the mountains of Lebanon, Palestine, Syria, and the north of Iraq and in the deserts of Arabia, they achieved a considerable degree of autonomy and freedom. Mount Lebanon, the most protected of these areas, not only had a high degree of village self-government, with secure land tenure, but an established and officially recognized "national" government which, at times, even carried on a separate foreign policy. Baron de Boislecomte, traveling about 1830, noted in his *Mission* that in many places the "cultivated valleys, separated from one another by the mountains and the great stretches of desert, form themselves into small republics." Writing of the bedouin "nations" in the Great Syrian Desert, Burckhardt observed that they were for all practical purposes autonomous states.

Bedouin tribes covered much of the land that is now agricultural. In the summer, for example, the valleys of Lebanon and Palestine and areas virtually within the shadow of the walls of Aleppo and Baghdad, were dotted with bedouin tents. In fact, as has been suggested above, a true picture of the Middle East at this period can be depicted in analogy to the sea: the agricultural areas and oases were the coast and islands in a vast sandy desert. Only occasionally could the people of the settled areas "go to sea," but the bedouin—merchantmen, privateers, fishermen—came and went at will. The sand sea was their natural element and in it they were safe from government tax collectors. Only rarely and temporarily could they be brought to heel by the forces of the government; in fact, they often are recorded as raiding and plundering the armed forces of the government whose valuable weapons were more targets than shields.

Between the tribes and the urban government, as between the upper and nether grindstone, was the peasant, accessible and defenseless, himself a domesticated animal, humbly submitting to the shears of the tax collector and the "brotherhood" extortion of the nomad. Where he could not defend himself, in the great river deltas of Egypt and Iraq or on the Syrian steppe lands, he paid the bill for both the town and the desert. Few families lived their entire lives in a single village. Great areas of agricultural lands had been abandoned and the so-called "frontier of settlement" had receded toward more protected areas. The Frenchman C. F. Volney remarked in his *Voyages*, "the peasant lives therefore in great distress; but at least he does not enrich his tyrant and the avarice of despotism is its own punishment."

Wherever possible towns were walled, and every man was a part-time soldier. Travel was expensive since each town, jealous of its autonomy and needing funds to pay taxes and hire guards, charged customs duties—in some cases little different from ransom—on entrants. Where the governor was strong, as in the city of Acre, he was really an autonomous prince although nominally an official of the empire. If he took a short-sighted view of his position he merely gathered as much treasure as he could, paid out to the empire or his overlords as little as possible, and retired to Constantinople. Jean Joseph Poujoulat, recounting his visit to Gaza, observed that the pashas looked upon themselves as travelers, camping out in their posts, never bothering to invest or repair. But this was not always the case. The pashas of the walled city of Acre encouraged the production of goods, both agricultural and industrial, which they monopolized, and taxed but tolerated the foreign merchant communities who settled in their midst. In some respects, Acre resembled a medieval Italian city-state.

With travel insecure and expensive, men moved mainly in caravans after careful preparation and along established routes. Some of these caravans were vast affairs. From Damascus, a city of 100,000, the Mecca caravan of 2000 camels departed once a year with 40,000 pilgrims; the Baghdad caravan of roughly a thousand camels made two or three round trips yearly. Ten to twelve thousand pilgrims yearly visited Jerusalem, then a city of 20,000.

Also because of the expense of travel, men tried to satisfy their wants locally. It is surprising to read the long lists of manufacturing "factories" of such little villages as Gaza, Dair al-Qamar, Homs, and Zubair. The important fact, however, is not the *scale* of economic life but the fact that for centuries men had accommodated to it and had found in it a satisfying pattern. Woven into their commerce, social organization, military service, and family life were their religious beliefs and their expectations from life. In a man's family, clan, or neighborhood was the seat of his loyalty. City dwellers found in trade and religious guilds what tribal life gave to the bedouin, a social matrix for individual life. Desires were limited because horizons were narrow. Weapons had changed little in centuries and they were usually inherited from relatives or made locally; the principal luxury item of clothing was the Kashmiri shawl and this too lasted at least one lifetime. Agricultural implements were made by the farmers—the hoe and the "stick plow" were the whole range—while those of the artisan in the town required little more investment of time and resources. Food was not more exotic or expensive. The staples were cracked wheat, vegetables, and yogurt. Meat was a luxury for the agricultural and urban population.

The elements of society interacted and met one another's requirements. The bedouin provided the villager with a market for his crops and sold him animal products; the towns brought the products of bedouin and peasant, fashioned them into leather, soap, cloth, and luxuries, and sent them out to the world on the backs of bedouin camels. The economic machine was a simple one which by modern standards was slow and inefficient, but it worked. The breakdown of this machine, even if it is to be or in some instances has been replaced by a vastly superior though much more complex and expensive one, is what is ascribed to the "impact of the West."

European contacts with the Middle East had never totally ceased in the Middle Ages. Venice and Genoa, even in decline, maintained merchants' "factories" along the Levant and Egyptian coasts. The Portuguese, reaching the Indian Ocean in the sixteenth century, rapidly established similar factories on the Persian Gulf. Gradually, as the British and French aspired to world empires, they too created, took over, or inherited centers of trade and influence. Even the most remote areas of the empire were visited by the traveler and the merchant. The French monopoly port of Marseilles and the British East India Company developed vested interests in the politics of the area for not only was trade with and within the Middle East of importance, but the Middle East was the road to India.

In France plans for the conquest of Egypt had been discussed since the reign of Louis XIV. Behind them were motives more often romantic than practical, but Egypt did offer a shorter route to India than the Cape of Good Hope. This became of great moment to the French government when, in the last years of the eighteenth century, it entered a mortal struggle with the British

Empire. Not only, it was thought, was Egypt capable of becoming the granary of France and a market for French goods, but from the port of Suez a French army could reach India in six weeks. This idea was first discussed by Napoleon in his correspondence with the Directory in the summer of 1797. With his customary dispatch he was ready to depart the following spring.

On July 1, 1798, a French army of 38,000 men disembarked from an armada of 280 ships off Alexandria. In a few hours Alexandria fell to the French force. The Egypt he found must have come as something of a shock to Napoleon. The population, living in the midst of the relics of ancient grandeur, was small and poor. It was, to the advantage of the French, divided into several, compartmented sections. The rulers, nominally Ottoman Turks but in practice the Turko-Circassian Mamluks, spoke a different language from the native population. The natives themselves were divided by religion, class, and education. The peasants, cut off alike from Islamic learning and from political experience, were, like the peasants of the rest of the Middle East, more objects than actors. The Copts, "Franks," Greeks, and Jews were the scribes, merchants, and tax collectors. And the literate, educated, Arabic-speaking Muslims tended to all matters of personal status and law. It was to them that Napoleon was to address his impassioned, nationalistic pleas for understanding and support. "People of Egypt, you are told that I come to destroy your religion. Do not believe it. Reply that I come to restore your rights, punish the usurpers and that I respect, more than the Mamluks, God, his Prophet and the Quran . . . Tell the people that we are friends of True Muslims. Is it not we who have destroyed the Pope who wanted to make war on Muslims? Is it not we who have destroyed the Knights of Malta because they believed that God wanted them to make war on the Muslims? Is it not we who have been throughout the centuries the friends of the Sultan (may God grant him favor) and the enemy of his enemies?" All Egyptians, Napoleon proclaimed, "are called upon to fill all the posts; the wisest, best educated and most virtuous will govern and the people will be happy."

In the Egypt of that time these were such outlandish notions as simply to be incomprehensible to the Egyptians. Indeed, even generations later the notion that the Egyptians were peasants, that rule was not their function or calling but rather was that of the Turks, was firmly held by very large numbers of people. The habit of centuries of foreign rule had deeply scored the Egyptian character. Their withdrawal from politics was to be incomprehensible to Napoleon throughout his stay in Egypt.

Much more startling to Egyptians was the ease with which Napoleon marched to Cairo with his large, disciplined, and modern force and in the famous Battle of the Pyramids, on July 21, in the space of an afternoon, utterly destroyed the colorful, dashing medieval army of the Mamluks. The next day the French army entered Cairo.

For Napoleon Egypt was a way station on the road of Alexander the Great to the Orient, but, realizing the necessity of consolidating this forward base, he entrusted to the Commission des Sciences et Arts the task of organizing an administration, surveying the country, regulating taxes and expenditures, in short, of performing all of the functions of a military government. For the most part the personnel and practices of the past were retained by the government; the major innovation, and the major failure, was Napoleon's attempt to enlist in the service of the government a council of native Egyptians. On October 21 the population of Cairo, led by the very men whose favor Napoleon had courted, the native Muslim, Arabic-speaking Egyptians, rose in revolt to throw out the French. Though they failed, they did shatter the liberation image of the French occupation.

Like most of the strong rulers of Egypt before him, Napoleon realized the importance to the security of Egypt of control over the Levant coast, and so early in 1799 he set out on the expedition to conquer Palestine and Syria and perhaps to open the route to the East. At the walled fortress-city of Acre he was handicapped by an English naval blockade and the outbreak of the plague. After an unsuccessful, fever-ridden seige, Napoleon turned back to Egypt in which, since it now was a jumping-off place to nowhere, he quickly lost interest. After one more major battle against an Anglo-Turkish force, in which he demonstrated again the tremendous superiority of his army, Napoleon left Egypt on August 23.

Napoleon's invasion, and the long-range threat it posed to British interests in India, marked a great turning point in the history of the Middle East. The impact, however, was initially less in the Arab East itself—changes there have been greatly exaggerated by writers caught up in the romantic image of Napoleon and provided with superb propaganda in the publications of the expedition—than in the policies of the great powers. The French, pushed out militarily from the East, never lost their aspirations to play a major role in the East. The Ottoman government, surprised by the tremendous superiority of modern armies, accelerated its own programs of modernization and of the reimposition of authority over its huge but anomalous empire. Lastly, and more importantly, the British, frightened by the possible loss of their Indian empire, redoubled their efforts to drive the French out of India and, by a deep involvement in the affairs of the Middle East, to block any future moves from Europe toward southern Asia. A British army assisted in the expulsion of the French from Egypt in 1801, and in the Persian Gulf, Iraq, Mount Lebanon, and Egypt itself the English presence, whether the consul, the merchant, or the traveler, began to be felt.

The major if somewhat delayed impact of Napoleon's expedition was that made on one of the great figures of the nineteenth century, Mehmet Ali Pasha, a Turkish soldier of fortune who had nearly lost his life fighting the French.

Mehmet Ali Pasha, born in the Macedonian port town of Kavalla in 1769, the son of a police officer, orphaned young, a man whose energy was matched only by his ambition, was fond of remarking, "I was born in the same year as Napoleon in the land of Alexander." Throughout Mehmet Ali's life Napoleon and the expedition to Egypt were to exercise a profound influence on him. Like Napoleon he was a foreigner in the country he was to make his own; like Napoleon he was to win a vast empire; like

Napoleon he was a superb opportunist. He realized, as few in the East in his time, wherein lay the real strength of the French, and his life was spent in attempting to acquire the modernization, the industrial and materials base, and the organization which had made a Napoleon possible.

By 1805 Mehmet Ali emerged as the leader of the most powerful faction within the Ottoman forces in Egypt and was able to seize power. He had his seizure of power ratified locally in Egypt rather than from the Ottoman Empire, by an assemblage of notables in Cairo—itself rather an unusual move—and then negotiated with the empire as to how his position could be confirmed. Confirmation as governor came in 1806. But the political situation was still very unstable in Egypt, where rivals watched as hungry wolves the leader of their pack. The attempted British invasion of Egypt in 1807, which ended disastrously for the British at the Battle of Rosetta, came at a dangerous point for Mehmet Ali and his "victory" was not of his design or execution but was due to peasant xenophobia, poor British planning, and thirst.

In this period the necessity for reform in Egypt was recognized by everyone. Napoleon's military force had so easily destroyed the flower of Mamluk cavalry as to produce a profound impression on the whole Middle East. The Mamluk beys themselves, particularly the two who emerged as Mehmet Ali's major opponents in these years, aped French uniforms, had their troops drilled in French style, and attempted to gain modern French power by appearing, insofar as they knew how, French. The first Ottoman governor against whom Mehmet Ali contended for power, Khusrev Pasha, who was later to be grand vizier, enlisted French officers to train a Sudanese regiment on the French system. So it took no unique insight on the part of Mehmet Ali to realize where the new road of power lay. Each contender for power recognized that if he were to survive in the kind of situation which had been created by Napoleon's challenge to Egypt, he must create a modern army. Mehmet Ali won partly by his reforms and largely by luck. But, having won locally, he knew he could survive only by a combination of modernization and expansion.

In 1815 he tried to introduce into Egypt the *Nizam Jadid*, the new-style army. But the opposition on the part of his own army was such that he was forced to drop this program, and it was not until a lengthy war in Arabia against the Wahhabis had virtually killed off the veterans of his existing force that he was able to undertake the imposition of a modernized military system. It happened that just about the time the political situation was ready in Egypt for the introduction of this system, a former French army officer, then a captain, by the name of Sève, who subsequently became known as Sulaiman Pasha, arrived in Egypt and offered his services.

Mehmet Ali ordered Sève to introduce into Egypt several schools for the training of soldiers on the French system. At first these schools were largely made up of Turkish and Mamluk young men. Subsequently, Sudanese were enlisted in the Egyptian army, and ultimately, apparently at the suggestion of a French adviser, Egyptian peasants, for the first time in many centuries, were conscripted into the army. The wars of Mehmet Ali made further and further demands for a larger and larger military machine. By 1833 there were about 190,000 men in the Egyptian army and auxiliary forces, and by 1839 one out of every ten Egyptians was in one way or another involved in the army. (This compares with only one in each 160 in 1967.)

It was the genius of Mehmet Ali that he recognized that it was not simply a matter of numbers, or of the drill, or the style of uniforms, or equipment of troops which made power in the new sense. It was rather the control over the *means of production* both of modern weapons and of modern soldiers which differentiated him for his rivals. He recognized that he could not rely on Europe for either but had to open schools to train soldiers and factories to equip them. Therefore he set out to build in Egypt factories to produce guns, ammunitions, and uniforms; arsenals to equip the army and the fleet; and ultimately shipyards to produce the fleet itself. The production of these things required not only a handful of technicians who could be hired in Europe, but also an intricate bureaucracy, a large number of literate, qualified, capable people, to run and organize all of the myriad services that a modern government required.

Mehmet Ali began quite early in his career to train his people abroad. In 1809 the first man was sent from Egypt to Europe for training, and in almost every year thereafter a new mission of students would be sent abroad. Very few of these were sent for what we would call "higher education"; most were sent for rudimentary technical training. Workers were sent to Italy to learn about the textile industry; others were sent to learn how to manufacture guns and equipment. Others were sent to military schools to learn not only tactics but engineering, medicine, and logistics. Although he apparently had not intended to do so, Mehmet Ali created a new generation, which was to come to the fore in Egypt after his death, of men who had begun to learn about the inner nature of European civilization.

Perhaps the most famous of these men was one who was sent to Europe not as a student but as the imam, or chaplain, of a group of students in 1824. This was Rifaa Rafi, who was born in the little Egyptian town of Tahta, where his father had been a fairly wealthy local landlord. So struck was Rifaa with the new world he discovered that while in Paris he set about writing a book which was intended to explain to the Egyptians what life was like in France. This book, called *The Journey* and published in 1834, went through three Arabic editions and a Turkish edition and was the most widely read of any book produced in the Middle East in the first half of the nineteenth century. It and that great classic of European description E. W. Lane's *Manners and Customs of the Modern Egyptians* present the most fascinating contrast of the intellectual contact between Europe and the Middle East produced in the nineteenth century.

When each Egyptian student returned from Europe, he was placed in the Citadel in Cairo and told to translate the textbook that he had been studying in France. So, somewhat casually, individual students made available to their confreres the works upon which they had relied during their European exposure. Ultimately, a special bureau was set up to translate a great corpus of European literature into Arabic. As manuals gave way to belles lettres the intellectual foundations of subsequent Egyptian history were laid.

The third aspect of Mehmet Ali's creation of power in Egypt lay in the field of economics. He recognized that it was necessary for the government to centralize agricultural, financial, industrial, and commercial control just as it had centralized military and political control. This was not the result of a sudden decision to undertake a new program. It was not comparable with the sort of decisions that are made in modern planning but came about as a purely pragmatic solution to a problem. Mehmet Ali had effectively eliminated his rivals, one by one, and finally in 1811 had massacred the Mamluk opponents of his regime and confiscated a great deal of their property. In 1816 he formalized the trend in centralization by subsuming land rights over all of Egypt. What these rights had amounted to was administrative control over a given area of land. The holder of this right (*iltizam*) would agree to pay to the central government a specified sum of money yearly in return for which he would be allowed to tax the people who lived on the land. He did not himself own, *de jure*, the land. The land was theoretically owned by the Empire. What Mehmet Ali did in broad outline was to take fiscal control over the land to himself and subdivide the rights to use the land among other people—in the main, peasants—who after 1816 produced crops for and paid taxes directly to the government.

Similarly, in the realm of urban finance, commerce, and industry, Mehmet Ali established a monopoly in 1816. Anyone desiring to buy Egyptian produce had to do so through a government agency. Ultimately, Mehmet Ali came to recognize that the government must undertake the stimulation of industrial growth. For this purpose the government sent industrial workers and students to Europe for training, hired European industrial workers and technicians to come to Egypt, furnished capital and raw materials, set production goals, purchased all finished goods, and paid the operating costs of the industry Mehmet Ali thought Egypt needed.

In Egypt in the 1820's, as in America at a later date, the textile industry formed the major thrust of the industrial transformation. Between 1818 and 1828 thirty cotton textile factories were opened. Additional woolen factories were built to provide uniforms for the army. Textiles continued to be the pace setter in Egypt and as late as 1952 accounted for 36 percent of the labor force in establishments of ten or more workers. Other industries lagged far behind textiles as Egypt lacked iron and coal. Here again there is continuity: in 1952 mining and manufacturing, of which textiles and food processing accounted for the bulk, still amounted to only 8 percent of the gross national product.

But in the time of Mehmet Ali as later, noneconomic factors caused the government to industrialize. In the 1820's and 1830's the Egyptian military machine, with about 130,000 men under arms, required the manufacture of artillery, small arms, powder, and other munitions. The growing navy demanded and got a rapid acceleration in the manufacture of naval vessels and stores in Alexandria. Troops and those who supported them had to be fed and supplied, so sugar refineries, dye works, glass-blowing factories, tanneries, paper mills, and chemical works were set up throughout the country.

All of these factories were supervised, financed, and controlled by the government. Many were under the immediate jurisdiction of foreign technicians but even in them Egyptians or other Orientals were trained to fill, ultimately, all the jobs. All of the personnel, including the directors, were government employees. The products were marketed by the government and all raw materials were procured by the government. Perhaps this government monopoly was necessary, as the growing and already far larger industries of Europe could swamp the area with their cheaper products, but the system, as the perceptive Egyptian writer Moustafa Fahmy has pointed out, did not permit the entry of a single capitalist or entrepreneur into industrial or, at times and in certain fields, commercial activity. This was to have profound social, economic, and political implications in later times.

In order to train the new personnel required by the government for its bureaucracy and its various other technical and military activities, Mehmet Ali also began a new venture or, more correctly, series of new adventures in education. Ultimately, over 10,000 students were enrolled in various government institutions, where they were given lodging, food, and stipends at a total yearly expenditure of approximately £150,000 or 5 percent of the then gross national product of Egypt.

In the enrollments one can see the obviously utilitarian aims. A school of languages, to train translators, was opened for 225 students; a school of secretarial service for clerks was opened for 300; a polytechnic institute had 300 pupils; artillery and medical schools had 300 each; a school for infantry officers enrolled 800; and a veterinary medical school, to minister to the cavalry, absorbed 120 young men. Upon graduation each young man was immediately taken into government service. Uniformly, and this was to remain a feature of the system until recently, education led directly to service in the government.

The number of salaried, permanent workers in factories reached approximately 30,000 in the 1830's and over a quarter of a million others worked in smaller establishments, or at their homes, on the government account. It has been estimated that between 1816 and 1850 the total number of industrial workers was at least 400,000.

At this same time rapid transformations were in process in Syria, which came under Egyptian rule in 1832. The population of the Syrian hinterland and coast was 1.3 million, of whom half were urban. In this area as in Egypt, commerce had always been an element in the economic life but relatively a secondary element. Following the French Revolution and during the French invasion of Egypt the violent and greedy rule of the Ottoman pashas based in Acre and Sidon caused a sharp decline in the international trade of the Levant. The French trading establishments were closed, the British had not at that time interested themselves in the Levant, and the American effort was then minor. On the eve of the Egyptian invasion even the British consul could not establish himself in Damascus so restrictive and xenophobic were its people. The people, as mentioned above, were content with the small world they knew and feared outsiders would destroy it. They grew, built, or inherited most of what they needed; and what little they got from outside was mainly from the Far East rather than from the West.

The effect of the Egyptian invasion of 1832 was to "open" the Levant to Western influence. This is a process which the author has described in detail in a recent book.* Here it is useful to point out that a change in tastes and technology distinguished the Egyptian period, as old ways, old tools, and old weapons were quickly judged to be outmoded. Cheap Western goods, the products of the new and booming industry of Europe, flowed into the Syrian market. Syrian handicraft industry was doomed. In the one year of 1833 an estimated 10,000 workers, mainly in textiles, were thrown out of work in Damascus and Aleppo. The smaller towns, which had to some degree specialized in particular local products, could no longer market their goods. Even the old caravan trade was hurt as clothing styles changed. The people of Damascus who would not allow the entry of one British official in 1830 were patronizing 107 shops retailing British goods in 1838. Even the great tribal groups in the deserts were affected as they found they could buy their headdresses and gowns from factories at Birmingham at less cost than they could weave them. Within a few years even the chief moneylenders of Damascus and other towns were British. The flood gates, once opened by the Egyptians, were never again closed.

In Syria, as in Egypt, the army was the principal agent fostering change. The soldiers were major purchasers. Officers were important investors. For the first time in Syrian history since Byzantine times the government, that is the army, undertook public works projects and gave security to the roads thereby encouraging trade and travel. As a direct result the Levant began to be tied to the world market on a massive scale and to acquire a taste for the goods and disquieting new ideas of the West. As the British agent John Bowring wrote in 1839, "The soldiery be-

* *The Opening of South Lebanon* (Cambridge, Mass., 1963).

came protectors instead of destroyers of property; they formed part of a structure of social improvement, which, with some attendant evils, brought an incomparably great portion of benefits. The effect of this better organization has been immense. Even in the populous parts of Egypt, before the time of Mahomet Ali, there was little security for life or property; in the Desert, none whatever . . . the Desert has been made as safe and secure as the high road of the Nile."

It is difficult to say what might have happened in Syria—or in Egypt itself—had Egyptian rule in Syria continued. This was not to be. At the height of his powers, after a series of campaigns that had taken his armies into Africa to conquer the Sudan, into Europe to attempt to retain Greece in the Ottoman Empire, and into Asia where they had conquered Arabia, Palestine, Lebanon, Syria, and half of Anatolia, Mehmet Ali had routed the forces of the Ottoman army and assumed control over the Ottoman fleet. The major Western powers were increasingly alarmed that the threat posed by Mehmet Ali to the empire would force the sultan into the arms of Russia. The English realized that they must weaken Mehmet Ali to get the sultan, and his prized Straits, away from the Russian grasp. Specifically, they must get the Egyptians out of Syria. Moreover, industrial England was actively in quest of markets and the restrictive practices of Mehmet Ali were frustrating British commerce. Mehmet Ali refused to allow the Commercial Code of 1838—which, having been negotiated with a weakened sultan, was extremely favorable to foreigners—to be applied in Egyptian-controlled areas, rightly seeing in it the ruin of Egyptian industry and the denationalization of commerce. "Monopoly," in free-trade England, was almost as damning a word as "Communism" is today. So, when the Egyptians had made themselves thoroughly unpopular and were in the midst of a civil war, the British assisted the sultan in driving them out of Syria, and forced Mehmet Ali to reduce his standing armed forces from over 130,000 to 18,000. With the *raison d'être* of the reform program removed, Mehmet Ali lost interest in the sweeping changes he had set in motion.

VII. The High Cost of Modernization: Coming of the West

The residual effects of Mehmet Ali's rule, both in Syria and in Egypt, were to be felt strongly by future generations. Mehmet Ali had created, albeit for his own limited purposes, the first of the successive groups of "new men" who were to come forward in Arab society over the next century.

What Mehmet Ali did was to unleash forces of economic change which had long-term but slowly maturing social consequences. He once referred to himself as "the armed missionary of European civilization in Arabia," trying to accomplish there what England was doing in India and what France was to try in Algeria. But Egypt lacked the power to sustain the effort, to control the process of change, or to replace older social institutions.

In 1824 Damascus alone had bought twice as much from the Orient (brought by the Baghdad caravan) as all Syria bought from Europe. When Egypt opened the Levant to Western trade, this situation changed drastically: by 1838 urban men were wearing fezes imported from France and drinking from glass made in Bohemia. By 1854 the French and Austrian steamers, plying the coastal Levant towns, had in the words of the British consul "annihilated the local carrying trade." New ideas from the West changed clothing styles, so that the key luxury import from the East, the Kashmiri shawl, went out of fashion. By 1857 the old Baghdad-Damascus caravan was finished. Routes of trade were either forgotten or reversed: Aleppo traditionally had got its coffee from Yemen but began to get it from Santo Domingo via France; pepper, which had come to Beirut from the East via Baghdad, was, after the advent of steam, sent to Baghdad via Beirut.

Specialization in the produce of the area led to entry into the world markets. This in turn led to the necessity of cultivating certain kinds of crops and of processing these in a way suitable for European use. Silk, long the staple export of Lebanon, had been reeled by hand, but by 1850 the requirements of the European industry had brought a drastic change in methods. Silk thread reeled by hand fetched only a quarter as much as silk reeled by steam power. This opened a new market for European investors who constructed large-scale filatures in Lebanon. Cotton, which was introduced on a national scale by Mehmet Ali in Egypt in 1831, was likewise affected by the European market. The short-staple cotton of Syria was useful only for producing wicks, while that of Egypt commanded a wider market.

However, cotton and other large-scale crops were affected by the vagaries of the world market. The Crimean War caused a rapid rise in prices but the return of peace in 1856 caused a fall of 50 percent in prices of cotton and other local produce in the Middle East. In 1860 the United States supplied over 80 percent of the cotton used in European industry; thus, when the outbreak of the Civil War cut the source of supply, a "famine" was caused in textile mills, which were the heart of British industry. In the year 1861–62 the price of raw cotton quadrupled and attention was attracted to alternate sources of supply, of which Egypt was the most promising. British purchases from Egypt increased from £8 to £22 million between 1861 and 1865. Such smart operators as Ismail Pasha, who was to become khedive of Egypt in 1866, made their fortunes in this period (Ismail is reputed personally to have made £1 million). But the slump which followed ruined many who had overinvested in lands and equipment.

Thus, the units of society began to change both absolutely and relatively. The bedouin alone held out, relatively unaffected by the slow pace of the new social revolution. But incursions into the nomad's sanctuary were made. Relentlessly the line of settlement was pushed out into the steppe and modernized armies became more efficient in hunting him down.

British and French consular dispatches of the 1840's and 1850's are filled with references to Ottoman punitive expeditions against the bedouin. Since the Ottoman administrators regarded the bedouin as pirates, they tried to drive them back into the desert, cut them off from trade with the towns, and where possible to kill them. Fairly typical of their efforts was a campaign in 1864. It was, wrote the British consul in Aleppo, "successful as far as regards the numerous tribes of settled Arabs, all of which have confirmed their submission to the authorities and consented to pay their annual taxes. The [nomadic] Anezi tribes, however, are during this season in the plains of Nejd or Central Arabia whither they withdraw regularly for the winter." The Ottoman policy, in short, was similar to the American policy toward the Indians, but whereas the Americans were a numerous and pioneer people, backed by a mobile army, the Ottoman government was represented by tax-collecting pashas with small and usually immobile military forces. Their proper target was the land-bound peasant, not the elusive nomad. It was only as the bedouin could be induced to settle and invest in immovable objects that they could be controlled.

Settlement of the bedouin had been one of the most interesting aspects of the Egyptian occupation of Syria. The Egyptians had a large and relatively mobile army which could overwhelm the nomads if necessary, but continual warfare was expensive. Moreover the Egyptians needed more agricultural production. So the Egyptian governor hit upon the solution of inducing tribes to settle. Purchase of land was made extremely easy, bedouin and peasants were assisted with government loans, and a ready market existed for the produce. In this way a great deal of land was brought into cultivation on the Syrian steppe. But following the Egyptian withdrawal the market for agricultural produce declined. A return to government exploitive practices induced many peasants to abandon their newly acquired lands and return to nomadic life. The British consul in Damascus reported the complete failure of the policy of settlement of the tribes when, in 1863, he noted that the bedouin "are being pursued by the Government troops in every direction without any reason other than they are nomadic tribes." It was not until the able and wise Ottoman Governor Midhat Pasha went to Baghdad in 1869 that the policy of inducing settlement was again tried and with some more success.

In Lebanon one of the principal effects of the Egyptian occupation had been the upset in the traditional relationship between the Christians and the Muslims and Druze. Lebanon, set apart by its mountains from the surrounding areas, had always been able to live an independent life. The position there of the Christians and other minorities was always stronger than that of their confreres in other areas. But at least in the southern half of Lebanon the Christians were second-class citizens in 1830. Often they were the clients and peasants of the Druze warrior class. Favored by a tolerant or even superficially pro-Christian Egyptian government, the Christians of Lebanon emerged in 1840 as landlords and creditors of their former masters. The Druze attempted when the Egyptians were driven out to regain their former possessions but were thwarted not only by the Christians, against whom they probably could have won a war, but by the European powers who undertook either to protect the Christians (in the case of France) or to hold the peace (as in the case of Great Britain). When the Christians invaded a Druze area, they were defeated, but the British and French stopped the Druze from following up their advantages. When Druze shaikhs tried to collect rents from their properties, their agents were killed by townsmen whose arms were conveyed to them by priests under French diplomatic protection. Indeed, the first Ottoman governor referred to the "innumerable French Missionaries . . . [as] the Pope's Light Irregular Cavalry Established in Lebanon, who under the garb of priests were in fact political Agents and Pertubators of the Public Peace."

Friction between the Christian and Druze communities invited outside intervention and led to a series of crises which culminated in the 1860–61 civil war during which the French sent a military expedition to restore the peace. Finally in 1864 Lebanon's unique character was enshrined in a *reglement organique* which acknowledged Lebanese autonomy under a Christian governor appointed by the Ottoman sultan but approved by the great powers. This was the formalization of Lebanon as a Christian and Western-oriented enclave which it has been to this day.

Foreign religious activity in the Middle East was facilitated by the organization of non-Muslim subjects of the Ottoman Empire into self-governing millets or "nations" on the basis of religion. Most of these had long existed. The separation from the rest of society and the relative internal cohesion engendered both by a common concern in community affairs and the existence of a single hierarchy or ethnarchy, which controlled not only matters of personal status but also the rate of taxation, made each millet a receptive partner for foreign political, missionary, and economic activity.

Lebanon—a land protected by its mountainous chain, relatively isolated from the East but open by sea to the West, whose population included religious minorities with a long tradition of contacts with the West—was an ideal place for early Western Christian missionary activity. The first American missionaries came to Lebanon in 1823, but it was not until 1831 that the mission was firmly established. Faced as they were by hostile Christians in long-established churches (until 1871 the Protestants were hampered by not being recognized as a separate millet with their own institutions), and unable to make overt efforts to convert Muslims, the Americans turned to educational activities. To succeed in these, they had to learn Arabic. Having done this, they were able to establish ties with local men of letters, some of whom became converts and in cooperation with whom they translated numbers of Western books and the New Testament. Gradually, they spread a network of schools over the Middle East and in 1866 founded the Syrian Protestant College, now known as the American University of Beirut. The French opened the Jesuit Université St. Joseph, and by the eve of the First World War the Levant coast had over three hundred foreign schools educating more than twenty-five thousand students.

Foreign intervention in the life of the Middle East characterized the second half of the nineteenth century. Whereas in 1830 a British consul had been unable to enter the city of Damascus, in 1840 another British consul actually picked the man who was to be governor of Lebanon. British consuls intervened even in the most minute political affairs of remote areas. For example, in 1854 in the port of Beirut a native and a foreign ship collided. No court then constituted could try the case. It was the British consul not the Ottoman governor whose powers were adjudged most nearly able to meet the requirements of the situation, and he constituted a mixed commission to assess damages and responsibility.

The commercial code of 1838 gave to European merchants great advantages over their native competitors, and they used these with the full support of their governments. The "capitulations" removed them from the jurisdiction of local courts. Capitulations had long existed. Originally, they were granted by the Byzantine Empire to encourage trade by allowing merchants to follow their own customs and laws while temporarily residing in the empire. This fit easily with the Islamic notion that nations or groups of people with a common religion should have corporate institutions of their own. The Ottoman rulers granted this privilege to the French in 1535, to the Austrians in 1567, and to the English in 1592. However, in the decline of the empire the capitulations became both a symptom and a cause of the denegration of Ottoman sovereignty. By the middle of the nineteenth century all foreigners enjoyed more privileges than do modern diplomats.

Foreigners on criminal charges could appeal their cases to courts in their native lands; even when their crimes involved natives, the local government was powerless to punish them. So flagrant were the abuses possible under this system that it was to be regarded as one of the great triumphs of Egyptian nationalism to get the great powers to recognize and participate in the creation and functioning of "mixed courts," in which Egyptian judges, though a permanent minority, could have a voice in the decision of cases involving their countrymen with Europeans. It was not until 1937 that Egypt was able to get the capitulations abolished.

The great stimulus to European investment in the Middle East in the nineteenth century was, of course, the huge Suez Canal project. This was the lifework of Ferdinand de Lesseps, who in 1854 was able to convince the Egyptian governor to grant him a concession to dig a canal to link the Mediterranean with the Red Sea. Lesseps was as ruthless, shameless, patient, and brilliant an entrepreneur as lived in a century of Morgans, Guggenheims, Rockefellers, and Rothschilds. The terms under which he began his operations in Egypt were almost the antithesis of those under which modern concessionaires work: The Egyptian governor was to purchase over half of the stock of Lesseps' company, but the stock gave him few rights and was held under various restrictions. Egypt was to get 15 percent of the net profits of the company but was to furnish a labor force of nearly 20,000 men to dig the canal. Then, as the company needed new sources of revenue, the Egyptian treasury was literally plundered of "untold amounts . . . for indemnities, fraudulent and semi-fraudulent claims, exorbitant prices to purveyors and contractors, and all manner of bribes designed to buy cheap honours or simply respite from harassment," writes Professor David Landes. In 1869 Lesseps was especially hard pressed for money, and this, in Landes words,

forced the ingenious entrepreneur to find other pretexts for an assault on the treasury. He found them without delay (the company cashbox did not admit of procrastination) in a catch-all of rubbish that was either no longer of use to the company or never belonged to it in the first place. By agreement of July 1869, the canal sold to the Egyptian government those barracks, hospitals and other structures built to serve during construction and no longer required; a stone quarry that the company had been *allowed* to exploit for purposes of building and maintaining the waterway . . . divers other imaginary "rights"; and, most important for Egypt, a renunciation by the company of any further claims . . . The Egyptian government paid 30 million francs for the package. Since it had no cash, it abandoned its rights to interest and dividends on its shares in the company for a period of twenty-five years. Lesseps in turn issued at 260 francs 120,000 assignment bonds covering the detached coupons; the gross yield to the company on the transaction was therefore almost 60 millions, while the purchasers of the assignments could hope for a total of about 110 million francs in interest alone during the period in question. As though this were insufficient, the Egyptian government also agreed to share with the company the proceeds of future sales of improved land along the canal, in spite of the fact that the Emperor's arbitration had specifically enjoined the company from seeking any profit from this source.*

The governor of Egypt, Ismail, made the opening of the canal in 1869 an occasion for Egypt to gain a sort of diplomatic recognition of independence from the Ottoman Empire. At vast expense he prepared a gala ceremony for the crowned heads of Europe, built palaces to accommodate them during their visits to Egypt, and commissioned Verdi to write an opera extolling the grandeur of Egypt—thereby giving us *Aïda*.

To meet the financial obligations he had undertaken, to buy his autonomy from the Ottoman Empire, and to satisfy his own wishes for luxury and for the development of Egypt, Ismail began contracting ever larger loans from the great European banking firms. It was this, wrote the later British proconsul Lord Cromer, that brought the British to control over Egypt. When Said Pasha died in 1863, the external debt of Egypt was £3.3 million; thirteen years later the debt totaled £94 million. Lord Cromer, who rarely minced words, wrote that "for all practical purposes it may be said that the whole of the borrowed money, except £16,000,000 spent on the Suez Canal, was squandered."

However, a contemporary English author, J. Seymour Keay, in a widely sold pamphlet called *Spoiling the Egyptians, A Tale of Shame,* and later historians have pointed out that of the vast debt, "only about 45,500,000 [pounds] were even nominally received" and on some loans the rate of interest was over 26 percent; indeed, one loan of £9 million was paid over to the Egyptians in defaulted bonds. Typical of the debts contracted was one in 1865 for £3 million. The Egyptians received £2.2 million and had to repay £4.1 million plus various fees and penalties. European sharp practice in Egypt was paralleled by European treatment of the Ottoman Empire, which between 1854 and 1875 borrowed the equivalent of $900 million of which it actually received not much more than $600 million.

* *Bankers and Pashas* (Cambridge, Mass., 1958), p. 316.

Ismail did "waste" a great deal of money—the festivities at the opening of the Suez Canal, for example, cost £1.3 million—but his big outlays were to the Ottoman Empire, an obligation forced upon him by the fact that Europe had refused to allow Egypt to become independent, to the European creditors whose pressures he could not resist once he was caught in the web of usury, and for the development of Egypt. During his reign the new basis of the Egyptian economy was laid. Apart from the Suez Canal Ismail Pasha constructed over 8000 miles of canals, 900 miles of railroads, 5000 miles of telegraphs, 430 bridges, the harbor of Alexandria, mills, factories, and lighthouses and reclaimed about 1.25 million acres of land. During this period Egypt's exports tripled in value.

By 1875 Egypt had sold its shares in the Suez Canal through the offices of Rothschild to Disraeli's government for a mere £4 million and had ceded to its creditors control over the collection of taxes and duties in large parts of the Egyptian economy. By 1877 about two thirds of the revenues of the Egyptian government were devoted to the debt, and Egypt was in effect, placed in receivership by its European creditors and their governments. Finally in 1879 Ismail was deposed at the instigation of the European powers and replaced by a weak and vacillating ruler who could be little more than a front for the Europeans who controlled Egypt.

As a part of the economy drive the new governor allowed an international liquidation convention to force him to issue a "liquidation law." Then he cut the pay of the native officers, newcomers to high command, in the Egyptian army. This brought on a rebellion led by a triumvirate of officers—the first Egyptians to rise to the rank of colonel—of whom the principal was Arabi Pasha. In 1882, to maintain his throne, the discredited ruler called upon the great powers and both Great Britain and France sent warships to Alexandria. On July 11 the British bombarded Alexandria, while the French withdrew. In September a British force invaded Egypt by way of the Suez Canal, routed the Egyptian troops at the battle of Tal al-Kabir, captured Cairo, and arrested Arabi Pasha.

Retrospectively Arabi Pasha has been magnified as a great national figure who tried to protect the independence of Egypt and who sought to enhance the position of the native Egyptians in the face of a corrupt, alien aristocracy. But in his own time Arabi was not a popular man; his limited intelligence and lofty pride were not solid foundations for national leadership, and the Egyptian people had not yet firmly grasped the concept of nationalism. In large part nationalism was to be a by-product of the British occupation.

The British seizure of power in Egypt was almost embarrassingly easy. The official justification for it, the bankruptcy of Egypt, could not be satisfied by an early withdrawal. Thus, though Britain immediately announced that it was planning to withdraw, British officials set about the reorganization of the country. Once involved in this program they found it more and more difficult to leave. The last British troops did not, in fact, leave until 1956.

The underlying reason for Britain's interest in Egypt was the one which took Napoleon there—Egypt dominated the route to India. It might, indeed, be argued that the construction of the Suez Canal made inevitable in an age of unblushing imperialism, as Mehmet Ali had predicted it would, the occupation of Egypt by some one or a consortium of European powers. It should be noted that 80 percent of the ships using the Suez Canal in 1882 were British. Thus it was that when the two immediate causes of the invasion were satisfied—Arabi was overthrown and the finances of the country restored, as they were by 1890—the British remained in Egypt. There was always some compelling reason to stay a bit longer. As Lord Cromer put it, "England did not want to possess Egypt, but it was essential to British interests that the country should not fall into the hands of any other European power . . . British diplomacy, which may at times have been mistaken, but which was certainly honest, did its best to throw off the Egyptian burden. But circumstances were too strong to be arrested by diplomatic action."

Having acquired a position in Egypt and built a cadre of able administrators there, Britain was inexorably drawn into all of the Middle Eastern affairs which had been the traditional concerns of rulers of Egypt. The affairs of the Sudan could not be neglected, so an Anglo-Egyptian force reconquered it from its native ruler in 1898 and established in it a new administration. The affairs of the Levant coast and Arabia, to which thousands of Egyptians went yearly on pilgrimage, became the concerns of the British. As a buffer to Egypt, the British government required the Ottoman Empire to cede the Sinai Peninsula to Egypt in 1906. During the First World War these area-wide concerns forced the British government to take a commanding role in the whole Middle East even at the expense of a partial estrangement from its principal wartime ally, France. The occupation of Egypt, then, may be said to have begun the political phase of the impact of the West while it set a seal on the first efforts of the Arabs to find their own way into the modern era.

The "impact of the West," whether the result of actions by Europeans or by modernizing Middle Easterners, resulted more in the destruction of institutions and old balances between resources and expectations than in the creation of new institutions and balances. But, of course, it was long before intellectuals in the Middle East were able to formulate their fears of this disruption. Essentially the question posed to those who would protect their way of life was how to recoup the strength of the East in order to protect it from the West.

Answers to that question could be found in many ways. There was some flickering interest in "love of homeland," as expressed in the *wataniyat* poetry of the middle of the nineteenth century, but this amounted to little. In Egypt at least, Islam seemed to be the best rallying point and found two able spokesmen in Jamal ad-Din al-Afghani, who spent the years 1871–1879 in Egypt, and Muhammad Abdu, who eventually became grand mufti.

Jamal ad-Din, the subject of intense suspicion and recent investigation, a person who, to escape being classed as a Shii in the Sunni Muslim world, claimed to be born near Kabul, Afghanistan, in 1839, was the great promoter of anti-Western movements. He traveled widely in the Islamic world and professed to find in Islam itself and in the community of the Islamic peoples the best hope of the East to defend itself. During his stay in Egypt, Jamal inspired a new generation of Egyptians with his interpretation of Islam and so gained the disfavor of the British and their Egyptian friends. In September 1879 the new pro-British khedive expelled Jamal from Egypt, as one of the first acts of his government.

Some of those associated with Jamal took part in the Arabi rising in 1881–82, and his foremost student, Muhammad Abdu, joined Jamal in Paris, where he was living in exile. In 1884 the two began publication of a weekly newspaper in Arabic called *al-Urwah al-Wuthqah* (the Unbreakable Bond) in which they urged Muslims everywhere to unite to save themselves from Western domination. The paper was short-lived, issuing only eighteen numbers, and was banned in Egypt and India. Nevertheless it had a profound influence on a generation which had begun to search for a means of identification and defense.

Secular nationalism was more difficult to project into popular concern. The government and all political figures were men of the well-to-do classes of the city, were cut off from the life of the people in the countryside, and were themselves too caught up in the process of modernization and Westernization to oppose it effectively. Indeed, such seemed to be the case all over Asia. To the Egyptians it came as a major shock to learn of modernizing Japan and particularly of its victory over Russia in 1905. Thus it was natural that the principal leader of the secular nationalist movement at the turn of the century in Egypt should have written a book called *The Rising Sun*.

Still, this was rather intellectual and esoteric fare. The average Egyptian peasant had benefited from British rule, and whether his benefit was due to investments made by the Khedive Ismail in the 1870's or to honest government under Lord Cromer in the 1890's mattered little. It was not until the 1906 Denshawai incident that public opinion was crystallized against the British on a mass emotional basis. The incident itself was small, resulting from a dispute between British officers and villagers during a

pigeon shoot near the village of Denshawai, but the violent, un-
fair, and bullying response, in which the British-controlled government sentenced three Egyptians to be hanged and others to
be flogged and thrown into prison, shattered the mask of benevolence to reveal the face of imperial power. The Egyptians were
never again able to focus on the benevolence, despite the best
efforts of the British to play down their power. This new aspect
of imperialism was to captivate Egyptian thought and lead them
to revolt in 1920.

Though it was Egypt that was the main threat to British interests in the area in 1800 and the main base of British activity in
the Middle East at the end of the century, Britain's major holding in Asia was India, and it was India that set the stamp on
British endeavor throughout the Middle East. This concern
tended to draw British activity into areas other than those of
even long-term interest to Egypt. Prime among these was the
Persian Gulf.

From the time of Napoleon the British were obsessed with the
thought that another European power—first France, then Russia,
then Germany, and then Russia again—might use the Euphrates
River–Persian Gulf route to attack India. This concept was
most clearly stated in the House of Lords in 1911 when Lord
Curzon said, "the Gulf is part of the maritime frontier of India,
and . . . in the politics of the Gulf are involved the security, integrity and peace of India itself." But as early as 1798 the British
Secretary of War wrote that "Bonaparte will, as much as possible
avoid the dangers of the Sea, which is not his element, but . . .
by marching to Aleppo, cross the Euphrates, and following the
example of Alexander, by following the River Euphrates and the
Tigris, and descending to the Persian Gulf will march on India."
The walls of Acre and the Royal Navy blockade stopped Napoleon but the memory of the real or imagined danger remained
fresh in the minds of successive British and British Indian statesmen.

Moreover, communications were vital to the retention of control over the Indian empire. Before the advent of steam the Red

Sea was regarded as a dangerous route, and the Isthmus of Suez was until 1882 in the hands of a potentially hostile or untrustworthy power. The route around Africa was excessively long for the carrying of government communications.

An alternative and rapid route was, therefore, what in modern policy pronouncements would be labeled a "vital national interest." Usually such a communication route was available on the Tatar post of the Ottoman Empire, but it was unreliable and was often subject to interference by agents of other European powers. Therefore, it was early realized that Britain must create its own service, the "British Dromedary Post," protected by the agents and consuls established at Basra (in 1764) and Baghdad (in 1798). One undertaking led to the next as the very mechanics of the problems of communications drew the British deeper into Middle Eastern affairs. A governor general of India complained in 1800 that "in the present year I was nearly *seven months* without receiving one line of authentic intelligence from England . . . Speedy, authentic, and regular intelligence from Europe is essential to the conduct of the trade and government of this empire." The Persian Gulf, although cleared of European rivals by the seizure of Hormuz in 1622, was still endangered by the pirates of Muscat. Indeed, these pirates raided India and the eastern African coast as far south as Zanzibar. After several expeditions the British established control over the gulf by 1820, suppressed piracy, and entered into treaty relations with the shaikhs of the "Pirate" (renamed "Trucial") Coast.

The desire to improve this route, and fear of Russian penetration, led the British government to send Lt. Francis Chesney to explore the Euphrates River with a view to establishing on it a steamboat service in 1830. In 1834 Chesney had two steamers on the river. Though the whole plan he had conceived did not prove feasible, he left behind a private company which operated a steamer on the Tigris River between Basra and Baghdad and provided the basis of British commercial penetration and development in Iraq.

If steamers were not the answer, the advent of the railroad seemed to offer renewed hope. The desert route itself was still in

use by camel riders as late as 1886. A Euphrates valley railroad
scheme was first discussed in 1840, but the British government
lost interest. By 1888 Constantinople was linked by rail to Europe. France, the principal banker of the empire after 1854, also
led the way in railroad development; by 1914 French investors
had 500 million francs in Ottoman railroads. But as early as 1872
an Austrian engineer, serving as a consultant to the Ottoman
sultan, had recommended that a rail net link Basra with the
capital. As the land was then sparsely populated, and such a project was not economically feasible, the engineer suggested that
two million Germans be settled along the route to develop the
resources of the empire. Although relatively latecomers to Turkey, the Germans plunged rapidly ahead. Several German authors
urged that ancient Babylonia was a proper area of German colo-
nization; expansion of trade was vigorously fostered; and through
military missions, Germany entered deeply into the affairs of the
Ottoman Empire.

The actual concession to build a railway was given by the
sultan in 1899 to a German company. By the outbreak of the war
in 1914, 1200 miles from Constantinople to Baghdad were completed. In 1901 the Germans began the construction of the railway from Damascus south to the Hejaz, to take pilgrims to
Mecca. Everywhere the Germans seemed to be pushing south-
ward. After 1890 German trade increased dramatically, and by
1910 it ranked just behind that of England and India.

The British felt secure south of Basra where they had agreements with the native rulers not to deal with foreign governments. In 1869 the first of these had been negotiated with the
Trucial shaikhdoms. Similar agreements were made with Bahrein
in 1880 and Muscat and Qatar in 1891. In 1898 the British used
their influence to deny to the French a coaling station in Muscat.
In 1899 the British and the Shaikh of Kuwait agreed to prevent
other foreign influence there. So, when a visiting German ship
arrived shortly thereafter in Kuwait, the shaikh did not receive
its captain, and when in 1900 a commission arrived to survey
Kuwait as a possible terminus for a railway, it was turned back.

The British interest could have been accomplished by holding the line at Kuwait except for two developments which drew the British deeper into Iraq. The first was the discovery of huge deposits of oil in Persia (Iran) to the east of Abadan in 1907. The increasing production from this field stimulated interest in possible fields in Iraq—who had not heard of the "fiery Furnace" —on which the British secured a concession on the eve of the First World War. The conversion of the Royal Navy to oil-powered ships and the rapid development of Persian oil led the British government to purchase control of the oil company operating in Persia just six days prior to the outbreak of the war. So important was this to become that Curzon was to say that "the Allies floated to victory on a wave of oil."

The second development was the growth of a belief in Europe that "Babylonia" could become the farm of Europe and a residence for the surplus and hungry population of India. The English expert on irrigation Sir William Wilcocks wrote glowingly in 1910 of the possibilities of agriculture in the Tigris-Euphrates valley to meet the wheat and cotton requirements of England and India. A few years later he wrote that "the delta of the two rivers would attain a fertility of which history has no record." A popular book of the period was J. T. Parfit's *Mesopotamia: Key to the Future*. And a senior British official, reflecting on this Garden of Eden, wrote that "there is no doubt that the land is the richest in the world."

VIII. The First World War: Midwife of Nationalism

The years before the First World War were filled with contests between the European powers, principally Britain, France, and Germany, for concessions and points of influence, but this rivalry in the Middle East had little to do with the actual outbreak of the war. Until the eve of the war itself the Middle Eastern issues seemed on the road to accommodation, particularly in the new oil industry, through the development of international consortia. Indeed, the Anglo-German Turkish Petroleum Company received its concession in Iraq as late as June 28, 1914. Like the causes so most of the events of the war were acted in other theaters. Here, four aspects of the war are of lasting concern, however: the situation on the eve of the war; the course of the war in the two separate and contrasting Arab theaters, the Arabian Peninsula–Syrian area and Iraq; the wartime arrangements, promises, and declarations of the participants which have left such a strong imprint on subsequent history; and the immediate aftermath.

But first a word of caution. The First World War ended one era and began another. It began half a century ago, yet even today a satisfying perspective is difficult to achieve, so embedded are the politics of our own times in the events of these years. And even if a clear and logical perspective is achieved, it will be profoundly unreal. A too-precise systematization of events and pronouncements results in a pattern which, though true in hindsight, distorts the context in which each decision was taken and each event occurred. In the midst of that vast and protracted crisis, the events were confused, the future obscure, and the actors imperfectly informed. It is, therefore, difficult and necessary to keep in mind but separate both the events and their subsequent implication.

It is now fashionable to inveigh against the Ottoman Empire as the corrupt, tyrannical, "sick man" of Europe, which lived by exploiting the sullen, resentful, and uniformly hostile non-Turkish population of Asia, and thwarted all progress in the East. The facts are otherwise. The government of the empire, with few resources in trained people or a developed economy, chronically insolvent, and hard pressed by foes and well-wishers alike, was able to control inexpensively a vast, heterogeneous area—a feat beyond the capacities of its richer successors—while retaining the *essential* loyalty of the several nations who were its subjects. The secret of its success was its toleration of *other* loyalties. To see what happened in the Arab areas, at least, it is useful to understand what these loyalties were and what they were not.

There was, first of all, no clear sense of territorial loyalty. The empire was divided into administrative districts, but these were in no sense nation-states and were not separated from one another by frontiers, linguistic barriers, or infrastructure patterns. Only Egypt, over which a British protectorate was declared in December 1914, had a discrete identity. There was no "Syria" or "Iraq" except in a geographic sense, as one might refer to an American Midwest or to the eastern seaboard. The "Syrian" moved easily to Baghdad, Mecca, or Cairo and felt no more alien than an American from Kansas City would in Los Angeles.

Such loyalties as transcended the family, clan, and tribe centered mainly on one's religious "nation" or millet, and this concept had no geographic expression. Members of the several Christian millets and of the Jewish millet were scattered all over the empire. The millet system did not divide Turks from Arabs and

Kurds as most of each group were Muslims. And, by extension, the millet of the Muslims was the empire itself.

Dissatisfaction with this conception of a polyglot, multinational, universal empire had grown gradually except in the Balkans, where it was accelerated in the nineteenth century as the Greeks (from 1821–27), the Bulgarians (in 1879), the Rumanians (in 1881), and others won recognition of their distinct nationalities. But even in the Balkans nationalism was often equated with religion—the Bulgarians, for example, won recognition in 1870 for a separate national church to distinguish themselves from the Greeks.

It was the Armenians who brought into the heartland of the empire, Anatolia, the notion of nationalism in the new, ethnic sense in the last years of the nineteenth century. This, in turn, stimulated the Turkish element in the empire to probe its own historical legacy for what came to be called Turkism. This new sense of particularism was a part of the drive in the Young Turk revolution of 1908. As the Young Turks assumed power they forced upon the empire their Turkishness in a way never before attempted by an Ottoman government. School systems throughout the empire began to teach in Turkish and to emphasize the virtues of the Turks. This new exclusiveness of the Turks compelled the Arabs to seek for themselves an identity which was different from Ottoman and different from Muslim.

From about 1890 onward Egypt was the cultural center of the Arabic-speaking Middle East. There, of course, *the* national enemy was the West as represented by Great Britain. Most Egyptians who sought a means of defense against this enemy turned to Islam as represented in part by the Ottoman sultan-caliph. Unaffected by the growth of *Turkism*, since the British posed a barrier between the Ottoman Turkish suzerain and their administration and school system, the Egyptians followed a different drummer than did the literate, vigorous, and modernizing Arabs of the Levant and Iraq, who were in contact with the new Turkish administration.

What the Syrians and Iraqis found exciting was that in Beirut, particularly at the American University, a sort of literary revival of Arabic was in process. This literary revival had meager origins and was of small influence. Much has been written to make it seem otherwise, but the intellectual archaeology of nationalist writers makes rather pitiful reading for the dispassionate foreigner.

Even the most friendly foreign observers have found little Arab nationalism before the advent of the Young Turks. However, the core of such a movement was there and its elements were clear. The major stimulus came from the ideas of Europe and America; religion was excluded as a prime differential since the Turks were also Muslim while many of the best Arab thinkers were Christian. It was to the rich, pre-Islamic heritage of the Arabic language itself that these Arabs turned for the basis of national identity.

In 1905 a young Syrian Christian Arab, who subsequently published a book in French called *Le Rèveil de la Nation Arabe*, issued a manifesto deploring the alien rule of the Arabs. "Encouraged by our servility, the Turks pretend to preserve the remaining independent tribes of the Arab nation. [But they plan to dominate all Arab lands] where they wish to construct railways . . . And what is even more degrading, they plan to do it with our money and our labor so that we ourselves will forge the chains of our own servitude." But, although the author claimed to speak for a vast network of secret organizations throughout the Middle East, few were interested.

In the first blush of the excitement of the Young Turk revolution of 1908 the Arabs had cooperated and even formed "Ottoman Arab" organizations to participate. When the Young Turks suppressed this form of organization, the Arabs retreated first to "literary" societies and then to secret societies. These, though very small in number, attracted the younger, active, literate Arab element in the Ottoman civil and military service. But the Arabs had no spokesman. None among their group had a "national" reputation, and, of course, no one transcended the religious barrier which divided their community. An early manifesto reflects this problem: "Muslim Arabs, this despotic state is not Muslim.

Christian and Jewish Arabs, unite with your Muslim brothers. Those who say that they prefer the Turks-without-faith to you are imposters and enemies of our race." Ultimately, however, it was a quasi-religious official of the empire, the sharif of Mecca, to whom the Arabs turned for leadership. But even if the young Arabs could have agreed among themselves on their ultimate objective, which they could not, they had little of any substance to offer the sharif, that cautious and skilled figure who had lived most of his sixty years under the close supervision of the sultan's police. It was not the Arabs but the British who tempted him to act on a grander stage.

We have seen how the impact of the West altered the traditional social relationships and created new aspirations in the more advanced parts of the Ottoman Empire. It would be a mistake, however, to exaggerate the size and influence of the groups who, on the eve of the First World War, had already been led to sedition by these changes. Nevertheless, some overtures to outside powers had been made. In 1913 a group of Arabs toured the European capitals to seek support for reforms in the empire, a tactic used by the Armenians before them, while another group visited Cairo to suggest that the British annex Syria. More important, Amir Abdullah, a son of the sharif of Mecca and a man whose name figures prominently in subsequent Arab history until his assassination in 1951, contacted Lord Kitchener in Cairo and laid the foundation of subsequent British-Arab negotiations.

These negotiations, and others with the French, led the Turks to warn their military governor in Syria, on the outbreak of the war, that "the news from Syria points to general disturbance in the country and great activity on the part of the revolutionary Arabs." This intelligence was confirmed when the Turks seized the papers of the French consulate in Damascus.

What distinguished this surge of resentment against the empire was the fact that the outbreak of a world war provided the opportunity for a revolt sparked by the growth of both Arab and Turkish national consciousness. Yet, it is notable that many Arabs continued to be loyal to the empire and to serve in its armed forces throughout the war.

The outbreak of the war in Europe in August 1914 was not immediately followed by war in the Middle East. It was not until November 5 that Great Britain and France declared war on Turkey. Great Britain then annexed Cyprus and on December 18, after nearly deciding on annexation, proclaimed a protectorate over Egypt. But in October, before the declaration of war, British troops and ships from India had sailed into the confluence of the Tigris and Euphrates rivers. In return for aid given by the shaikh of Kuwait, Great Britain recognized its independence under British protection on November 3. On November 6, the Anglo-Indian force seized the town of Fao in what is now Iraq.

The British and French governments were profoundly worried at that time about the effect on the large Muslim populations in India and North Africa of the proclamation of a holy war by the sultan-caliph of the Ottoman Empire. Pan-Islam was then credited by Europeans with great popular appeal and the dangers of a massive Muslim revolt, in the midst of the war, were never far from the minds of the British policy planners. On November 14 the sultan-caliph did, in fact, issue a call to holy war but the sharif of Mecca, who should have joined in the appeal, kept his silence. The British now hoped that the sharif could be persuaded to espouse the Allied cause, which would at least mitigate the threat of a Muslim revolt. This was the basic aim behind the correspondence between the British government on the one hand and on the other the sharif of Mecca, the so-called Husain-McMahon Correspondence, which set the terms upon which some of the Arabs entered the war on the Allied side.

It is important to remember that the First World War was a hard and bitter contest, fought over vast distances by huge armies from many nations, and that the issue was in doubt until almost the very end. The battle plans for Europe had been conceived in great detail years before the war, but the fighting brought a revolution in military tactics. Early in the war the British considered making the Middle East a major front, to attempt to bring the Balkan states into the war on the Allied side. Had this been done, not only Middle Eastern history but also the course of Russian history might have been profoundly changed. In a sort of compromise, in April 1915, a British invasion force landed at Gallipoli, but the Turks held firm. Russia remained effectively cut off from Allied assistance. It seems possible, from what is now known, that had this force landed on the Syrian coast, a native uprising might have assisted it to bring the war in the East to a more speedy close. The Turkish military governor, who should have known, later wrote that after finding in the French consular records evidence of Arab plans to revolt he had quickly shifted the local Arab units in the Turkish army away from Syria. He was, he said, "certain that to the executions [of Arabs suspected of nationalist sedition in 1915 and 1916] alone do we owe the fact that there was no rising in Syria."

In the history of what was rather than what might have been, Syria did not revolt and the Turkish armies on all fronts fought determinedly and bravely. In February 1915 a Turkish force reached the Suez Canal and in the same month pro-Turkish tribesmen in western Iran cut the oil pipeline from the fields to the port; the threat thus posed at both ends of the British holdings in the Middle East required the British to garrison large armed forces in the Middle East throughout the war. In August 1915 the British army in southern Iraq attempted to push northward, to capture Baghdad, and so to relieve the pressure on the oil fields. Just south of Baghdad, however, they ran into a strong Turkish force which turned them back with heavy losses and ran them to ground in the town of Kut in December. There, after a siege of four months, in which the attempts to relieve the besieged garrison cost the British over 7000 casualties, the 13,309 men of the garrison surrendered. It was not until March 1917, after a bitter struggle in which 40 percent of the 40,000 attacking British and Indian soldiers were casualties, that Baghdad was taken. On the Egyptian front, likewise, the fighting was hard. The British would not agree to American suggestions to urge the Turks to make an honorable peace. It was December 1917 before the British took Jerusalem and October 1918 when they took Damascus.

Of course, at the beginning of the war the British could not have known how hard-fought it would be, but prudence alone would have encouraged them to seek all the local support they could muster. And thus it was that on October 31, 1914, the British government offered Sharif Husain of Mecca a conditional guarantee of independence.

As a result of these factors—probable Turkish might, supposed Muslim restiveness, and actual Russian hunger—the Allies, led by Britain, entered into a series of agreements of a "tactical" nature to contribute to victory. Within two years Britain had made three major (and several lesser) commitments or proclamations of intent. To one of these the Arab allies were to rally as the fount of their rights in the Middle East. To another Zionists pinned their hopes; and on yet a third the French based their claims to realize their traditional desires for a French enclave in the Levant.

First in point of time came the letters exchanged between the Arab Sharif Husain of Mecca, who was then an official in the Ottoman administration, and the British high commissioner of Egypt, Sir Henry McMahon. This is the Husain-McMahon correspondence, which contains the terms upon which the Arabs revolted and entered the war on the Allied side.

In the first letter in the series of eight, dated July 14, 1915, Sharif Husain demanded British recognition of the independence of the Arab provinces in an area now divided between Syria, Iraq, Jordan, Israel, Saudi Arabia, and a part of Turkey. These demands were countered in a letter from McMahon, dated October 24, 1915, which excluded as not "purely Arab" the districts of Mersin and Alexandretta and portions of Syria lying to the west of the districts of Damascus, Homs, Hama, and Aleppo. The British also reserved their position, established by treaty, with other Arab chiefs and in Basra and Baghdad. Further restrictions were made in the series of letters to protect the interests of France. The last letter was dated January 30, 1916, and the Arab Revolt began on June 5, 1916.

The Husain-McMahon Correspondence has been the object of detailed and searching criticism. The letters were not officially published until 1939, when a special Anglo-Arab committee was set up to evaluate its importance to Palestine. The existence of the exchange was known, however, and the terms had been printed in part in 1919, in the Paris newspaper *Le Temps;* but, in spite of the subsequent urging of Earl Grey, who was Foreign Minister during this period, the British government refused for twenty strife-torn years to publish the full text.

At the close of war a dispute arose over the phrase excluding from the area promised to the Arabs the land to the west of the "districts" (*wilayat;* the Arabic plural) of Aleppo, Hama, Homs, and Damascus. The later British contention was that *wilayat* meant here both "town" in the cases of Aleppo, Hama, and Homs and the Turkish administrative district known as a vilayet in the case of Damascus. If the word means the same in all four instances, then it must mean only town or township, since the towns of Hama and Homs were in the same vilayet and only the sea is to the west of the vilayet of Aleppo. West of the district of Damascus is Mount Lebanon. If by the *wilayah* (the Arabic singular) of Damascus was meant the whole of the vilayet of Syria, then excluded from the Arab area was the whole Levant coast including Palestine. Summing up the British government opinion in 1939, the Lord Chancellor said he had

been impressed by some of the arguments brought forward in regard to the exclusion of Palestine under the phrase "portions of Syria lying to the west of the districts of Damascus, Homs, Hama and Aleppo." He considers that the Arab point of view as regards this aspect of the question has been shown to have greater force than has appeared hitherto, although he does not agree that it is impossible to regard Palestine as covered by the phrase.

The vilayet of Baghdad was, likewise, left until the end of the war for disposition. Distinct from the British pledge were agreements with other Arab chiefs. These included Kuwait, the Idrisi Sayyid of Sabya in Asir and the Amir Ibn Saud of Riyadh, who later founded the Kingdom of Saudi Arabia.

At the same time, in Europe, negotiations were begun with France to clarify postwar aims. These were spelled out in an agreement, known for its drafters as the Sykes-Picot Agreement, in which the parts of the Middle East here under consideration were divided into five parts: (1) the Levant Coast which the French claimed; (2) the Syrian hinterland which the French would assist (the word used is *soutenir*); (3) a zone in Palestine which would be internationalized; (4) British-protected Arab areas of Transjordan and much of Iraq; and (5) British-controlled areas of Baghdad and Basra.

The Arabs had heard of the agreement by way of diplomatic hints before, but it was not until the Bolshevik government published the Russian Foreign Office Archives late in 1917 that the Arabs knew the full extent of the agreements. This information was obligingly passed by the German General Staff to the Turks, who relayed it, with an offer of a separate peace, to Husain. To his credit, Husain turned the message over to his British ally with a request for an explanation. In reply the British informed him that the Sykes-Picot Agreement was merely a series of exchanges of views which in any case no longer represented the situation because of the Russian withdrawal from the war. It was, however, put into effect at the end of the war in Syria.

The second, and much more important, European undertaking was the Balfour Declaration of November 2, 1917. During the subsequent thirty years this was to the Zionists what the Husain-McMahon correspondence was to the Arabs: the final rallying point in the struggle for supremacy over British policy on Palestine. The declaration is disarmingly simple and delicately balanced in phraseology; is described as an "expression of sympathy"; and is only sixty-eight words long. Yet, it was the result of months of discussion in the British cabinet and was carefully and deliberately constructed to thread the thinnest rail on the fence of political indecision. Like the pledges to the Arabs, it must be seen in context.

The key figure among the group of advocates of Zionism in England, Chaim Weizmann, supported by the Secretary of the War Cabinet on Middle Eastern Affairs, Mark Sykes, and others, made a concerted effort to convince the government of the value to Britain of a pro-Zionist declaration. Their efforts could not have come at a more favorable moment. In the first place, European Jewry was naturally suspicious of the Entente, for the same reason that the Turks were hostile to it: tsarist Russia was a member. To the Turks, Russia was the aggressor par excellence; and to the Jews, it was the land of the pogrom. Russian oppression had displaced many East European Jews—including Weizmann himself—and sent them into the West, where some had reached positions of influence. Thus, to a considerable extent Great Britain and France labored under the bad reputation of their ally. Germany, on the other hand, then had perhaps the best record in Europe of treatment of the Jews. There Jews found not mere toleration but acceptance. Many Jews had achieved national prominence, and the Jewish community as a whole was more assimilated than in almost any other European country. Germany had not yet had her pogroms or even her Dreyfus case. When World War I broke out, the Zionist Organization declared itself neutral but retained an office in Germany.

The Russian Revolution somewhat reversed the situation in Russia by bringing a number of Jews into key positions. The strong sentiment in Russia for leaving the war was an important element in the Revolution, and both the British Foreign Office and the German General Staff thought that Jews in Russia were leaders of this move. To encourage this feeling and to win over those who wavered, the Germans put pressure on their Turkish ally to grant concessions to Jews wanting to colonize Palestine. Turkey delayed, perhaps fearing to antagonize those Arabs who had remained on her side in the war, but eventually, as her armies were being pushed out of Palestine, granted the Zionists a concession there similar to the Balfour Declaration.

At the time the Germans were making a determined effort to win Jewish support, Britain was worried both about keeping Russia in the war and about American neutrality. In both cases British statesmen came to the conclusion that Jewish support could greatly aid British policy. As early as March 1916 Lord Grey had suggested to the Russian and French governments the utility of a pro-Zionist arrangement on Palestine to "bring over to our side the Jewish forces in America, the East and elsewhere which are now largely, if not preponderately, hostile to us." Mark Sykes was alarmed by the American position and thought pro-German Jews to be the cause. And Prime Minister Lloyd George noted that "their [the Jews'] aid in this respect [financial affairs] would have a special value when the Allies had almost exhausted the gold and marketable securities available for American purchases." Consequently, Lord Robert Cecil encouraged the English Zionists to request a British-Jewish Palestine. It thus would appear likely that the Balfour Declaration is rightly to be regarded as a declaration *through* rather than *to* English Jews, many of whom were opposed to Zionism. The real audiences were in Russia, Germany, and America. To inform them of the Balfour Declaration millions of leaflets were dropped by air, circulated by hand, and printed in the press. In the Middle East, however, the declaration was withheld by military censorship until May 1, 1919, when it was read in Nablus, Palestine, by Allenby's successor.

The Declaration reads as follows:

I [Balfour] have much pleasure in conveying to you [Lord Rothschild] on behalf of His Majesty's Government the following declaration of sympathy with Jewish Zionist aspirations, which has been submitted to and approved by the Cabinet:

"His Majesty's Government view with favour the establishment in Palestine of a National Home for the Jewish People, and will use their best endeavors to facilitate the achievement of this object, it being clearly understood that nothing shall be done which may prejudice the civil and religious rights of existing non-Jewish communities in Palestine, or the rights and political status enjoyed by Jews in any other country."

I should be grateful if you would bring this declaration to the knowledge of the Zionist Federation.

In this form the declaration was approved, before issue, by President Wilson and subsequently was endorsed by the French and Italian governments. It was reaffirmed at the San Remo Conference in 1920, was written into the Mandate instrument for Palestine and so passed by the Council of the League of Nations, was unanimously passed by both Houses of the American Congress, and was approved by the Vatican. In 1922 the British Colonial Office declared it to be the basis of policy in Palestine and as such "not susceptible to change."

It was to prove a most difficult sentence to divide by a comma.

Among the less famous Allied commitments are the following. 1) The proclamation of General Maude (also written by Sir Mark Sykes) upon the capture of Baghdad, in which the British government set out its aim in grand but imprecise phrases, "that the Arab race may rise once more to greatness and renown amongst the peoples of the earth and that it shall bind itself to this end in unity and concord . . . Therefore, I am commanded to invite you, through your Nobles and Elders and Representatives, to participate in the management of your civil affairs in collaboration with the Political Representatives of Great Britain who accompany the British Army so that you may unite with your kinsmen in the North, East, South and West in realizing the aspirations of your race."

2) In January 1918 the British government ordered Commander Hogarth to deliver a message to Sharif (then King) Husain which stated that "The Entente Powers are determined that the Arab race shall be given full opportunity of once again forming a nation in the world. This can only be achieved by the Arabs themselves uniting, and Great Britain and her Allies will pursue a policy with this ultimate unity in view." Continuing, the message embodied some of the language of the Balfour Declaration and urged the Arabs to consider that "the friendship of world Jewry to the Arab cause is equivalent to support in all States where Jews have a political influence. The leaders of the movement are determined to bring about the success of Zionism by friendship and cooperation with the Arabs, and such an offer is not one to be lightly thrown aside."

3) The June 1918 "Declaration to the Seven" was a statement on British policy addressed to seven Syrian Arab leaders then living in Cairo. It affirmed that British policy was to "recognize the complete and sovereign independence of the Arabs" inhabiting areas free before the war and those liberated by Arabs during the war "and support them in their struggle for freedom." In regard to areas liberated by the Allies, the declaration reaffirmed the proclamations issued at Baghdad and Jerusalem by the occupying armies which stated that "It is the wish and desire of His Majesty's Government that the future government of these regions should be based on the principle of the consent of the governed

and this policy has and will continue to have the support of His Majesty's Government."

4) Sir Edmund (later Field Marshal Lord) Allenby officially assured Amir Faisal, the Arab leader in Syria, that all military government arrangements were provisional and would not prejudice a final settlement. "I reminded the Amir Faisal that the Allies were in honour bound to endeavour to reach a settlement in accordance with the wishes of the peoples concerned and urged him to place his trust whole-heartedly in their good faith."

5) A joint Anglo-French Declaration of November 7, 1918, affirmed a policy for "the establishment of national governments and administrations deriving their authority from the initiative and free choice of the indigenous populations . . . Far from wishing to impose on the populations of these regions any particular institutions they are only concerned to ensure by their support and by adequate assistance the regular working of Governments and administrations freely chosen by the populations themselves."

These pronouncements were, with official encouragement, given extremely wide distribution in the press and on handbills. It seems highly probable in retrospect that without this official encouragement the population would have settled for far less, but with encouragement their aspirations soared.

Mr. Balfour, in a confidential memorandum to the Foreign Office, wrote on August 11, 1919:

France, England, and America have got themselves into a position over the Syrian problem so inextricably confused that no really neat and satisfactory issue is now possible for any of them.

The situation is affected by five documents . . . Each can be quoted by Frenchmen and Englishmen, Americans and Arabs when it happens to suit their purpose. Doubtless each will be so quoted before we come to a final arrangement about the Middle East.

. . . The four Great Powers are committed to Zionism. And Zionism, be it right or wrong, good or bad, is rooted in age-long traditions, in present needs, in future hopes, of far profounder import than the desires and prejudices of the 700,000 Arabs who now inhabit that ancient land . . . Whatever deference should be paid to the views of those who live there, the Powers in their selection of a mandatory do not propose, as I understood the matter, to consult them. In short, so far as Palestine is concerned, the Powers have made no statement of fact which is not admittedly wrong, and no declaration of policy which, at least in letter, they have not always intended to violate.

It is easy to exaggerate the part played by the Arabs in the war. The glittering romance of Lawrence of Arabia is far more real to most people—both Arab and non-Arab—than is the murky reality of the war. *If* the Allies had landed at a Levant port instead of Gallipoli, the Arabs of Syria *might* have risen in revolt. But the British did not. As a result the Syrians suffered through the war in hunger and disease but did little to win their freedom.

In the desert the Amir Faisal's Arab army did isolate Yemen, capture most of Arabia, and harass the Turkish supply lines in what is now Saudi Arabia, Jordan, and Syria. By British consent they captured Damascus. (This was in accord with General Allenby's interpretation of the Sykes-Picot and Husain-McMahon agreements.) But probably the most important contribution made by the Arabs was as Muslims in deflecting the threat of a religiously inspired insurrection against the Allies on the part of their huge Muslim colonial populations.

When the war ended, there was a profound contrast between British-occupied Iraq, where the population was hostile and still quite pro-Turkish or at least anti-Western; Syria, where an Arab government had been installed at least nominally by Arab arms; and Palestine and Lebanon, where foreign armies of occupation were greeted as liberators by the inhabitants.

In the East the war came to an end with the Armistice of Mudros on October 30, 1918. Subsequently, however, the British forced the Turks to evacuate Mosul, in north Iraq, which they still held. The armistice was ultimately formalized in the Treaty of Lausanne which was signed on July 24, 1923.

The war in the East had been costly. Typhus, smallpox, and starvation had taken a heavy toll in the areas long under blockade. The British had committed almost 1.5 million men and had spent about £750 million (of which £6 million were used to subsidize the Arab Revolt). The French had relatively little part in the war in the East but had, of course, borne the brunt of the war in Europe and, at the end, demanded that their rights under the Sykes-Picot Agreement be honored on this basis. The British were not eager and the Arabs were strongly opposed, but it was a French naval unit which occupied Beirut and its hinterland.

In Iraq, little of value could be drawn from Ottoman precedent for the empire had vanished, records were packed and taken away, and the administrative personnel was gone forever. Necessity was the mother of the new government. The job of supporting an army makes harsh and immediate demands. Shortage of shipping space made it imperative to grow produce, especially cereals, locally. India, then facing another famine, could feed its army in Iraq only with the greatest difficulty, and every ton of shipping space that could be saved was vital. So the occupation force was immediately faced with nonmilitary demands in a situation in which it had the assistance of neither local personnel nor guides. If necessity was the mother, India was the father. Since the British forces came from India, it was not only natural but inevitable that British India would become the exemplar of Iraq. Large numbers of Indian laborers and clerks from the civil service and soldiers from the army were brought into Iraq. Moreover, the officers of the army and civil service were either directly trained in the Indian service or inspired by men who were. Many of these made distinguished careers for themselves and played a key role in the events over the next two generations.

In Egypt the war had brought prosperity and, at last, independence from the Ottoman Empire in name as well as in fact. Egypt became the farm for vast armies in Europe and the Middle East, and the peasants grew rich. But the political life of the country was stifled by a powerful and determined military government which, with a war to be won, could not be bothered with immature nationalism. What had been intended to be a request for volunteer help ended as confiscation and enforced labor. Thus, the Egyptians came out of the war, as did many new nations, embittered and determined to achieve independence.

So it was that a former protégé of Lord Cromer, Saad Zaghlul, approached the British Residency, the seat of power, on November 13, 1918, at the head of a delegation (Arabic: *wafd*) to demand the right to petition for freedom in London and Paris. When he was refused, Zaghlul organized committees throughout Egypt, circulating petitions calling for an end to British rule. These committees grew into the Wafd party. This was in violation of martial law, and the British authorities, who always held a low opinion of Egyptian will and daring, warned Zaghlul to stop his activities. When he refused, he was deported to Malta on April 7, 1919.

Few then realized the strength of the nationalist movement or the bitterness which years of wartime suppression and social contempt had engendered in the Egyptians. On the day after Zaghlul's arrest Egyptian students, in the first of their forays into the streets of violence, began what was to become a full-scale national rebellion.

In Syria the war had ended on strident notes of national liberation but muted voices of national organization. Everyone was restive with new aspirations, but among the Arabs there were few with the sophistication to move to the grand stage of Europe where the future was being decided.

Amir Faisal, who had led the Arab Revolt, was then thirty-five years old but quite inexperienced in international politics. He knew his limitations but thought he had some hope, as he put it himself, with Zionist money, connections, and *savoir-faire*. It was immediately evident that the Zionists had these. The Zionist Organization had secured the appointment of a pro-Zionist as the chief political officer in the Arab area, had the support of Lord Balfour and other senior British officials, and had a powerful American delegation, close to President Wilson, led by Justice Louis Brandeis. During Faisal's visit the British officer closest to him, Colonel Cornwallis, reported, "I understand that Dr. Weizmann, in return for the Emir's help in Palestine towards realization of Zionist aspirations, proposes to give money and advisers, if required, to the Arab Government and claims that the Zionists can persuade the French Government to waive their claims of influence in the interior." At a dinner given by Lord Rothschild, Faisal himself was reported to have said to a Jewish audience:

> Dr. Weizmann's ideals are ours, and we will expect you, without our asking to help us in return. No state can be built up in the Near East without the goodwill of the Great Powers, but it requires more than that. It requires the borrowing from Europe of ideals and materials and knowledge and experience. To make these fit for us, we must translate them from European shape to Arab shape—and what intermediary could we find in the world more suitable than you? For you have all the knowledge of Europe and are cousins by blood.

It is clear that at this period Faisal was far more worried about French intervention in the Levant than he was about any possible future clash with Zionism. France had laid claim to most of the Levant coast. Faisal realized before he left the Middle East, that even if the French chose not to push into the interior their geographical position would give them a strangle hold on the Arab state. The British Foreign Office seemed to want to set aside the Sykes-Picot Agreement, on which France's claims rested, but seemed equally firm on insisting that the Balfour Declaration must stand. Faisal realized, as few Arabs have since, that in these circumstances politics is indeed the science of the possible. So he came to a provisional agreement with Dr. Weizmann. The agreement was written up as a formal document in eleven articles. In brief, the two recognized the need to work together to achieve mutual aims, to give effect to the Balfour Declaration, to facilitate Jewish immigration provided the rights of the Arab peasant and tenant farmers be protected, to ensure freedom of worship and protection of the Holy Places, to provide Jewish economic help to the Arabs, and to constitute the British government as their arbiter. To this agreement Faisal appended in Arabic, above his signature, the following condition: "Provided the Arabs obtained their independence as demanded in my Memorandum dated the 4th of January, 1919, to the Foreign Office of the Government of Great Britain, I shall concur in the above article. But if the slightest modification or departure were to be made I shall not then be bound by a single word of the present Agreement which shall be deemed void and of no account or validity, and I shall not be answerable in any way whatsoever."

Faisal realized that the local population of Palestine strongly opposed the creation of a Jewish state, but he thought he could act on his own, compromising as necessary in order to save his state from the French. Like other figures at the Peace Conference, Faisal lost touch with the mood of his countrymen. In Palestine itself, the visit of the first Zionist commission had roused the strongest antagonism and fears in the population. The British political officer in Jerusalem warned in August 1919 that "if we mean to carry out any sort of Zionist policy we must do so with military force."

Faisal was not alone in being confused as to the desires of the population. The Middle East was far away from Western Europe and America, unknown save as the Bible Land to all but a few, and even that small band violently disagreed. The American and British delegations were in favor of an international commission to ascertain the wishes of the natives, in the spirit of the various wartime statements on self-determination issued in the names of all the Allied governments. The French were opposed to a commission unless it were understood, as the senior French representative in the Levant put it, that its purpose was "to keep Faisal in the dark while partition of Syria is being arranged." British forces then held the north of Iraq and Palestine, large parts of which areas had been promised to the French under the wartime Sykes-Picot Agreement. At the Paris Peace Conference, France demanded that the commitment be honored, but the British, aware of the need to control the north of Iraq to make the Iraqi state viable and of the need for more territory than the area around the port of Acre-Haifa to honor the Balfour Declaration, refused to go by the letter of the Sykes-Picot Agreement. After a serious diplomatic crisis between the two countries, the issue was resolved in September 1919 by Prime Minister Lloyd George and Premier Clemenceau. It was agreed that Mosul should be given to Iraq, Palestine should come under British control, the British should withdraw from Syria, which would come under French control, and France should share in the exploitation of Middle Eastern oil.

French accusations that the British were trying to make it impossible for the French to enter Syria embarrassed the British and caused them to give up urging the appointment of an investigating commission. But President Wilson unilaterally appointed his own, the King-Crane Commission. It visited the Middle East in the summer of 1919 but its report was probably never read by President Wilson and was not published for nearly four years. The report was, however, reproduced in British diplomatic reports. Essentially, the King-Crane Commission found that the population of Syria was strongly opposed to a French mandate, wanted, above all, independence and unity, but would settle for an American or British mandate. Its methods of gathering impressions have often been criticized (mainly by those who were unhappy at the results) but its findings are borne out by the investigations of all the experienced British political officers then resident in the Middle East.

Meanwhile, Faisal's popularity was slipping badly in Syria. He had made no progress in keeping out the French, who were massing forces on the Levant coast, and he had been reported to have virtually given away Palestine to the Zionists. His understanding with the Zionists was in the words of the political officer in Jerusalem, "a noose about Faisal's neck . . . he is in favour with [the Arabs only] so long as he embodies Arab nationalism and represents their views." Indeed, the Arab congress at Damascus did repudiate the substance of his agreement with Weizmann.

When he returned to London in September, Faisal informed the Zionists that he could agree only to limited immigration and that he had intended that the Jewish homeland be thought of as a province of the larger Arab state. "I quite understand," he said, "the desire of Jews to acquire a country, a homeland. But so far as Palestine is concerned . . . it must be subject to the right and aspirations of the sentiments of the present possessors of the land." Jewish rights he brushed aside as the sort which would give the Arabs a right to take over Spain, which they had ruled for as long as the Jews had Palestine.

Another trip to Europe was equally fruitless. The French were determined to extract their pound of Syrian flesh and the British bluntly informed Faisal that he must go to Paris and make his terms. As Lord Balfour later told the chief political officer, "We had not been honest with either French or Arab, but it was now preferable to quarrel with the Arab rather than the French, if there was to be a quarrel at all." British troops gradually pulled out of Syria and Lebanon, turning over their positions to the French on the coast and to the Arabs in the interior; the British monthly subsidy of £150,000 (upon which Faisal's state depended) was cut in half with the understanding that the French would then begin to contribute £75,000. Faisal, meanwhile, was not allowed to build up his army or police force and received no new equipment; his own position was by then so compromised that in the north of Syria a strong movement was begun to re-create the Ottoman Empire and the army passed into the control of Arab officers whose sympathies and service had been on the Ottoman side during the war.

At the eleventh hour Faisal recognized that there was no future in his course of moderation. Since he could expect nothing but sympathy from the British and obviously nothing from the Americans who, due to the illness of President Wilson, had virtually dropped out of the Peace Conference, Faisal threw himself into the ranks of the nationalists. He completely repudiated his understanding with the Zionists—which had always been conditional upon the granting of Syrian independence — and in March 1920 had himself proclaimed King of Syria and Palestine by the Arab congress at Damascus; he was not recognized as such either by the French or the British. The San Remo Conference in April awarded a mandate over Syria to France. The French army at this time had concentrated some 90,000 troops on the coast. A minor incident in July led to a French ultimatum that the mandate be accepted, the outbreak of hostilities, an invasion of Syria by the French, and the overthrow of the Arab government. The seeds were sown for a harvest of hatred of the French which was to be reaped yearly for a quarter of a century.

PART FOUR   DEVELOPMENT OF THE ARAB STATES

IX. The Mandates: Iraq, Syria, Lebanon, and Transjordan

Neither in Lebanon, which benefited from French protection and favor, nor in Transjordan, whose primarily nomadic population was loosely governed, was much opposition initially expressed to the mandates. Both in Iraq and Syria the mandate period began badly. In both, significant portions of the population regarded the mandates, as did many European statesmen, as "a substitute for old imperialism."

In Syria the tone of the whole mandate period was set in the initial contacts between the French and the Arabs. As we have seen, Sharif Faisal, as head of a state, had participated in some phases of the Paris Peace Conference, had negotiated with the British and French governments, had accepted the title of king from the General Syrian Congress on March 7, 1920, and was in control of the government in Damascus. The French, at the same time, were in control in Lebanon and had gradually built up strong military forces there. After their long, frustrating, and bitter contest with the British at the Paris Peace Conference, at Sèvres, and·at San Remo over the division of spoils in the middle East, the French were not prepared to be stopped by a motley crowd of semi-savages, as they regarded the Arabs, and on July 14, 1920, issued an ultimatum to Faisal. Among the demands listed were reduction of the Syrian army, acceptance of the French mandate, punishment of those who had opposed France, acceptance of the French-controlled currency, permission to station French garrisons in most Syrian cities and important towns, and prior acceptance of other, then undisclosed, demands which the French might make later. Three days were allowed for compliance.

Recognizing his inability to resist, Faisal tried to temporize but finally on July 20 agreed to submit. At this point Arab mobs attacked the government and demanded that it fight for national independence. Whether for this reason or others, the telegram of capitulation from the Syrian government to the French high commissioner General Gouraud took seven hours to reach Lebanon. When it arrived the French troops had already marched. To the Arab negotiator who tried to get the invasion stopped, the French set forth a new schedule of demands. Clearly, the French were intent upon a definitive assumption of power, unhampered by any conditions or restraints. On July 24, after a skirmish at Maisalun, the French moved toward Damascus whose occupation they completed on July 25. Faisal tried to compromise, even at that point, but was rebuffed and on July 29 went into exile in the British zone of what is now Jordan.

Meeting much hostility in the interior of Syria, primarily from the Muslim Syrians, the French acted to create for themselves a more pro-French and more powerful Lebanon. On August 31 General Gouraud issued a proclamation which recast the frontiers of "Greater Lebanon" so that it became about four times as large as the Lebanon which had existed prior to World War I. Though this move made some of the Lebanese more pro-French, it accentuated the divisions both between the religious groups in Lebanon and between Christian Lebanon and Muslim Syria, divisions which underlay the 1958 Lebanese civil war and which even today are the source of bitterness. In the short run the French policy appeared successful, but, ironically, the inclusion of large areas wherein the population was predominantly Muslim has made Lebanon less secure as a Christian state.

The rest of Syria was dismembered also. The coastal area north of Lebanon, centering on the port of Latakia, was split off and put under a separate administration and even, in 1922, temporarily made a separate state. Alexandretta, on October 20, 1921, was separated and put under a special administration which eventually resulted in its incorporation in Turkey. Jabal ad-Druze, south of Damascus, was made autonomous under the mandate. Finally, Aleppo and Damascus were separated with each as capital of an autonomous area. From an administrative point of view these attempts to divide and control local opposition were so expensive that within a year the French rejoined three of the areas in a federation.

Throughout the French mandate period, although one administrative division after another was tried, the threat of violence was never far behind the outward face of events. Damascus, invaded in 1920, was bombarded in 1925, 1926, and 1945, and martial law was enforced periodically until the very end of the mandate. Constitutions were tried and suspended and independence was proclaimed or promised time after time until finally gained in 1945. Divisions between religious groups and districts were certainly not created by French policy, but were as certainly magnified by it. It would be fair to categorize the mandate period as less a school in government than one in administration wherein tendencies toward unrest, rather than being corrected by political means, were temporarily restrained but ultimately increased in violence. The bitter harvest is still being reaped.

In Iraq the situation was quite different. As we have seen, between November 22, 1914, and October 30, 1918, the British were in the process of capturing Iraq from the Turks. During this period they were forced to lay the base for what became the state they helped to create. Efficient military government was necessary to the conduct of war: lack of sufficient shipping space required the maximum amount of local production, especially of cereals, and the maintenance of forces required the construction and management of such facilities as ports and railroads. Above all, public security had to be established and maintained. Half a government was clearly impossible. Moreover, the British, unlike the French in their subsequent efforts in Syria, had a workable model in the Indian empire. Cadres of men familiar with problems of public security on the Northwest Frontier and in the Persian

Gulf were imported into Iraq to handle analogous problems. In the caliber of these men is one of the most striking contrasts to the French in Syria. Included in the British forces were many of the Englishmen who, for a generation, dominated Western writings on the Arabs and who became legends in their own rights. But having said this, one must also say that their overt paternal system could not and did not work.

Sir Arnold Wilson was the very personification of the government of Iraq. Highly intelligent, well educated—his two-volume memories of his difficult years in Iraq is a model of its genre— strongly principled, inspiring, and personally liberal, he was an authority on the Persian Gulf area. Under his control the government was honest, efficient, and paternal. His aim was order and economy. He tended to divide the country into three groups: the bedouin and the Kurds, who composed the first, were the noble savages; the second, the peasantry, were pitiful and in desperate need of succor; but the third, the urban literati—the "town Arabs"—were deceitful, dangerous, pompous, inept, and best kept out of all affairs. If let into government, the town Arabs would only strip the bedouin of his nobility and would complete the ruin of the peasant. Neither the peasant nor the bedouin could rule; so the British must. Any other view was simply naïve and irresponsible.

Naïve and dangerous was Sir Arnold's description of the "romantic" policies which had flowed from President Wilson's declarations on self-determination and from the British promises to the Arabs. Without these Britain and France could rationally have carved out spheres of interest, and Britain's share would have been of great value to its empire in India. Wilson's bête noire was Colonel T. E. Lawrence, a flamboyant newcomer to the area who had captured the public imagination and the ear of senior British officials in London. But it was not Lawrence so much as a tired and nearly bankrupt England on which the plan for a greater Indian empire went aground.

Lacking the force to garrison the whole of Iraq while they also fought the determined and brave Turks, the British tried to create order in the countryside by "promoting" the shaikhs of clans or

sections of tribes, the largest *effective* units of tribal life, to paramount status, making them responsible to the government for
public order. To keep an eye on the shaikhs and their tribesmen,
political officers with small detachments of locally levied police
forces were stationed throughout the country. Since communications were often unreliable and always slow, the political officer
relied largely upon his personal daring and bluff to maintain his
authority.

Announcement in Iraq, at the end of the war, that Britain intended to assume the mandate for Iraq led to widespread popular
discontent. Pro-Ottoman sentiment was not dead, and the Syrian
government had dispatched a small group of nationalists who,
calling themselves the Northern Iraq Army, had tried to capture
Mosul in May 1920. Agitation against the government, particularly because of its measures of taxation and its friends among the
new tribal paramount chiefs, increased during the summer. Finally, on June 30, a minor incident set off the great tribal rising
which spread all over southern Iraq. As railroads were cut and
trains derailed, the scattered and partly immobile British force
was unable to act promptly to relieve the outlying detachments.
For a while, indeed, only the area immediately surrounding Baghdad was secure. Not until mid-October, after the loss of 1654
British men, the expenditure of £40 million—or more than six
times the total given to the Arab Revolt in the First World War
—and the infuriation of the war-weary and impoverished English
government, was order restored.

In a letter to the London Sunday *Times* in August 1920, T. E.
Lawrence stung Wilson's imperial policies where the hurt was
worst, the purse: "Our government is worse than the old Turkish
system. They kept fourteen thousand local conscripts embodied,
and killed a yearly average of two hundred Arabs in maintaining
peace. We keep ninety thousand men, with aeroplanes, armoured
cars, gunboats and armoured trains. We killed about ten thousand
Arabs in this rising this summer. We cannot hope to maintain
such an average: it is a poor country, sparsely peopled. But Abd
el Hamid would applaud his masters, if he saw us working . . .
How long will we permit millions of pounds, thousands of im-

perial troops, and tens of thousands of Arabs to be sacrificed on behalf of a form of colonial administration which can benefit nobody but its administrators?"

It was the power of the purse that moved Iraq toward freedom. To the great credit of the British, they recognized, after a severe shock of tribal war, that they could not afford to govern Iraq directly as a colony, and they found a less overt system, with English advisers behind an Arab façade, which was more economical. In recognition of this fact, Sir Arnold Wilson was withdrawn from Iraq.

On October 21, 1920, the newly arrived civil commissioner, Sir Percy Cox, announced the formation of a provisional government under Arab ministers with British advisers. Meanwhile, the British sought a head of state. As provisional president of the Council of Ministers, they chose an old and venerated religious leader under the umbrella of whose prestige they set about organizing a government and administration. As the tribes submitted they were amnestied. At this time about 250 of Amir Faisal's supporters, many of whom had served in the Turkish forces, but who were born in the area which had become Iraq, petitioned to return. Wisely, the British decided to make them into an asset. In the first group, which returned early the following year, was Nuri Said, who was to serve as prime minister many times until his assassination in 1958.

At Cairo, in March 1921, Winston Churchill met with senior British advisers and worked out, essentially, the administrative arrangements that were to endure for the next forty years. Recognizing the need to cut expenditures and the fact that the mandate was unpopular in Iraq, Churchill decided to negotiate a treaty with Iraq, parallel to that between Britain and Egypt, which would, bilaterally and in name at least, end the mandate (although in the eyes of the League Iraq remained a mandate) and give Iraq that degree of nominal independence which would lessen the danger of hostilities or civil war. Recognizing also that Britain's position in Iraq would, in large part, depend upon the selection of a ruler, Churchill decided to move vigorously for the selection of Sharif Faisal, so lately king of Syria. To this end, a program was worked out to ensure his election in the forthcoming referendum. "Popular" support was mobilized and Faisal's only serious opponent was arrested and deported on vague charges of sedition. Faisal arrived in Iraq in June 1921, met with a disappointingly cool reception, but was declared king on July 11, 1921.

Thus the British imported into Iraq, to make possible their indirect rule, the very man whom the French had at the cost of an invasion expelled to make possible their direct rule. Herein lay an essential contrast in methods. Throughout their period in the Arab East, the British sought the cheap ways of rule, making virtues of necessities and assets of rivals, while the French plunged on, often into unnecessary and costly clashes with nationalism. Whereas the French never consolidated their position, the British success is striking: reductions in British personnel in the Iraq government reached such proportions that by 1927 they controlled the country with only a handful of civil servants and small detachments of the Royal Air Force.

Like Lebanon, Transjordan was created as a separate unit without serious opposition by the local population. Transjordan was the product of Churchill's Cairo Conference. Its territory had been originally a part of the mandate of Palestine, as approved by the League of Nations, but was always administered under a separate regime and on May 26, 1923, was formally separated. Since April 1, 1921, it had been controlled by the Amir Abdullah, brother of King Faisal, who agreed to give up his plan to attack the French in Syria, to avenge his brother, if he were given control over Transjordan. The British, whose relations with France were still strained, agreed. They also had another reason. The British declared that Transjordan as constituted, was not subject to the Balfour Declaration and that Jews were forbidden to buy land there; thus the British could feel that in Transjordan they had honored their wartime promises to the Sharif Husain.

It is not important for our present purposes to follow in detail most of the developments of the mandates in the four countries. Major trends in the control of the hinterland, in the development of national markets, in the development of organizational cadres of the new states, and in the rise of education are, however, of such a formative influence on the area and the people of today as to require close attention.

Possibly the most significant aspect of the mandate period in Jordan, Iraq, and Syria was the spread of urban control over rural and desert areas. From time to time, under powerful and able governors, public security had been secured, but normally, as one left the Mediterranean coast it steadily declined. As we have seen, the nomadic tribes were autonomous "nation-states" which lived beyond the reach of urban government. As long as they were mobile, the tribes constituted a danger to public security; only when they had invested in immovable objects, particularly land, could they be brought to heel.

The great tribal rebellion of 1920 was the rock on which the British dream of empire had broken: it simply was far too costly to retain Iraq as the imperialists within the British government wanted. To cope with the tribes, the British relied upon two methods. On the one hand, they made clear that they had the power and the will to enforce public security in those areas of importance to them; and on the other, they appointed responsible chiefs to whom they gave incentives to control the tribes. Since all of the other clan chiefs would conspire against the government-appointed paramount chief, the British high commissioner, in a report to the League of Nations, reckoned that "as the authority of the central government increases, the problem [of security] should be logically solved by the gradual dissolution of the tribal bond." The first job, however, was to cope with the tribes militarily.

The British at the end of the First World War, like Egyptians in Lebanon in 1832, profited from a revolution in arms technology. Between 1840 and 1918 the Turks lacked a clear superiority in arms. The rifles they used were about the same as those used by the tribes. Their position was not dissimilar from that of the American army when the American Indians began acquiring repeating rifles. The First World War introduced several new sorts of weapons. The first was the armored riverboat which enabled the British to bombard fortified towns in the Tigris-Euphrates delta. The stunned Arabs whose mud forts crumbled had to surrender, lamenting that, in the words of one old warrior, "but this is not war." A second weapon and perhaps the most striking of all was the airplane. The rapid development of the airplane came just at the end of the war in Europe and air power got its first major test in the Middle East.

To control the vast expanses of steppe and desert, both the British and the French came speedily to rely on air power. For example, in 1924 occurred the last of the great tribal raids out of Arabia. In this raid, which was not unlike the original Arab invasion after the rise of Islam, some 26,000 sheep were seized and taken from southern Iraq and Syria to Arabia. The devastating effects on the tribes within Iraq and Syria, which had been more or less brought under government control by that time, was immediately recognized by officials. The Royal Air Force in Iraq was then called upon to police the vast frontier land of the great Syrian desert. Thereafter, the RAF patrolled the frontiers so that a bedouin tribe would be spotted as it got anywhere near the frontier area. If an "invader" were seen, the plane would radio to alert ground troops who rushed to the area in "armed Fords." The armed Ford was simply a truck with a machine gun mounted on the top, but between it and the camel was a gulf as wide as that between a Jenny and a jet. This combination of air power and mobile ground units gave the government the ability to reach out into the desert as no government ever had in the past.

In a report from the high commissioner of Iraq in 1923 the effect of this new power is vividly described: "a main factor in the pacification of the country has been the Royal Air Force. By prompt demonstrations on the first sign of trouble carried out over any area affected, however distant, tribal insubordination has been calmed before it could grow dangerous . . . In earlier times punitive columns would have to struggle towards their objectives across deserts or through difficult defiles, compelled by the necessities of their preparations and marching to give time for their opponents to gain strength. But now, almost before the would-be rebel has formulated his plans, the droning of the aeroplanes is heard overhead, and in the majority of cases their mere appearance is enough. By its means (air power), it has been possible to achieve a highly centralized yet widely understanding intelligence which is the essence of wise and economical control."

The building of roads and the rapid rise of public transport made it unnecessary for notables to retain expensive bands of retainers. The local political officer in Kurdistan remarked in a report to the League in 1928 that in the town of Sulaimaniya one could see a good example of the pacifying influence of the motorcar. "Formerly, a tribal chief from the vicinity of the Persian border having business at administrative headquarters would make the two days' journey accompanied by a large escort of armed horsemen. Following the construction of a pioneer motor road, with police posts, from Sulaimaniya to [one of the administrative posts], a regular taxi service has sprung up. The tribal chief, finding that he can take a seat for three rupees and perform the journey without fatigue in two hours, ceases to entertain large bodies of expensive armed retainers. The practice of carrying arms thus tends to grow less." Thus, not only was it possible for the central government to move more rapidly and dramatically against rebellious people, but the people gave up a part of their means of rebelling.

The opening of roads tended to bring about the creation of national markets. This trend had been stimulated by the wartime conditions. Since shipping was everywhere at a premium and supply of large numbers of troops was difficult, the military administrations tried to organize sufficient production to meet local needs. The demands of war forced the administration to create a cash crop economy to replace the honeycomb cells of largely autarkic groups of villages and to encourage production of cereals needed by the army. This was a trend which the settlement of tribes, the building of roads, and the creation of an export market in the following decade was greatly to extend.

Moreover, British troops brought with them the desire for, and small supplies of, the accouterments of Western civilization: kerosine lamps, flashlights, pocket knives, cheap cotton cloth,

automobiles, and trucks. These became objects of intense desire
for the wealthier civilians not only for their utility but, no doubt,
as status sumbols of a civilization that was so obviously powerful
and successful. The British army was not, however, able or willing to supply such things to the local inhabitants. So it was natural that a new commercial class should spring up on the foundation of large-scale purchases by the army and casual spending by
troopers which had pumped money into the economy. New styles
were introduced as influenced by the army: sandals to headdress,
the Iraqi shed his Arab dress for Western. His Syrian cousin was
not far behind.

As roads were built across the desert from Damascus to Baghdad along the Euphrates route and connecting the various Iraqi
cities, the areas which had been largely autarkic, which had supported themselves and had a considerable degree of economic
autonomy, came to sell their goods one to the other and to buy
from central points those things which they could not produce
as economically. The Kurds in the northern area of Iraq, for example, who had prior to this time bought very little from the
outside world, began to buy cotton goods from England or India,
chinaware from Japan, cigarettes from Baghdad. As they acquired
new tastes, locally produced goods were no longer satisfying to
them, and they were anxious to move in and out of the places like
Baghdad and to acquire the accouterments of European life.
Markets grew in strategic locations throughout the country and
more and more people were drawn into the system which the
state itself represented. Thus, more and more people came to have
a stake in supporting the political existence of the state. It is interesting that Basra and Beirut, where this commerce developed
earlier and most rapidly, saw almost none of the armed unrest
that some of the northern areas of Iraq and Syria witnessed.

As the city governments extended their control over the countryside, townsmen extended the limits of their cultivation far beyond what had been considered relatively safe in Ottoman times.
Of course, this meant that townsmen took over many of the
watering places and extensively used farming lands of the semi-
nomadic and nomadic tribes. Particularly in Iraq, something com-

parable to the "enclosures" of eighteenth century England or the changes brought about on the American range by the advent of cheap barbed wire happened during the first decade of the mandate.

In all of the mandates, but particularly in Iraq, the development of the economy was dependent upon security in the rural areas. Not only physical security, of the sort that could be supplied by military means, but also security of investment was essential to get money out of strong boxes and into the land.

As early as the enactment of the new land code in 1858 the Ottoman government had recognized the utility of the security of tenure. In 1869, during his short stay in Iraq, Midhat Pasha, the greatest of the Ottoman governors of the nineteenth century, tried to bring order into the system of land tenure. Similar efforts were made in Lebanon in the decade of the 1850's and in Palestine somewhat later. The details of the Ottoman system are complex, but the general purpose was twofold: to give sufficient title to those who would invest in the land and hire others to farm it, and to give the nomadic tribes lands on which to settle.

Before this time the Ottoman governments had concentrated their efforts in the towns and left the countryside to itself until the harvest, when tax collectors, accompanied by military escorts, collected what they could from the unwilling peasants. The effective law of the countryside, except when taxes were collected, was local custom. Peasants cared little what the records in the distant cities might say; they knew who owned the land. Even when encouraged to register their lands, they feared to do so since they suspected that land registration might be a government ruse to raise their taxes or to conscript their sons into the army.

Profiting from this disaffection from government of the peasant and the tribesman, the larger merchants and officials obtained formal rights to vast tracts of tribal and village lands. Later, when the Iraqi land system was studied by Sir Ernest Dowson, he found that "with the introduction of tapu tenure many village areas appear to have been wholly or partially registered as the personal possessions of local notables, without any consideration of the immemorial rights of those who had regularly occupied and tilled the land or pastured the flocks thereon. The pinch in these cases seems to have been mainly felt when the lands were pledged, and forfeited, to town-dwelling merchants for debt."*

As to tribal lands themselves, the Turks regarded them as government-owned, merely being used by the tribes with no rights of ownership. Taking up the Turkish definitions of ownership and the Turkish records, the Iraqi courts according to the high commissoner's report to the League for 1925, reached the momentous decision that "all lands excluding urban mulk (freehold) properties belong primarily to the State and that good title to such lands can only be obtained in consequence of alienation by Government . . . acquisition of title to lands by long and undisturbed possession, is a legal impossibility in Iraq." This one blow placed the tribes on the danger list. Their lands could be encroached upon at will by city dwellers who could arrange with the government to buy or lease land. The tribesmen involved were forced to emigrate or to settle. Whereas in Turkish times they had been able to keep their lands by making it impossible for others to take possession, in 1925, under the droning of the airplane, they were powerless.

During the period 1920 to 1932 great tracts of land along the rivers which had in the past been lightly used by semi-nomadic and nomadic tribes as grazing, water, and winter-wheat areas became regularly cultivated private property. In 1921 along the Iraqi rivers were 140 water pumps, irrigating a total of 72 square miles; by 1929 the number of pumps had risen to over 2000 and the area irrigated to over 2670 square miles. In the three years from 1927 to 1930 some 1057 new pumps were installed with a substantial increase in the size of the area cultivated. The pumps were mostly owned by city men who expected to get from the government rights to the land. And, in fact, according to the land sales of the period, they did. In the year 1927, for example, the government sold 7917 pieces of government land and 448 pieces of mortgaged land. As the report to the League of that year described the development, a gradual transition to an enclosure of arable land was being promoted. "The prospective pump-

* Sir Ernest Dowson, *An Inquiry into Land Tenure and Related Questions* (printed for the Iraqi government by the Garden City Press, Ltd., Letchworth, Eng., [1932]), p. 20.

owner is usually an enterprising capitalist townsman, lacking land and anxious to develop a portion of the Domains already subject to tribal occupation."

The policy of the government was to grant a limited term tenure to the shaikh as the representative of the tribe, but in practice title to the land often passed to the shaikh, so that what had been in fact tribal land became in law his land. This, and the large investment necessary for irrigation, tended to produce a heavy concentration of land. Ultimately nearly 70 percent of the arable land of Iraq was held in blocks of over 250 acres. In southern Iraq the concentration was even more impressive. In one province 75 percent of the land was in units in excess of 2500 acres and only 6 percent in units less than 125 acres.

Shortly after achieving independence in 1933 the new national government passed a law which virtually converted the formerly free tribesmen into serfs. The key to the relationship between the owner and the tenant in the new land was debt. So widely was it defined that it is almost inconceivable that any peasant could ever be out of debt. The peasant incurred a debt for any work done by the owner, any seed advanced, any work *not* done by the peasant. If the peasant tried to leave the land, the owner was entitled to call out the armed forces of the government to have him brought back. Then he was blacklisted so that he could get no other job.

The shaikh who in the time of the peasant's father or grandfather had been the honored elder, the generous host who dared not inflict the most trifling punishment on the poorest man in the tribe, had become an absolute master, perhaps a member of Parliament, who lived far away in the city and who had all of the power of the government behind his word. This was nothing less than a social revolution, one whose legacy was to have profound —and violent—influence in the midst of the Iraqi revolution of 1958–59 and, perhaps, will again. At the least, it has been largely responsible for the creation of those vast concentric rings of slums which lean on Arab cities.

In all four mandates the governments were pressed to organize relatively cheap means of control. In general they sought to recruit local people to work for the government so that the more expensive Europeans would be required only for senior positions. This was particularly evident in the area of public security. Britain, as we have seen, was strongly opposed to the continued outlay of large amounts of money on public security and demanded a cut in the size of the British garrison in Iraq. Transjordan never had more than a handful of British officers and no sizable force.

The French, to the contrary, throughout their tenure in Syria and Lebanon were compelled to retain very large military establishments. In 1921 the French had over 50,000 troops in Syria and shortly after the two-year rebellion of 1925–27 sent in even more. Additionally, from 1921 the French began recruiting Syrian and Lebanese auxiliaries and by 1925 had over 7000 of these under arms. Ten years later, at the high point, these *troupes spéciales* totaled 14,000. Until the bitter end of French rule in Syria in 1945, when they formed the basis of the incipient Lebanese and Syrian armies, the French were to retain control of these troops. To patrol the steppe and desert, they also formed in 1921 camel companies under French officers. But French efforts were always expensive since they could not entrust any significant role to the Arabs of Syria.

The British position was quite different. After the 1920 Iraqi revolt, the more settled areas of Iraq were relatively peaceful. Only in Kurdistan and in the desert areas was public security seriously threatened. Security in these areas, after the inauguration of the government of King Faisal, was the concern of the government of Iraq, with which the British had treaty relations (although under the terms of League they formally exercised a mandate). This government had primary responsibility and was assisted to create and sustain its own military force under British guidance.

In 1926 the mandate government organized an "armed Ford police unit" to control the great bedouin tribe of the Shammar, and in 1928 a similar group was created in the south of Iraq. So successful was it that it became the model for changes in all the frontier guard forces organized in the area. In Transjordan the former commander of the Egyptian camel corps had formed a desert patrol in 1920 to fend off tribal raids from across the border and to bring a degree of security to the desert. The force, however, was not entirely successful as it could not gain the cooperation of the bedouin and had to meet raiders on their own ground with their own weapons. It was the scheme of enlisting bedouin into a special highly mobile desert force that made John B. Glubb (Glubb Pasha) famous and brought order and security never before imagined into the desert.

In Iraq the British had formed units of Assyrian and Kurdish levies to assist in the garrisoning of the country during the war. These forces proved loyal to the British during the 1920 revolt and by 1925 reached a strength of 7500. Since they were under British officers, paid by the British, and drawn from the non-Arab minorities, it was decided that they could not be a proper nucleus for an Iraqi army. However, throughout the mandate period they matched or overshadowed the young Iraq army. The Iraqi army, itself, was formed in 1921 under the command of former officers of the Ottoman army of whom the chief was Nuri Said, later to be prime minister. A military college was also opened. By 1925 this force had reached 7500 (just matched by the levies 7500) and was able to replace departing British ground units.

The young Iraqi army was impelled into politics sooner than any of the other forces of the mandates since it had early "tasted blood" in the Kurdish revolt and then in 1933 had attacked and massacred large numbers of Assyrians whom the British had used as the base of their power in Iraq. In the 1930's, as later, the Iraqi army was always close to or involved in political power. Seven times between 1936 and 1941, it made or supported coups d'etat. The reason is not difficult to find. The army was by all odds the most efficient organization in the country. Its dedication and discipline contrasted as sharply with the often self-seeking politicians and their merchant allies as did its ability to communicate and move with the rest of the population. Moreover, it was used and permitted itself to be used by the government as "a valuable means of fostering a true National Spirit." From this position in the mid-twenties was no great step to the military coups of the mid-thirties.

One can argue that what happened in Iraq in the mid-1930's occurred twenty years later in Syria, delayed by the nature of the French-controlled military structure there. In the late 1950's the Syrian army began to intervene decisively in politics. This is a phenomenon which came to distinguish virtually all of the Arab countries by 1960.

With the exception of Syria, which had existed as an inde-pendent kingdom, though with uncertain frontiers and a rudi-mentary administration for two years until the French invasion, and to a lesser extent Lebanon, whose nucleus of Mount Lebanon had enjoyed autonomy for several centuries, the new mandate states did not exist even in the minds of the leaders of Arab nationalism in 1920. Tribal groups were divided—often bitterly —amongst themselves and held both their urban cousins and members of the minority groups in contempt. In Iraq the Shii community was politically attached to Iran, dependent upon its charities and culturally Persian. In northern Syria pro-Turkish sentiment was sufficiently strong to allow Turkish guerrilla bands a free hand. In Lebanon the several groups whose religions divided them still thought of their churches as their "nations." And in Transjordan statehood was a mockery, opposed by the Palestin-ians, both Arab and Jewish, scorned by the bedouin, and referred to by the British as "Churchill's inspiration."

It was long before any of these governments was to achieve a sense of identity. Even today the issue of nationality—whether a man of Damascus is a Syrian or an Arab or, if both, which is the object of his deepest loyalty—is unresolved. Even King Faisal, the hero of the Arab Revolt and the popular victim of French tyranny in Damascus, was far from accepted. A British report to the League of Nations for the year 1922–23 admitted that "Faisal and his government could not be maintained without British support and friendship." The real job of the mandate period, then, was the schooling of the Arabs in the requirements of statehood.

The creation of states, each distinct from its neighbors, was in large part a mechanical process. The growth of administration created jobs and careers; to travel a man had to have a passport which bore the name of his country; the forms and procedures of daily life developed in different patterns. Linguistic differences resulted from the fact that technical vocabularies, created to give instruction in fixing trucks or filling out government papers, were patterned on different models. The Iraqi army manual was unintelligible to the Syrian gendarme. Even the goods available from Europe differed as each copied the European metropole— the French radio using 110-volt electrical current would not work in Baghdad where the British installed 220. And, at least as important, each area developed its own enemy: The Syrians carried an abiding hatred of the French but remembered Britain with some favor, while the Iraqis who had never seen the French but who were captivated by stories of Paris felt no anger toward the French but were resentful of the British. Transjordanians, on the contrary, rather liked the British and, at least in the early days, admired the gallant band of Englishmen who knew the desert and the bedouin like the best of Arabs. The Lebanese, profiting from French benevolence and attracted by French culture while fearing Syrian nationalism, threw themselves almost wholeheartedly to the French. So, on the "new politics" the Arabs of Beirut, Damascus, Amman, and Baghdad literally had no common language.

From this to statehood, however, is a long jump.

Many small impulses contributed to that jump but none was more important than education. As an American educational consultant informed the Iraqi government some years later, "Without a public school system it is obvious to everyone that an independent nationality could not be maintained even if established."

Education in the Turkish era had been directed toward government service. Special schools were established to enroll the sons of tribal shaikhs—with the double purpose of impressing the young men with the power of the empire and holding them hostage for their fathers' conduct. Those of the city men who did not go abroad and wanted more than the religious schools could offer were obliged to learn Turkish. With little developed native industry or commerce, moreover, the roads of advancement led through government civil or military service. Most of those who achieved prominence in government service in the generation after the First World War had been Ottoman army officers. It was a principle of the British administration, but not of the French administration, to bring these young men right into responsible posts as early as possible.

Since the Ottoman craft of state aimed at creating essential public security, raising tax revenues, and maintaining territorial integrity at minimum cost, it is not surprising to find that little was done in the field of education. The few schools which Iraq had were mostly on the primary level and all, after the Young Turk revolt, offered courses in Turkish. In 1913 about 6000 students were registered but probably most of these were only part-time and very few got beyond the first two or three years of classes. Religious schools taught recitation of the Koran and literary Arabic; weak and unimpressive as they were, they did preserve in Iraq some unity of form in Islam and, for a very small part of the population, a standard of the written language.

When the British surveyed the educational system, they found little other than the buildings to be of any use. Most of the relatively modern teachers were not qualified to teach in Arabic while those who could teach in Arabic did not know the subjects needed by the class of clerks and administrators the British wanted to staff the mandate government and business enterprises. In 1920 less than one half of one percent of the population was registered and in attendance in the schools. In that year the government opened two secondary schools—one with seven and the other with twenty-seven students. The British viewed education in highly specific and utilitarian terms. In its 1923–24 report to the League of Nations the mandate government stated its view that "in this country, it is neither desirable nor practicable to provide Secondary education except for the select few."

In that same year some 15,000 students were in Iraq's 300 religious schools and about 5000 adults were enrolled in anti-illiteracy classes. But pressure of necessity forced the government gradually to increase its outlay from 3 percent to 8 percent of the budget in the field of education. However, even as late as 1932, when the mandate ended, the average rural school child got only two years of schooling, and of the 154 existing government schools only 14 had as many as six grades. Whole districts of Iraq had no schools with six grades.

In Syria the situation was similar but for different reasons. The French defined their mandate as an obligation to bring European, that is, French, culture to the benighted natives; it made little difference that the natives were Arabs, with a vast literary heritage. That heritage was eschewed to the extent possible. Students were encouraged to study French and the best among them found their ways to French universities and institutes. But caution was the keynote. Since the French attempted to retain for themselves a far larger share of administrative and political power than did the British, they regarded education as a dangerous fuel for the fires of nationalism.

It is significant that the number of students in school rapidly increased when Iraq obtained its independence. By the end of the British mandate Iraq had 19 secondary schools with 129 teachers and 2082 students; within three years the number of students doubled, and by the eve of World War II it had reached nearly 14000. But even more significant was the change in the materials of instruction: school books became increasingly directed at fostering nationalist feeling. The function of these schools, as seen by the Iraqi government, was to "select and train leaders for all the essential phases of life of [the] nation."

The British educational adviser was not rehired and the example of Germany came increasingly to attract Iraqi educators. Education, always considered as a means to the end of national betterment in the larger sense, became so in all points of detail. For example, the aim of teaching history was to "strengthen the 'national and patriotic feeling' in the hearts of the pupils." This was to be accomplished in Iraq, as in the Palestine school system of the same period, by means of study of Arabic literature and with "stories about famous Arabs and their qualities . . . taught in such a way [as] would lead to the growth of national feelings."* This was a difficult task, for far from burning with a sense of national mission, the students were apathetic. An American consultant wrote that "there is evident among teachers and pupils no great patriotic fervor for their new nationalism . . . Somehow the youth of the secondary school and their teachers must get a vision of what the nation demands of them and an inspiration from these new possibilities of national culture and political achievement. These things they do not seem to have, nor does the school experience contribute in any extent to them."†

This lack of purposefulness in what they were doing and disappointment with their much advertised new "democracy" were to be of great significance in the troubled days of the 1930's. As in Europe so in Iraq, the failure of democracy to put the meat of practice on the bone of pronouncement left the educated elite with little more than whetted appetites and sore teeth.

Consciousness of the apathy of the Iraqi people and shame at the weakness of the nation before Europe was a potent political mixture in the 1930's in Iraq. Despairing of adults, the government encouraged the rise of paramilitary youth groups. Even the Boy Scouts were involved and grew by 1930 to 12,000 members. But the most significant was the *Futuwah*—the name evoked the memory of the efforts of the last Abbasid caliph to restore his regime to its former glory on the eve of the Mongol conquest, but the spirit was more akin to the fascist youth movements of Europe—whose director urged Iraqi youth to "get tough for ease spoils virtue." "That nation," he admonished Iraqi high school students in 1933, the first year of independence, "which does not master the art of death with steel and fire will be trampled to death [shamefully] under the hooves of cavalry and the boots of foreign soldiers." Essentially, this "art of death" was an attempt to state in a modern and national form the famous pre-Islamic verse

* Matta Akrawi (later director general of education of Iraq), *Curriculum Construction in Economic, Social, Hygienic and Educational Conditions and Problems of the Country* (New York, 1942), pp. 186–187.

† Paul Monroe, *et al.*, *Report of the Educational Inquiry Commission* (Government Press, Baghdad, 1932), p. 37.

memorized by generation after generation of school children: "Who holds not his foe away from his cistern with sword and spear, it is broken and spoiled: who uses not roughness, him shall men wrong." This inculcation of pre-Islamic values, which ultimately made up the whole syllabus of the humanities in the public school system of all the mandates, was in part an attempt to find a national image which could transcend the bitter and divisive religious problems of the Sunnis and the Shiis, of the Christians, Jews, and Muslims.

Education was the road to advancement through government service, but few wanted to get their hands dirty in the process of building the nation. The law college, the high road to government, prospered, but in the agricultural state of Iraq in 1930 an agricultural college was closed for lack of students. The glittering lure in the educational system was a tour abroad. To imbibe Western learning at its source was to be on the road to success in Iraq.

In a broad sense the entire mandate system was conceived as a sort of giant school in self-government. In no sense had the Turkish government aimed at such tutelage. And, as in any school, the "students" eagerly pressed for graduation.

In its report to the League of Nations in 1928 the mandate government noted that "From the beginning, the idea of a mandate has been abhorrent to nearly all educated elements in the country, and it was this fact which, in 1922, caused the British Government to negotiate with the 'Iraq Government a Treaty of Alliance to define Great Britain's relations with 'Iraq. It was not long, however, before the view became prevalent in 'Iraq that the Treaty of Alliance was in effect only the mandate in another form and it was approved by the Constituent Assembly in 1924 on condition that negotiations should be opened with a view to amending it."

Iraq achieved its formal independence in 1932 when it joined the League of Nations. The Syrians, remembering with pride their prior independence, pressed for their freedom, and it was only with great difficulty, at considerable cost in lives and property, that the French were able to hang on. Ironically, Syria was economically a losing proposition for them since it was British trade which always predominated in the Syrian market and French administration was always expensive. A full-scale civil war raged in and around Damascus in 1924–25. Damascus and other Syrian towns were bombarded three times during the mandate. Finally, after another outbreak in 1944, Syria and Lebanon achieved their independence.

Many of the problems which the mandate system was designed to solve were merely deferred and still form a part of the Middle Eastern scene.

X. Arabia and Egypt: Isolation or Humiliation

Egypt and the Arabian Peninsula present a sharp contrast in their development in the twentieth century. In their experience with the West, this contrast is particularly instructive and illustrates another aspect of "the impact of the West." Egypt profited in its relations with the West by gaining the most advanced Arab economy and by passing rapidly into the modern era, but has paid a heavy price in the psychological scars so evident in its political life. Arabia, unscarred, was also unassisted and unorganized by imperialism. While enjoying what has been termed "the ancient and comfortable right to be let alone," the states of Arabia have paid for their seclusion. None of the infrastructure associated with the mandate system or Western tutelage was created and, especially in those areas of the peninsula where oil was not found—in Yemen, for example—the people suffer from material and cultural backwardness.

The geography of Egypt is an invitation to invasion; and the regulation of the Nile irrigation system requires strong, centralized authority. These two facts have dominated Egyptian history. After suffering a series of invasions by the so-called Hyksos in the midst of its classical period, Egypt was invaded by the Persians in 525 B.C. and then conquered by Alexander the Great in 332 B.C. Never again, until after the First World War, when Egypt attained formal independence, or, as many Egyptians aver, after the Second World War, when the British troops were evacuated, did Egypt live under Egyptian rule. Its rulers were Greeks, Romans, Arabs, Armenians, Abyssinians, Turks, Circassians, French, and British. So deeply ingrained was the notion that it was not the métier of Egyptians to rule that, as we have seen, Napoleon's attempt to get native Egyptians to accept official responsibility was violently rejected. Forty years later, in the midst of the rule of Mehmet Ali Pasha, Egyptians told visitors that they were unsuited to rule themselves, that rule was the profession of others while they, the Egyptians, excelled in the law of Islam and in arts, crafts, and agriculture.

Egypt to Mehmet Ali Pasha and his successors was a base of power, not a homeland. Thus, though Mehmet Ali's dynasty rid themselves of the Albanian, Circassian, and other foreign slave or mercenary troops, they did so because these men refused to modernize, were expensive and unreliable; though they recruited native Egyptians, they did so because the Sudanese did not perform well and the Egyptians were available. Yet, Mehmet Ali Pasha and his more vigorous successors were personally if not nationally vitally interested in the growth of Egyptian power and in the achievement of Egyptian independence.

Twice during his long rule, Mehmet Ali had the Ottoman Empire in his grasp but both times the European powers forced him to let go. European statesmen realized, during most of the nineteenth century, that the sudden and dramatic breakup of the Ottoman Empire would endanger European peace and stability in a way unacceptable to them all. Thus, as has been said, British policy aimed at keeping the Ottoman Empire strong enough to withstand Russian pressure in the north but not so strong in the south as to constitute a barrier to the thrust of British commerce or imperialism. Russia wanted either no Ottoman Empire or one amenable to Russian policy; therefore, it alternated a policy of aggression with one of support against the aggression of others. France lacked such a clear conception of its national interests. Napoleon III sent an expedition to Lebanon in 1860 but withdrew, and in 1882 the French sent ships to Alexandria with the Royal Navy but took no part in the bombardment or the invasion of Egypt which established British power there. In general France tried to maintain friendship with the empire and its rivals, suffusing both with French culture and assisting in the development of both through commercial loans and entrepreneurial activity.

Mehmet Ali realized that his only security of tenure rested on his military power. Other rebels before his time in Egypt and elsewhere throughout the Ottoman Empire had gained a measure of autonomy only to lose their heads on the executioner's block. Safety lay in the acquisition of such power as to rival or replace that of the empire itself. Therefore, Mehmet Ali undertook his program of modernization of the army and the economy. To gain foreign exchange, he introduced cotton, encouraged agriculture, built and manned factories, sent missions of students and technicians abroad for training, and hired foreign specialists. Recognizing the geographic facts of Egypt, he instituted a strong, centralized regime, becoming himself the "landlord" of Egypt to get the most out of the country, and invaded surrounding areas to protect the open, defenseless Nile Valley. At the peak of his power, he ruled much of the Middle East and had armed forces totaling nearly 10 percent of the population of Egypt.

After the British-led invasion of Syria and the retreat of the Egyptian army in 1841, Mehmet Ali was forced to cut his army to 18,000 men, to give up a large part of his fiscal policy, particularly the monopoly system which sustained his industry and prevented the influx of cheap European manufactured goods, and to forgo the attempt to rival the Ottoman Empire. With his road to independence blocked and in declining health, Mehmet Ali lost interest in his reforms. In his last years and under his successors Egypt, in the words of an Egyptian historian, "was going slowly to sleep again."

But if this was true of the government, it was not true of the country as a whole. The growth of export agriculture, particularly in cotton, had tied the Egyptian to the world market. Even more significant was the intellectual ferment, at first affecting very few people, occasioned by the creation of a group of men who had been exposed to European culture and who, upon their return, infused their fellow countrymen with information and curiosity concerning Europe. In the shock of discovery of Europe, Egypt came, gradually, painfully, and partially, to recognize itself. Avant-guarde Egyptian writers began to speak of the nation, love of the homeland, and nationalism as something Egyptian. It was long, however, before the seeds thus planted were to take hold and grow in the soil of Egypt.

Meanwhile, Egypt had much to learn of the power and influence of Europe. The lesson began in earnest in 1854 when the ruler of Egypt granted to Ferdinand de Lesseps a concession to dig the Suez Canal. The sorry story of this episode, in which the Suez Canal Company, backed by a powerful consortium of Europeans and uncontrolled by inexperienced or venal Egyptians, committed grand larceny, has been told above. Oriental delight in pomp and circumstance and the genuine need to develop the Egyptian economy led the ruler of Egypt deeper and deeper into the trap of the great European banks. And the refusal of the European powers to allow Egypt to break loose from the Ottoman Empire saddled it with additional expenses. Prime Minister Disraeli announced to the House of Commons on March 23, 1876, that the khedive had requested that the report of an inquiry into Egyptian finances be suppressed. This was the coup de grace to the unsound finances of the country. Ultimately, Egypt was literally placed in receivership with its government under the control of a debt commission. This sparked native resentment against the weak Egyptian government and its European masters. A coup against the Egyptian government by a group of Egyptian army officers was put down by a British invasion and Egypt became in fact though not yet in name a British protectorate.

Immediately after their assumption of power over Egypt, the British announced that "although a British force remains in Egypt for the preservation of public tranquility, Her Majesty's Government are desirous of withdrawing it as soon as the state of the country and the organization of proper means for the maintenance of the Khedive's authority will admit of it." As the years went by the British government, according to a British historian, promised some 66 times to evacuate the country. Britain finally withdrew its last base in 1956 only to attempt later in that year to invade the country again.

British administration of Egypt was always a curious arrangement. The British did not claim possession or even protection over Egypt for three decades, the senior British official was the "consul-general," and Egypt remained a part of the Ottoman Empire. Essentially, British rule over Egypt was the quintessence of enlightened imperialism: It was the international version of government by a city manager. Under Consul-General Lord Cromer, who ruled Egypt from 1883 until 1907, improvements in irrigation, notably the completion of the first Aswan Dam in 1902, made possible an increase in the cropped area from 4.7 million to 7.7 million acres, debts were repaid to the full face value, and many substantial improvements were made in the government. Following the reconquest of the Sudan in 1898, Egypt was made a nominal partner in the Anglo-Egyptian Condominium established to rule it. Egyptians have complained, and rightly, that little was done in the field of education and that they were excluded from participation in social as well as administrative affairs.

But Egyptians, having acquired a better educated minority, stirred by a native religious revival which at the least encouraged a belief that in the Arabic-Islamic past there was much of which to be proud, and watching the national assertiveness of Japan and Turkey, aspired to a larger control over their own destiny. Political parties espoused the slogan, common in sentiment to others in many parts of the world, "Egypt to the Egyptians." To some degree the British found this political agitation useful to keep the ruler, the khedive, more dependent upon them. In any case the nationalists posed no serious threat as they were merely a small group of urban professional and trades people without much popular backing. It was not until the Denshawai incident of 1906 that hatred of foreign rule stirred the average Egyptian.

Successors to Lord Cromer were somewhat more willing than he to allow Egyptian participation in government or, at least, expression on political affairs. In 1907 the first national congress

was held, and more encouragement was given to education.
Again, however, the government tightened down on public
demonstrations, enacting a press censorship law in 1909 and in-
stituting exile as a punishment for undesirable politics. Thwarted
resentment found an outlet in the assassination of the Coptic
prime minister Butros Ghali, whom many regarded as a puppet
of the British.

Egypt had become more prosperous. The government had
been extremely frugal and had managed to cut most taxes and
duties to the bone. Yet income increased as more lands were
brought under cultivation as a result of the Aswan Dam, and the
population increased by nearly 30 percent. By the First World
War exports had increased 30 percent over Lord Cromer's best
year.

When the First World War broke out, both the khedive and
the British agent were out of the country—the khedive in Constantinople and Lord Kitchener in London. In November, when
Britain declared war on Turkey, Kitchner joined the British war
cabinet. The cabinet voted to annex Egypt, but British officials
resident in Cairo were opposed. In December Egypt was declared
a protectorate, with all ties to the Ottoman Empire severed, and
its pro-Ottoman khedive deposed.

Ironically, it was to be Lord Cromer's protégé, Saad Zaghlul,
who was to lead the charge against the British. Zaghlul, picked to
be minister of education in 1906, was commended to the Egyptian people by Cromer as one who "possesses all the qualities
necessary to serve his country."

We have noted above Zaghlul's petition to the British, and
how, when he was refused, Zaghlul set about organizing committees throughout Egypt and circulating petitions for an end to
British rule. The arrest and deportation of Zaghlul led in March
1919 to nearly a month of violence in which the British won all
the battles, but the Egyptians won the war. Caught, as in Iraq, between expensive civil strife and frugal war-weariness, the British
invited the Egyptians to submit proposals for reform and announced in April that Zaghlul was to be released. A state of
tension continued with one prime minister after another resign-

ing, so the British government appointed a commission of inquiry to investigate the causes of the disturbance and to plan for a more peaceful future.

On its arrival in Cairo in December 1919 the commission met with a silent boycott from all Egyptians outside the palace since its terms of reference had restricted it to modification of arrangements *within* the protectorate rather than allowing it to consider independence. Again the pace of violence was stepped up, with a steady procession of terrorist attacks on British soldiers and on those Egyptians who cooperated with the British.

Zaghlul, who had failed to achieve anything in Paris, then approached the commission of inquiry in London and attempted to negotiate with the British for what he had failed to get in Paris. A memorandum was drawn up to show what the British were prepared to accept, but Zaghlul, impelled by now by the very public emotion he had helped to create, found consideration of any proposal short of outright British evacuation impossible.

The main items in the British proposal called for Egyptian independence, a mutual defense treaty between Great Britain and Egypt, British right to maintain military forces in Egypt, Egyptian assumption of control over financial affairs, centralization of the capitulations under British control, and Egyptian right to discharge foreigners employed by the Egyptian government at a future date. These points are important both in that they indicate how far Egypt was from true independence and in that they form the base line for all future Anglo-Egyptian negotiations. The very fact that Britain was willing to negotiate thus with a man who had no official standing in Egypt—Zaghlul was not then even a member of the government—was itself tantamount to a British admission that the government of Egypt was a sham. This served to strengthen the nationalist movement and to concentrate still further the leadership in Zaghlul's hands.

Failing to work out an acceptable pact with the nationalists, the British government agreed in December 1921 to negotiate Egyptian independence. To ensure that events went smoothly, the British again arrested and deported Zaghlul. But at this point the British government, despite the urgent pleas and even threats

to resign by its able high commissioner, Lord Allenby, again delayed. Again Egypt was torn by violence. Finally, on February
28, 1922, London unilaterally announced the independence of
Egypt, leaving "absolutely reserved" four areas: British imperial
communications, Egyptian defense, protection of the minorities
and foreign interests, and the Sudan, over which, in theory,
Britain and Egypt exercised a condominium.

It is a part of the tragedy of the contrast between the ruler
and the ruled, the powerful and the powerless, the donor and
the recipient, that events which appear to the one in one guise
do not so appear to the other. As the British saw it, after frustrating and often infuriating negotiations, undertaken in good
faith by the British but punctuated by violence in Egypt, the
Egyptians, acting with the encouragement if not under the direct
leadership of the very men carrying out the negotiations, refused
a reasonable and logical solution in which Britain agreed to independence, reserving for itself only those matters of vital national interest or international moral concern.

From the perspective of the Egyptians, the events appeared
quite the contrary: In the midst of a great war, ostensibly and
vocally proclaimed to be for freedom—so ringingly announced
by President Wilson—the great powers showed, under their thin
new masks, the old faces of greed, oppression, and cunning. At
the Peace Conference in Paris when it suited their purposes they
dealt with half-savages or phony representatives, but would not
meet the legitimate demands of representatives of such advanced
and civilized peoples as the Egyptians for self-determination.
After so constituting all of the "legitimate" avenues to power as
to exclude the true representatives of the people, they accused
these of breaking the law when they resorted to the course of
true patriotism in the face of tyranny. Finally, when violence
became too costly, they gave in, but did so with such cunning
as to produce a stillborn state with matters of integral national
concern like self-defense, maintenance of public security, and
control over the headwaters of the Nile withheld. If any lesson
had been learned, it was that Britain respected only force. Such
was the Egyptian view.

Zaghlul was allowed to return to Egypt in September 1923. In the elections for the new parliament, the first conducted on a mass basis, he won an overwhelming victory with 190 out of 214 seats. Zaghlul was asked to form the cabinet and was invited by the British to negotiate a new treaty; he agreed to form a cabinet but refused to enter negotiations with the British unless there were no "absolutely reserved" points. On this, negotiations again broke down, and Zaghlul, flushed with what he thought was the proximity of victory, threw his Wafd into demonstrations in Egypt and the Sudan. In the atmosphere of hostility and passion the British officer who was commander of the Egyptian army and governor-general of the Sudan, Sir Lee Stack, was assassinated in Cairo on November 19.

The British reacted in a white fury, presenting an ultimatum to the Egyptian government which, after stating that "this murder, which holds up Egypt as at present governed to the contempt of civilized peoples, is the natural outcome of a campaign of hostility to British rights and British subjects in Egypt and the Sudan, founded upon a heedless ingratitude for benefits conferred by Great Britain," demanded "ample apology," "condign punishment" for the criminals, suppression of all "popular political demonstrations," payment of a fine of £500,000, withdrawal of all Egyptian officers from the Sudan within twenty-four hours, and notification of the Sudanese (that is, British) government that it could draw unlimited water from the Nile—thus appearing to strike at the jugular vein of Egypt. Moreover, Egypt was to "withdraw all opposition in the respects hereafter specified to the wishes of His Majesty's Government concerning the protection of foreign interests in Egypt."

The Egyptian government immediately agreed to apologize amply, to punish the criminals, and to pay the fine, but refused the other demands. In reply the British instructed the Sudan government forcibly to eject the Egyptians there and to renounce restrictions on its use of Nile waters. The British seized a part of the Alexandria customs to ensure Egyptian fulfillment of conditions. Further, the high commissioner suggested that hostages should be taken to be shot in the event of further assassinations.

Powerless to react but too proud to remain, Zaghlul resigned as prime minister and was replaced by a government that was little more than a British puppet. In December Parliament was dissolved and new, carefully rigged, elections were staged, but even in these the Wafd won almost half the seats. So Parliament was again dissolved. In yet another election the Wafd won 144 out of 201 seats but a British show of force, fear of palace intrigue, and, probably, weariness caused the 67-year-old Zaghlul to take a moderate position until the end of his life in 1927.

Once again, the Wafd took power in 1928 but was dismissed on charges of corruption and scandal—often more potent political weapons than gunboats—and in confusion, the Egyptian nationalist movement seemed itself in danger of being as discredited as were the very institutions of popular participation in government, the Parliament and the ministries. It appeared that long before it had reached its goals, the Wafd "sold out." Indeed, the man who followed Zaghlul as leader of the nationalists, Nahhas Pasha, was deeply involved in the scandals and corruption which so divided his party.

So Egypt faltered through the early 1930's, having lost all the élan of its nationalist period, led by men with an increasing stake in the status quo, dissatisfied but apparently, even in seeming victory, unable to achieve real independence. By 1936 the government was ready to sign a treaty with Great Britain which gave Britain essentially what she had asked for in 1922, military control, joint participation in British control over the Sudan, and British endeavors to end the privileged position of other foreign powers in Egypt. In 1937 on this basis Egypt was able to join the League of Nations.

Egyptian frustration and anguish is perhaps best documented in the rise of such extremists as fascist youth groups and the Muslim Brotherhood. The Egyptians, now really leaderless and with uncertain or complex goals, were unable to find a path to their future. Although formally independent they did not find themselves to be free.

Egypt broke diplomatic relations with Germany when World War II began and with Italy when Italy entered the war in the summer of 1940, but did not declare war. The country became a huge armed camp for the British Eighth Army as the western desert became a major theater of operations, and in the exigencies of the situation such freedom of action as was possessed by Egypt was quickly subordinated to the demands of the British military. Egyptian reticence or sympathy for the Axis, widely shared in the Arab world, was overcome by a coup de main in which British forces surrounded the palace of King Farouk in February 1942 and threatened to depose the king unless he named a prime minister of their choosing. Ironically, the government so installed was of the Wafd, long since tamed and friendly to the British.

Even those who have criticized the British admit that they acted under the most extreme conditions, with the war apparently being lost in most theaters and the beginnings of a German drive in North Africa which would bring Field Marshal Rommel's tanks to a point within 70 miles of Alexandria. But British actions in Egypt as in Iraq and elsewhere did lend reality to the contention of nationalists that so long as British forces remained on Egyptian soil, Egypt was a good deal less than fully independent.

Perhaps as potent a factor in Egyptian thought as any that could be adduced in economics or politics was the scar tissue caused by the blatantly evident and utter scorn felt by many Europeans for the Egyptians. "Wog"—Wily Oriental Gentleman—and "Gypo" became soldiers' taunts; the words of the Egyptian national anthem were redrafted as a smutty joke on the Egyptian king and queen. The typical English-Arabic phrase book always prominently featured the words "Get out," *imshee*, and "Beat it," *yalla*, and were largely restricted to those words used by an impolite patron to a waiter. But perhaps most of all, the central and most inviting piece of real estate of Cairo, the island in the middle of the Nile, was largely taken up by a sporting club which was restricted to Englishmen and, toward the end, to acceptable Europeans and Americans. Even the king of the country was unwelcome. Later there was to be no prouder victory of nationalism, even the Egyptianization of the Suez Canal or the National Bank of Egypt, than the capturing of the board of directors of the Gazira Sporting Club.

As the tides of war changed, after the battles of El Alamein and Stalingrad, the British position eased considerably. Britain not only was prepared to allow more autonomy within Egypt itself but encouraged Egypt and other Arab states to move toward the realization of at least a part of their aspirations for some form of federation. It was in Alexandria in October 1944 that the Arab Unity Conference was assembled under the chairmanship of Egypt. And, in order to be allowed to join the United Nations, Egypt in February 1945 finally declared war on Japan and Germany.

Once again, Egypt emerged from a war with appetite whetted for real independence. Students and members of the Muslim Brotherhood and other groups dominated the streets of Cairo for some months. The Egyptians were able to begin negotiations with the new Labour government on a revision of the 1936 treaty, but the Wafd, attempting to recapture its faded youthful vigor and purity, refused to be bound by the negotiations or to take part in them. In beginning the negotiations Great Britain agreed to evacuate all of Egypt except for the Suez Canal Zone, which became the major British base in the Middle East, but the future of the Sudan, which the Egyptians regarded as a part of Egypt since, at least, the 1899 convention establishing the condominium, led to a break in the talks. Egypt then took to the United Nations her case against the 1936 treaty, which she held was negotiated under duress, and against British moves to alienate the Sudan, but the Security Council was unwilling to do more than urge continued discussions between the two parties.

Almost immediately upon the heels of the defeat at the United Nations came the Palestine War in which Egyptian forces, after glowing speeches by leaders of the Egyptian government, were defeated. The bitter consequences of this humiliation were not long delayed for a government by now almost devoid of the respect of its people.

The Arabian Peninsula, where Islam was born, ceased to be the major stage of Islam in the time of the fourth caliph, Ali, when the capital of the empire was shifted to Kufa in what is now Iraq. But Arabia, with Mecca as the target of prayer and goal of pilgrimage and Medina, the birthplace of the Islamic state, never lost its sentimental and religious hold on Muslims. Particularly after the bedouin "defected" from the caliphate, returning to their pre-Islamic ways, in the second century of Islam, Arabia remained the "blood bank" of Arab civilization. From it all but Arabs were excluded and to it the faithful sent their pious donations to support religious and cultural institutions. Indeed, as the routes of commerce and the centers of industry were concentrated elsewhere, religion became the major "business" of Arabia. Little scope existed for agriculture, for few areas other than Yemen and the southeastern coast had sufficient rainfall or springs—Arabia has no rivers—to support more than occasional farming, and until this century no other significant resources were exploited.

Periodically in Islamic history, a reform movement has come from Arabia, paralleling the rise of Islam. The last, and greatest, of these is the Wahhabi revival of fundamentalism.

A successor in spirit if not in fact to other attempts to return to the bases of the faith, Wahhabism was begun in Arabia in the eighteenth century when a religious reformer, Muhammad Abdu'l-Wahhab, made common cause with the shaikh of the princely tribal family of Saud. The classic Islamic combination of the "Book and the Sword" which thus resulted led to a wave of conquest and tribal raids into Syria, Iraq, and all parts of Arabia in the early nineteenth century. Temporarily suppressed in the second decade of the nineteenth century by the Egyptian armies of Mehmet Ali, Wahhabism survived in the highlands of Nejd and on the eastern shores of Arabia. Its influence was, however, contained by the rise of a rival Arabian dynasty, the Rashidis of Hail, and by the Ottoman protection and support given to the office of the sharif of Mecca. In 1890 the Rashidis forced the Sauds to flee from the Nejd, to seek safety under the protection of the shaikh of Kuwait. In 1902 the late Abdu'l-Aziz ibn Saud, with a small band of Kuwaiti and Nejdi retainers, in a predawn coup de main, recaptured Riyadh. The Rashidis, weakened by internal disputes, were unable to cope with the revival of Wahhabi power not only in the Nejd but also in the Ottoman province of al-Hasa which the Saudi forces captured in 1913.

In December 1915 the British government signed a treaty in which it agreed to recognize Ibn Saud as sultan of the Nejd and to grant him a subsidy of £5000 monthly. Essentially, the British were interested in keeping Arabia quiet internally so that the Arabs under the influence of the sharif of Mecca, the British chosen instrument, could carry the war to the Turks in the Hejaz and in what is now Jordan and Syria.

The British were at the same time negotiating with Sharif Husain on the terms under which *his* Arabs would enter the war. In the Husain-McMahon Correspondence the British had specifically undertaken to restrict his activities from interference with other Arab rulers with whom they had treaties. Consequently, the British refused to recognize Husain's claim to be "King of the Arabs." Meanwhile, an Arabian force under Husain's son Faisal captured Damascus and took over Syria.

However, in Arabia supporters of Husain and Ibn Saud clashed in 1918, and Ibn Saud decisively defeated the Hejazis in 1919. Preoccupied with his Rashidi rivals until 1921 when he overcame their last resistence, Ibn Saud made no move against the Hejaz until 1924. In that year, after the abdication of Husain in favor of his eldest son Ali, the Hejazi forces were defeated again and both Taif and Mecca taken. A year later, in December 1925, Ibn Saud completed the conquest of the Hejaz, taking Jiddah, and King Ali went into exile. In 1927, in the Treaty of Jiddah, Great Britain recognized Ibn Saud as King of the Hejaz in return for his recognition of Faisal as King of Iraq, Abdullah as Amir of Transjordan, and the special status of the British-protected shaikhdoms on the Persian Gulf. Except for a brief Saudi war with Yemen in 1936 the Arabian Peninsula was at peace from 1927 to 1961 when a coup d'etat in Yemen developed first into a civil war and then a "civil war with outside intervention" as Egyptian troops landed in Yemen and the Saudis assisted the Yemeni royalists.

The British and the Ottoman Turks were almost the only foreigners in Arabia until the end of World War I, when interest in the possibility of oil brought in Americans. The major British interest in Arabia, until the discovery of oil in this century, has been the route to India. The Persian Gulf was a link in the

Euphrates-Mediterranean route and so involved vital communications. We have seen that one effect of Napoleon's invasion of
Egypt was to accentuate the importance of securing the northern
Persian Gulf gate of the route, Kuwait, just as an earlier rivalry
with the Portugese and then the Dutch had brought the British
to the lower end of the gulf and the Island of Hormuz in 1622.
By 1639 the British had secured rights to open a trading post at
Basra, and by 1764 had a consul there. By the end of the century
the British placed a resident in Baghdad to superintend the post
route to Europe. By 1820 they had established complete control
over the Gulf, suppressed piracy, and entered into treaty arrangements with the shaikhs of the "Pirate" (renamed "Trucial")
Coast.

From the time of Napoleon the British were deeply worried
about the use by other powers of the Euphrates–Persian Gulf
route to attack India. At first Russia was thought to pose such a
danger and then Germany. One after another the petty shaikhdoms came under increasing British influence and protection. In
1869 the Trucial shaikhdoms agreed not to deal with foreign
governments except through Great Britain; this was extended to
Bahrein in 1880, Muscat in 1891, and Qatar in 1916. Kuwait, from
the middle of the nineteenth century the key port on the gulf,
was originally planned as the Persian Gulf terminus of the Berlin–
Baghdad–Persian Gulf railway; but in 1898 it was effectively
removed from the Ottoman Empire when, finding that the
Russians intended to establish a logistics base there, the British
entered into treaty arrangements similar to the others concluded
with the gulf shaikhdoms in previous years.

The shaikh of Kuwait was recognized by Great Britain to be
independent under British protection on November 3, 1914. On
April 30, 1915, the Idrisi Sayyid of Sabya in Asir was recognized
similarly. These areas were backwaters in the general war effort,
which was concentrated in western Arabia, in the Hejaz, where
Sharif Husain instituted the Arab Revolt. But they were areas of
immediate concern to the government of India and consequently
their special status was reserved in the British commitment to
Husain.

Aden, on the southwest tip of Arabia, was also affected by the thrust of Napoleon toward the East. In 1799 a British force occupied the island of Perim, which forms a sort of stopper in the mouth of the Red Sea, and then moved to Aden. In 1802 the British concluded a commercial treaty with the sultan. Relations later were strained and an incident involving the passengers and crew of a wrecked British ship gave the British a pretext in 1839 to bombard and seize the town of Aden. In an ensuing peace treaty a stipend was allotted to the sultan, but five times before 1857 the town came under attack. Aden became a crown colony in 1937. As a part of the South Arabian Federation, which was formed in 1959, even today Aden is the object of a three-way tug of war between the British, the Arabic-speaking natives, and the large Yemeni community resident there.

Yemen, "Arabia Felix" of the classical writers, is the second largest of the states of the Arabian Peninsula. With a climate quite different from the rest of the peninsula and cut off by vast deserts from the north, Yemen has been strongly influenced by its nearer neighbors in Africa. But it has also been ruled by Ethiopia and Persia. The legendary seat of the Queen of Sheba, Yemen has the longest settled and recorded history of any part of Arabia. Its relatively heavy rainfall has made settled agriculture possible, and this has caused men to invest in the land in a way quite different from the use of nomadic areas to the north. Both Judaism and Christianity have, at periods, dominated the religious life of the country. Following the advent of Islam, Yemen became Muslim but most of the people espoused a non-Orthodox branch of Islam, the Zaidi Shii sect, which has had its "patriarch" the ruling imam of Yemen from the ninth century to the present time.

In 1517 Yemen was nominally conquered by the Ottoman Empire, but more effective threats to the autonomy of the area came from the Europeans, mainly the Portuguese, who alternated trade with piracy and imperialism. Invaded in the nineteenth century by the Egyptians, who drove out the Wahhabi tribes of Arabia, restored the imamate, and re-established Ottoman suzerainty, Yemen served in World War I as the base for Turkish operations against the British in Aden. In the Armistice of Mudros, Yemen achieved its independence. Although Yemen had a treaty with the Soviet Union in 1928, it was not recognized by the United States until 1946.

Internally, the history of Yemen is a sordid and bloody tale, but the country has been so isolated from the outside world and so poor in resources or strategic value as to preserve not only a large measure of autonomy but also a culture and a way of life. Well might a commentator say, when civil war broke out after the death of the old imam in 1962, "Yemen is rushing headlong into the fourteenth century."

When the "impact of the West" came in Arabia, it came not in the uniform of the soldier, in the ledger of the European banker, or with the humiliating attitude of the imperialist, but with the magic wand of the oil drilling rig. Far from refusing to let the Arab into its posh clubs, the oil industry was delighted to sit as a guest in the bedouin tent or to build for the Arab Western, air-conditioned cities, railroads, schools, and hospitals in return for the privilege of being allowed to drill in the desert wastes for oil. Undreamed of wealth poured into the peninsula—by 1967 nearly $2 billion yearly. The sudden infusion of wealth was initially intoxicating. Lacking the institutions or the trained people to manage the new income, the petty states wasted much. However, some, notably Kuwait, have not only learned rapidly to invest productively at home and abroad but also have created funds to assist in the overall development of the Middle East.

What the Arabian peninsula lost in missing the colonial period —training, building of infrastructure, and the imposition of constitutional institutions—was, at least in part, compensated for by what it also missed in the trauma of the deep wounds of national humiliation. The pride that the poorest of Bedouins has retained is only now being regained, at great cost and effort, by the richest of the Egyptians.

XI. Palestine: The Promised Land

On February 18, 1947, the British government announced to the world what had been evident to many long before, that "there is no prospect of resolving this conflict [in the Palestine mandate] by any settlement negotiated between the parties . . . We have . . . reached the conclusion that the only course now open to us is to submit the problem to the judgment of the United Nations."

As with so many simple and straightforward statements in international relations, behind the words lies a complex, emotion-fraught, and bitter story, many of whose ramifications lie far outside the scope of this book, yet one whose influence permeates the whole history of the modern Middle East—and the world—and which, therefore, commands out greatest and most sensitive attention. It is not incumbent upon the author or the reader to join the emotional fray—quite enough authors and readers have already done this—but it is essential for anyone who aspires to understand the Middle East today to know the sources, the extent, and the depth of those emotions in order to be the better able to cope with the events and men they have so profoundly affected.

The history of the Palestine problem is a long and spotty one; for the present purposes, only a few things need to be said about it: (1) though Palestine remained the emotional center of Zion, the Jewish population was almost totally expelled or drawn away from Palestine under the Roman Empire; (2) the Arab invasion in A.D. 636 brought relatively few new people to Palestine, so that the ancestors of most of today's "Arabs" were actually converted (either to Islam or to use of the Arabic language) over the centuries of Arab and Turkish rule; and (3) the immigration of Jews, other than the small number who came for religious reasons over the centuries, began in the late nineteenth century and was the result of persecution in Europe.

During the First World War, as we have seen, much or all of what subsequently became the Palestine mandate, entrusted to Great Britain under the League of Nations by the Paris Peace Conference in April 1920, was promised to France under the May 1916 Sykes-Picot agreement, to the Jews for "the establishment in Palestine of a National Home for the Jewish people" in the November 1917 Balfour Declaration, and, at least under one reasonable reading, to the Arabs by the Husain-McMahon Correspondence of 1915–16. The war ended with Great Britain in control of the area and the other three contenders attempting to secure their rights. A serious diplomatic clash with France over what the French regarded as British bad faith on the issues of Palestine, Syria, and Mosul was settled in Paris. This left two contenders, the Zionists and the Arabs, with the British holding an uneasy and unstable balance for nearly thirty years.

Initially, as we have seen, the Arabs were less concerned with opposition to the Zionists than to the French. The Arab leader Amir Faisal thought that if he came to terms with the Zionists, they could persuade the French government to waive their claims of influence in Syria. In a formal understanding with Dr. Weizmann, Faisal agreed, on behalf of the Arabs, to work together with the Zionists to achieve their mutual aims, to give effect to the Balfour Declaration, to facilitate Jewish immigration provided the rights of the Arab peasants and tenant farmers be protected, to insure freedom of worship and protection of the Holy Places, and to constitute the British government as their arbiter, provided the Arabs achieved their independence. Also a part of this agreement was Jewish economic aid to the Arabs. But the Arab Congress at Damascus repudiated the essence of Faisal's agreement with Weizmann, saying: "We regard their claims as a grave menace to our national, political and economic life. Our Jewish fellow-citizens shall continue to enjoy the rights and bear the responsibilities which are ours in common."

Faisal, himself, had little more time on the world stage as spokesman for the Arabs of the Levant. On July 14, 1920, French troops invaded Syria and, after routing the small Arab forces sent to oppose them, seized Damascus and overthrew the Arab government. Never again were the Arabs of Palestine to find a spokesman of international stature, and not for years were they to be represented by an Arab state with even the shadowy authority enjoyed by Faisal's Syrian kingdom.

Meanwhile, events in the occupied territory of Palestine had begun to assume, as they had in Iraq, a shape of their own. As in Iraq, so in Palestine, it was discovered that the administration was in a state of chaos. This was particularly evident in Palestine in questions of land ownership. Not only had the retreating Turks taken with them most of the administrative personnel but also had either taken or destroyed official registers of land holdings. Confusion was compounded. In Palestine, due to the Turkish ban on foreign ownership of property, dual sets of land ownership records had been maintained since the middle years of the nineteenth century. The many foreigners who had bought land registered it in the name of a subject of the empire. Over the years the land might have been sold or inherited several times. Moreover, since the Ottoman land tenure system was superimposed on local usage, rights of various sorts were often exercised by different parties in any given piece of land. In some instances land cases begun in the immediate postwar years were hardly settled by the end of the Palestine mandate.

The first chief administrator of Palestine urged that the Zionist program be dropped as inimical to public security in Palestine. The King-Crane Commission, which President Wilson sent to the Middle East to ascertain the wishes of the population, of which about 10 percent was Jewish, reported an overwhelming rejection by the population of Zionist aspirations. But before the end of the military administration and the inauguration of the mandate, upwards of 5000 Jewish immigrants were allowed to enter the country, and Hebrew was adopted as one of the official languages.

Meanwhile on July 1, 1920, authority in Palestine was handed to Sir Herbert Samuel as the first high commissioner of the mandatory government. But it was not until 1923 that Palestine legally ceased to be a part of the Ottoman Empire and became a mandate of the League of Nations. A little over a month after taking power the new civil government issued the land transfer ordinance which reopened the registry office so that lands once more could be bought and sold. The first major purchase of land, by the Jewish National Fund and the Palestine Land Development Company, Ltd., encompassed seven Arab villages in Galilee.

At the same time Sir Herbert Samuel, who had been a principal supporter of Zionism in England during the war, set the quota for the first year's immigration of Jews at 16,500. Just before the publication of the quota on immigration, occurred the second of what was to become a series of Arab-Jewish clashes. In the following year, in May 1921, immigration was suspended after another series of Arab attacks on Jews and Jewish settlements. Everyone, even among the Arab moderates, feared that sooner or later a Zionist state would be created if a sufficiently large number of Jews had moved to Palestine. This was the finding of an investigation commission. However, immigration was allowed to continue the following month with fewer restrictions than prior to the outbreak.

Thus, in 1921 two precedents were set by the government which were to be followed for the next quarter century. In the first place, in the face of acts of violence, the government *did* temporarily accede to the aims of those committing the acts of violence: it did temporarily suspend immigration. In the second place, after the situation had been brought under control and an investigating commission had studied the underlying causes of the trouble, the government *did not* address the identified causes in its subsequent policy.

In 1922, after further Arab outbursts against Zionism, the high commissioner requested that the Colonial Office define exactly the meaning of the phrase "a National Home." The then Colonial

Secretary, Winston Churchill, replied with a statement of policy. After affirming that the Balfour Declaration was to remain the bedrock of British policy, he restricted, more narrowly than any senior British official had to that date, what was meant in the Balfour Declaration: "Unauthorized statements have been made to the effect that the purpose in view is to create a wholly Jewish Palestine. Phrases have been used such as that Palestine is to become 'as Jewish as England is English'. His Majesty's Government regard any such expectation as impracticable and have no such aim in view . . . They would draw attention to the fact that the terms of the Declaration referred to do not contemplate that Palestine as a whole should be converted into a Jewish National Home, but that such a Home should be founded in Palestine."

In 1922 the British government decided to separate Transjordan legally from the mandate of Palestine. Transjordan, said the British government, was not included in the Balfour Declaration and Jews were forbidden to buy land there. This move satisfied no one. The Zionists felt that if their historic claim was justified in principle, it was justified in its particulars; so they argued at that time, as they had previously argued at the Peace Conference, that Transjordan was necessary for the development of their National Home. The Arabs, in their turn, argued that Britain's act tended to weaken the position of those who lived in the Palestine mandate by appearing to settle the Arab claim to the dubious benefit of the small number of nomadic tribesmen moving about in the Jordan desert. Further, they pointed out, this action gave a larger degree of independence and self-government to Arabs far less advanced than they, and so sapped the idea of tutelage in statecraft inherent in mandate conception.

In Palestine itself the high commissioner tried in 1922 to establish a government agency in which Arabs would have a voice—at least in lesser issues of policy. The plan called for a council of twenty-three members, including the high commissioner. Ten of the other twenty-two would be official appointees; of the remaining twelve elected positions, two would be Christian, two Jews, and eight Muslims. The Arabs opposed the plan since they would have only ten votes—a permanent minority—on such matters as land policy, immigration, and Zionism. In the face of Arab hostility the high commissioner dropped the whole project. The following year he suggested that the Arabs form "an Arab Agency" analogous to the Jewish Agency, so that the Palestine Arab community would have voice in the affairs of government. This also the Arabs refused.

There can be no doubt that the Arabs were mistaken in not accepting this proposal, for their refusal deprived them of all effective concentration of their activities in the Palestine mandate. Again and again in the following years the Arabs refused to be involved responsibly in political affairs. They argued to themselves that if they accepted responsibility for any part of the affairs of the mandate they would thereby acquiesce in the basic policy of creating a Jewish National Home and would become actually, as the mandate suggested they were politically, but a single part of the population of Palestine.

In Palestine, as in the other mandate states, noteworthy developments in education, public works, health, and other "social overhead" facilities took place. In the excitement of the developmental activity so evident within the mandate, the political questions appeared briefly in the 1920's to have been shelved.

This is true to a certain extent because the worst fears of the Arabs had not been realized. The country had not been "swamped" by Jews, a Jewish state seemed no nearer to establishment than in 1922, and as long as times were good, everyone was prepared to deal in the present and leave the future worries for bad times. Then, somewhat curiously, the arrival of a sharp economic depression, which resulted partly from a collapse of the Polish currency, instead of increasing Arab discontent tended to lessen Arab fears. From 1925 to 1928 no meetings of the Palestine Arab Congress were held, and no protests were voiced over Jewish immigration. The immigration figures themselves provide an index.

The year 1925, when a series of Arab protests were made to the mandate authority, was the largest immigration year to that date, with a net Jewish immigration increase of 31,650. In the next year, however, only about one sixth as large a net immigration was recorded. The Arabs reached the conclusion that with their high birth rate they were not in danger of losing their majority of the population. In 1927 the Jewish community had 2358 more emigrants than immigrants. By the Arabs this was taken as a sign that the National Home had failed, the Jews were leaving, and the Arabs could relax in victory. In the following year, however, the trend was reversed; a very slight net gain was made. And in 1929 the net gain was 3503. The optimism of the Arabs was shattered. They also observed that the Zionist crisis had tended to heal the breach between the Zionist and non-Zionist Jews and even led to an enlarging of the Jewish Agency.

The relative calm of the middle years of the 1920's was ended by a riot in 1929, begun when a number of Zionists organized a demonstration at the Wailing Wall in Jerusalem in the course of which the Zionist flag was raised and the Zionist anthem sung. Within two weeks of violence 472 Jews and 268 Arabs were among the casualties. The commission which investigated the disturbances noted: "The Arabs have come to see in the Jewish immigrant not only a menace to their livelihood but a possible overlord of the future . . . and the result of Jewish enterprise and penetration have been such as to confirm that they will be excluded from this soil."

After questions were raised in the League of Nations Permanent Mandate Commission, the British government decided in May 1930 to appoint a special commission under Sir John Hope-Simpson of the League of Nations Refugee Settlement Commission for Greece, and formerly of the Indian Civil Service, to investigate the underlying causes of the recent disturbances. The Hope-Simpson report recommended an immediate halt to immigration, but suggested that it might become possible again on a limited scale in future years.

The British government accepted the report and on the basis of it issued the Passfield White Paper which went even further toward granting Arab desires than did John Hope-Simpson's report. Jewish reaction was both immediate and effective. Zionist leaders protested to the Colonial Office, and the president of the

Jewish Agency, Chaim Weizmann, resigned in protest. From a wide variety of public figures, including the leadership of the opposition Conservative party, protests flowed in. In hasty retreat, the British government took the unusual step of redefining its action in a letter published in *The Times* in which the prime minister denied that the government intended to stop the development of the National Home. Subsequent speeches in Parliament and statements to the press further modified the intent of Passfield White Paper. In February 1931 the British prime minister, in a letter to Weizmann which was published in *The Times*, proclaimed that immigration "can be fulfilled without prejudices to the rights and positions of other sections of the population of Palestine," and so repudiated the Passfield White Paper.

Coming as this letter did, only as the result of protests by one group in Palestine and their supporters, without benefit of another government study or commission, it was naturally taken by the Arabs as concession to political pressures. They called it, in bitter jest, the "Black Letter" which canceled the White Paper. For the first time Arab hostility began to be directed at the government rather than toward the incoming Jews.

The immediate result was an Arab boycott and a refusal to work together with the Jewish community on civic affairs. But on a positive program, the Arabs spoke with many voices when they spoke at all. Lacking a constituted representative, as the Jews possessed in the Jewish Agency, the Arabs divided into a number of mutually hostile groups which were ineffective in expressing their desires to the government. Moreover, the minimum Arab program was independence, end of immigration, and restriction of land sales. On these terms the government had shown itself unwilling, if not unable, to negotiate. As a result, moderate Arabs could have no concrete and positive program to urge upon the government.

Meanwhile, with the rise to power in Germany of the Nazis in 1932, a new sense of urgency and, eventually, desperation was felt by the Zionist organization, and its ability to act was stiffened by the increasing scale of immigration from Germany. Between

1932 and 1933 the number of immigrants tripled. As the subsequent royal commission pointed out: "As the National Home expanded from 1933 onwards, so the Arab hate and fear have increased." The attitude of the Arab leaders became more hostile toward the government, and the tone of the Arab press more bitter. In the autumn of 1934 the Arab executive submitted to the high commissioner a formal expression of its view that the safeguards for Arab interests embodied in the mandate had broken down. In the single year of 1935, 61,854 Jewish immigrants arrived. This figure was as large as the total immigration of the first five years of the mandate, and in the four years from 1932 to 1936 the Jewish population of Palestine quadrupled.

Meanwhile, in other Arab countries, notably Egypt and Syria, the British and French governments appeared to give way before violence and nationalist demonstrations. So once again, the Palestine Arab community resorted to direct and violent action. On April 13, 1936, a series of terrorists attacks began throughout the country. Violence bred further violence between the Jewish and Arab communities. Throughout Palestine committees were formed in the Arab towns to demand the establishment of a representative government, prohibition of sales of land to Jews, and end of Jewish immigration. The normally mutually hostile Arab political leaders were forced by their rank-and-file supporters to form a united front and call for a general strike. This time, the government refused to submit to pressure and on May 18 issued an immigration schedule which was somewhat higher than in any previous year. The general strike quickly developed into a civil war. Two trains were derailed, a bridge blown up, and guerrilla bands which included soldiers from Syria and Iraq began to operate in the hill country. On May 23 mass arrests of Arab leaders were made, and in June members of the Arab Higher Committee were interned in a concentration camp.

In June 1936, 137 Arab senior officials and judges in the Palestine government presented a memorandum in which they set out their contention that the disturbances were caused by the fact that the Arab population of all classes, creeds and occupations is animated by a profound sense of injustice done to them. They feel that insufficient regard has been paid in the past to their legitimate grievances, even though those grievances had been inquired into by qualified and impartial official investigators, and to a large extent vindicated by those inquiries. As a result, the Arabs have been driven into a state verging on despair; and the present unrest is no more than an expression of that despair.

The fact must be faced that that feeling of despair is largely to be traced to loss of faith on the part of the Arabs in the value of official pledges and assurances for the future, and to the fact that they are genuinely alarmed at the extent to which His Majesty's Government have from time to time given way to Zionist pressure. Their confidence was severely shaken as far back as 1931, when the Prime Minister's letter to Dr. Weizmann was issued as an interpretation of the White Paper of 1930. But more recently, when the projects regarding the Legislative Council and the restriction on sales of land were hotly challenged in Parliament, their loss of confidence turned to despair.

Coming as this did from the most moderate, committed, and responsible members of the Arab community, the memorandum made a considerable impression both on the government and on the royal commission which was subsequently sent to investigate the cause of the disturbance.

By September 1936 some 20,000 regular troops had been sent to Palestine to try to re-establish public security. Severe punishment, including the destruction of villages and the quartering of troops, was meted out to those accused of harboring rebels. Arab casualties amounted to over 1000. Both Amir Abdulla of Transjordan and the prime minister of Iraq offered to mediate, but the British government could not allow mediation to include the issues of any of the terms of the mandate or the goal of the establishment of a National Home. Their offer of mediation having been refused, the rulers of the other Arab states advised the Arabs of Palestine "to rely on the good intentions of our friend Great Britain who has declared that she will do justice." By mid-October the strike had ended and the Arab bands had dispersed.

A royal commission, appointed to investigate the underlying causes of the disturbance, arrived in Palestine in November 1936.

After careful study of the situation the commission decided that the mandate was unworkable in its existing form. Their conclusions, published in 1937, are still worthy of attention.

An irrepressible conflict has arisen between two national communities within the narrow bounds of one small country. About 1,000,000 Arabs are in strife, open or latent, with some 400,000 Jews. There is no common ground between them. The Arab community is predominantly Asiatic in character, the Jewish community predominantly European. They differ in religion and in language. Their cultural and social life, their ways of thought and conduct, are as incompatible as their national aspirations. These last are the greatest bar to peace . . . The War and its sequel have inspired all Arabs with the hope of reviving in a free and united Arab world the traditions of the Arab golden age. The Jews similarly are inspired by their historic past . . . In the Arab picture the Jews could only occupy the place they occupied in Arab Egypt or Arab Spain. The Arabs would be as much outside the Jewish picture as the Canaanites in the old land of Israel. The National Home . . . cannot be half-national . . . This conflict was inherent in the situation from the outset. The terms of the Mandate tended to confirm it [and] the conflict has grown steadily more bitter . . . In the earlier period hostility to the Jews was not widespread among the fellaheen. It is now general . . . The intensification of the conflict will continue . . . it seems probable that the situation, bad as it now is, will grow worse. The conflict will go on, the gulf between Arabs and Jews will widen."

The recommendation of the royal commission was that Palestine be partitioned between the two communities since the only alternative appeared to be a rule of repression which would lead nowhere. The British government accepted the royal commission's report and issued a White Paper announcing that partition would be the basis of British policy. In the debate in the House of Lords, however, Lord Samuel, the first high commissioner, pointed out that the Jewish state, as small as it necessarily would be, would contain a population of Arabs almost equal to that of the Jews. Later he wrote that "the Commission seems to have picked out all the most awkward provisions of the Peace Treaty of Versailles, and to have put a Saar, a Polish corridor, and a half a dozen Dansigs and Mamels into a country the size of Wales." Such a monstrosity, he warned, would be impossible either to administer or to defend. After an initial cool reaction, the hostility of all parties to the conflict hardened against the plan. The Zionist Congress refused it outright. The League of Nations was not in favor but, in the final analysis, could do little but accept the advice of the British government. Those Arabs whose districts would be lost to the Arab state brought pressure on their leaders to oppose the plan. To see if a better redrawing of the map of Palestine might not be possible, a partition commission was appointed and sent to Palestine.

Meanwhile, in September 1937 the acting district commissioner of Galilee, which under the royal commission proposal would have been given to the Jewish state, was murdered by Arab terrorists. On October 1, a week after the assassination, the government outlawed the Arab Higher Committee and all national committees, ordered the arrest and deportation of six leading Arab figures, and froze the funds of the Pious Foundation which had supported Arab political activity. Almost 1000 people were interned. During the year, 438 attacks with bombs or fire arms were made on police posts, Jewish settlements, and Arab houses.

When the partition commission arrived in Palestine in April 1938, the leaders of the Arab community were for the most part under detention, but the community itself was united as never before and not one Arab collaborated with the commission. To counter Arab hostility, the government armed nearly 5000 Jews as active and reserve police, but the period of Zionist cooperation with the government was short-lived. Following the June 1938 hanging of a Jewish revisionist terrorist convicted of firing on an Arab bus, the Jews attacked government buildings and bombed Arab markets. In one such attack in Haifa 74 Arabs were killed and 129 others wounded.

During 1938 the government reported 5708 "incidents of violence" including over 1000 attacks on troops or government facilities. Some 2500 people, almost all Arab, were interned, and it was estimated that at least 1000 rebels had been killed by the police and army.

The partition commission published its recommendations in November 1938. After admitting that "the Arabs remain inflexibly hardened to partition" and that "it is impossible to divide a country of its size and configuration into areas the frontiers of which, having regard to the conditions of modern warfare, will have any real military significance," the commission presented three plans for partition. The unsolved dilemma was simply the need to create a Jewish state of sufficient size as to be economically viable and yet one which would not have an Arab majority.

The ensuing government White Paper admitted that "the political, administrative and financial difficulties involved in the proposal . . . are so great that this solution to the problem is impracticable."

The next British move was to summon yet another conference —this time only of the more moderate Arab leaders and those of the Jewish community—to London in February 1939. There, the government decided to review the basis of the Arab case including the Husain-McMahon Correspondence which, for the first time, was made public. A committee was established to evaluate the correspondence as it related to Palestine. Though this committee was not able to agree, the British government representative admitted that the Arab condition was found to be stronger than was thought before. The conference adjourned without having reached any agreement, and with both Jews and Arabs resolved to resist any limitation on their rights. The Arab rebellion continued in the hills of Palestine with covert and overt support from Arabs in surrounding countries. At the same time Jewish legal and illegal immigration was greatly accelerated.

To cope with the dilemma in which it found itself, the British government decided to issue a new statement of policy in which it proposed to adhere to *its* original contention that Palestine was not included in the area promised to the Arabs, but that neither was it the intent of the Balfour Declaration to convert Palestine into a Jewish state against the will of the Arab population. Therefore, the British government offered a plan whereby Palestine would, if possible, within ten years, be given representative institutions and a constitution. After five years Jewish immigration would cease, and Arab land sales would be permitted only within selected areas. The White Paper ended with a plea that both Jews and Arabs take note of the reverence "of many millions of Muslims, Jews and Christians throughout the world who pray for peace in Palestine and for the happiness of her people."

In Palestine the Jewish community was outraged. The transmission lines of the broadcasting station were cut so that announcement of the White Paper was delayed. Government offices were burned or sacked, police were stoned, and shops looted. The government thus found itself under attack from both the Arab and Jewish communities at once.

Meanwhile, in Europe the lights were dimming, and on September 1 the Second World War began with the march of the German army into Poland.

In Palestine reactions to the war were mixed as members of both communities rallied to support the British government against the Germans. Altogether some 21,000 Jews and 8000 Arabs served in branches of the British armed forces. However, both Jews and Arabs did maintain their opposition to the local government, and demonstrations and terrorist attacks never ceased throughout the war. Shortly after the immediate German threat to the Middle East was ended with the British victory at El Alamein in 1942, public manifestations of hostility increased. Members of the Stern Gang clashed with the police in a number of instances. On August 8, 1944, a Jewish attempt was made to assassinate the high commissioner, government installations were raided and looted, and the commander-in-chief of the British forces in the Middle East was moved to issue a communiqué pointing out that the "active and passive sympathizers of the terrorists are directly impeding the war effort of Great Britain and assisting the enemy." On November 6, 1944, the British minister of state resident in Cairo, Lord Moyne, was murdered by two members of the Stern Gang. In the late spring of 1945 the incidence of attacks on the government and on British army units greatly increased. Raids were made with great precision on arms dumps, banks, and communication facilities. As Europe emerged from the war, Palestine took up war in earnest.

As the full horror of the war in Europe and Nazi massive murder of Jews came to the public attention, the already critical situation was inevitably further inflamed in Palestine. The British government was blamed, because of the restrictions on immigration which followed the 1939 White Paper, for the death of hundreds of thousands of Jews who failed to escape from Europe.

With an unbroken record of failures in its attempts to settle the Palestine problem the British government asked the United States to participate in one further inquiry. The resulting Anglo-American committee of inquiry had as a key part of its terms of reference instructions to inquire into the *European* Jewish community's needs. So it was at the assembly points for the survivors of Nazi bestiality that the Anglo-American committee began its short life. The heart-rending tour was an emotional gauntlet for the committee members who eloquently described in the report "the depths of human suffering there endured."

In Palestine the committee found the observations of the royal commission to be valid, as valid in 1946 as in 1936. Hostility of the Arabs to Zionism was unanimous. The major difference between the two dates was the new and increasing power of the Jewish Agency with its unofficial army, the Haganah, then estimated at 60,000. The committee's description of Palestine will be recognized by all who saw it in these violent days. "Army tents, tanks, a grim fort and barracks overlook the waters of the Sea of Galilee. Blockhouses, road barriers manned by soldiers, barbed wire entanglements, tanks in the streets, pre-emptory searches, seizures and arrests on suspicion, bombings by gangsters and shots in the night are now characteristic."

While awaiting the report of the Anglo-American committee the government of Palestine had set the immigration quota at 1500 monthly and tightened up on penalties for armed attack, possession of firearms, and membership in terrorist groups. These police measures did little to calm the situation.

On the night of June 16 the paramilitary activity in Palestine became more concentrated as the commando group of the Haganah, the Palmach, destroyed nine bridges in different parts of the country. The next night the Stern Gang attacked railway installations in Haifa, and on the eighteenth the Irgun kidnapped six British army officers and held them as hostages. The government published a series of intercepted telegrams which showed that the Jewish Agency was involved in the activities of the terrorist groups as well as of its own army, the Haganah. On June 29 the government arrested a number of key figures in the Jewish Agency and occupied its headquarters long enough to seize a part of its files. Twenty-seven hundred people were arrested, of whom about seven hundred were detained after questioning. Most of the personnel of Palmach was included among those arrested, and large supplies of arms were discovered and seized by the British troops. In reprisal the Irgun blew up the King David Hotel, where the senior staff of the government of Palestine was housed, on July 22.

Meanwhile, in London, American and British officials discussed the possibility of solving the problem of Palestine in a way which went far beyond the cunning of Solomon. The proposal was to divide the Jews and Arabs into separate zones or provinces but to leave these provinces as autonomous members of one state. This was actually a contingency plan worked out some years before by the Colonial Office as a last resort. The plan was considered in London by representatives of the Arab states, who rejected it. Neither Palestine Jews nor Arabs even accepted the British government invitation to discuss the plan. The Arab position remained that Palestine should become an independent state ruled by its native majority with due protection for the rights of the minority. The Zionist position likewise was familiar: Palestine should be a Jewish commonwealth, open to Jewish immigration as controlled by the Jewish Agency.

As yet another attempt at compromise, the British government suggested in February 1947 that Palestine be administered for five years as a trusteeship with substantial local autonomy in areas with Jewish or Arab majorities, the protection of the minority being the responsibility of the British high commissioner, with provision for nearly 100,000 refugees to enter the country in the first two years. This proposal was rejected by both the Arabs (including the Arab Higher Committee) and the Jewish Agency.

In these circumstances, failure, heavy expenditure of men and money, and what the British regarded as American irresponsibility—in 1946 both the Democratic and Republican parties attempted to win Jewish electoral support by declarations favoring mass immigration into Palestine—Britain decided to turn the problem over to the United Nations. Speaking in the House of Commons on February 18, 1947, Ernest Bevin said the government had "been faced with an irreconcilable conflict of principles. There are in Palestine about 1,200,000 Arabs and 600,000 Jews. For the Jews, the essential point of principle is the creation of a sovereign Jewish State. For the Arabs, the essential point of principle is to resist to the last the establishment of Jewish sovereignty in any part of Palestine. The discussions of the last month have quite clearly shown that there is no prospect of resolving this conflict by any settlement negotiated between the parties . . . We have, therefore, reached the conclusion that the only course now open to us is to submit the problem to the judgment of the United Nations . . . We shall then ask the United Nations . . . to recommend a settlement of the problem. We do not intend ourselves to recommend any particular solution."

The United Nations had previously taken official recognition of the problem of Palestine, in the Security Council and General Assembly, but it had not itself investigated the situation. On May 15, 1947, the General Assembly voted to create a Special Committee on Palestine (UNSCOP), to submit not later than September 1, 1947, "such proposals as it may consider appropriate for the solution of the problem of Palestine."

UNSCOP members arrived in Jerusalem on June 14. Once again the Arab Higher Committee showed itself inflexible by refusing to participate in the meetings of the special committee. The Arab states, however, did make their views known by repeating arguments they had previously advanced.

The Jewish Agency, to the contrary, cooperated in full with UNSCOP and provided its members with extensive documentation and appeals. Even the Irgun, then engaged in a game of hide-and-seek with the whole of the British forces in Palestine and not always on friendly terms with the Haganah, managed to hold a lengthy meeting with the chairman of the committee.

The committee found little that was different from what its predecessors had reported. It pointed out that Palestine was a small country and of its limited extent of somewhat over 10,000 square miles, only about half was inhabitable by settled people. although the country was principally agricultural—65 percent of the population gained a living directly from agriculture—some 50 percent of the cereals used by the population had to be imported. Palestine, it noted, "is exceedingly poor" in all of the resources needed for modern industry. The population was then 1,203,000 Arabs to 608,000 Jews or about 2 to 1. Since the Arab birth rate was much higher than the Jewish, by 1960 these figures would probably become by natural increase, if immigration were stopped, 1,533,000 to 664,000—or almost 5 to 2. Lastly, to complicate the problem of any sort of partition, UNSCOP found that there "is no clear territorial separation of Jews and Arabs by large contiguous areas." "Jews are more than 40 percent of the total population in the districts of Jaffa (which includes Tel-Aviv), Haifa and Jerusalem. In the northern inland areas of Tiberias and Beisan, they are between 25 and 34 percent of the total population. In the inland northern districts of Safad and Nazareth and the coastal districts of Tulkarm and Ramle, Jews form between 10 and 25 percent of the total population, while in the central districts and the districts south of Jerusalem they constitute not more than 5 percent of the total."

Unquestionably the problems involved in partition were great, yet the urgency of the problem was even greater than in the previous year. Some 17,873 illegal immigrants were under detention and 820 Palestinians were under arrest for security reasons; if anything the situation reported by the Anglo-American committee had worsened. "The atmosphere in Palestine today is one of profound tension . . . In the streets of Jerusalem and other key areas barbed wire defenses, road blocks, machine gun posts and constant armoured car patrols are routine measures. In areas of doubtful security, Administration officials and the military forces live within strictly policed security zones and work within fortified and closely-guarded buildings."

The British administration found that virtually its whole energies had to be devoted to public security and eventually, in all truth, to self-defense. "The right of any community to use force as a means of gaining its political ends is not admitted in the British Commonwealth. Since the beginning of 1945 the Jews have implicitly claimed this right and have supported by an organized campaign of lawlessness, murder and sabotage their contention that, whatever other interests might be concerned, nothing should be allowed to stand in the way of a Jewish State and free Jewish immigration into Palestine."

This being the situation, UNSCOP recommended that the mandate be terminated "at the earliest practicable date," that independence be granted, and that until independence the United Nations assume responsibility. It further recommended that the international community assume *its* responsibilities in assisting the 250,000 Jewish refugees assembled in Europe so as to relieve the pressure on Palestine. Finally the committee urged that whatever other divisions be made in Palestine, it be preserved as an economic unit. The majority of UNSCOP voted to approve a plan of partition with economic union. The states thus created would have the following populations: Arab state, 10,000 Jews and 725,000 Arabs and others; Jewish state, 498,000 Jews and 407,000 Arabs and others; internationalized district of Jerusalem, 100,000 Jews and 105,000 Arabs and others.

This was about the best UNSCOP felt it could do. The Arab state would contain a 1½ percent Jewish minority but the Jewish state would contain a 45 percent minority of Arabs (not including an estimated 90,000 bedouin). In the international zone there would be an almost 1 to 1 equality. The United Nations Secretariat estimated on the basis of past returns for the various districts of Palestine that the Jewish state would have a revenue three times larger than the Arab.

A minority of the committee—India, Iran, Yugoslavia—proposed that a federal state be created. The major motive behind this solution was to "avoid an acceleration of the separatism which now characterizes the relations of Arabs and Jews in the Near East, and to avoid laying the foundations of a dangerous irredentism there, which would be inevitable consequences of partition in whatever form." Moreover, the UNSCOP minority pointed out that the vast majority of both Jews and Arabs opposed partition. The Arab and Jewish states within the federal state should have full powers of self-government under the federal constitution. The boundaries suggested differed slightly from those proposed by the majority.

At the United Nations, before the proposals of UNSCOP were published, Soviet delegate Andrei Gromyko expressed the Russian position on the Palestine issue. He stressed the "bankruptcy of the mandatory system of administration of Palestine." In this he agreed (except, perhaps, in choice of words) with almost every observer of the problem from the royal commission onward. He then went on to support the "aspirations of the Jews to establish their own State." However, he agreed with the Arabs that the responsibility for this state of affairs was European, was due to the "fact that no western European State has been able to ensure the defense of the elementary rights of the Jewish people." Finally he supported the sort of dual state proposed in the minority UNSCOP report. The British and American delegates wanted to avoid discussing the possible solutions until the UNSCOP report was available and clearly wanted to avoid any approach to solution that might involve Russian entry into the Middle Eastern sphere.

When the UNSCOP proposals were published, the British government announced its intention to remove its military installations from the Palestine–Suez Canal area deep into central Africa, to an area which then seemed relatively quiet, Kenya. In effect, Britain was getting ready to wash its hands of Palestine. As desperately as everyone had wished this in the past, there was an immediate realization that such action would precipitate a grim and bloody struggle, that as violently condemned as the British had been, they had exercised the only existing restraint.

The Jewish Agency could be satisfied in having gained recognition of its early claim to independence and a much larger slice of territory than ever before offered, except in the limited "National Home" sense suggested in the Balfour Declaration. The Arabs felt that they had lost everything, and they publicly announced that they intended to resist the implementation of UNSCOP's proposals by force. The Egyptian newspaper *al-Ahram* predicted in September 1947 that "the Palestine Arabs will launch a relentless war to repel this attack on their country, especially as they know that all the Arab countries will back and assist them, supplying them with men, money, and ammunition."

The rival communities prepared for war, the Arabs in two—rival—paramilitary organizations neither of which proved to amount to much when tested. The Jews of course had large cadres of men who had served in the British army or the American army and air force during the war, and they already had standing, if concealed, armies in the Haganah, its Palmach elite corps, the Irgun, and the smaller Stern Gang. Quantities of equipment and ammunition were being seized from British stores and soon the Jewish purchasing agents were able to send into Palestine considerable amounts of American and Czech equipment.

At the United Nations both the United States and the Soviet Union supported partition, and by agreement, arrived at on November 10, decided that the British mandate should end May 1, 1948, and that the two states would be established by July 1. The British delegate announced that the British army would have evacuated the country by August 1, and that Britain would thereafter not participate in whatever efforts were made to police partition. When the General Assembly met on November 26, Sir Alexander Cadogan announced that Britain wanted to make quite certain that the General Assembly realized it could not count upon British forces to impose its decisions on either Jews or Arabs.

In the Middle East outside of Palestine itself, the growth of anti-Zionism among the Arabs had reached a fever pitch. Ugly demonstrations broke out in many points all over the Middle East. In points as widely scattered as Aden, Libya, and Baghdad a growing feeling of anger over Palestine which could not be expressed against the distant Palestine Jewish community was vented locally upon Jews who in most cases had little or no contact with Zionism. The Jewish communities in their turn recoiled in fear from the nations in which many of them had participated, often at the highest levels of government. This ugly situation in the ensuing months led to a large-scale migration from Iraq and Yemen which further increased the immigration pressure upon Palestine.

After study by various subcommittees and lengthy debates on the floor at the United Nations, a proposal was made to partition Palestine, in general according to UNSCOP's recommendations with minor frontier changes (the main feature being to include Jaffa within the Arab state). Finally on November 29 the partition proposal was passed by a vote of 33 to 13 with 10 abstentions. The end of the mandate was in sight.

In Palestine the Arabs managed to gain a semblance of unity by reverting to their 1936 model of local national committees. The first of these was established in Jaffa just before the United Nations voted partition. Arab attacks on Jews and Jewish settlements and Jewish reprisals and attacks on Arabs began at the end of November and rapidly gained in intensity. In January 1948 Arab volunteers from other states began to enter Palestine. The Arab leader of the 1936 revolt was again in Palestine with about 5000 volunteers in scattered and uncoordinated bands. The streets of all towns and many villages were already forests of barbed wire, and only the foolhardy and the combatants moved about at night.

As the British troops exposed themselves less and less and began to withdraw from remote positions, Arab bands raided settlements and even managed to cut the road from Tel Aviv to Jerusalem, but they soon showed they were no match for the Jewish military units. Both Jews and Arabs set up shadow governments by drawing on the personnel of the mandate government and their respective organizations. In the Jewish Agency, of course, the Jewish community had a ready-made government. The Arabs were more restricted in their experience. They never had an organization comparable to the Jewish Agency, and even their few leaders had been absent for a decade.

The day-to-day events in Palestine from December 1947 to May 1948 belie the arbitrary classifications of peace and war. There were 5000 casualties—one in every 350 people in the country—in this five-month period, and the damage to property may be estimated in the millions of dollars. In some days as many as fifty "incidents" were reported all over Palestine. Trains were blown up, banks robbed, government offices attacked, convoys ambushed, and mobs and gangs looted, burned, and clashed with troops or rival mobs.

The surrounding Arab states prepared for war, and their presses proclaimed in lurid and strident tones that they would resist to the death the UN decision. However, on March 21, the political committee of the Arab League unexpectedly made a bid for a compromise peace. It decided to insist that the original British proposal, which the American government was also considering, be enforced. This would have put Palestine under a temporary trusteeship. The committee further urged that the Jews then on Cyprus be accepted into the several Arab states as immigrants and that those in Palestine be assured of their rights as a minority in an Arab state. If the proposal was in earnest, it was certainly too little and too late. Psychologically no one could retreat, least of all the Arab governments.

On the surface the Arabs appeared infinitely stronger. After all, the whole Arab world was publicly pledged to intervene in the war. Egypt, Iraq, Syria, Lebanon, and Transjordan all had standing armies and were receiving surplus British or French equipment. Public enthusiasm, especially among students and the middle class, was high. Yet, it was already evident how weak the Arab governments were. None of the governments was "popular" in its own home, and subsequent events proved that corruption was not only prevalent but existed to such an extent as to all but incapacitate most of the Arab forces. The army commands proved inefficient particularly in logistics but lacked initiative in tactics as well. The troops were poorly trained and often poorly led. And finally, even in dire need, the Arab governments proved that their jealousies and personal quarrels were of much more importance to them than their declared interest in Palestine. None of the Arabs, Palestinian or other, except the Arab Legion of Transjordan, could begin to match the level of technical competence of the Jewish forces. Moreover, among the Arabs of Palestine they found little support. These had been virtually leaderless since 1938 and had never really recovered from their rebellion of 1936–38. By the end of the mandate, they had become terrorized, psychologically defeated mobs, fleeing in all directions.

Early in April the pattern of events began to assume some shape. British forces had been steadily pulling out of the country. The March 20 statement by the Secretary General of the Arab League, that the Arabs would accept a truce and limited trusteeship for Palestine if the Jewish Agency would agree, was rejected out of hand by David Ben-Gurion "for even the shortest time." Fighting raged over most of Palestine. On March 27 Jewish aircraft had begun to participate in the fighting for the first time. Then on April 8 the most active and popular Arab leader, Abd el-Qadir Huseini (who was then chief of the Arab national guard) was killed. On April 10 the Irgun with the help of the Haganah attacked and took the village of Deir Yasin. After the Haganah left, the Irgun, in a deliberate attempt to promote terror among the general Arab population, massacred all the village inhabitants and widely publicized its action. Arab attacks on settlements and Jewish areas began to be beaten off and on April 15 the Haganah launched a major counterattack against the main Arab army under Fawzi el-Qawaqchi. From then on the Arab forces began to fail in their attempts and to assume the defensive. On April 19 the Haganah took Tiberias as the British evacuated its Arab population. April 21 saw the Irgun and Haganah offensive on Haifa, which surrendered and was evacuated by the Arab population. Early in May Jaffa was declared an open city under Haganah control, and on May 14 the Haganah captured Acre. Staggering from these defeats, Arabs were pouring out of the country by every road. On May 14 in the afternoon at Tel Aviv, David Ben-Gurion proclaimed the establishment of the State of Israel.

The mandate had ended.

XII. Formal Independence: A Short Flight on Fledgling Wings

The end of World War II marked the close of a period of overt and covert guidance and restraint by the West and the emergence of the Arab states into the community of nations. On the surface this statement is simple enough. However, the precise definition of the time framework and the realities of power which lie behind it pose the key issues of Arab politics of the last generation.

Though no part of the Arabian Peninsula was under Western domination or tutelage, the entire economic life of that area was financed, managed, and developed according to the decisions of the international petroleum industry, and rightly or wrongly—in scorn or envy—Arabs then as now ascribe to that area something less than full independence. More significant and more measurable, however, was the Western impact on the political history of the other, more advanced, and more populated Arab states.

Egypt, which had been declared a protectorate at the outbreak of World War I, entered into a treaty with Great Britain in 1922 which gave it formal independence with four "absolutely reserved" areas of British control. In 1936 this treaty was revised so that Egypt got more independence of action, and in 1937 she joined the League of Nations. However, British troops remained in Egypt, and from the perspective of Egyptians they were the trump card which made the British the final arbiters of Egyptian affairs. In 1942 the British did, *in extremis*, use their military power to impose upon the Egyptians a prime minister of their choosing. At the end of World War II Egypt finally declared war on the Axis, joined the United Nations, and got the British to agree to withdraw their troops from Cairo and to restrict their military presence to the Suez Canal Zone. It was not until 1954 that the bulk of the British troops withdrew from the Suez Canal, and in 1956 the British and French made an effort forcibly to re-enter Egyptian affairs.

In Iraq the story was similar with a few changes in dates and names. After a costly attempt to rule Iraq as a province, loosely attached to the Indian empire, the British organized a national government in 1921, installed a more or less popular monarch of their choosing, and accepted a mandate from the League of Nations. The mandate was, however, so unpopular in Iraq that while maintaining it vis-á-vis the League Great Britain negotiated a treaty in 1922 in which Iraq's special status was recognized. In 1930 a new treaty was negotiated which gave to Iraq sufficient independence for it to join the League of Nations in 1932. The British continued to maintain garrisons there. These made no attempt to intervene in the political unrest of the mid-1930's, but when in 1941 a pro-Axis government came to power, the British and their Arab allies invaded the country to replace the government with one composed of Britain's friends. Iraq declared war on the Axis in 1943 and joined the United Nations. An attempt to negotiate a new treaty in 1946 (the Portsmouth Treaty) led to an outbreak of riots in Baghdad. The treaty was dropped, but behind the shield of the monarchy and the astute political leadership of Nuri Said, British interests remained safe. As Iraq joined the Baghdad Pact in 1955, the British relinquished more of the form of their special position.

Transjordan, which had been separated from the Palestine mandate in 1922 and placed under the rule of Amir Abdullah, remained a client state of Britain. In 1946 it was declared independent but was in fact dependent upon Britain for financial support and for the leadership of its army. Growing resentment at the recognition of this dependence led to the ousting of Glubb Pasha, the British general who commanded the Arab Legion from

1939 to 1956 and to attempts to find other sources of revenue, including Egypt and Saudi Arabia and, after the failure of these, the United States.

Lebanon, which had benefited from French favor in 1920, when its area was multiplied in size, became in that year a French mandate. In 1926 it was given a constitution, but this was amended twice and suspended in 1932. After a period of direct French rule the Lebanese government was restored but with strictly limited powers. The constitution was reestablished in 1937. The period before and immediately after the outbreak of war saw French power retained but operating behind a façade of Lebanese political activity. Then, following the Franco-German armistice in June 1940, Lebanon and Syria went under the Vichy government, and a year later both were invaded by a British–Free French military force. At that time Lebanese independence was promised, and this promise was repeated and reaffirmed in various forms until in 1945 when the British ordered the French to evacuate their military forces. At that point Lebanon joined the United Nations.

In Syria the story parallels that of Lebanon, but the actions were at each stage considerably more bitter. Syria was not augmented by the French in 1920 but rather was invaded and then divided into a collection of petty states. In 1924–25 the Druze and others revolted against French rule, and the French retaliated by bombing villages and shelling Damascus on two separate occasions, in October 1925 and May 1926. In 1928 a constituent assembly was convened in Damascus, and the constitution was put into effect in 1930 but suspended in 1932. In 1936 Syria was rent by a general strike, attended by considerable violence and national agitation, which the French met with an attempt to negotiate a treaty, patterned on those the British had made in Iraq and Egypt. If concluded, this would have made Syria a member of the League of Nations with certain military facilities left in French hands. But the French government refused to ratify the treaty.

Syria, like Lebanon, was invaded by the British and Free French forces in 1941 and received the same assurances of inde-

pendence. Continued delays in the implementation of these assurances created an atmosphere of smoldering resentment which
burst into flame in May 1945 when, after a general strike and
sporadic outbursts of violence, the French shelled and bombed
Damascus and other Syrian cities. On June 1, 1945, the British
ordered the French to cease all military actions and to withdraw
all their forces. Syria at last achieved de facto independence
which was symbolized by participation in the San Francisco
Conference of the United Nations.

As a move toward the realization of the generally held aspira-
tion of Arab unity, the Arab states, with the encouragement of
Great Britain, in 1945 formed the Arab League. Actually, as
early as May 29, 1941, alarmed by the pro-German activities of
the Iraqi government, Anthony Eden, in a widely publicized
speech at Mansion House, encouraged the Arabs to look to
Britain as a friend of Arab unity aspirations. "This country has
a long tradition of friendship with the Arabs . . . It seems to me
both natural and right the cultural and economic ties between
the Arab countries, and the political ties too, should be strengthened. His Majesty's Government for their part will give their
full support to any scheme that commands general approval."
Taking up this encouragement, Nahhas Pasha as leader of the
Wafd and Prime minister of Egypt spoke of "the bonds which
bind us to the Arab and Eastern peoples [as] many beyond
numbering and strong beyond sundering . . . with Egypt in the
forefront [they will build] a powerful and cohesive bloc." Somewhat later, in January 1943, in announcing the Iraqi declaration
of war on the Axis, toward which, as the enemy of Britain, many
Iraqis were still sympathetic, Prime Minister Nuri Said proposed
the formation of a new state, composed of Syria, Lebanon, Transjordan, and Palestine—"Greater Syria"—with which Iraq would
join to form an Arab League. Finally, after consultations and
negotiations among all of the Arab leaders, delegates of the several Arab states and the Palestine Arab community met in September 1944 at Alexandria and agreed to form a League of Arab
States.

Thus, it may be said that the end of World War II marked a real beginning of independence and self-assertion in the Arab countries. With the departure or the formal "nationalization" of the military and paramilitary forces which had been created in the mandate states, national governments had more real power but also accepted more real responsibility than ever before.

At this point the old objects of national struggle became irrelevant: little merit attached to anti-French activity in Syria when the French had departed. A single new issue of nationalism took the center of the Arab stage, an issue for which all of the Arab governments eagerly sought responsibility and to which they turned all of their suppressed energy and ardor of nationalism. That issue was Palestine.

Not only through the Arab League, whose attentions were largely devoted to the Palestine problem during the immediate postwar period, but singly each Arab government became deeply involved in the issue in consultation with the British government, at the United Nations forums, and in virtually every public media in the Arab countries. Even the religious leaders of the Mosque-University of al-Azhar declared a Holy War. An irregular "Arab Liberation Army," financed and condoned by the Arab governments, of some six or seven thousand men, infiltrated into the Palestine mandate. As the mandate drew to a violent close, the Arab radio and press publicized the plight of the Palestine Arab community, particularly the massacre at Dair Yassin in which almost the entire village population was killed, and thereby stimulated Arabs everywhere to demand action by their governments.

On May 14, 1948, when the mandate ended, the Arab governments had to try to implement their decision to intervene. However, no government was really prepared to act. The most effective force, that of Transjordan, consisted of only four battalions with very little ammunition or other supplies and was under the command of British officers. It had virtually no logistical base or transport. The other Arab armies were ill-equipped and ill-trained. Their commands, moreover, were timid and mutually antagonistic. The governments behind them were suspicious of one another. The Egyptians, fearing King Abdullah's ambition to take over Palestine, deliberately took action to undercut Transjordanian effectiveness by seizing military supplies destined for Transjordan.

Military forces of Egypt, Transjordan, Syria, Lebanon, and Iraq were sent to Palestine. After a month of fighting the Arab states agreed to a truce which the United Nations undertook to monitor. This period, which lasted just a month, was used to bolster the fighting capacities of both forces, but truly herculean efforts on the part of the Israelis enabled them to emerge at the end of the truce far stronger than they were before. However, the public announcements by the Arab governments led their peoples to expect an early victory and the Arab governments refused to extend the truce.

Fighting broke out again on July 8 but the Arab armies were hopelessly disorganized and had no common plan of action. Israeli forces used the next ten days before the second truce greatly to enlarge their area of occupation. During the truce itself, an "Arab Government of All Palestine" was proclaimed in September, recognized by all the Arab governments except Transjordan, which organized a rival "National Congress." The open split between the governments of Kings Farouk and Abdullah encouraged the Israeli military command to concentrate all their strength against the Egyptian forces, and after winning air superiority the Israelis captured the southern area of the former mandate in October. Yet another cease-fire was proclaimed on October 22 in the south, but on that day fighting which spilled over into Lebanese territory broke out in the north. Meanwhile Abdullah had been declared by his supporters to be King of Palestine, and this led to violent reactions in the other Arab countries. Again the Israelis hit the Egyptians on December 22 and penetrated Egyptian territory.

In Cairo public outcries, at first directed against foreigners, quickly turned against the government whose ineffectiveness, despite propaganda and censorship efforts, had become clear. On

December 28 a member of the militant Muslim Brotherhood assassinated the prime minister. At this point, seeing that hostilities
threatened its interests, Great Britain announced that it would
invoke the 1936 treaty to intervene unless Israel withdrew her
forces from Egyptian territory and some stability were achieved
in Egypt. The Egyptian government wished to avoid British intervention above all, and notified the United Nations that it was
prepared to discuss an armistice.

Armistice agreements were negotiated bilaterally between the
Israelis and the *separate* Arab countries in the early months of
1949. In the midst of the negotiations the Iraqi government withdrew its forces and so exposed the Transjordanian forces' flank;
consequently the Transjordanian government, under threat of a
resumption of the war, was forced to cede to Israel additional
territory. The Syrian government was unable seriously to undertake armistice negotiations until April, when the others had been
concluded, due first to violent public demonstrations leading to a
fall of the government and then to a military coup. The latter
almost caused Iraqi and Jordanian military intervention in Syria
and further split the Arab governments.

The fact, however dressed up or explained, was simply that the
Arab states were beaten in the Palestine War.

Fairly uniformly, there was the realization that below the
façade of government and authority little real power existed.
"But how could this be" was the implicit question behind the
outpourings of the critics. The governments of the Arabs who
created Islam, who conquered half the world, whose caliphate
shone with the bright glow of civilization while Europe slept in
the ignorance of the Dark Ages, and whose vast corpus of literature and rich language were admired all over the world, were
spotlighted as impotent, backward, corrupt bombasts. The shock
of this discovery created a trauma from which Arabic society
suffered for a decade. Many sought excuses—the governments,
mere puppets left behind in the wake of imperialism were rotten;
the arms furnished the Arab armies were worthless; Israel was a
front for a combine of the great powers and of course the Arabs
were not able to defeat this combine. Radio propaganda warfare,

with each state blaming the "other" Arabs for the defeat in Palestine, started in late 1948 and was increased in violence in 1949. Since then it has been a regular feature of the Middle Eastern scene. Many Arabs blamed the West: Israel was the "last stage" of imperialism, was the stepchild of the West, was the way Westerners, shamed by the horrors of the Nazi "final solution," sought to repay the Jews (at the expense of the Arabs), and so forth.

Other Arabs sought the causes in more complex problems of Arab society and politics. A bitter critic of the failure of the Arabs, the former ambassador of Syria to the United States and president of the National University in Damascus, Constantine Zurayq, wrote immediately after the events in 1949, in *The Meaning of the Disaster*, "Seven Arab states declare war on Zionism in Palestine, stop impotent before it, and then turn on their heels. The representatives of the Arabs deliver fiery speeches in the highest international forums, warning what the Arab states and peoples will do if this or that decision be enacted. Declarations fall like bombs from the mouths of officials at the meetings of the Arab League, but when action becomes necessary, the fire is still and quiet, the steel and iron are rusted and twisted, quick to bend and disintegrate. The bombs are hallow and empty. They cause no damage and kill no one." Equally bitter was the statement by the Palestinian Musa Alami, who had helped to found the Arab League, "In the face of the enemy the Arabs were not a state, but petty states; groups, not a nation; each fearing and anxiously watching the other and intriguing against it. What concerned them most and guided their policy was not to win the war and save Palestine from the enemy, but what would happen after the struggle, who would be predominant in Palestine, or annex it to themselves, and how they could achieve their own ambitions. Their announced aim was the salvation of Palestine, and they said that afterward its destiny should be left to its people. This was said with the tongue only. In their hearts all wished it for themselves; and most of them were hurrying to prevent their neighbors from being predominant, even though nothing remained except the offal and bones."*

* *Middle East Journal*, 3 (1949):385.

Most Arabs found it hard to disagree and the press was filled with bitter reproach against the Arab governments. In an oft-quoted passage, from his *Philosophy of the Revolution*, Gamal Abdul Nasser later wrote: "In Palestine I met only friends that shared the work for Egypt, but there I also discovered the thoughts that shed their light on the road ahead. I remember the days I spent in trenches pondering over our problems. Falougha was then beseiged and the enemy had concentrated his guns and aircraft heavily and terribly upon it. Often have I said to myself, 'here we are in these underground holes besieged. How we were cheated into a war unprepared and how our destinies have been the plaything of passions, plots and greed. Here we lay under fire unarmed.' As I reached that stage in my thinking my feelings would suddenly jump across the battlefront, across frontiers to Egypt. I found myself saying, 'What is happening in Palestine is but a miniature picture of what was happening in Egypt. Our Mother-Country has been likewise besieged by difficulties as well as ravaged by an enemy. She was cheated and pushed to fight unprepared. Greed, intrigue and passion have toyed with it and left it under fire.' "

The events of the period from the winter of 1948, when it was obvious that the war was lost, onward make clear how widespread was the feeling of malaise in the Arab world. To take Egypt as an example: On November 9 an attempt was made to kill former prime minister Nahhas; on November 13 the printing plant of the major European-language Egyptian newspapers was blown up; on November 28 the leaders of the Muslim Brotherhood were arrested; and on the same day police opened fire on a demonstration in a provincial city; on December 4 the Cairo chief of police was killed by a hand grenade; on December 28 the prime minister was assassinated; and on February 12 the leader of the Muslim Brotherhood was killed. Riots, attempted bombings, and threats were almost daily occurrences. Minor episodes were the divorce by the unloved King Farouk of his popular wife and the bitter, degrading, but revealing fight in the Egyptian parliament over passage of Egypt's first progressive income tax in February 1949.

The first government to collapse, however, was not in Egypt but in Syria where on March 30, 1949, a Kurdish colonel seized power in a bloodless and rapid coup. In all likelihood the coup was "popular" since the public was sick of the failures and ashamed of the weakness of the old regime. But the Syrian parliament refused to legalize the new government and was dismissed. Dismissal of a discredited parliament was not enough and the new government could not build a base of popular support; on August 14, in his turn, the colonel was arrested, tried, and shot by another military clique. The ensuing government was greeted with less warmth than apathy by the Syrian public. This government, in turn, was overthrown by an army lieutenant colonel on December 19, 1950.

Egypt in January 1950 held general elections, won by the Wafd party, which had been out of office during the Palestine War and which now promised a program of basic reforms. Education in particular was to be brought to the whole people as never before, but the government also promised to modernize the army and industrialize the country. These were bold programs and deeply stirred the Egyptian public, for the Wafd, despite many tales of corruption, still had a powerful organization and, comparatively, some luster of its nationalist days in the 1920's.

Recognition that more was wrong with Arab society than a government, or a collection of governments, was made manifest in the United Nations–sponsored conference on social welfare in Cairo in November 1950. Explicit was the notion that poverty and backwardness were direct results of structural defects in Arab society, and implicit was the notion that governments could act to remedy these if they had the will and the intelligence. Titles of many of the papers given at the conference centered on "How should a . . . project" be undertaken or "The practical steps which can be undertaken."

In concluding the conference its chairman, the Egyptian minister of social affairs, said: "This [giving of needed social services and raising the standard of living of the mass of the population] is their right from the State. The time is passed in which social services were rendered as a form of charity. The responsibility of the States has developed; it is no longer confined to matters of order, security, defence and the like, but its prime duty is to secure the welfare of its people, by providing possibilities of employment and adequate wages for a decent living, together with social services including education, medical care, suitable housing, and so forth . . . This is the prime responsibility of the States." This admission, not particularly important in itself, was typical of many which all of the Arab governments made either explicitly as here or implicitly in beginning programs of development as Iraq did in 1950.

Once made, the admission of responsibility, and possibility, raised further questions: If development is, in fact, possible and if the well-being of the citizenry is the "prime responsibility of the States," then does not the blame for past weakness, misery, lack of development, and humiliation fall upon those same states? If development is possible now, was it not possible before? And if it is now possible, is it not possible faster and more fundamentally? Is the development going to be real or merely the subject of wordy conferences? Can it be carried out by parliaments which represent those groups in society—landlords and tribal shaikhs—most firmly and obviously opposed to change? These were the questions of political discussion in the press, where it was free, in the army officers' messes, the coffee houses, and in every gathering of students.

As if in partial answer to the feelings behind such questions, the Wafd government had passed in July 1950 a law making journalists liable to a year in prison and a fine for publishing even innocent information on the biggest Egyptian landlord, the royal family, without government consent. Censorship, fear of confiscation or retaliatory action, caused the press to moderate its attacks, except on the "fair game"—governments in neighboring states. But throughout the area discontent was seething. No one who visited Egypt could miss it. As Sir Malcolm Darling wrote in the Manchester *Guardian* on December 7, 1950, "In the village ignorance may not be bliss, but it is some protection against discontent. Now, however, a new wind blows. With the greatly increased facilities of communication and the steady if very gradual spread of education the seed of new ideas, of new hopes, is carried from town to village. Ignorance of the outer world is no longer universal, but almost universal poverty remains. Herein lies the danger. Poverty and ignorance can lie down more or less happily together, but not poverty and education. That nowadays is likely to be an explosive mixture."

The peasants, themselves, did nothing to overturn the regime, but in the ruling class a split rapidly became manifest. The students, as they often had, led the revolt. Street demonstrations were common during this period, and the government retaliated by cracking down on the students. The Wafd government, originally a product and benefactor of student violence, imposed fines and jail sentences on anyone who incited students to demonstrate. Even professional men had to be banned from striking. By suppression of legitimate protest and itself stimulating the desires of the people for reform, the government contributed to the rise of violence. By December 1950 the press reported agitation in the army of a group known as "The Free Officers."

Meanwhile, the Egyptian government proved unable to win any concessions from the British government on a revision of the 1936 treaty, but encouraged the activity of paramilitary groups against the British army in the Suez Canal Zone. When the British refused Egyptian demands, however, the government turned on those who had supported its anti-British program.

Caught between its own nationalist propaganda, its weakness in dealing with the British forces, and the militancy of its own people, the Egyptian government faltered and fumbled from one mistake to another. While continuing its violent verbal attacks on the British, it ordered the police to fire on demonstrators who repeated its slogans and closed schools and universities where the agitation was carried on. Encouraging a belief that reform was possible and publicly condemning senior officers of the army and even members of the royal family for corruption in supplying faulty arms to the Egyptian forces in the Palestine War, it failed to produce any tangible results of reform or progress.

In July 1951 King Abdullah of Jordan was assassinated by a Palestinian Arab in Jerusalem. This was an act of violence which ripped away the already thin and tattered veil of kingship which had held at least some of the rulers aloof from the sorry plight of their peoples and what an increasing number of army officers and students regarded as the sordid gluttony of the politicians. Revealed were weak men with tarnished scepters. At once they were pulled knee-deep into the muck of corruption and intrigue.

Finally, on January 26, 1952, "Black Friday," anti-Western and anti-privileged-class mobs raced through Cairo, burning, pillaging, and killing. Among the casualties was the world-famous Shepheard's Hotel in Cairo. The Wafd government fell, only to be replaced by a series of weak and less popular teams of ministers. Just hours after the last of these was announced, the army led by the "Free Officers" seized power on July 23, arrested many senior officials, and forced King Farouk to abdicate and leave the country.

XIII. Coups, Conflicts, and Conferences

The coup of July 23, 1952, in Egypt was an event of the greatest significance in the Arab countries. Even at its inception, it was viewed by other Arabs as qualitatively different from the coups which had punctuated Iraqi politics in the 1930's or Syrian politics in 1948–50. To many it seemed, from its beginnings, the most needed reform—total abolition of the old regime—before real progress could be made.

In a mood of jubilation other Arabs demanded revolution *à l'Egyptienne*. Even in Lebanon, where cooler heads have created a tradition of commercial shrewdness since the time of the Phoenicians, editorials called for a "complete revolution" which would sweep away the past and all its memories, to bring immediately power, progress, and above all dignity. Plagued by scandals of truly epic proportions, threatened by general strikes, and not supported by the army, the president of Lebanon resigned on September 19, 1952. The chief of staff of the army became prime minister *ad interim*, and a new president was elected by the Chamber of Deputies on September 23. In Lebanon, however, the army refused to stay in politics; in fact, so quickly was power turned back to civilian politicians that the new president had to come to terms with the very forces and vested interests, as represented in the parliament, he presumably had come to office to supplant. The poisonous plant of discontent, so vigorous in the

Lebanon of 1952, was pruned but not extirpated; it was to grow again and to bear the bitter fruit of civil war in 1958.

In Iraq, meanwhile, the process of development had begun under the development board formed in 1950. The rather sudden infusion into the economy of massive oil royalties, as both production and profits soared in the early 1950's, produced a shock to the whole society. The vista of a real and proximate new world seemed to open ahead. Everything appeared ready to sail forward on a wave of change. Yet, the current was neither uniform nor rapid enough to suit many.

Young women, held apart from society more strictly than their cousins in the Levant or Egypt, suddenly emerged into educated society. They, like their brothers, began to win government fellowships for study abroad, and they were "liberated" from the long black gown, the *abba,* which had symbolized their confinement and social disability. But the end of confinement, in some spheres, led to great emotional stress, to the accentuation of a sense of doubt, loneliness, frustration, and fear which haunted and distorted Iraqi intellectual life in the 1950's. In the spring of 1952 a young Iraqi woman was expelled from her college for writing a short story depicting a young woman's hunger for meaning in a time of "tasteless emptiness" in which an "ignorant, leaderless people" still clung to "crippling and immoral social mores."

Similarly, the Iraqi young men returning from long periods of education abroad ran head-on into the roadblocks of Iraqi society and bureaucracy. The backward Iraq to which they returned both embarrassed them and spurned them. They were prevented from putting into effect their new learning and felt themselves to be aliens in their own homes. A best seller in those years was an Arabic translation of Turgenev's *Father and Sons,* which was set in a Russia of comparable anguish and dislocation. But, in the early 1950's the number of able, energetic, and uncommitted people in Iraq was very small; by the end of the decade it had become powerful. In 1951–52, for example, Iraq had only five native mechanical engineers, but so many of Iraq's more able people were abroad studying that by 1958 it had over a hundred mechanical engineers. Changes of proportional magnitude were in train in all the professions and in other parts of the society as well.

Movement and change were "in the air" in Baghdad. At first each individual rushed headlong toward a better future. There was no focus to the obvious discontent. Times were clearly better. But the "new men" of Iraq were cramped by the contrast of a potential future and an actual present. It was only as the government got more efficient and devoted more resources to the development program that its end was hastened. The irony of Iraq lies precisely in this fact: Iraq had the resources and the capital and was developing the people for the inevitable overthrow of the government. If it lacked any of these, the old regime might still exist.

The government was led by Nuri Said, a wise and experienced stalwart, trained in the Ottoman army, who had fought in the Arab Revolt. He had weathered many a storm and three times fled for his life from (and returned to vanquish) more powerful enemies than what he regarded as mere children of some education. Nuri guided the Iraqui government with a sure hand. Even his enemies respected him, and so popular—or so accepted—was he that his most bitter opponents admitted that he would have won even a free election. He knew what he wanted and how to get it. But Nuri's government was creating a new Iraq in which he and men of the old school would have no place. Great economic and social change was unmatched in political life, which, like a dam, held back the forces of protest. Pressures built steadily until 1958.

The military officers who had engineered the coup in Egypt in July 23, 1952, were clearly unsure what to do with their power. They *were* sure they had to destroy the power of the monarchy and so forced King Farouk to abdicate and leave the country within a few days. It was eleven months, however, before the monarchy was formally abolished. The relationship of the older politicians to the new order was more open-ended. First the government was entrusted to a "clean" politician of the old regime, but the officers also moved to destroy both public recognition of the old elite, by abolishing titles connected with the monarchy, and the base of its power, the ownership of huge tracts of fertile, irrigated lands along the Nile. On September 7 the army took over formal power as General Nagib, the figurehead of the "Free Officers," became prime minister. Most of the ministers, however, were civilian, and as late as March 1954 the officers were still flirting with a return to civilian rule.

It appears clear, in retrospect, that the Free Officers really did not have any precise notion of the structure of the new Egypt they sought. They wanted to abolish much of the old structure, but just how much was determined more by the events of the first two years after they seized power than by any preconceived ideas. For example, it appears that the land distribution program was suggested to the Free Officers *after* the coup as a popular move, one needed for any real progress in the country and the sure way to sap the foundations of their potential opponents, the men of the old order. They did not seize power to carry out land reform, but having seized power set about learning what they could do to improve their chances of staying in power and of uplifting the country. Similar was their attitude toward civilian politicians. It was not until the Muslim Brotherhood militants had tried to assassinate Gamal Abdul Nasser on October 26, 1954, that rival political groups began to be suppressed. And in pressing to get the Sudan recognized as a part of Egypt and to get the British to evacuate Egypt, the new government was carrying forward, more vigorously perhaps, policies espoused by Egyptian governments for over half a century and in other forms for time out of mind of man.

Nasser has suggested that he never thought his group would have to build a new regime, but that he conceived of his job as one of destroying the old. In his *Philosophy of the Revolution* he speaks bluntly of his "shock," "sorrow," and "bitterness" at the lack of support for the coup. "Prior to that date I imagined that the whole nation was on tip-toes and prepared for action, that it awaited the advance of the vanguard and the storming of the

outside walls for it to pour down in a solid phalanx marching
faithfully to the great goal . . . After July 23rd I was shocked
by the reality. The vanguard performed its task; it stormed the
walls of the fort of tyranny; it forced Farouk to abdicate and
stood by expecting the mass formations to arrive at their ultimate
object. It waited and waited. Endless crowds showed up, but
how different is the reality from the vision! The multitudes that
arrived were dispersed followers . . . We needed discipline but
found chaos behind our lines. We needed unity but found dissen-
sions. We needed action but found nothing but surrender and
idleness . . . Personal and persistent selfishness was the rule of the
day. The word 'I' was on every tongue."

It is not really necessary to question whether or not the military had always intended to retain power: even if they wished
to turn it back to another group, the Free officers could hardly
have done so safely, for having seized the tiger by the tail they
had to hang on or be eaten themselves. The question was not
whether to retain power but who would exercise it and for what
ends. This brought to the surface a power struggle between
General Nagib and Lieutenant Colonel Nasser which involved
the army, the Muslim Brotherhood, and civilian politicians. Ultimately, after much covert and some overt struggle and maneuver,
Nagib was ousted from power and placed under house arrest on
November 1, 1954. But the regime was still very far from having
an established and agreed policy on domestic issues. Up to that
time its energies had largely been absorbed in consolidating
power.

The most emotion-laden and popularly watched if not important issue with which the new regime had dealt grew out of
its relations with Great Britain. When the British evacuated
Cairo in 1945–6, the bulk of their forces, at times as large as
80,000 men, moved to bases in the area of the Suez Canal. Successive Egyptian governments tried to get them to leave Egypt
but to no avail. Appeals to the United Nations were unsuccessful.
As we have seen, the inability of the last series of precoup governments to satisfy nationalist goals, in large part stimulated by
the same governments, was a major factor in their being dis-

credited. After lengthy negotiations the new government achieved this aim in the October 1954 Anglo-Egyptian treaty. By April 14, 1956, the British had evacuated the last of their Suez installations.

The regime was less successful in its attempt to reunite the Sudan and Egypt. The importance of the Sudan to Egypt had long been recognized: it was the conduit through which the Nile River passed and from which Egypt historically derived cheap labor. The Sudan was conquered by the forces of Mehmet Ali Pasha in 1821 and indifferently ruled until it revolted in 1881. When the British came to Egypt, they and the Egyptians reconquered the Sudan in the battle of Omdurman in 1898. After 1899, when it was administratively separated from Egypt, the Sudan was ruled as an Anglo-Egyptian Condominium. Reacting to the nationalist agitation following World War I, when Sir Lee Stack was assassinated in Cairo, the British almost totally excluded the Egyptians from participation in the Sudanese government.

Thus, while Egyptian cultural contacts, particularly through the spread of Islamic teaching from Cairo's Azhar Mosque-University, remained strong, the Sudan began to develop a separate system of administration, to deal directly with Great Britain, and to achieve some sense of separate national identity. Economic activity was sparked by the creation of a rich cotton-growing agricultural area at the confluence of the Blue and White Niles. This brought a degree of prosperity to the Sudan but raised two problems in Sudanese-Egyptian relations: was the amount of water taken from the Nile for use in the Sudan harmful to Egyptian agriculture and was the amount of cotton grown in the Sudan a threat to Egyptian exports. These issues were debated regularly in the press and in various intergovernmental conferences up to 1952 when Britain decided to allow the Sudanese self-determination.

At that time the Egyptians made a determined effort to woo the Sudanese into a union with Egypt. The British and the Egyptians agreed to allow the Sudanese to elect a provisional government which would, after a three-year period, decide whether or not to join Egypt. It is easy to see why this was a

serious tactical mistake for the Egyptians: once the Sudanese
had tasted the sweet fruit of self-government, they were unwilling
to give it up.

Syria also was unable to achieve a sense of identity or national
cohesion. The sequence of coups of 1959 was followed by an
interlude in which a civilian government served as a façade for
military power. Then Lieutenant Colonel Adib Shashakli openly
took power in December 1951, became president in July 1953,
only to be ousted from power in February 1954. A civilian government returned to office but the real nature of its power was
probably only the relative exhaustion of the many rivals.

Whether Syria was to be an independent state, a part of
"Greater Syria," in union with Iraq and/or Jordan, or ultimately
a part of the United Arab Republic was a question for which
Syrians found no answer in the 1950's and which is still under
debate.

The issue which pointed this up most clearly was the Western
attempt, particularly from 1953 to 1955, to get the Arab World
into an area defense pact. Following the Korean War the United
States sought to forge a "shield" of interlocking alliances from
Europe to the Far East. It was United States policy to encourage
its allies to take the leadership wherever possible in forging these
alliances. Since the Middle East was an area of British influence
and expertise, Britain's advice and leadership were sought. In
British thinking Egypt was the center of military power. Britain's
base at Suez contained the major military facilities for the whole
area. Therefore, Britain sought, as early as 1951, to bring Egypt
into an alliance. But London was unwilling to meet Egyptian
demands on the Sudan and the weak and corrupt government
of Nahhas Pasha could not compromise on this issue.

American thinking on Middle Eastern defense turned increasingly to what came to be called "the Northern tier," Greece,
Turkey, and Iran. This resulted in United States military assistance programs and bilateral military pacts between Turkey and
Pakistan in the spring of 1954. At that time the United States
began giving military aid to Iraq, but the suggestion that Iraq
might join such a pact was strongly attacked by Egypt. Through-

out the summer of 1954 it appeared that Egypt might, itself, be receptive to some sort of alliance with Turkey, but her incentive was sharply reduced when Britain, unilaterally, agreed to withdraw from Suez. By December it was clear that Egypt was opposed to other members of the Arab League joining any Western-oriented military pact.

In Iraq, however, the motivations of the government were quite different. Nuri Said, whether in the government or working behind the scenes, was firmly committed to a pro-Western orientation. Iraq, moreover, had begun to benefit by United States military assistance and was on the eve of its great "leap forward" through the development plan, with which it needed Western help. Iraq had its "Suez" also. It sought to get the British to terminate the 1930 Anglo-Iraqi treaty. Great Britain agreed to do this if Iraq joined in an open-ended collective security pact with Turkey. So in February 1955 the Baghdad Pact was born, and in April Britain terminated the 1930 treaty. This led to a violent outburst from Egypt, which accused Iraq of having betrayed the quest for Arab unity. In riposte Egypt sought compensatory stronger ties with Syria and Saudi Arabia and, for a time with Jordan.

The whole relationship of Arabs one to another remains the key unresolved issue in Arab politics. The ideological basis of this problem is discussed below but here it should be pointed out that moves toward some degree of Arab federation or unity had been made or talked about since 1919 when Sharif Husain of Mecca proclaimed himself "King of the Arabs." During the latter phases of World War II, as described above, the Arab states had founded an Arab League. But the Arab League was always as much a cockpit as a coordinating committee. It had effect on the policies of its members only on key issues and then only sporadically. It tried to achieve a coordinated approach to the Palestine War, but it failed. Its attempts to establish what sort of entity "Arab Palestine" should be only high-lighted the profound differences between Kings Farouk and Abdullah. Subsequently, as King Farouk was ousted and Egypt acquired a militant, reforming government of young men while Iraq and Saudi Arabia remained under the control of what the Egyptians regarded as old regimes, the lack of accord became painfully obvious.

As the *Economist* Middle Eastern correspondent Tom Little wrote of the October 1955 meeting of the Arab League in Cairo "The Arab League met in Cairo in October in 'an atmosphere of cordiality.' To judge by reports of every meeting it has held in the eleven years in its existence, it has never done otherwise . . . the simple fact that the League met at all, after the violent polemics between Egypt and Iraq during the first nine months of 1955, was enough to warrant satisfaction of the Arab statesmen . . . Arab unity does not exist. I question whether it has ever existed . . . The Arab League revealed from the outset this historical condition of the Arabs: their persistent inability to unite politically but their abiding belief that union is a natural condition of their peoples which only required political formulation. In the Arab League, the Arabs trod a little too heavily upon their own dreams."

Meanwhile, the Palestine problem continued to occupy the attentions of the Arabs and others. When Secretary of State John Foster Dulles visited the Middle East in 1953, he found that whenever he attempted to discuss the Communist menace, his Arab counterparts rejoined with what they considered the more immediate danger of Israel.

Peace, indeed, had never really come to the Middle East. Despite the armistice of the Spring of 1949, the borders of Israel were fronts rather than frontiers. Raids and counterraids, intelligence probes, commando attacks, or foraging expeditions were the order of the day, almost every day. Shootings back and forth across the Syrian-Israeli, Jordanian-Israeli, and Egyptian-Israeli frontiers were normal operating procedure. The United Nations Mixed Armistice Commissions were kept busy sorting out conflicting claims and charges and passing judgment, or recommending censure by the Security Council, for acts of aggression. Between 1949 and 1955 thousands of incidents occurred.

Armistice lines, drawn to fit a haphazard pattern of military events rather than to meet economic, social, or even strategic criteria, make notoriously bad frontiers. In this case they cut off from their normal means of earning a living, either their places of employment or their fields, an estimated 150,000 Arabs. These people, technically not refugees since they still retained their dwellings, were the most grievously hurt of all of those who lost in the Palestine War. As such, they constituted an angry, hungry, and desperate element in the political life of Jordan where most lived.

The others, the legally certified refugees, almost a million strong, were scattered in the surrounding Arab countries. The bulk were in refugee camps maintained by an agency of the United Nations at a cost per person—including everything they got—of less than $2 monthly. That gave them medical attention and food measured at 1600 calories daily. But they were idle, miserable, and sustained by intoxicating memories of an idealized past and enervating dreams of an unlikely future. Idleness became the dry rot of character. As more "refugees" were born each year and the older refugees died off, the number who had ever known a life outside the confines of the camps declined. Able to do little for themselves—few had any skills to sell while most fell into that already saturated economic category of landless agricultural laborers—they bitterly reproached their Arab hosts for their plight. It was a refugee who killed the Arab statesman regarded by non-Arabs as the "most sensible" and realistic on the Palestine issue, King Abdullah. This lesson was not lost on the public figures in the other countries. Everywhere, even if inarticulate, passive, and humbled, the refugee was a reminder of the Arab humiliation and shame in the war and a living indictment of those who had promised to protect him.

Israel had embarked upon a policy of "massive retaliation" for Arab border violations. Demonstrations of this policy came in Israeli raids with regular army units against Nahhalin, Jordan, in March 1954 and Gaza in February 1955. In the latter case the Gaza headquarters of the Egyptian army was the target, and there were sixty-nine Egyptian casualties. Apparently that raid alarmed the Egyptians as no previous raid had and made obvious to them their need for better equipment. When this was not forthcoming from the Western powers on the schedule, on the terms and in the amounts desired, Egypt decided to explore other sources. In September 1955 Nasser announced that Czechoslovakia would supply large quantities of late-model military equipment to Egypt on terms not then known.

It speedily became apparent that the United States viewed this development with alarm, for it appeared that the "northern tier" had been hurdled. But the Arabs, still conscious of a long and often unhappy history of relations with the West, were gleeful. Nasser had done what no other Arab had thought possible. He had used the Cold War to internationalize Arab affairs and so, apparently, gained a lever to extract better terms from both the West and the East.

Meanwhile border friction grew rather than lessened. Israeli forces attacked Syrian positions on October 22, Egyptian positions on November 2, and Syrian outposts on December 11. For these attacks Israel was censured by the Security Council. For its impartiality in voting for censure, the United States got less credit than an outsider would have thought due. The Arabs regarded Israel as a Western state, and Arab, particularly Egyptian, propaganda grew more bitterly anti-Western. In Jordan demonstrations were held in December against the pro-Western government and the Baghdad Pact. The government fell and violence continued well into 1956 until finally, on March 2, the British officer who commanded the Jordanian military forces, Glubb Pasha, was discharged by King Husain in what was perhaps the most popular move made by a Jordanian government. In his place the king named a young Jordanian Arab nationalist. Putting aside the colorful bedouin headgear of the Legionnaires, he dressed them in the drab but "modern" caps of Western armies.

In Iraq, in a bid to win more popularity, the government decided in April 1956 that it would shift its development emphasis from massive but remote and unseen projects, such as it had undertaken, to "impact" projects in the populated areas. But the Iraqi government remained politically and emotionally isolated from the currents of change in the Arab world—for example, in June 1956 it banned a visit by a popular Arab hero, the young Algerian nationalist leader Ahmad ben Bella.

Worsening relations between Egypt and the West induced Secretary of State Dulles to announce on July 20, 1956, that the United States would withdraw an offer to lend Egypt $200 million toward the construction of the Aswan "High Dam." In riposte Nasser nationalized the Suez Canal on July 26.

Western reaction was swift and sharp. The foreign ministers of Britain and France and the American secretary of state met in London on August 2 and organized the first conference of "user states" for August 16. This group sent a mission to Cairo in the first week of September to attempt to work out a compromise solution. None proved possible. Egypt continued to run the canal despite the removal of most of the pilots. Threats and the freezing of Egyptian assets abroad failed to move Nasser. Egypt offered to pay compensation to shareholders in the company but insisted that the canal had been and would continue to be Egyptian. After various moves and pronouncements by all the parties, which will be described in Chapter 17, Israel attacked Egypt on October 29, despite warnings from the United States. Great Britain and France issued an ultimatum ostensibly to both sides and then on October 31 bombed Egypt and on November 2 invaded the canal zone. On November 5 the Anglo-French force captured Port Said but agreed to a United Nations–ordered cease-fire on November 7.

Insofar as there had been careful Allied planning, it presumably had as an immediate object the fall of Nasser. That did not happen. The Egyptians—particularly the guerrilla and paramilitary forces—fought better than had been expected, and there was no attempt at a palace coup.

As the dust settled it was clear that major changes had taken place in the Middle Eastern scene. Suez was going to remain Egyptian; Egypt was going to pay any price to get what it regarded as adequate arms to prevent another defeat; the Jewish, English, and French communities of Egypt, as minority communities always do in such circumstances, paid the price for the acts of those associated with them, had their property sequestered, and for the most part left Egypt; and Israel gained one objective, unhindered passage through the Straits of Tiran to her port in the

Gulf of Aqaba, Elath. The failure to enshrine this new situation in a treaty and the subsequent assertion, by Egypt, of its right to close what it regarded as territorial waters to Israeli shipping, was a major contributory cause to the outbreak of fighting a decade later in June, 1967. The United Nations was brought into even closer contact with the Palestine problem as a United Nations Emergency Force (UNEF) was established to monitor the withdrawal of Israeli troops. Again, while this arrangement was to last for a decade and was generally successful in preventing the outbreak of fighting between Egypt and Israel, failures in its initial implementation were to have profound consequences. First, Israel's refusal to allow UN troops on the Israeli side of the frontier exposed the Egyptians to the taunt that "they were hiding behind the skirts of the United Nations." Moreover, while the UN force did act as a buffer, its creation was retrogressive in the sense that the Mixed Armistice Commissions had involved Egyptians and Israelis in daily negotiations. However, for Egypt, the withdrawal of British and French forces symbolized the end of a century of foreign interference—one of the first things Egyptian troops did upon entering Suez was to blow up the statue of Ferdinand de Lesseps.

The Suez crisis had made Nasser an Arab hero. Before his nationalization of the Suez Canal Company and his purchase of arms from the Soviet Bloc, Nasser had been regarded by many Arabs as a strong but colorless modernizer, but weighed in Arab scales, Suez was Stalingrad, El Alamein, and the Battle of Britain rolled into one. In the Arab view Egypt had stopped Britain, France, and Israel and Nasser had defied the world and won. In expression of support for the Egyptians, the Lebanese cut the oil pipeline at Tripoli and the Syrians blew up the Iraq Petroleum Company pipelines. ARAMCO, as an American company, was unharmed. So strongly, in fact, did this emotional wave of pro-Nasser feeling carry the Arabs that young King Husain of Jordan, believing he was about to lose his throne to it, himself struck against the more extreme nationalists in April 1957, dismissing his prime minister and the chief of his army and installing a government in the style of his grandfather, King Abdullah.

Continued Syrian instability led, in February 1958, to a merger of Syria with Egypt to form the United Arab Republic. Moves toward some sort of closer association between the two countries were begun in 1956. In January of that year the new Egyptian constitution proclaimed that the Egyptians were "a part of the Arab nation," and the Syrian parliament, in July, voted to set up a negotiating committee to explore plans for a federal union with Egypt. After an interval of some months, November 1957, a joint parliamentary session was held in Damascus. This group urged further steps toward a federal union. Finally in February, when the Syrians grew alarmed at the rise of Communist power in Syria, the formation of the United Arab Republic was announced. Other Arab states were invited to join in a larger union called the United Arab States. Rather curiously, Yemen, alone among the other Arab states, decided to adhere to this new, and largely theoretical, entity.

Stung by the challenge the formation of the UAR seemed to offer to their security, integrity, and pride, the governments of Iraq and Jordan speedily, on February 14, formed the Arab Union, taking as their flag the banner of the Arab Revolt. Little that had made them separate states was actually affected. It was clear that the initiative and the leadership were in the hands of President Nasser of the United Arab Republic, and the Arab Union aroused few patriotic sentiments.

In Saudi Arabia, where the sudden and vast inflow of riches had produced something like an Arabian nights dream come true, mounting criticism of extravagance, corruption, and decadence led, in April 1958, to a gentle, intrafamily palace coup in which King Saud, the son of King Abdul Aziz, who had died in 1953, handed over power to his brother Crown Prince Faisal.

Just a month later the political and religious factions of Lebanon, which had been at one another's throats since the 1830's, broke into open warfare again. The issue this time was the extent to which Lebanon should be overtly committed to the West, through the Eisenhower Doctrine, or be attached to the major powers of the Arab World, particularly Egypt and Syria. These and other issues tended to divide the country along religious lines with the Christians, in general, favoring closer ties with the West, and the Muslims, with the Arab countries. In these troubled waters the Egyptians and others were fishing. The president of Lebanon, himself a product of the coup of 1952, sought to retain office beyond the constitutional limit and invited the help of the United Nations and ultimately of the United States to this end. All eyes were upon Lebanon when, suddenly and with no apparent warning, the Iraqi army overthrew the government of Nuri Said.

The American reaction was quick and powerful: within hours the first contingents of American marines began landing from the Sixth Fleet. And Britain put air units into Jordan. Unlike Suez, this intervention came at the request of the government and came promptly. But like Suez, it was harder to stop than to begin, more complex to withdraw than to mount. What ultimately made possible a graceful American withdrawal was a Lebanese compromise by which the commander of the Lebanese army, General Faud Shihab, agreed to become president of the country, and the incumbent agreed to step down.

In Iraq Abdul-Karim Qasim's new government, born of a violent coup and conceived in a social revolution, differed markedly from that of Nasser in Egypt. The king, the crown prince, and the prime minister were hunted down and shot, amidst scenes of great brutality and mob hysteria. The military forces which had seized power quickly split amongst themselves. The moderate, nationalist forces which had set the tone of the movement in the fall and early winter were replaced in 1959 by groups which moved more and more to the radical left. A countercoup was tried in the spring of 1959; when this failed, it was followed by a savage repression in Mosul and Kirkuk. The government became paralyzed, and the development program ground to a near standstill as the government failed to move on new contracts and defaulted on previous engagements.

The Kurdish followers of Mulla Mustafa Barzani rose against the Iraqi government in the late summer of 1961, rapidly seized the whole of the mountainous area of northeastern Iraq, Kurdistan, and prevented government forces from moving off the plains. In reply Qasim's government bombed Kurdish villages and issued an endless stream of communiqués announcing that the revolt had been completely crushed or soon would be or both. In August 1962, to show the world—and the Iraqi people—their power, the Kurds blew up the oil pipeline which connected Iraq to the Mediterranean. The inability of the Iraqi army to put down the revolt reflected both the lack of trust in the line officers on the part of Qasim, who insisted on controlling all operations, and the inability of his regime to act decisively. Finally, this issue, in conjunction with the other mistakes he had made, was to precipitate a coup which on February 8, 1963, resulted in the fall of Qasim's government and his own execution.

In Syria the United Arab Republic was not destined to last as it had originally been constituted. On September 28, 1961, a junta of army officers revolted, established a national government, and ordered all Egyptians to leave the country. On October 19 Syria was readmitted to the Arab League. On December 1 a general election was held, but on March 28, 1962, the new government was overthrown by a military coup.

Yemen, the most isolated and backward of the Arab countries, had experienced many coups and attempted coups in its bloody past. In 1948 the then ruler of the country, faced with rebellion, had called in the tribes of the north to sack the city of Sanaa. In March 1955 an attempted coup against the imam failed. Those involved in plots against the government were always few in number and were ruthlessly, often savagely, put down. Finally, on September 19, 1962, the old Imam Ahmad died of natural causes. His son, Crown Prince Badr, who was widely thought of as a comparatively liberal man and by some as a friend of President Nasser, became imam. Then on September 27 the chief of the army, Abdullah Sallal, a man of humble origins, led an attack on the palace, narrowly missed capturing the new imam, and proclaimed a republic. The imam himself fled from Sanaa to the tribal territory in the north from which he has organized and commanded a guerrilla army since that time. Meanwhile, Sallal, with few troops loyal to the government in comparison to the numerous and well-armed tribes, and with fewer other resources, appealed to President Nasser for help. Egyptian troops began pouring into the country to fight in the war against the supporters of the imam, and Egyptian technicians to help "bring Yemen into this century." No end to either effort seems in sight.

It can be said that the first decade of the "new era" of Arab freedom, neutrality, and assertiveness ended as it began, with the major questions of national life yet to be answered. In the interval, major changes had occurred in the society and the economy of the Arab world and to these we shall now turn.

PART FIVE THE MATRIX OF
THE NEW ARAB

XIV. The Accelerating Social Revolution:
The New Men

In the Arab World are many divisions. Traditionally, the bedouin have thought of mankind both in terms of kinship, with all mankind viewed in a pyramid of kindred from the family to the clan to the tribe to the races descending from the sons of Noah, and in terms of social economy with the bedouin sharply distinguished from the settled peoples. In the Koran men are divided religiously and by language. We in the West tend to think of divisions by income and class. But in analyzing the nature of the social revolution in the Arab countries, it is more useful to distinguish men of the traditional society from the "new men."

Both the new men and the traditional men can be seen in all social, religious, and economic groups and at all levels of society. The new men form a sort of "vertical" society, composed of all classes. They have an inner similarity and share certain values despite the obvious differences in economic, educational, and political attainments of their members.

The growth of this core within Middle Eastern society is one of the most significant changes in recent years. But viewed historically, what we observe today can be seen to be but a recent phase in a much older process.

The traditional society is not, of course, completely static. Contemporary hallmarks of conservatism in the traditional society were, in their way, often marks of social or aesthetic advance.

This is as true of social values as of such superficial signs of social usage as the wearing of a fez or tarbush. Regarded by recent reformers as the very symbol of reaction, the fez was a revolutionary innovation when introduced in the third decade of the nineteenth century to replace the more cumbersome and time-consuming turban. When the Lebanese Amir Bashir put aside his turban and effected the fez, he was symbolizing his entry into a new age; when the Egyptians later banned the fez they meant this as a symbolic step toward secular modernization. Likewise, on a more profound level, Islam was in its youth certainly revolutionary, with new ideas on the status of women, the brotherhood of believers, and the role of government. Yet modern Middle Eastern nationalists and modernizers have found in Islamic values a barrier to rapid modernization and have sought in secular nationalism a replacement for some aspects of Islam.

Like the tastes and the ideas, so the new men of each generation tend to fade, relatively speaking, into traditional society as they are overtaken and surpassed by a new generation. This is not, necessarily, to say that their role as modernizers has ended; some have come to be appreciated only long after their times. Moreover, some of the most significant innovations in the Middle East have been brought about by men who were, personally, deeply committed to the old order.

To gain some perspective on the current situation, let us briefly review the nature of earlier social change.

Writing in the first half of the nineteenth century, that remarkable observer and student of Egyptian life E. W. Lane echoed the thoughts of many previous writers when he pointed to lethargy as a hallmark of the people of the Nile. Since the then three or four million Egyptians could so easily support themselves on their fertile land, lacked a major inventive to devote themselves to industry, and found their simple and often crude products satisfactory, they could afford the luxury of backwardness. The picture painted by Lane and others is of a people whose lives were minutely regulated by established custom and whose appetites were as yet unwhetted for the new and the exotic produce of the Industrial Revolution, for the stimulating if disquieting ideas of the Renaissance, the Reformation, or the Enlightenment.

In the Syrian hinterland and the Iraqi basin, likewise, the people had accepted traditional approaches to life. Every man had his place in society. If that place were not entirely satisfying, it was God-ordained. To attempt to change it was unnatural. Indeed, even the word "change" (*ghaiyara*) carried the implication of "to corrupt" or "change for the worse." What was, was right, and the limits of acceptable human endeavor were narrow. As Professor Joseph Schacht in *The Arab Nation* has written: "One ancient Arab idea, arising from the very core of the mental endowment of the Arabs . . . became the central concept of Islamic religious law and theology . . . The Arabs were, and are, bound by tradition and precedent; they were, and are, dominated by the past . . . Whatever was customary, was right and proper; whatever their forefathers had done, deserved to be imitated."

The facts of life lent weight to this natural bent toward conservatism. The bedouin already had a highly sophisticated approach to a most difficult environment. To change his pattern of life, the bedouin would be required to change his environment. Only by nomadism can the extensive resources of the desert be utilized. Significantly, one of the Arabic words meaning "to settle" (*qantara*) al.ɔ means "to possess a hundred-weight," for when a man becomes acquisitive, he must settle.

The villager, tilling a small plot of land, consuming most of what he produced, in need of only the most rudimentary weapons, tools, and consumables, and fearful of outside influences, was content within his small world. Much of his culture, the villager shared with the bedouin, but whereas the nomad ranged widely over vast, if not markedly different, expanses of the world's surface, the villager stuck close to a narrow, confining world. Surrounded by kinsmen with whom he shared his means of livelihood, the villager was intent on *protecting* his water rights, marketplaces, and common pasturage. Deeply wedded to his land, the villager married within his village and called it his "nation" (*watan*). Oppressed or ravaged from the one side by

the rapacious nomad and from the other by the equally rapacious
tax collector, the villager sought to retain and enjoy rather than
to expand his means of livelihood. Seldom it was that he attempted to market his produce or to communicate with people
outside of the small autarkic clusters of villages which were the
limits of his world.

The city dweller, likewise, was enmeshed in a world of narrow scope, but known satisfactions. The mosque was his school,
his club, and his parliament. In craft and religious guilds and
brotherhoods, his relations with his fellows were drawn tightly
together. His neighbors, like those of his village cousin, were
often his kinsmen. They and he were segregated from other
neighborhoods by walls and were ruled internally by men at least
in part of their choosing. In the city as in the village or the
tribe, man was never isolated but was able to find a stable, understood, and reasonably satisfying pattern of life.

The government was distant and its local agents were often
foreigners, partaking of little of the local life and adding less to
it. The government agent was himself a sort of nomad, camped
in his headquarters, but little concerned with the life around him
except in the collection of taxes.

More exposed, less secure, and less integrated were the minority groups. Some of these groups shared religions or languages
with foreigners. Not the Muslim, therefore, but usually the members of the minorities were most open to change.

The British agent Dr. John Bowring, in his report on the
"Commercial Statistics of Syria" in 1839, said that he found the
Muslims to be the most backward as a group since they "accumulate little capital and fail to practice the arts progressively"
whereas "most of the commercial establishments . . . (were) in
the hands of the Christian or Jewish population." The merchant,
he wrote, "is rarely an honored being—the power of the sword
and the authority of the book—the warrior and the Ulema (religious leadership) are the two really distinguished races of society. All productive labour—all usefully employed capital is
regarded as belonging to something mean and secondary."

The Christians, particularly of the Levant, had been in contact with European missionaries and many had studied European languages. The Jews were less aided by European powers or organizations but were freed from many of the inhibitions of Islamic politics and were somewhat affected by European contacts. Moreover, the Christians and Jews were able to enter into professions that the Muslims despised. In the Levant, for example, Jews and Christians were money lenders; the men who served as the equivalent of ministers of finance to the pashas of Saida were Jews and Christians, and the prevalence of such names as Katib, Haddad, Najjar (scribe, blacksmith, and carpenter) among the Christians testifies to their economic activity. The rulers of Egypt traditionally used the Copts as their tax collectors and as the cadres of their civil service. As late as 1910 almost half of the civil service of Egypt was drawn from the 15 percent Coptic minority.

Traditionally, in Islamic countries, education was not a function of the state but of the Islamic institution. In Egypt it was not until 1869 that the government tried even to inspect the schools, and only in 1925 did the state open half-day primary schools.

Egypt has been a pacesetter for the Arab countries in recent generations—even today half the literate Arabs are Egyptians —so it is instructive to observe trends there in some detail.

Between 1913 and 1945 school attendance in Egypt rose from 206,000 to 477,000 boys and 26,500 to 418,000 girls. In 1931 six public schools catered to 2500 secondary students of whom none were girls, whereas in 1945 fifty-three schools enrolled 33,000 boys and 3000 girls. During the same period the number of private schools increased from five to seventy-four. Higher schools increased their enrollment during that period from 1500 to 15,000. In 1952 only 45 percent of the children of proper ages attended schools, but following the 1952 revolution the figure rose to 65 percent and present plans call for facilities for all children by 1969. Total enrollment in 1950–51 was 1.5 million; by 1960–61 it had reached 3.1 million; it is expected by 1970 to reach 5.4 million. During that same period, university-level technical students almost tripled in number, and the secondary schools graduated more students yearly than the total enrollment in 1945–46.

In Iraq, one of the key factors when the British established their control in the last stages of World War I was the need to create a sufficiently large cadre of skilled men to administer the country and to work its industry. Particularly after the expensive revolt of 1920 had raised serious protests in London it was decided that economy must be the rule. Therefore, the British were anxious to pull out their relatively expensive foreign personnel as rapidly as possible. The Indian clerical help the British had imported during the war was, for political reasons, not regarded as a feasible alternative. However, India could be taken as a model for the small core of senior British officials who set policy for Iraq and supervised its execution by a local staff.

In Iraq as in India, the British faced what ultimately was an insolvable dilemma: they needed a skilled bureaucracy but deeply distrusted the urban literati who were its only native source. They felt that if this superficially Westernized group were allowed to gain control, it would corrupt the simple nobility of the "good Arabs," the bedouin, and would further impoverish the miserable peasantry. In any event, British interests would suffer. Therefore, a fine line had to be drawn between training for bureaucracy and education for government. The British therefore put major emphasis on primary schools. Their plan was to restrict secondary education to the "select few" needed by the administration.

In Kuwait, the coming of oil can be seen graphically in the rise of the education budget from $90,000 in 1942 to $33 million in 1960.

Other states are making major strides. Yet serious education problems remain. The population of the Arab states is still largely illiterate, and even that part of the population which is "educated" is still largely untrained in disciplines which are readily employable. But the efforts of the modernizers in Middle Eastern countries to educate the next generation for industrial and technical occupations are already showing results. Though statistics vary for the different countries, they all show the same emphasis on expansion of the technical qualifications of Arab society. In 1960–61 enrollment in preparatory and secondary vocational schools in four countries was as follows.

	Schools	Students
Egypt	181	114,693
Iraq	34	6,732
Jordan	14	1,281
Syria	32	6,830

And Saudi Arabia had 1081 abroad in schools. These figures do not include trainees in industry or apprentices, such as those in oil installations or other plants throughout the area. Occasionally, this kind of training has been on a massive scale. For example, the British forces in Egypt employed some 80,000 skilled or semi-skilled workers in World War II.

Today the emphasis placed on science and technology, in the schools and out, has greatly increased as several countries have set out to industrialize. It was estimated in 1961, by the Higher Council for the Sciences, that 38,000 Egyptians had graduated in the natural sciences and technology from Egyptian faculties. Of these 10,000 were engineers, 9700 agronomists, 9000 physicians, and 5000 scientists.

In addition to the more formal education in schools there was, of course, a major if less formal educational development in the increasing awareness of the outer world which was fostered by the presence in Iraq, Lebanon, Syria, Jordan, the Palestine mandate, and Egypt of large numbers of foreigners who brought with them distinctive habits. The goods and services which these foreigners imported, the administrative structures which they built, and the industry and commerce in which they engaged tended to impart education in the broader sense of the word to the native populations.

It is instructive to compare the former mandates and the colonial countries of the Middle East and other areas with those which have not had the disruption and benefits of foreign rule. A wound has been inflicted in the former colonial and mandate states' "national psyche." On the other hand, such countries as

Yemen, in which there has been no outside rule, have missed the beneficial aspects of foreign tutelage. Foreign powers did leave a sense of "structure" or organization and set styles for the new men who alone could run them.

In Iraq, there was an early recognition that the army was a school of nationalism. In its report to the League of Nations in 1926 the mandate government noted that "the army is proving a valuable means of fostering a true national spirit." Even the paramilitary groups, including the Boy Scouts, played an important part in the growth of national identity on the new model.

It was this same spirit which subsequently caused an Egyptian army officer, Sharaf ad-Din Zabalawi, to write in an article entitled "Military Education and Character Training": "Military life is the school of the people; it is an advanced school in public, social and national aspects of life, for the first lesson that a young soldier learns is self-denial and to exert all his efforts toward a noble cause. It is the repudiation of personal interests in favor of the public interest. The individual becomes a sound ideal citizen."*

It was logical that modernizers should assign this role to the army. We have seen that in the time of Mehmet Ali the army was in fact a vehicle as well as a reason for reform.

Today in many of the Middle Eastern countries the army is viewed as the guardian of national virtue, the sole force capable of and interested in pushing forward those reforms which alone will give dignity, strength, and justice. In part the army and modernization programs fulfill the role of creating the "image" which the military modernizers would like to project to the world —an industrialized, militarily powerful, state, respected in the world community.

Traditionally, of course, this was not the case. The military establishment, as we have seen, was restricted to a very narrow stratum of the society. In Egypt it was an alien force which did not even share the language or customs and certainly thought little of the well-being of the population. Egyptians only grad-

* Quoted in Morroe Berger, *Military Elite and Social Change* (Princeton, 1960).

ually won admission to its service and then, in the time of Mehmet Ali Pasha, usually as common soldiers. Indeed, it was not until 1936 that the Egyptian government opened the military academy to all social ranks. The nature of the change of the social composition of the army, as it grew larger and more "national," has been well expressed as one "from Praetorian Guard to Advance Guard." The armies, alone among the institutions of the societies, were organized along nationalist, modern, and secular lines without commitments to the past. The military alone has a defined code, a clear line of command, channels of communication, mobility, force, and, ultimately, will. The better an instrument of the state it became, the less committed it was to the state. As Professor Halpern in his *Politics of Social Change* has perceived: "The more the army was modernized, the more its composition, organization, spirit, capabilities, and purpose constituted a radical criticism of the existing political system . . . In civilian politics, corruption, nepotism, and bribery loomed much larger. Within the army, a sense of national mission transcending parochial, regional, or economic interests, or kinship ties, seemed to be much more clearly defined than anywhere else in society . . . As the army became modernized and professionalized, the traditionalist elements within the civilian sector found army service less to their taste."

Whereas in Western society the army has tended to be equated, at least in part, with the middle class, in the Middle East until recently this has not been the case. In the first place what we would call, on economic grounds, the middle class was often in large part composed of non-Muslims or even alien minority communities. This was particularly the case in Egypt where the Copts and large foreign communities of Greeks, Italians, and others predominated in the middle reaches of the economy and society. The Egyptian middle class in 1947 was estimated to comprise only about 6 percent of the population or half a million people. Of these about 51 percent were thought to be merchants, 26 percent clerks, 19 percent professionals, and only 4 percent businessmen. Very few were the new men who sought to remake the country.

In part, at least, the role taken upon itself by the Egyptian army has been the *creation* of a middle class. The middle class, composed of managers, administrators, teachers, engineers, journalists, scientists, lawyers, and army officers are, for the most part today, employees of the state. Where new state organs have been established, they are often staffed by men who were recently army officers. This is true of the Suez Canal Authority and the oil refinery and many of the nationalized business concerns.

The middle class in the modern Middle East is rather different in several ways from the Western middle classes we associate with the Industrial Revolution and democratic government. It is not distinguished by a dedication to private ownership, rights of self-expression, or a particular political credo. It uses and agrees to be used by the state for whose well-being it strives. And the new middle class is highly pragmatic in its approach—espousing "socialism" or whatever seems to offer solutions to baffling social problems. In these ways it differs significantly from the traditional sector which shares its "middleness" in economic terms, for example, the landlords and merchants.

Today the lack of a technical education effectively blocks the forward progress of men even within the middle class. Men who are well trained but trained in the traditional subjects do not have the assets to move upward socially and economically. Significantly, the acquisition of a foreign education, preferably at the source in a Western university, not a man's social rank or wealth, is the surest passport to advancement. This is the field of education in which one can note the most spectacular progress in the years since World War I in several Middle Eastern countries.

To take Iraq as an example, in 1921 nine Iraqis were sent abroad to acquire a Western education; by 1928 the number had risen to 93; by 1939 it had reached 238. By 1931 over 200 young men had spent periods of study abroad and had returned; by 1950 the number had reached almost 2000. In the one year of 1962 nearly 7000 were abroad at Western schools, colleges, and universities. As increased numbers were sent, and as governments committed higher proportions of money to education both on the lower and the higher levels, the young men and women were drawn from more humble social strata. Thus, in education as in the army, social class origins became less important. And, perhaps more significantly, whereas education *inside* an Arab country involved a limited exposure to the West in an Eastern context, the student on a mission abroad might spend upwards of eight years living in the West, acquiring new habits of life and far higher expectations; upon return, a sense of bitterness, extreme criticism, and frustration were common.

Curiously, this sort of contact with an alien society seems to have affected the humble more strongly than those at the top of the social ladder. Perhaps it was partly that the young man from a humble family could more fully commit himself to a new life and, because less bound, more readily accept its ways and values, and partly that upon his return from a relatively comfortable well-paid, and challenging experience, he viewed his own former position more bitterly, having less means of action and less protection—in family and money—from a harsh adjustment.

But those who went abroad and learned, at the prestigious source, a profession or new technical field were able to move ahead economically, politically, and socially more rapidly than those who stayed behind. Thus, even men of wealth and family who stayed behind gradually became socially inferior to those of more humble origin who went abroad and returned with a marketable skill. The graduate of a Baghdad college was destined for inferior jobs, perhaps as a primary or secondary schoolteacher, whereas the graduate from Oxford or Harvard could teach in the colleges, practice his profession, or take a responsible government position. Here it is possible to see the very sharp differentiation between the new men and the more traditional.

Likewise, one can observe this differentiation among the groups which we would categorize as lower class. In their study *Human Resources for Development in Egypt*, Harbison and Ibrahim distinguished several groups of workers. The largest is unskilled, landless, and without capital. The second, much smaller, consists of skilled or semiskilled traditional artisans who are technologically increasingly unemployed. The third group, perhaps now less than 10 percent, is made up of men with some degree of modern skills. Although all would be lower class because of the sharp contrast they present to men of the rest of the social order, they are clearly distinguished from one another by salary, regularity of employment, and morale. In Egypt, where, as in most countries of the underdeveloped world, unemployment and underemployment are common, a mechanic, for example, earns three times as much per diem as a day laborer and is assured of continual employment—so his real wages may be many times that of the day laborer. Everywhere the differential has been very high, and apparently the aim of a number of the Arab governments is to increase it.

Aware that a technologically backward and poor population is unable to form a solid base for the growth of national dignity and power, the two cherished goals of the modernizers of the Middle East, both the Iraqi and the Egyptian governments in the 1950's embarked upon programs to create new men not only in the cities but also in the countryside. This was the essence of the "Liberation Province" scheme in Egypt and the resettlement and housing experiments in Iraq.

Roundly, and perhaps rightly, criticized as an economic fiasco or as an example of ambitious political planning without the requisite technological and economic foundation, Liberation Province does give a clue to how the government felt about the need to build a new Egyptian. In the words of the director of the Social Affairs Department, M. Gamal Zaki: "Settlers are selected scientifically on social, medical, psychological tests. As social qualifications, applicants must possess one wife, no dependents except children, and no property; they must have been married only once, and must have finished their military service. Of 1,100 applicants so far, all have the right social qualifications, but only 382 families were accepted medically, because while most of the men were healthy enough, the women and children fell far short of the standard. Only 180 families survived the psychological test . . . of these 132 are now undergoing a six-month training, which included a three-month probation period. We must consider both people and land to be under reclamation."*

* Quoted in Doreen Warriner, *Land Reform and Development in the Middle East* (London, 1957), pp. 50–51.

The new man of Liberation Province was marked off from the traditional Egyptian peasant by a new standardized uniform in place of the traditional gown—the new version of the fez for the turban or the cap for the fez—by a much higher caloric intake of food, and by a salary four times the average rate in Upper Egypt. In addition, the workers were to put their children into a boarding school, as in the Israeli kibbutzim, which presumably would enable teachers to ensure a better and modern upbringing for the children. Moreover, like the rest of Egypt, Liberation Province was to become a mixed rural and industrial economy with factories interspersed throughout the agricultural area.

Liberation Province has had a stormy career and has certainly fallen short of goals intended for it, but the purpose was clear, and one may see this purpose, if less clearly specified, perhaps much more uniformly carried out, in certain other ways. For example, as mentioned above, the army has long been regarded as a school in civic virtues. In addition, today the army has also become a school to impart modern skills, a hospital to cure the ills of society and turn out healthier men, and a source of discipline. Each year approximately 20,000 Egyptians are inducted into the army for three-year enlistments; in Syria about the same are called up for two years. From 1957 to 1963 perhaps as many as 130,000 Egyptians have passed out of the armed forces into civilian life. When one considers that larger-scale, modern Egyptian industry in 1961 employed roughly 250,000 workers, the impact of this group of ex-soldiers can be appreciated.

Not very much is known about these new men when they return to civilian life. It is clear, however, that they are possessed of a rudimentary technical training, a sense of discipline, an indoctrination in nationalism, and certainly a far higher standard of health than are those who have not had army experience. All of these things are rare and prized possessions in a rapidly evolving and industrializing society.

At the upper echelons, the former army officer is the "doer" of the new order. He may aspire to cabinet rank, or take a key managerial job in the apparatus of government-run industry or commerce. As a factory manager or a senior bureaucrat he will play a dominant role in modernizing the country. In the middle

levels, it is probable that the former noncommissioned army officers and junior officers take on lower-level administrative and industrial functions and former private soldiers are probably readily
absorbed into industry. It is doubtful that many return to village
communities where their skills are not in demand and where the
life they have learned to lead, or at least aspire to, is impossible.
As yet little is known in specific terms, but, in the round, it is
possible to see that in the making is a multiclass, nontraditionalist,
as yet politically or philosophically uncommitted, pragmatic, disciplined, privileged core of new men.

In all of the Middle Eastern countries, revolutionary and conservative alike, it is the aim of governments to increase both
absolutely and proportionately the sector of the "new men." This
is the political constituency of the modernizing governments and
is the group upon whom all governments, conservative as well as
modernizing, must depend for the development of national power.
With the rapid growth of the school system and the perpetuation
of conscript armies, it seems likely that the influence of this group
will be felt conclusively throughout the society of each country:
not only will the governments come to represent these relatively
more effective citizens, as their absolute numbers increase, we can
already perceive the outlines of a different kind of politics. Probably by the 1980's, if not sooner, most of the Arab countries will
have, as never before, mass political parties. Thus, in two generations, politics in the Arab countries will have evolved from a
situation in which the bulk of the citizenry will participate either
actively or passively, either constructively or destructively, either
democratically or in totalitarian masses, in politics. How, we cannot foretell, but that the social base of Arab politics has been
profoundly altered is already evident.

XV. The Economy of the Arab World

The economy of the Arab World is profoundly affected by international politics and can only be understood in this perspective. To illustrate this point, it may be useful to think in terms of a piece of real estate. To a homeowner the value of property depends largely upon the comfort, income, or other satisfactions it gives, but for outsiders the value may be largely a matter of location and the virtues of the building may count for little or nothing.

Historically, the "real estate" of the Arabs has presented them with an irony. In it, they have found little of the ease of life to be gained from ample water, a moderate climate, or a balanced endowment of minerals. However, the Middle East, athwart the trade and communications routes joining Europe, Asia, and Africa, with important religious and cultural influence in Africa and Asia, with an agricultural season different from Europe's, and, in this century, with the discovery of vast deposits of oil, has been of great strategic value to others.

Until recently the contrast of inner poverty with strategic value worked to the disadvantage of the Arabs. Now, it has become a major asset if not the major hope for the Arab's future. The contrast of the present with the past is evident in commercial relations. One side of the coin is the Suez Canal, which was dug by Egyptian labor, is located on Egyptian territory, and was largely paid for by Egyptian capital, yet from which Egypt received almost no return for this first sixty years of its operations.

Immediately before the outbreak of fighting between the Arab
states and Israel in June 1967, the Suez Canal was yielding Egypt
a revenue of $250 million in hard currencies annually. The other,
bright, new side of the coin is oil. Foreign companies have paid
vast treasures simply for the privilege of being allowed to explore
some of the most inhospitable and barren land on this planet.
When petroleum was found, as it usually has been in vast quantities, they have paid enormous and increasing revenues to the lucky
government, providing fringe benefits in public services and
employing local citizens in oil field facilities. The result, in some
countries, has been miraculous: Abu Dhabi has suddenly become,
in terms of per capita income, the world's richest state with only
20,000 people sharing approximately $500 million yearly.

An even more striking change, however, is in the actions of the
outside powers. Mehmet Ali had opposed the digging of a canal
at Suez because he rightly perceived that it would make foreign
domination of Egypt inevitable. His attempt to industrialize
Egypt was opposed by the European powers, which sought markets for their own produce, and, ultimately supported their bankers and merchants commit what amounted to grand larceny in
Egypt. Today, the great powers compete to assist the Arab countries with grants, loans, special trade arrangements, and technical
assistance on an unprecedented scale. They also give or sell great
quantities of military equipment. The strategic value of the Middle East has now become its major natural resource.

In the years since 1945 the United States has granted $795
million, lent $583 million, and given military equipment worth $88
million to the Arab states. During this period the Soviet Union
has given or lent about $1.2 billion in economic aid and in excess
of $1 billion worth of military equipment. Other Western states
have lent or given the Arab states about $700 million worth of aid.

The domestic resources of the Arab World, as we have seen,
are extremely meager. Only in a few places—mainly in the north
of Syria and Iraq—does sufficient rain fall to sustain agriculture.
In the Arabian Peninsula, an area a fifth as large as the United
States, only one tenth of one percent—an area about twice the
size of Long Island—is arable. Egypt, as Herodotus said, is the

"gift of the Nile"; without the Nile the 3 percent which is now arable would be as barren as the 97 percent which is now desert. Iraq owes most of its agriculture to the Tigris and Euphrates rivers which rise in the Turkish and Kurdish highlands where more than eight inches of rain falls. Elsewhere, agriculture areas are islands in a vast, waterless sandy "sea."

The economy of the Arab countries of the Middle East has gone through three discernible stages and is now in the early stages of a fourth, characterized by major efforts at development. In the first, which lasted until the 1820's in Egypt, the 1830's in Syria, and perhaps the 1860's in Iraq and the 1930's in Arabia, the economy was largely fragmented into clusters of villages and tribal groups which, in the main, were self-sufficient and in which a balance existed between nomadism, agricultural life, and small-scale urban industry. This first phase was followed by a second characterized by the rapid introduction of cheaper Western goods and more attractive Western styles as a result of the European industrial revolution, of the development of public security, and of the weakness of the Ottoman sultans who, in the commercial code of 1838, virtually turned over to Europeans the commerce of the empire.

In the third phase, which began in Egypt at the end of the First World War and later in Iraq, Syria, and Lebanon, and is just starting in Arabia, the Arabs set about creating an industrial base. As described above, a false start was made in this direction in the 1820's and 1830's in Egypt, when Mehmet Ali tried to create an industry, but Egypt lacked both the skilled manpower and the resources to sustain the development. It is possible that this attempt set Egypt back by shutting out private initiative. It did definitely channel all efforts into monopolies which were politically unworkable. A somewhat different attempt was made later in the century, under Ismail Pasha, to create the "social overhead" or infrastructure of development. This was successful, but the results were long delayed and too costly.

The feeling has never died that until the Middle East has its own industrial base, it will be nothing more than a "country cousin" of Europe. Moreover, it was clearly not acceptable in terms of national self-respect merely to have industry *in* the Middle East. The British and French had filatures in Lebanon and small-scale factories in Egypt before World War I, but leading Arabs felt strongly that the institutions of modern capitalism must be in part native. So strong was this feeling that an Egyptian trade and industry commission secured major government support in 1920 to found the first Egyptian-owned and Egyptian-directed financial and industrial promoter, the Misr Bank.

Egyptian industry never was able to match Egyptian agriculture in competition for private capital, however. Cotton was king. Any Egyptian with money put it into land. Egyptian industry was new and untried, and with international commitments preventing the government from creating tariff barriers, infant industry was not an attractive investment. By 1927 only about 5 percent of Egyptian gross national product came from industry and mining. In the 1930's, however, the collapse of cotton prices and the continued rise in Egyptian population without compensatory rises in agricultural area or production led to a renewed interest in industrialization.

Textiles were the front runner in Egyptian industrial growth. Production increased from 9 million square yards at the end of World War I to 20 million in 1931 and 159 million in 1939.

But it was not really until the Axis blockade during World War II and the presence of a huge Allied army—whose expenditures totaled 25 percent of Egyptian National income—that the major stimulus to local production was felt. In Egypt 80,000 skilled and semiskilled workers were employed to supply the British Eighth Army.

A major part of the activity of Egyptian industry was stimulated by the Misr Bank, which participated in the founding of some twenty-seven companies. But the bank was always short of capital, even though used by the government to pump loans into industry, so in 1949 the government founded an Industrial Bank in which it owned 51 percent of the stock. Even though somewhat freer in the lending of capital, this institution fell short of the needs of the economy and tended to accentuate the growth of larger-scale industry to the detriment of medium- and smaller-scale companies.

The Iraq government began in 1927 to allow the import of industrial equipment without duty and in 1929 passed a law to encourage industry by granting some tax exemptions if the industry to be started were above a certain size and used power-driven rather than hand-powered equipment. In 1933 Iraq imposed high tariffs on those industrial goods which could be supplied locally. And in 1936 an Agricultural and Industrial Bank was formed to initiate industrial schemes.

The war made a major impact in Iraq as elsewhere. The military expenditures of the Allied forces there in 1943 were about three times the size of the government budget for that year. The existence of ready cash and the lack of imported goods caused a wartime spurt of industrial activity.

Not only was the war a short-term stimulus to industrial activity in the Arab countries; even more significant was the long-term impact it left as a school in fiscal and commercial control. This "school" was the Middle East Supply Centre. The Supply Centre was established by the British government in 1941 (and made a joint Anglo-American project in 1942) to ensure that the population of the Middle Eastern countries would continue to get essential supplies despite the wartime shortages of goods and shipping space. Essentially, the Allies sought to cut imports and particularly those whose bulk or shortage was a critical factor. The key measure of success in Allied strategic terms was the reduction of imports from about 6 million tons in 1939 to 1½ million in 1944.

The principal means of accomplishing this reduction were two. In the first place the advice of experts was sought on means to expand local production. Since the major bulk imports were agricultural and the primary danger was famine, a premium was put on agricultural development. Investments were made in studies, farm extension programs, and means to control the distribution of fertilizer, resulting in considerable short-term increases. The most lasting results, however, lay in the second major means available to the wartime military authority: government regulation of industry, commerce, and agriculture. As elsewhere, so in the Middle East, the war provided a justification and a need for forms of government activity which were continued long after the war ended. All import goods had to be licensed, currencies were controlled, and elaborate plans and machinery were established to allocate goods and services. Even for those who assumed that the purpose of the Middle East Supply Centre was to exercise foreign control over the area's economies and that its heavy emphasis on agriculture was motivated by a desire to keep the Middle East backward, the principle of central control was not abhorrent. At least in part the Middle East Supply Centre was a school in the fundamentals of state economic control.

In Iraq, Syria, and Lebanon, meanwhile, little industry had been started until the end of World War II. Characteristically, textiles led the way. In Iraq the oldest plants processed cotton and wool which were sold in large part to the government for army use. What little industry there was in Syria before World War II was primarily handicraft, but the shortages and high prices of the war and immediate postwar years served as a stimulus to the development of native industry. This, in turn, was encouraged by the newly independent government as a means of achieving economic independence to match political independence. Protective tariffs were introduced in 1949 alongside low-interest, state-guaranteed loans for industry. In 1952 the importation of a number of articles that could be manufactured in Syria was prohibited and import quotas imposed on others.

The problem faced immediately in Syria and Iraq was the creation of industry in the general absence of capital or skills in the population. Whereas in Egypt both had evolved over a number of decades, Syria and Iraq wanted to find short cuts to catch up with the West. In Syria the government was further hampered by the fact that the little capital it had was channeled through the Banque de Syrie et du Liban, then controlled by France.

But everywhere in the Arab countries, industry was a small part of the economy. Just what it amounted to in terms of gross national product of the several countries is at best a guess before recent years. In fact, relatively little was known of the economy of the Middle East as a whole, despite the efforts of the Middle East Supply Centre, until the Palestine War posed, in the displacement of nearly a million Arab refugees, economic problems of such magnitude and immediacy that a special United Nations Economic Survey Mission, the Clapp Commission, was created to study the problem.

The report of the commission, published in December 1949, pointed out that "the solution of the problem of the poverty and unemployment of the refugees is . . . inseparable from a solution of the problem of poverty and hunger as that already affects a large section of the population of the Middle East." Apparently affected by the talks with the new nationalist officials they met on their travels, the members of the commission felt called upon to say in their introduction that a "higher living standard cannot be bestowed by one upon another like a gift. An improved economy does not come in a neat package to be sold or given away in the market place . . . The highly developed nations of the world did not make their way by wishing. By work and risk they forced the earth, the soil, the forest and the rivers to yield them riches. They pooled their energy and resources by taxation and mutual enterprise . . . There is no substitute for the application of work and local enterprise to each country's own resources. Help to those who have the will to help themselves should be the primary policy guiding and restraining the desire of the more developed areas of the world to help the less developed lands."

The report pointed out that the area is "and for a long time to come will remain, agricultural." The first requirement was said to be the need to develop its potential to feed its people and increase export crops. Only limited industry was seen to be immediately required. Needs apart, besetting any large-scale projects were many obstacles. "The region is not ready, the projects are not ready, the people and Governments are not ready, for large-scale development." The conclusion was that pilot projects should be begun, with international assistance, while governments of the area organized themselves to mobilize their resources and focus their talents on national development plans and agencies.

The advice given to the Arab governments had two immediate effects, one good and one not. On the one hand the report pointed out the potentials of the area and indicated a road toward their realization; it encouraged local enterprise and promised external help; and, while eschewing unrealism, it underlined projects that could be undertaken immediately in the interval before larger developments could be launched. This was a valuable endowment. On the other hand, the mission was viewed with a jaundiced eye by the critical and suspicious Arab, suffering from the humiliation of the Palestine War. He saw external assistance as a means to salve the conscience of the West for the fate of the Arab refugees while emphasizing agricultural development to keep the Middle East merely the "farm" for Europe.

The first country to profit from the advice offered by the Clapp Mission was Iraq, which in 1950 created a Development Board charged with the planning and execution of schemes to develop the country. To carry out its projects, the board was to receive 70 percent of the government's revenue from oil. At that time this sum was about $12 million; it rose rapidly over the next few years to nearly $180 million yearly. Recognizing its need for large-scale technical assistance, the government of Iraq began to recruit foreign experts and asked the International Bank to send a team to study the economy. Upon the report of this group, the first development plan for the period 1951–56 was based.

At the time, also, Iraq entered into an agreement with the United States government under which the United States gave Iraq technical advice on the development of its resources. A part of this project led to a further broad study by a technical consulting firm on industrial development and to a myriad of project plans by other consultants. Indeed, while much useful work was done in the many studies and plans, planning became virtually an end in itself as the headquarters of the Development Board commissioned whole teams of contractors to design facilities which required or catered to talents and personnel not then available in Iraq.

But Iraq was fortunately situated between the two extremes of the Arab countries, those with dense population and shortage of capital, led by Egypt, and those with proportionally vast capital resources but little into which to invest it locally, typified by Kuwait.

Among the many problems associated with development is the acquisition of sufficient foreign exchange to hire or buy the equipment and skills needed to build the physical plant and train the personnel for modern economic activity. In the Middle East, during the past three decades, oil has been the magic source of this foreign exchange.

Used on a small scale for thousands of years where it bubbled to the surface, as at Nebuchadnezzar's "fiery furnace" near Kirkuk, oil was first discovered in commercial quantities in Iran in 1908. Since at that time the Royal Navy was changing from coal- to oil-burning ships, the British government, at the insistence of Winston Churchill, on the eve of the First World War acquired 51 percent of the stock of the corporation set up to exploit Persian oil production. In large part it was the existence of the Iranian oil fields and the need to protect them from the Turks that led to the Anglo-Indian invasion of Iraq in November 1914. While American and other companies acquired leases in the Ottoman Empire, the government of India arranged with the Arabian shaikhdoms under its protection to withhold concession rights from any but British nationals. An Anglo-German enterprise, the Turkish Petroleum Company, acquired a concession in Iraq on June 28, 1914.

After the war it was in part the desire of the Turkish Petroleum Company to control the areas around Mosul that led the British government to get French agreement to a revision of the Sykes-Picot Agreement which had awarded Mosul to French-controlled Syria. In return for the inclusion of Mosul in Iraq and transit rights across Syria for oil, the British agreed in the San Remo Conference to let French interests take up a part, later reduced to roughly a quarter, of the combine which later became the Iraq Petroleum Company. Turkish acquiescence to the inclusion of Mosul in Iraq was purchased for a consideration of 10 percent of Iraq's oil revenue for a 25-year period.

In America, at this time, there was a panic over oil, with talk of American reserves being depleted in four to six years; the government was, in fact, so alarmed that it considered entering the oil business itself as the British government had done. But American companies, some of which had concessions from the now defunct Ottoman regime, were excluded from areas of British and French influence. After long and somewhat acrimonious diplomatic negotiations, the British agreed to let American companies operate in the Middle East, and in 1925 American companies took roughly a quarter of the stock of the Iraq Petroleum Company. With the major oil interests included, in 1928 a monopoly area of the Middle East was created for the Iraq Petroleum Company alone.

Meanwhile, American companies not a part of the 1928 agreement tried to get concessions in the Arab areas. In 1932 the Standard Oil Company of California, having found a loophole in British restriction on foreign enterprise in the Persian Gulf by establishing a Canadian company, struck oil on Bahrein Island. Stirred by this enterprise, it acquired a concession in Saudi Arabia in 1933. Joined by the Texas Company, which had a stronger market for oil, it struck oil in Saudi Arabia, near Dhahran, in 1938. Meanwhile, in 1933, the Gulf Oil Company in partnership with the Anglo-Iranian Oil Company, which held the concession in Iran, acquired a concession in Kuwait and struck what eventually became recognized as the world's richest oil field, the Burgan Sands, an area of thirty square miles, fourteen miles from the coast, and only 3400 feet deep in 1938.

World War II interrupted the development of Kuwait's oil before it had achieved commercial production. The real stimulus came in 1951 when Anglo-Iranian Oil lost its concession in Iran and turned to Kuwait in search of another source of supply. From 1950 to 1954 Kuwait production tripled and additional oil was discovered. Today it is estimated that Kuwait has proved reserves in excess of 62 billion barrels or 25 percent of the world's total. Near the surface, adjacent to the sea, and of extremely high quality, this oil has made Kuwait a golden land. At the present time oil revenues are approximately $500 million yearly in a country whose population totals only 340,000. In past times Kuwait had small trading and pearl-fishing industries, which in 1938–39 earned the government about $290,000, but these were literally forgotten in the incredible deluge of prosperity. From a prewar gross national product per capita of about $40, the current rate has risen to $3360. Kuwaitis rapidly became the landlords of Cairo, Beirut, and Lausanne apartment houses, and Kuwaiti deposits in London became an important factor in the stability of the pound.

Kuwait quickly came under heavy criticism among the Arabs for its inability to spend its vast riches to their satisfaction. Iraq, in serious financial trouble, in 1958 resurrected the claims made repeatedly by successive Iraqi governments that Kuwait was a part of Iraq. In the face of a threat to invade the country, Britain rushed in troops and equipment in 1961 until the Arab League took action to replace them with a mixed Arab force. For the Kuwait government the lesson was clear that it must give other Arabs collectively a stake in its security. Thus, Kuwait created in 1962 an Arab Development Fund, with assets now totaling nearly $1.8 billion, to lend to other Arab states.

Libya, after only five years of production will overtake Kuwait and Venezuela by exporting over $2 billion worth of oil in 1971. Total export of Middle Eastern oil products is estimated to reach $8 billion by 1972. Even Syria, with Russian help, and Egypt, with American help, after years of unrewarding search, have become oil producers.

The Iraq Petroleum Company is one of the world's great cartels. Among its owners are Royal Dutch Shell, British Petroleum (which is 56 percent owned by the British government), Cie. Française des Petroles (35 percent owned by the French government), and a consortium of American petroleum "giants." The Arabian American Oil Company is jointly owned by California Standard, the Texas Company, Standard Oil of New Jersey, and Socony; the Kuwait Oil Company is jointly owned by Gulf and British Petroleum. The maze of interlocking and separate research, refining, marketing, shipping, production, and exploration companies controlled by these groups and their vast assets and armies of employees make them literally empires within the petty states of the Middle East and silhouette them bleakly against the simple economic horizons of the countries in which they operate. Irrespective of the enormous contributions to Middle Eastern de-

velopment and the usually enlightened public relations policies
of the companies, this fact has created a highly charged political
atmosphere both for the governments and the companies.

As the governments have begun to develop cadres of men with
some knowledge of the petroleum industry, they have naturally
aspired to control and exploit this single national resource of
worldwide importance. They have found that the companies
usually can afford to pay almost any demand, after a decent
period of bargaining, because the stakes are so enormous: the
goose has been hard to kill and the golden eggs seemingly unlimited. Oil royalties have gone up from token payments in the
1930's to a flexible definition of a 50-50 split today with higher
charges in special circumstances. The Arabs have concerted with
the other members of the Organization of Petroleum Exporting
Countries (OPEC) to find ways further to increase their income
from petroleum. A favorite idea of some Arabs is that fully integrated companies—"from the well head to the gas station pump"
—should exist to give the Arabs a share of profits at each stage
of the operation. However, discovery of oil in North Africa and
increasing Soviet exports of oil have tended, to a degree, to inject
into company-country discussions a note of caution on the health
of the goose. It is clear that the relations between companies and
countries today are far more healthy, in inverse proportion to that
of the industry, than some years ago. Nevertheless, so long as the
oil industry is *the* Middle Eastern industry, its political position
is exposed and dangerous.

Leaving aside the oil boom, the basic economy of the Middle
East is still agricultural. In most of the Arab countries roughly
two out of every three people are directly dependent upon agriculture for their livings. Moreover, most of the foreign currency
earned by the nonoil countries is from agricultural production.
Yet agriculture accounts for one quarter to one third of the gross
national product of Iraq, Syria, Jordan, and Egypt.

Agriculture is lacking in both social and political prestige.
The nationalists of the Middle East do not propose to be Europe's
farm, and the Arabs traditionally have despised the menial lot

of the peasant. However, since the major foreign exchange earner apart from oil and strategic location (which earns revenues in aid and in rental of the Suez Canal, transit facilities for oil, and so forth) is agricultural produce, economic development is largely dependent upon its sale on the world markets. The infant industries of the area simply cannot yet compete on the world markets whereas cotton, dates, and other commodities can.

Ironically, one must conclude, the more successful the Arabs are in their industrial projects, up to the time they became capable of competing on the world market, the more they will depend upon agriculture, since more raw materials, more components, and more machines will have to be imported at greater and greater cost in foreign exchange. This means more strains on the agricultural base which furnishes the bulk of the foreign exchange.

Further, the economic and political situation is dynamic: yesterday's dream is today's norm and tomorrow's failure. The "revolution of expectations" is continuing and accelerating. The "new man" in part brings about and in part is a result of the growth of industry.

Improvement in agricultural output and marketing, therefore, is vital to the success of the development effort. How possible is it? The answer cannot be given in purely economic terms.

For many centuries the *fellah* or peasant had been treated as a domestic animal, a part of the sultan's flock, to be shorn of his yearly produce by tax collectors, usurers, and casual robbers under various titles. His attitude toward government was one of sullen hatred, fear, and—when one of his many ruses succeeded—contempt. For him, as for the very rich, the best government was the least government. In no way did the government benefit him. Regulation of his personal affairs, guidance in matters of law, and what little succor or education he received came from the religious establishment, from the village custom and its council of elders, or from his own numerous kindred.

The villager and many of his city cousins lived apart from government and according to rules different from its formal laws. In the eyes of the government the village lands belonged to the state and the villager enjoyed an insecure tenure upon payment of various sorts of taxes and fees to someone rich or powerful enough to contract with the government for the right of a tax farm (*iltizam*). The tax farmer obligated himself to pay a fixed fee or render military service to the government in return for the right to extract anything he could from the peasants.

Let us take Egypt as the example as the history there is the most precise. When Mehmet Ali became pasha of Egypt in 1805, he was in conflict with the previous ruling group, the Mamluks, and undertook to undercut their authority in various ways. One way was in the abolition of the *iltizam* titles. As in his military reforms, he had to move somewhat slowly and it was not until after his massacre of the Mamluks in 1811–12 that he was able to destroy the system.

In 1812 the *waqf* lands—lands devoted to a foundation though the former owners continued to enjoy the produce—in upper Egypt (and shortly thereafter in all Egypt) were confiscated and their former beneficiaries given compensation. Lands were then turned over to village communities, in accord with the customary, as distinct from formal, law in many parts of the empire; the villages became responsible for the payment of taxes to the state. What the individual "owned" was the right to cultivate certain plots of land, and this right was passed from father to son.

Having destroyed the "feudal" class and established a direct relationship between the state and the land, Mehmet Ali began in 1829 to encourage the development of uncultivated lands by granting tenure to army officers, merchants, and others willing to invest in them. Apparently, he also sought in this way to create a new landed aristocracy. Gradually, over the years, as the role of the state in the economy declined, laws and degrees converted tenure rights into something approximating full ownership. Then as crops for export, notably cotton, became more common in Egypt, title to the land became more firm.

Meanwhile, great improvements in land productivity were made. After the introduction of cotton in 1821 the rich lands of Egypt became golden. The American Civil War, which took American cotton off the world market and produced a financial panic in industrial England, made Egypt prosperous and lured to the land large amounts of capital. Finally, even a peasant could own and sell or mortgage his lands.

What this did to the peasant is clear: he achieved more mobility, but his ties to the land were weakened so that in bad years he risked losing both his new title and his age-old usufruct. In the slump following the end of the American Civil War the smaller operators in Egypt went heavily into debt or lost their lands to larger companies. As the government became desperate for revenue, particularly in the days of Ismail Pasha, it was willing to play fast and loose with law and tenure, so that the wealthy were able to buy titles to land, and rights over the peasants on them, by the payment of back taxes.

Foreigners were encouraged even in the time of Mehmet Ali to invest in the land of Egypt, and by 1901 they individually and through land companies had acquired about 11 percent of the agricultural land of the country.

As dams and canals were built by the state, marginal lands came into production and passed into the hands of larger capitalists and land companies.

The amount of land devoted to agriculture increased from 4.8 million acres in 1893 to 5.4 million in 1906. It has undergone little lateral expansion since, although more control over flooding and irrigation has resulted in double cropping (vertical expansion) and thus more real agricultural area.

Perennial irrigation, however, decreased productivity since it halted the infusion of large amounts of silt which had yearly renewed the fertility of the lands and required heavy use of fertilizers which the peasants could not always afford, often did not know how to use, and periodically, as in World War II, could not obtain. Moreover, the steady waterlogging of the delta has presented major problems of salting and so required expensive canals. And the constant availability of water has promoted the spread of the debilitating disease of bilharziasis and various sicknesses spread by flies and mosquitoes.

The lot of the peasants was always difficult at best. If the year was bad—in Egypt the key factor was the size of the Nile flood

—the peasant had little to eat, and as the crop became specialized, usually in cotton, he could not even eat his produce. (For this reason peasants bitterly opposed extension of cotton plantations.) If the year was good the unit price for his goods fell and the state demanded higher taxes from him.

In Egypt as in Syria and Iraq men fled from the land when the government or the landlords pressed too hard. Conscription or forced labor (*corvée*) were added incentives for men to quit the land or to migrate to protected lands or to the lands of those who could protect them from what amounted to kidnapping for army service or labor gangs. Moreover, due to the Islamic laws of inheritance, there was a steady tendency to subdivide lands, resulting in plots too small to support a farming family. In Egypt in 1910 6.7 percent of the agricultural land was in units of one acre and 18.3 percent in one- to five-acre plots; by 1950 13.1 percent was in units of one acre and 22.2 percent units of one to five acres.

The policy of the government, in Egypt as in Syria, was to force bedouin tribes to settle on the land. To lure the tribes, tax exemption and land ownership was offered. In Egypt as later in Iraq the bedouin shaikh normally became in law and gradually in custom the landlord while his formerly equal tribesmen became his peasants.

By the end of World War II conditions in rural Egypt had become unbelievably bad. At the end of a careful survey in 1946–47 the English economist Doreen Warriner wrote, in *Land and Poverty in the Middle East*, "Near starvation, pestilence, high death rates, soil erosion, economic exploitation—this is the pattern of life for the mass of the rural population in the Middle East. It is a poverty which has no parallel in Europe, since even clean water is a luxury. Money incomes are low—£5 to £7 per head per year—but money comparisons alone do not convey the filth and disease, the mud huts shared with animals, the dried dung fuel. There is no standard of living in the European sense —mere existence is accepted as the standard."

The man-land ratio declined drastically, as population rose from 6.8 million people on 4.7 million real acres or 6.2 million

crop acres (since some land produced two crops) in 1881 to
12 million people on 9.7 million crop acres in 1914 to 16 million
people on 8.4 million crop acres in 1937 and 19 million people on
9.1 million crop acres in 1948. Today the population is about 32
million and the agricultural area has increased only slightly to
10.3 million crop acres. Little further increase is possible from
the Nile waters, yet the population is doubling each 25 years.
This has resulted both in a massive migration to the cities, whose
populations are rising at a rate beyond that of the country as
a whole, and the conversion of the Egyptian countryside into a
quasi-urban area with population densities of approximately 2000
per square mile.

Miss Warriner went on to say that while "it is fashionable to
praise the Egyptian fellah for his industry and frugality, in fact
the conditions of his life are of unrelieved horror. The fellaheen
are physically wretched . . . they are an almost slave population."
It was partly to alleviate the horror of rural wretchedness and
partly to break the power of the landlord class (as in 1812) that
reforms, including the change of titles to the land, were undertaken in 1952 by Nasser's new regime. To the surprise of the
government it was quickly discovered that only about 8 percent
of the land was held in blocks of over 200 acres and that a real
increase in the standard of living of the people could not be
achieved simply by cutting out the big rich. Redistribution was
undertaken, however, and by 1962 nearly one sixth of the agricultural land of Egypt was made subject to the program and
nearly 240,000 farmers had received land. Since an acre of delta
land yields about $150 net profit yearly, this injected into the
agricultural sector of the population a considerable potential for
new income.

In the interval, there has been a major increase in the well-
being of the people in large sections of the Arab countries.
Disease has fallen and public health facilities—rudimentary by
Western standards yet revolutionary in local terms—have been ex-
ported from the cities to the rural areas.

The problem posed by the social history of the rural Arab,
however, may require solutions which are unconventional by

Western standards. It is true that acre for acre, American methods of cultivation produce more than do those of the Arab peasant, but the American methods depend on a level of technology that is not matched in the Middle East. Thus while in American terms "vertical expansion" and the use of better seeds, fertilizers, and methods are more economic, these may not produce the same results in the Arab countries. Not only is the peasant poor and uneducated but he is suspicious of government, unwilling—perhaps sensibly so—to experiment with methods he does not know and cannot understand, and prizes above all else the acquisition of additional land. "Horizontal" expansion of agriculture, even when this involves heavy investment in dams, irrigation and drainage canals, and eventually desalination facilities, may therefore offer the best hope for a higher agricultural output in the near future.

Lebanon has become the financial center, not only of the Middle East, but of worldwide importance. It is, indeed, the Switzerland of the Middle East.

Meanwhile, every Arab government is planning its future. And in every plan the emphasis on expansion of industry is paramount. Industry is a thing of the modern world; to be modern, it is thought, one must industrialize. The index of success, therefore, is the speed with which each state can acquire an industrial plant. In Egypt, for example, between 1939 and 1947 the value of industrial production rose 50 percent, from 1947 to 1954, 40 percent, and from 1954 to 1960, a further 50 percent. Yet this was mainly a result of increased capital investment per worker. Industry has, as yet, proved unable to absorb the large numbers of unemployed and underemployed people for whom there is insufficient land. A serious political problem is thus to find a means of increasing the number of jobs created by industry. Shorter hours and emphasis on industry requiring a higher input of labor is a partial answer. But often the pressures behind the urge to industrialize work in the opposite direction: it is the huge steel factory, which requires a high capital input and little labor, rather than the consumers' goods factory, requiring little capital and much labor, that gives prestige.

Lastly, it must be said that the building of an industrial plant and the infrastructure of the modern state will not sustain a developmental revolution: none of the Arab states has found ways to create markets—which alone will make possible a sufficiently large-scale production to encourage their infant industry. The great economic problem of the Arab countries is not how to build factories and get men to run them, or "build better mousetraps," but how to get people buying the goods of their industry, so that the economy, in Walt W. Rostow's famous phrase, can "take off."

The future appears to offer both hope and irony. As the technology of salt water conversion improves, it is by no means inconceivable that in the coming generation vast areas of the deserts of the Middle East may become fertile agricultural areas. The cost of desalinization has fallen in the past decade from approximately $2 to 15¢ per thousand gallons. Taken together with the remarkable contribution of the Rockefeller Foundation in plant genetics, and the tremendous solar energy of the desert, the Middle East may be on the brink of an agricultural revolution. Coinciding with this trend, perhaps by 1990, nuclear power should become sufficiently inexpensive to replace petroleum for fuel. At that point, petroleum will have become too valuable as a source for petrochemicals, in any case, to be burned. Then, the principal factors of the Middle East economy—the worthlessness of vast deserts and the prime value of petroleum—will be almost reversed: the single most valuable resource in the Middle East will be its intense sunshine.

Perhaps the most severe challenge in the coming generation, however, will not be notably different from the past: the production of enough men with the skill, the daring, the dedication and the tenacity to bring about the basic economic revolution which modern technology will make possible. It is still possible to fail, but now, as never before, there is a bright ray of hope in the contemporary atmosphere of misery, poverty, and backwardness.

XVI. The Arabs and the World: A Quest for Identity and Dignity

Arab politicians and thinkers have set out to answer two basic questions: "who are we?" and "how can we get the world to respect us?" These have been implicit in most of the speeches, books, and actions of the Arab leaders since the end of World War I, and are still burning issues today. It was not very long ago that they were explicitly stated in all significant Arabic-language books. Most began with an attempt to define who the Arabs are: Are Egyptians to be considered Arabs? If so, to the same degree as men of Arabia? Are Christians *really* Arab or must an Arab be a Muslim? Is a man of Damascus more an Arab or more a Syrian? How does the Westernized Lebanese compare in "Arabness" to the isolated Yemeni? Is there *one* Arab nation despite the obvious diversity and conflict of the several Arab states? And, if so, how can the Arabs so express this nation in political, economic, and social terms to give it reality?

The political experience of the several Arab countries, as we have seen, has been remarkably different. This fact has profoundly colored both Arab reactions to the situations in which they found themselves and their intellectual formulations of their goals. The surer road to understanding starts from a description of the Arab situation than from an analysis of the ideas. Many of the ideas were borrowed from Europe and are, in reality, more in the nature of flags of convenience than precise ideological formulations.

Egypt was geographically and culturally the most coherent of the Arab states. Compressed into the Nile Valley, cut off from the other Arabs by great distance, and after 1805 ruled by a strong national, if not Arab, government and after 1882 by a British government, Egypt was subjected to intense, beneficial but intellectually disquieting Western influence. Thus it was to achieve, more surely and easily than the other Arab states, an awareness of itself as a separate entity. Not only were other Arabs far away and living at least economically very differently from the Nile dwellers but the Egyptians, living in the shadow of monuments of their ancient grandeur, developed a sort of Aïda complex. Egypt as Egypt, rather than as an Arab country, had a continuous and recorded history for 4000 years, and whatever changes the successive invaders had made, each layer of foreign influence was built on the same Nilotic core. In contemporary squallor and weakness before foreigners, Egyptians were awed by the majesty of the past, their past, a non-Arab past. These feelings were accentuated by the exciting archaeological discoveries of the late eighteenth and the nineteenth centuries, particularly when the decipherment of hieroglyphics suddenly opened a wide window on the ancient civilization.

Nevertheless Mehmet Ali's attempt to create an Egyptian power failed in 1841 when the European powers forced Egypt to give up its military machine and the economic organization which had sustained it. Thereafter, Egypt "slowly went to sleep again" as Europeans took over more and more aspects of the national economic and cultural life and the more energetic and better educated Egyptians competed in becoming European.

By the 1870's Egypt had no real "line of defense" against the West in political, economic, or even cultural affairs. It was at that time that Jamal ad-Din al-Afghani came to Egypt, inspiring all he met with the notion that Islam could offer a coherent and powerful identification and means of defense. As a result of his influence and that of his disciple Muhammad Abdu, the hope of a revival of Islam and the identification of Egypt as a part of the enduring Islamic civilization became cardinal elements in successive Egyptian efforts to achieve a sense of identification and dignity.

A contrary force was evident, however, in the extensive Westernization of urban Egypt. This was evident in the political movements before World War I and was codified, in the 1930's, by the Egyptian scholar, novelist, and statesman Taha Husain, who stressed the Mediterranean base of Egyptian civilization and urged Egyptians to think of themselves as having a culture in common with Europe rather than with Africa or Asia. Even on the eve of the foundation of the Arab League, Egyptian statesmen echoed this sentiment and described the role of Egypt as a bridge between East and West. But the East was not exclusively the Arab East. If East and West could not meet in Kipling's Suez, they might in Taha Husain's Cairo, which was, in fact, a remarkably cosmopolitan city in a remarkably discrete land. This tendency in modern thought was in the main stream of the urban, polyglot, tolerant, cosmopolitan tradition of the golden age of Islam.

In Syria the environment was quite different. In the first place, before World War I the government was the Ottoman Empire, an Islamic state, so that Islam offered no means of achieving a separate identity. Moreover, a number of the pioneers of nationalism were Christians. Obviously, the Christian minorities could not hope, except to a limited extent in Lebanon, to achieve power or even security as Christians. The only things which they shared with their Muslim neighbors were the Arabic heritage and Syrian residence. In historical memory the shared residence achieved major importance only as the seat of the Umayyad Arab kingdom. That kingdom was not only little associated with Islam but was viewed by many Muslims almost as a secular, indeed as a pre-Islamic, pagan Arab state. The post-Umayyad Arab heritage had, of course, become intertwined with Islam. Thus to avoid the divisive religious issue and to capitalize on such elements of Syrian "nationalism" as existed in the Arabic heritage, modern Syrians had to go back to pre-Islamic Arabism to find a common base. That base could only be the notion of folk nationalism (*qawmiyah*) with a glorification of Arabism (*Arabiyah*).

In Iraq, for reasons quite different from those in Syria, the emphasis was also placed on Arabism. Like Egypt, Iraq had a rich and long past; unlike the Egyptians, however, the Iraqis were not so conscious of their pre-Islamic, pre-Arab past as to find in it the basis of a separatist nationalism. Like the Syrians, the Iraqis could not oppose the government, the Ottoman Empire, in the name of Islam since the Ottoman sultan was also the Muslim caliph. Unlike the Syrians and the Egyptians, however, the Iraqis had not one but two Islams: whereas the Syrians and Egyptians were almost exclusively Sunni or Orthodox Muslims, the Iraqis were divided between the Sunnis and the Shiis. Many of the Shiis were Persian or culturally oriented toward Iran and differed profoundly from the Sunni Arabs, who, in turn, differed significantly from the Sunni Kurds. Iraq also had a sizable Jewish population, some of whose leaders were active in the process of building the state—a good deal of the prosperity of the Iraqi state was due to the wisdom of a Jewish minister of finance— before the violent clash between the Arabs and Zionists after World War II. All of these factors tended, as in Syria and Lebanon, to de-emphasize religion as a basis of national identity. Consequently, as in Syria, nationalism came to have an ethnic and cultural coloration.

Arab nationalism received its first major challenge in the Middle East in Palestine; there a competing ethnic nationalism, Zionism, was the challenger. Impressed as they were by the vigor of this challenger, Arab writers, particularly of the 1930's, sought to meet the strengths of Zionism point by point in a revival of Arabism. And it was just at this time that the spread of public education, made possible in large part by the mandate system, required authentic Arabic cultural materials to form a humanities program for the increasing numbers of students. What could this program be? It could not, with Western notions of the separation of Church and State and with serious religious cleavage within the Arabic-speaking population, be Islamic. Whereas Islamic schools had taught pupils to read by reciting the Koran, public schools could not. There was no modern literature. The only acceptable answer was, therefore, pre-Islamic. This was the classical basis of the culture of all Arabic-speaking peoples of whatever religion or whatever region. Thus it was, with little thought of the political consequences, that the public school system injected into the population on a mass basis the elements of pre-Islamic, pan-Arab values as embodied in classical Arabic literature.

Meanwhile, inhabitants of the Arabian Peninsula, cut off from the disturbing intrusions of foreign thought, relatively secure from the tyranny of the Ottoman Empire and the imperialism of the European powers, and almost completely Sunni Muslim, were little concerned with what the outside world thought of this culture. They knew themselves to be tribal, Muslim Arabs and, like members of a small club, never were concerned with identifying badges.

The mandate system posed new barriers between the separate units of the Arab World. The young man of Iraq acquired English as a second language and was influenced by European formulations of ideas and information as these were filtered through English thought and institutions. The Syrian, to the contrary, viewed the world through a French window. The Egyptian either attended one of his own national universities, the first founded in the Arabic-speaking areas, or picked freely from Italian, French, English, German, or American institutions. Culturally he was apt to be influenced by France, but politically he dealt with the English. The Saudi Arabian usually went to an American school, often under the sponsorship of an American oil company, but was less motivated to learn foreign ways than his Iraqi, Syrian, or Egyptian cousin since, he discovered, his oil made foreigners willing to learn his own difficult language and to respect his customs.

Ironically, in this diversity was a force for unity. Arab students meeting in London or Paris were impressed by their foreignness from the English and the French and with their common identity as Arabs. Measured by their cultural distance from the Europeans, their differences from one another as Syrians, Iraqis, Saudis, or Egyptians paled into relative insignificance.

Meeting in Brussels in December 1938, a group of Arab stu-

dents tried to reach an agreed definition of "Arab" and "Arab
Homeland." The very cumbersomeness of their definition provides an index to the seriousness of their problem. An Arab, they
decided, is anyone "who is Arab in language, culture and *wilā'*,"
the last term being defined in a footnote as one who has "nationalist sentiments" (*ash-shu'ūr al-Qawmi*) while nationalism (*qaw
miyah*) is defined as "sensitivity to the existing necessity of lib-
erating and unifying the inhabitants of the Arab lands in view of
the unity of the homeland and language and culture and history."
Interestingly, a decade later the Syrian Baath party, in many ways
the most ideological of the Arab political movements, had not
got much further with an attempt at definition. It regarded as
Arab one who lives in an Arab country, speaks Arabic, and
believes in his connection with the Arab nation.

The desire on the part of the several Arab governments to
cater to the popular sentiment for some degree of Arab unifica-
tion, added to their determination to improve their own bargaining position, impelled the Arabs to organize the Arab League
during the later phases of World War II. The principal test of
that organization came in the Palestine conflict, and that test, as
we have seen, was a trauma for the whole Arab body politic.
The Palestine War severely challenged the previously acceptable
concept of separate states in a loose confederation; consequently,
great stress came to be placed upon the unity of the Arabs. Disunity was branded as a holdover from the bad old days of
Western colonialism.

Yet long after the departure from the Middle East of instruments of Western influence and power and even after the overthrow of the government of Nuri Said in Iraq and the withdrawal of Iraq from the Baghdad Pact, unity was still unattained.
The union of Egypt and Syria was short-lived, and its disintegration clearly had nothing to do with Western policy or
pressures.

The fact is that the "artificial" states into which the Arabs
have been divided have their separate existence enshrined in the
whole complexity of Middle Eastern life. Consequently, however

profoundly united the Arabs may feel themselves to be culturally, they have not been able to formulate even intellectually an acceptable basis of political or administrative unity.

There can be no simple answer to the question "what is an Arab?" or, as phrased in the beginning of this chapter, "is a man of Damascus more an Arab or more a Syrian?" In his political acts he shows himself to be both—and many other things, which impinge upon the precise frontiers he would put around *his* Arabness.

In this book on the Egyptian coup of 1952, *Egypt's Destiny*, Muhammad Nagib, the first president of Egypt, said, "We seized power because we could no longer endure the humiliation to which we, along with the rest of the Egyptian people, were being subjected." Another figure of the revoluion, Anwar Sadat wrote, similarly, in his *Revolt on the Nile* that "the humiliation, frustration and anger aroused by the incompetence of the men who had led Egypt to defeat instead of victory, provoked a passionate desire to overthrow a régime which had once again demonstrated its complete impotence."

Remarks of this sort filled the press in the Arab states in the aftermath of the Palestine War. It had been clear to some intellectuals since World War I that the West had not taken the Arabs seriously. Periodically—as in Egypt following the murder of Sir Lee Stack in 1923, or in Iraq in putting down an anti-British government in 1941, or in Syria in bombarding the capital city in 1925 and 1945—the new national pride of the Arabs was wounded. But it was in countless smaller ways that Westerners hurt the Arab pride the most. The facts that Egyptians were not allowed in the British sporting club in Cairo and were subjected to continuous and biting satire in cartoons, songs, and books were particularly galling.

The "quest for dignity" has, therefore, been at the heart of virtually every political movement in the area. But what gives dignity to a people? Obviously, there are many answers. No one answer is acceptable to all Arabs. But, there are three points on which there is a striking degree of agreement. One is negative and the others positive.

First, none of the modernizers of the Arab lands is prepared to accept the coherence of traditional society as the source of dignity. The "dignity" of a village elder or a Muslim shaikh or the haughty pride of a bedouin, so often admired by Western visitors, seems to the modernizer a consequence of ignorance. The attitude of the Westerner toward these people, moreover, seems to the modernizer to be compounded more of condescension than admiration. In short, the modernizers regard the "colorful bedouin" or the "quaint villager" in the same light as American Negroes regard "Uncle Toms."

Second, the Arabs must be united in order to achieve the strength and coherence which causes others to respect them. This was the lesson of the Palestine conflict. Unity is a complex quality, however obvious may be the manifestations of disunity. The failure of the union of Egypt and Syria showed just how fragile the elements of unity were. Clearly, the lack of unity was not simply a factor of foreign opposition or the lack of agreement between Arab rulers—although both are believed by Arabs to be significant—but depended in part on many other factors: economic organization, political orientation, trade, military doctrine, relations with outside powers, and so forth. It seemed manifest, after the breakup of the union of Egypt and Syria, that only when the Arabs became united in a myriad of cultural, economic, social, political, and military ways could this unity be expressed in a governmental form, and that the expression of the form would not necessarily give reality to unity. Thus, while all Arabs remain vocally committed to union, they differ on questions of the terms, the leadership, and the speed and the profundity of the measures.

Third, most if not all of the modernizers are willing to use the full apparatus of the state to carry their reforms into effect. This does not, in the Middle Eastern context, imply the same sort of ideological commitment as it would in Western Europe. It is not, as some observers aver, pragmatism—a willingness to experiment with various answers to problems—but is a commitment to use all available power. It is this which links Mehmet Ali Pasha to Gamal Abdul Nasser. On this basic point there is no significant ideological disagreement.

Why should this be so?

We in the West are so conscious of our own norms as often to seek to use these too precisely as measures for the actions of others in different cultural patterns. The split we find to be normal between Church and State, for example, we do not find in quite the same form in Arab society. Nor has there been in the political and economic spheres of life in Arab society the sharp distinction between the state and individual endeavor. It is important to be clear about this.

In the great river basin economies of the Near East, the role of the state in economic life was not only predominant but both minute and active. The state controlled water, the state set the standard in taxation and rent of land, the state decided what should be planted and when; in industry, the state owned the factories, bought the raw materials, employed the workers, set output quotas, and collected and distributed the production; in commerce, the state was often the sole merchant, monopolizing virtually all distribution of imports and exports. This was a pattern common to the ancient pharaohs, the Mamluks, and Mehmet Ali and is today the pattern adopted by "Arab socialism."

In this pattern there is no major role for the initiative of the individual, except as he operates within the state machinery, and no respect for or toleration of separate bases of power. Private property is not deeply rooted in either the Islamic or the Middle Eastern past: men have traditionally had usufruct of income producers but the state retained ownership. Land, for example, was the possession (*mulk*) of the state even though individuals either as favorites, payers of taxes, or holders of office, ex officio, had rights to some of the revenue of the land.

Property, per se, was regarded as exploitive rather than creative. It was what God did, through rain and sun, that made land yield under the hand of the peasant, himself virtually a "natural resource," rather than what a manager or investor did that gave value.

In nomadic society the land was the gift of the superhuman forces which control the fall of rain and the changes of the seasons. Herds of animals depended upon teams of men, the clans, for their guidance and protection. No man could accumulate very much because he could neither protect nor use more than a certain amount. For the individual real wealth and power came from membership in a rich and powerful "nation-state," his clan.

The peasant often had an understanding with his fellows on allocation of resources for he, like the nomad, could not exploit or profit from more than a certain amount of land and water. Even less than the nomad could he protect wealth. Consequently, in many parts of the Arab World, as in the Russian village commune, the *mir*, land was periodically reallocated. It was less in a particular plot of land than in a village community that the farmer had a share. He had, of course, no major incentive to invest in the particular plot that was his this year and might be someone else's next. When he had to invest, as on the mountain sides of Lebanon where terrace walls had to be built and maintained, property tended not to be reallocated and tenure to be clearly defined.

The landlord, similarly, could not count on possession of land for long periods. The estate which he "owned" came to him primarily in his capacity as tax collector for the government or to give him an income while he exercised an office or supplied soldiers. His relationship to the land was thus that of an exploiter rather than an investor or entrepreneur.

Finally, the merchant and manufacturer lived on the bounty and at the whim of the governor. It was essentially the control of competition, through the customs and marketing outlets, that decided success or failure of a venture. The business man, therefore, became a sort of agent of the ruler rather than an independent contributor to public prosperity.

Thus, as tolerant as Islam and pre-Islamic society have been of religious or kindred diversity, they never found congenial the notion that ownership of property or creation of wealth alone entitled men to any special toleration. Nor did they understand or condone the division between the individual and society or the individual and the state in ways familiar to us. These are factors of major importance in understanding the Arab Middle East of today.

Two other factors contribute to the emphasis on the role of the state in economic affairs. On the one hand, the modernizers in Egypt, Syria, and Iraq, particularly, came to power to speed up the modernization process. Their competitors for power were the men of the existing regimes, and these men, under the liberalizing influences of European mandate or guidance, had tried to diminish the role of the state and to foster the rise of private business initiative. Ownership of property had not yet created a vigorous, reforming "middle class," but had been adopted as a protection of privilege by the old power elite. The landlords of Iraq and Egypt and Syria had seized control of parliaments and had used their power to evade taxation and to tighten their control on the rural areas; to break their power the revolutionary regimes logically as well as sentimentally turned to programs of land distribution and sequestration of property.

Secondly, the "new men" wanted to move quickly and dramatically to catch up with the industrialized West and to solve problems of unemployment. They needed investment of a sort that private capitalists were unwilling to make. What the nation needed, in the eyes of the new men, was not necessarily, or even probably, going to have a good investment-profit ratio. What Egyptian capitalist could be Egypt's Carnegie to build the Helwan steel mill? With Iraq's oil fields already farmed out to the international consortium, the Iraq Petroleum Company, Iraq had no scope for a Rockefeller.

Moreover, if the Arabs are to catch up with the industrial areas of the world, they are going to have to make massive investments quickly in "social overhead" facilities which are traditionally, even in Western society, the domain of the state. Schools, hospitals, dams, and bridges are a felt need for the present, and in most of the Arab countries these have virtually been begun from the start in the last generation. Not only was the state, therefore, the organizer and motive force but it had to operate on a scale and in a period of time which made it preponderant: the Arab World has not had time for an Oxford, much less a Harvard or even such a new university as a Stanford, to evolve; what it needed, it needed quickly and on a huge scale.

Over the course of sixty years, for example, the Egyptian educational system has moved from no government schools to a
system which, by 1970, will enroll five million students, from the
first grade to postdoctoral work in nuclear energy. Only the state
could make such progress; in this, men as different from one
another as Lord Cromer and President Nasser have agreed.

Contributing to this emphasis on the role of the state, also,
was the other major impulse of the modern Arab scene, the need
to acquire military power. Clearly, this was a proper role for the
state. Private armies did exist in Egypt until about 1805, and, in a
sense, still today exist in Saudi Arabia, but these guards units and
"White armies" do not and cannot command the plethora of
expensive and complex equipment which distinguish modern
armies. Only a state can afford to buy and maintain a Mig-21 or a
T-54 tank. But, as Mehmet Ali realized long ago to own the
machine is very different from having power. Power comes from
control over production of the machines, the generation of economic capability to sustain them, and the training of men to use
them. Thus, the growth of military establishments has led most
of the Arab states into the myriad of associated problems of
logistics, creation of maintenance facilities, and, ultimately, the
development of factories to make all the tools of modern armies
and air forces. In Egypt this has now reached the point of developing and building rockets and jet fighter planes. These efforts
have led the state into many activities which in earlier, less complex times in the West contributed to the establishment of a
sphere of economic activity in which the state played a lesser,
more detached role. There is, therefore, no place for a Du Pont,
a Krupp, or a Nobel in the Arab World today.

On this basic point of the role of the state there is today very
little difference between any of the Arab governments, whether
monarchies or revolutionary "new men." What then are the principal points of difference?

The major differences are in the tactics to be adopted to
achieve agreed aims: the speed and control of the modernization
process and the political involvement of the individual in the
state. On these points there are profound differences of emphasis

and direction particularly between the "postrevolutionary" or "intrarevolutionary" states of Iraq, Syria, and Egypt (and Algeria in North Africa) on the one hand and on the other the more conservative, nonrevolutionary states of Lebanon, Jordan, Kuwait, and Saudi Arabia (joined by Libya, Tunisia, and Morocco in North Africa). Neither group feels safe as long as the other continues its programs and both have made strenuous efforts to persuade or force the other to adopt its model.

Involvement with outside powers likewise distinguishes the Arab states. From membership in the Baghdad Pact in the spring of 1958 Iraq swung very close to the Soviet Bloc in the spring of 1959; Saudi Arabia and Jordan depend heavily upon the West; Lebanon and Kuwait are usually able to call their own terms but each has ultimately shown to all that its security rested upon Western protectiveness. Egypt and post-Qasim Iraq have charted a more or less middle course which has been termed, by President Nasser, "positive neutralism." Essentially, this involves two elements: maintenance of political independence and extraction of all possible aid and assistance from both sides in the Cold War. Egypt, to date, has managed to get nearly $2 billion worth of arms and $2 billion worth of economic assistance from the USSR while banning the Communist party in Egypt, and while nationalizing foreign and domestically owned industry convinced the United States that it was to the American national interest to assist with a large aid program. The reasons for this willingness of outside powers to help Egypt, despite the unwillingness of the Egyptians to cater to foreign desires, are clearly not transferable to other areas and other peoples. Nevertheless the Egyptian program of neutralism has exercised a strong attraction not only in the Arab World but all over the Tropical belt of modernizing nations.

These are, obviously, tremendous areas for disagreement. They are the elements of Arab politics and interstate relations today, but as important as they are they come after a basic agreement that *the* objective is the achievement of a place of dignity for the Arabs in the world.

PART SIX THE UNITED STATES AND THE ARAB WORLD

XVII. A Decade of Discovery

Two aspects of United States relations with the Arab World call for our attention. Essentially these are merely different ways of approaching the same subject. The first is the history of the relationship and the second is a catalogue of what the United States seeks.

Unlike Latin America, Europe, and the Far East, the Middle East held little commercial or political interest for Americans in the nineteenth and early twentieth centuries. It was the missionary, for whom the Middle East was the Land of the Bible, who set the style of American involvement there. But the early missionary found its people so ignorant of their heritage and so borne down by the ills of this world as to be unwilling and unable to aspire to a higher calling. Consequently, starting in 1823, small bands of American missionaries began laying the foundations of what by the end of the century grew into a network of schools, colleges, and hospitals in Syria, Anatolia, and Egypt. In times of crisis, the Americans were sustained by British consuls. Rarely was much notice taken of them by the United States government except that it occasionally augmented its own small diplomatic corps by appointing missionaries as part-time consuls.

The United States did not declare war on the Ottoman Empire in World War I. But during the war President Wilson's declarations on self-determination led to a belief on the part of others that the United States would accept a large measure of responsibility for the achievement of a just and enduring peace in the Middle East, based upon the applications of its own domestic political ideals. There was a period in which the United States seemed to be moving in this direction. At one time she was deeply involved in the Armenian question. Suspicion of the intentions of Britain and France caused the United States government to send to the Middle East the King-Crane Commission to ascertain the desires of the native populations. At the Peace Conference an American Zionist delegation persuaded President Wilson to urge the application of the Balfour Declaration. But with the American return to isolationism, these efforts amounted to little. A bill urging an American protectorate for Armenia was killed in Congress; the report of the King-Crane Commission was probably never seen by Wilson, was not published in the United States until the end of 1922, and had no perceptible effect in the Middle East; and though the American Congress passed the first of several resolutions approving the Balfour Declaration, it was unprepared to commit the power of the United States to realize its terms.

The return to isolationalism was not, however, complete. Oil interests, already grown strong within America, were pressing for free entry into the new and promising field of the Middle East while their British, Dutch, and French competitors were anxious to keep these areas to themselves. In this case, for the first time, the American State Department took an active part in securing American access to the area. But the chief motivation behind the United States action, fear that American reserves were near exhaustion, was weakened by successive petroleum discoveries on the North American continent. Consequently, the United States government took little further part in Middle Eastern affairs until the coming of World War II.

During World War II, with the notable exceptions of stimulating Saudi Arabian oil production and establishing the Persian Gulf–Iran route to Russia, America took a decidedly secondary role in Middle Eastern activities; the area was British, and the United States was otherwise occupied. Where useful, the United

States would associate itself with Great Britain, as in the Middle East Supply Centre or in the moves to evict France from Lebanon and Syria, but the United States was, as it traditionally had been, far more concerned with other areas.

At the end of the war the United States government resisted British attempts to draw it into a responsible position in Middle Eastern politics. With its own overseas might being severely contracted, its deep sense of involvement in the Far East and Europe, and its people's desire to return to their homes to enjoy the fruits of wartime prosperity, was joined the conviction that Great Britain had both the power and the experience to handle the problems of the Middle East. Few Americans in 1945 thought otherwise. Thus, though President Truman on April 6, 1946, warned of the area's weakness and instability and its importance to the West, he was willing to work only through the United Nations, as in the Iranian dispute, or to offer mediation, as through the Anglo-American Committee of Inquiry in Palestine. He was not willing to accept direct responsibility.

A situation was being created, however, which impelled America to intervene. The Soviet Union refused to participate in the supervision of elections in war-ravaged Greece in 1946 while the Greek Communist party led the rebels in civil war. Soviet territorial demands upon Turkey in 1945 and the prolonged stay of Russian troops in Iran into 1946, emphasized as these were by events in the Balkans, convinced the American government that America must—as Britain announced in February 1947 that it could not—counter Soviet pressure. As the President said: "If Greece should fall under the control of an armed minority, the effect upon its neighbor, Turkey, would be immediate and serious. Confusion and disorder might well spread throughout the entire Middle East."

It was because of the Soviet Union, then, that America first undertook direct and large-scale responsibility for events in the eastern Mediterranean. It did so in default of Great Britain, to whom it had preferred to leave responsibility for the area. And through its European commitments in Greece, America was drawn into an involvement in the Arab World.

Despite the intensity of interest which it had evoked, the Palestine problem was long in calling forth a clear expression of official American policy. The reasons are basically three. In the first place, the Palestine problem has involved, more than any other of the overseas endeavors of the United States, an extension of domestic American politics. Both American Zionists, with well-directed, large-scale campaigns to influence the public, and American liberals, shocked and outraged by the brutality of the Nazis and fearful of future anti-Semitism in Europe and America, have taken to heart the issue of the settlement of Jews in Israel. This interest clashed with that of other groups, particularly those with ties to the Arab World. In the second place, in relation to the growing American concern with the Soviet Union, the problem of Palestine seemed to challenge no basic and vital American interest; whereas the United States government was not prepared to allow Greece or Turkey to slip into the Soviet orbit, it was prepared, within limits, to tolerate hostilities in Palestine. In the third place, the Palestine issue, as it still faces the world, may be said to have been molded at a time when the United States was not responsibly engaged in the Middle East.

When Great Britain indicated that it was unable to resolve the Palestine conflict and intended to turn it over to the United Nations, the United States played a major role in pushing through the General Assembly, in November 1947, a modification of the latest partition plan. However, the United States government was unable to lend the United Nations the force which *might* have made partition possible without war. Its military establishment was depleted and those planning American policy believed that they could not count on congressional or party support for an active policy.

Unable to move forward with any confidence, the government on March 19, 1948, suggested at the UN that action on partition be suspended and that a trusteeship be established over all Palestine to delay final settlement. When this was refused, both by the Soviet Union and by Great Britain, the United States again strongly advocated partition and recognized the State of Israel within minutes after it was proclaimed. Meanwhile, the United

States urged the creation of the UN Palestine Conciliation Commission. When the Commission was established in December 1948, the United States, in its first direct acceptance of responsibility in Palestine, agreed to serve as a member (along with France and Turkey). To support and to resettle the Arab refugees, the United States cooperated in the formation of the UN Relief for Palestine Refugees.

Outside of the United Nations, the United States joined Britain and France in issuing the May 25, 1950, Tripartite Declaration on the security of Middle Eastern frontiers, out of "the desire to promote the establishment and maintenance of peace and stability in the area and . . . unalterable opposition to the use of force or threat of force between any of the states in that area." This undertaking has remained a part of American policy for fifteen years.

Returning from the Middle East in May 1953 Secretary Dulles said he had ascertained that the Arabs were "more fearful of Zionism than of the Communists" because they thought that "the United States will back the new State of Israel in aggressive expansion." The new administration clearly perceived that this fear, and the suspicion it promoted of pro-Israeli policies, inhibited American action in the Middle East.

Israel at this point of her statehood was dependent upon American governmental and private aid. Private aid was pouring into Israel in loans and U.S. income tax–deductible gifts. In the fiscal year 1953 American aid still accounted for an estimated 35 percent of all imports into Israel. The new administration saw this factor as one of considerable leverage in influencing Israeli policy and used it.

When, in the early summer of 1953, the Israeli government began to move its offices to Jerusalem from Tel Aviv the United States government protested that this violated the 1947 UN partition resolution which, inter alia, recognized Jerusalem as an international city. Shortly thereafter, the UN Truce Supervision Organization, acting on a Syrian protest, requested that Israel not undertake a hydroelectric project on the Jordan River at Banat Yaqub, but Israel in September refused to halt work. On October

14–15 the Israeli army raided the village of Qibiya and killed fifty-three Arabs. Joined by France and Great Britain, the United States brought this issue to the Security Council, and Secretary Dulles, noting that the United States had "played an essential part in creating the State of Israel," admonished Israel that "this was clearly an occasion to invoke the concept of decent respect for the opinion of mankind as represented by the United Nations." At the same time it was announced that since September 25 the United States had been withholding an aid allocation because Israel was acting in defiance of the UN. On October 27 Israel suspended work in the demilitarized zone, and the next day Secretary Dulles recommended a grant of $26,250,000 in economic aid for that fiscal year.

Plain speaking on the Palestine issue drew hostile comments from both Israel and the Arab states. Assistant Secretary Byroade in particular was criticized for setting out American policy in 1954 in the following terms:

To the Israelis, I say that you should come to truly look upon yourselves as a Middle Eastern state and see your own future in that context rather than as a headquarters, or nucleus so to speak, or world-wide groupings of peoples or a particular religious faith who must have special rights within and obligations to the Israeli state. You should drop the attitude of a conqueror and the conviction that force and a policy of retaliatory killings is the only policy that your neighbors will understand. You should make your deeds correspond to your frequent utterances of the desire for peace.

To the Arabs I say you should accept this state of Israel as an accomplished fact. I say further that you are deliberately attempting to maintain a state of affairs delicately suspended between peace and war, while at present desiring neither. This is a most dangerous policy and one which world opinion will increasingly condemn if you continue to resist any move to obtain at least a less dangerous *modus vivendi* with your neighbor.

Border tension continued to increase with clandestine raids on the one side and on the other the announcement and fulfillment of Israel's policy of retaliation. The February 28, 1955, attack on Gaza was the high point of these clashes; for it, the Security Council censured Israel on March 29. Since the Gaza raid may be taken as the key event in the build-up to the Czech arms deal, it will be useful at this point to leave the Palestine problem to turn to a second sequence of moves, the attempt by the United States government to improve the economies of the Middle Eastern states.

The experiment with "pump priming" under the New Deal was perhaps the most extensive government economic endeavor in American experience. Moreover, wartime spending accustomed the public to large outlays by the government of funds and the use of these funds for the creation of new industries. The first major application to foreign affairs of government economic initiative was in the 1947 Marshall Plan for European Recovery. The basic ideas there were elaborated and carried a logical step forward in the famous Fourth Point of President Truman's inaugural address in 1949: "We must embark on a bold new program for making the benefits of our scientific advances and industrial progress available for the improvement and growth of underdeveloped areas . . . Our·aim should be to help the free peoples of the world, through their own efforts, to produce more food, more clothing, more materials for housing, and more mechanical power to lighten their burdens."

Already, in fact, between 1945 and 1950 Export-Import Bank loans to Middle Eastern and Asian states had totaled $266,110,000. Also the United States had already undertaken a share in the responsibility for the Palestine refugees' economic future.

The American government realized, of course, that the Arab refugees could not be permanently supported on an international dole and that a capital investment would be required if they were to be reintegrated into the economy of the Middle East. To this end, the State Department urged the UN Conciliation Commission for Palestine to send to the Middle East an economic survey mission under the leadership of Gordon R. Clapp, the chairman of the Tennessee Valley Authority. Out of the Clapp Commission report came the establishment of the UN Relief and Works Agency and, not less important, a broad scheme for the economic development of the whole area due to the recognition that "solu-

tion of the problem of poverty and unemployment of the refugees is . . . inseparable from a solution of the problem of poverty
and hunger as that already affects a large section of the population of the Middle East."

The United States government undertook to assist in both
programs. It contributed $45 million to the initial UN Relief
and Works Agency and yearly since has met over one half of
the agency's budget. The 1950 Act for International Development set aside $34.5 million for technical assistance, and the 1951
Mutual Security Appropriation Act set up a $160 million fund for
technical and economic assistance and allocated $21.5 million for
general Point IV aid. In addition the United States contributed
$12 million to the UN technical assistance program for the eight-
een months from July 1, 1950. By the end of the fiscal year 1963
the United States had advanced some $795 million in grants and
$584 million in loans for economic and technical assistance. (Dur-
ing this period, the Soviet Union gave or lent approximately $1.2
billion to the Arabs.)

In presenting the argument for the Mutual Security Program
for the fiscal year beginning July 1, 1952, the government stated
that "Political unrest and intense nationalism characterize many
of the countries in this area, and in part reflect deep-rooted social
and economic ills . . . The poverty resulting from these factors
together with a disease and illiteracy contributing to them, form
a vicious circle which we can help to break by the application of
technical skills." Given this analysis, the policy of the United
States was to "assist the people and governments of the area to
achieve not only greater military security, through the Middle
East Command and limited military assistance, but also to assist
responsible leaders in getting under way orderly reform and
development, in which the energies of the people can find constructive expansion. Our purpose is to demonstrate to these
countries, by concrete cooperative effort, that they themselves
can achieve their desires for economic and social progress as a
part of the free world. People who have evidence of this will not
turn in desperation to Communism."

Initial reception in the area was good: Israel, Libya, Egypt, Saudi Arabia, Lebanon, Jordan, and eventually Iraq entered into Point IV or subsequent aid agreements.

The change of administration brought no drastic changes in American policy; the Middle East was not mentioned in President Eisenhower's Inaugural Address in January 1953. The tide of United States involvement ebbed in the Middle East but flowed in the Far East. Under the impact of the Korean War American thinking increasingly followed military paths in its quest for security, and American funds were forthcoming mainly for military projects.

From the period following the Palestine War American aid has been used to damp down intra-area hostility and to build economies strong and progressive enough to resist the lure of Communism. American policy planners never changed in their close attention to what they regarded as the overriding goal, to counter or contain the Soviet Union. The policy of containment had been closely linked with economic aid. In the Mutual Security Program recommended to Congress by President Truman on May 24, 1951, the union of these concepts was clearly spelled out. Aid to the Middle East was necessary, said the President, because the Soviet Union was applying to the area "steady and relentless pressure" which the area was unable, alone, to withstand. "Endangered by political and economic instability, the security objective in the area must be to create stability by laying solid foundations, now, of economic progress and by establishing, now, confidence that further advances can be made." But, increasingly, after 1952 money was to be put directly into the creation of military strength rather than into programs to build economic strength. Of the $540 million proposed for 1953 for the Middle East, exclusive of economic assistance given to Greece and Turkey, $415 million was to be spent on military aid, mainly for Greece, Turkey, and Iran. Even at this date the government was clearly most concerned with the military aspects of what Secretary Dulles was later to call the "northern tier of nations," and in September and October invited Turkey and Greece to make arrangements to join in the military planning work of NATO. Both accepted and in the following September were invited to join as full members.

The rest of the Middle East presented a pact-maker's nightmare. Iran, already in serious financial troubles, was involved in the dispute which ended in the nationalization of the oil company and so in conflict with the British government. It was, therefore, a most unlikely partner in a British-led pact. Israel was an unlikely choice since its participation would automatically exclude the Arab states. The center of military strength at that time was at Suez, and in British thinking Egypt was the pivot of Middle Eastern power. Therefore, Egypt seemed to be the logical place to start. Consequently, on October 13, 1951, Great Britain, France, Turkey, and the United States invited Egypt to help found the Allied Middle East Command. If Egypt were prepared to join and to permit the use of her facilities, including the Suez base, Great Britain would agree to suppress the Anglo-Egyptian treaty of 1936 and would withdraw all British forces not assigned to the Allied Command. Britain made clear, however, that Egypt's demands on the Sudan would not be met.

Given the political climate in Egypt, neither the formula nor the time was propitious. Prime Minister Nahhas' weak government, under attack for domestic corruption, sought to protect itself with safe patriotism. It was publicly committed to the "unity of the Nile Valley" and could hardly give its domestic enemies the weapon they could have fashioned from a Wafd deal with the British. Nahhas immediately rejected the proposal and then pressed a counterattack by abrogating, unilaterally, the 1936 treaty under which British troops were in Suez. Thus, not only did the West not get a better coordinated defense arrangement, but it seriously weakened, at least de jure, its existing position.

The United States government was not prepared to give up. Despite the Egyptian rejection and Soviet protests that the United States was trying to draw the Middle East into the "aggressive Atlantic bloc," the government tried to keep the project alive until the May 1953 visit of Secretary Dulles to the Middle East.

Returning from that trip, Mr. Dulles indicated that he had come to the conclusion that it was not then feasible to attempt to create a Middle East parallel to NATO. There was, he found, "a vague desire to have a collective security system, but no such system can be imposed from without. It should be designed and grow from within out of a sense of common destiny and common danger." No two senses could be further from the thoughts—and nerves— of the Arab states. Mr. Dulles found that American fear of Communism was paralleled by Arab fear of Israel. But in Greece, Turkey, and Iran, he took hope. The implications of this finding represented less of a new departure in American policy, which had throughout the period included heavy contributions to Greece, Turkey, and Iran, than a departure from the ideal strategic model of the British, based upon Suez, a concept, incidentally, upon which the Arab League Collective Security Pact has been partly based.

Extension of the "northern tier" concept into the Baghdad Pact was a development in which the United States government took the keenest interest without playing an overt part. It was thought in Washington that however much use of the carrot and the stick were required, the states involved must pull or at least seem to pull their own loads. By late 1953 the United States had begun to plan a military assistance agreement with Pakistan which materialized in May 1954; on April 2, 1954, Turkey and Pakistan signed a military pact. When Pakistan joined the Southeast Asia Collective Defense Treaty in September, it became obvious that in the making was a belt of defense treaties from Europe to the Far East. The United States extended military assistance to Iraq in April 1954. In February 1955 Turkey and Iraq signed the Mutual Cooperation Pact which was opened to all members of the Arab League and other states concerned with peace and security in the Middle East. The United Kingdom adhered to this agreement on April 4 and terminated the Anglo-Iraqi treaty of 1930; Pakistan joined on September 23 and Iran on October 11.

Since the new pact bypassed the Arab League and was based in Baghdad whose government was hostile to President Nasser, it brought about an immediate deterioration of American relations

with those Arab states in which President Nasser had strong influence, first Syria, then Saudi Arabia, and for a time Jordan. This
development, coupled with the growing tensions along the Arab-
Israeli frontier, with the United States' unwillingness to supply
arms on terms acceptable to Egypt, and possibly with internal
pressures in the Egyptian army, caused Nasser to conclude the
arms purchase agreement with Czechoslovakia. President Nasser
announced the arrangement on September 27, and on September
28 an American emissary was sent to Cairo to reactivate and make
more acceptable the earlier American arms offer. The Egyptians
were not swayed, but the American response to the Russian move
set what President Nasser was to regard as a precedent—the key
to American motivations—when he came to negotiate aid for the
Aswan High Dam.

As the United States government saw the Czech arms deal, it
was sure to touch off an uncontrolled arms race; American arms,
it was thought, would not, even if they were given to Egypt,
since they were legally tied to specific uses. Furthermore, the
United States pointed out, it estimated that the likely terms upon
which the arms were acquired would mortgage the Egyptian
economy to the Soviet Union far into the future. Lastly, it
brought the Cold War into Arab-American relations as never before. These arguments failed to impress the Egyptian government,
which pointed out both that it had tried unsuccessfully to acquire arms from the West and that it thought the Czech deal was
a good swap for Egyptian cotton. Syria and Saudi Arabia indicated their willingness to make similar arrangements. In the
United States the fear grew that the "northern tier" had been
hurdled.

The Palestine problem remained, as it remains today, a focal
point of all the separate problems of the area and, therefore, of
American efforts to assist in the achievement of peace and stability
there. To the Council on Foreign Relations on August 26, 1955,
Secretary of State Dulles had set out one possible approach to
this complex issue. Mr. Dulles suggested that an international loan
might enable "Israel to pay the compensation which is due and

which would enable many of the refugees to find for themselves a better way of life." He further offered American assistance in determining satisfactory frontiers which the United States would then guarantee against aggression.

Eric Johnston had been appointed in 1953 as a special representative of the President to work on the problem of the Jordan River waters and was then in the midst of protracted negotiations with the Arab states and Israel. These did not produce any agreement but did lay the basis of American aid efforts. In effect, the United States indicated that it was willing to assist both the Arab states and Israel to complete projects which were in accord with the Johnston proposal; thus, though the Johnston Plan was not in principle accepted, it was in practice largely implemented.

It was not until the new administration that the next major public effort by the United States was made in the mission of Joseph E. Johnson as Special Representative of the United Nations Palestine Conciliation Commission. Johnson visited the Middle East in September 1961 and again in April and May of 1962 to attempt to find a solution to the refugee problem.

But in the Arab states there was no appreciation of Western attempts to be impartial. Egyptian anti-Western propaganda grew in bitterness, and this propaganda played an important part in creating an atmosphere in which Great Britain lost its control over the Jordan army. In other Arab states responsible political leaders privately expressed their fears that President Nasser had found his model not in Arabi Pasha but in Mehmet Ali Pasha—that his aim was not liberation of Egypt but regency over the Arabs. To the American public and Congress Nasser began to assume the shape of a villain and the possible range of State Department actions in regard to him narrowed.

Meanwhile, the Egyptian government, anxious to secure the necessary hard-currency funds to construct the Aswan High Dam, had approached the International Bank for a loan. The bank had agreed, contingent upon British and American participation to the amount of $70 million, to lend Egypt $200 million. In December the United States had been prepared to agree to this, but Egypt did not at that time accept. When the president of the International Bank went to Cairo the rumor was "leaked" that agreement with the Soviet Union, on much better terms, was near. If this was a ploy to get the same reaction as in the Czech arms deal, the ploy did not work. The grant from the Soviet Union did not, at that time at least, materialize; then, when President Nasser tried to reopen discussions with the United States by sending an ambassador to Washington to close the agreement, he met with a sharp and, in Egyptian eyes, humiliating rebuff. Secretary Dulles, having already found, but not countered, opposition to such a loan in Congress, announced on July 20 that the United States could no longer consider participating. In its statement, moreover, the United States government questioned "the ability of Egypt to devote adequate resources to assure the project's success" and also indicated its unfavorable view of the increasingly close ties between Egypt and the Soviet Union. Infuriated by the "public insult," President Nasser struck out at the only available large target, the Suez Canal. In his Alexandria speech of July 26, he announced that the Universal Suez Maritime Canal Company had been nationalized.

Reaction to nationalization of the company was swift. The foreign ministers of the United States, Great Britain, and France met in London on August 2, and the first London Conference of the "user states" was held from August 16 to 23. It was there agreed that a five-man delegation be sent to Cairo to present to President Nasser the proposals agreed to by eighteen of the users. The delegation visited Cairo from September 3 to 9 but failed to reach any agreement. The United States froze Egyptian funds in the United States, on the plea that it must be able to indemnify shippers who, while paying tolls to the Egyptian government at Suez, might also be sued for tolls by the Canal Company in Europe.

Up to this point, the reaction had been so swift as to startle the Egyptian government. But already a fatal weakness appeared in the Western position. Greece refused to attend the conference, and there was, within the conference, obvious disagreement as to the ways to negotiate a settlement and on the extent of pressure to be applied to Egypt. The attitude of Sir Anthony Eden was unmistakable, but that of Mr. Dulles was overtly, at least, imprecise. The United States would not recommend to its citizens that they continue to serve in the canal, as other Westerners resigned from their posts, but it also would not urge its shipping lines, all highly susceptible to government pressure as the recipients of its subsidies, to boycott Suez. In these circumstances President Nasser made every effort to keep the canal in operation, so as to avoid charges of obstruction or incompetence, and waited for further disagreements to turn the de facto Egyptian control into one recognized as de jure.

On the eve of his departure for the Second London Conference Secretary Dulles took what must have been read in Europe as a threatening tone toward Egypt. He went on to outline his answer to the problem, the Canal Users Association, the precise nature of which was to become the major point of discussion at the Second London Conference. And at this conference Mr. Dulles issued a statement in which the main lines of American policy are clear—but clear in their exact emphasis, it must be admitted, only in restrospect. "Now we are faced here with a problem whereby great nations are faced with a great peril. It is a peril that they could readily remedy if they resorted to the methods which were lawful before this charter was adopted. Then, we wouldn't be sitting around here—perhaps somebody else wouldn't be sitting where he is, either. But those days, we hope, are past. There has been exercised, and is being exercised, a great restraint in the face of great peril. But you cannot expect that to go on indefinitely unless those of us who appreciate the problem, who are sympathetic with it, rally our forces to try to bring about a settlement in conformity with the principles of justice and international law."

On September 21 the United States subscribed to the Co-operative Association of Suez Canal Users which later was called the Suez Canal Users Association. Five days later the United States announced that it would back the United Kingdom and France in the forthcoming United Nations debate. In his press conference on that day Secretary Dulles commented that "the decision of the United States, at least, as I put it, [is] not to shoot its way through the canal." He went on to say that "there are pressures which gradually grow up, not artificially stimulated but as quite natural and inevitable . . . But I do not believe that the situation is such now as to call for any drastic action like going to war."

In the rush of events and in the circumstances, as now known, within the British government and the French government, these remarks did rather less than clarify exactly what the United States would agree to. The position of the United States was, in fact, throughout opposed to the use of force, but each statement, such as that of Secretary Dulles on October 6, was so worded as always to hedge with a "But those who are concerned about peace ought to be equally concerned about justice."

Apparent indecision in the United States government was certainly matched by confusing moves by the British government; only the French and Israeli Governments appear, at the beginning of October, to have had clear plans. On October 10–11, when Israeli forces attacked Qalqilya, the British government reaffirmed its treaty obligations to Jordan despite the fact that Jordan was obviously and rapidly moving in the direction of closer ties with Egypt. (On October 26 a unified military command of Jordan, Egypt, and Syria was established.) The British and French governments certainly did not, however, keep the United States informed of what plans they had. Former Secretary Acheson said bluntly in 1958, in his *Power and Diplomacy*, that "the British Government did not inform ours of its plans to use force. It is fair to go further and say that, at that stage, its conduct was deceitful."

When reports of an Israeli mobilization reached President Eisenhower, he sent a personal message to Prime Minister Ben Gurion "expressing my grave concern and renewing a previous recommendation that no forcible initiative be taken which would endanger the peace." On October 28 the President again wrote to the Prime Minister. It is now known that already at that early date the United States was applying strong pressure on Israel not to act. But the Israeli army struck the next day; the following day came the Anglo-French ultimatum, and on the thirty-first, the Anglo-French invasion.

On the day of the ultimatum the United States took the issue to the Security Council (where its resolution was vetoed by Britain and France) and the President made a national radio and television address on the events in Hungary and the invasion of Egypt. In the course of his talk, Mr. Eisenhower said: "We believe these actions to have been taken in error . . . The actions taken can scarcely be reconciled with the principles and purposes of the United Nations to which we have all subscribed. And beyond this, we are forced to doubt even if resort to war will for long serve the permanent interests of the attacking nations . . . There can be no peace—without law. And there can be no law—if we were to invoke one code of international conduct for those who oppose us and another for our friends."

At the General Assembly, to which the United States had taken its vetoed resolution from the Security Council, Secretary Dulles on November 1 summed up, as perhaps no other statement he had ever made did more truly, the feelings of many Americans: "I doubt that any delegates ever spoke from this forum with as heavy a heart as I have brought here tonight. We speak on a matter of vital importance, where the United States finds itself unable to agree with three nations with whom it has ties, deep friendship, admiration, and respect, and two of whom constitute our oldest, most trusted and reliable allies."

The General Assembly adopted, 64–5, the United States resolution calling for an immediate cease-fire and withdrawal. But on November 3 this was rejected by France, Great Britain, and Israel. Negotiations were conducted by the UN Secretary General with Israel and Egypt, but both the United States and the Soviet Union took strong independent action. On November 4 the Soviet government delivered a note to the British government in which it "emphatically protests against these illegal actions by the United Kingdom and France and declares that the responsibility for all the possible consequences of those actions rests with the Governments of the United Kingdom and France." At the UN the United States supported a draft resolution introduced by Canada, Colombia, and Norway to establish the United Nations

Emergency Force. On the same day Soviet Foreign Minister Shepilov sent a note to the UN Security Council president declaring its readiness to send to Egypt "the air and naval forces necessary to defend Egypt and repulse the aggressors." Soviet Premier Bulganin wrote at the same time to President Eisenhower proposing "joint and immediate use" of the strong naval and air forces of the two powers to end the attack. In a statement from the White House, the United States immediately rejected the proposal saying that "neither Soviet nor any other military forces should now enter the Middle East area except under United Nations mandate . . . The introduction of new forces under these circumstances would violate the United Nations Charter, and it would be the duty of all United Nations members, including the United States, to oppose any such effort." The United States note went on to contrast the Soviet attitude on Egypt with the Soviet intervention in Hungary.

On October 7 Prime Minister Ben Gurion, far from indicating any fear of the Soviet attitude, which had included the withdrawing of the Soviet ambassador to Israel, spoke of the "glorious military operation . . . an unprecedented feat in Jewish history and . . . rare in the world's history." But on the same day the General Assembly once again called upon Israel to withdraw, and President Eisenhower again wrote to express his "deep concern" at the refusal of the Israeli government to withdraw its army from Egyptian territory. In reply, the following day, in the face of strong American pressure, Ben Gurion agreed to comply but indicated that the problem of the Sinai hostilities could not be separated from the context of the whole aftermath of the Palestine War. As Israel saw the steps toward peace, they must include, along with evacuation of Sinai, an end to the economic boycott of Israel, direct negotiations between Israel and the Arab states, and freedom of passage for Israeli ships through the Straits of Tiran and through Suez.

Israeli demands were regarded with sympathy in Washington since it was the opinion of the United States government that Egypt had done much to provoke the attack and that a return to the status quo ante was dangerous. Yet, the United States also was worried about the implications of a solution brought about by the use of force, for if the invasion could be reckoned a success, even indirectly, then the dangers of coups de main were certainly increased. Consequently, both in public and in private, the American government assured Israel that it would do all in its power to settle the outstanding problems of the status quo ante, but that, as Ambassador Lodge said in the General Assembly on several occasions and Secretary Dulles affirmed in dispatches to the Israeli government, the United States agreed with the Secretary General that "withdrawal is a preliminary and essential phase in a development through which a stable basis may be laid for peaceful conditions in the area."

The United States government felt, possibly, less sympathy with the British and French position, in that the actions of such close allies—particularly in the context of NATO—put the United States in a position of acute embarrassment. It was felt also that the Anglo-French invasion had at least mitigated the effects of the brutal Soviet repression of Hungary and was thus not only irresponsible but tragic. Considerable relief was felt in Washington when the last of the Anglo-French force was evacuated on December 23, the United Nations Emergency Force began their forward movement into Sinai. The last Israeli troops left Egyptian territory on March 1, 1957.

It was at this point that the United States had to try to pick up the tangled lines of its various alliances and to reassess the general context of its foreign policy. If the United States was to attempt to hold together a broad and at times mutually hostile coalition of Europe and Asia, it must have firm, clear, and definite policy assumptions and goals by which crises could be controlled. The Eisenhower Doctrine was an attempt to accomplish this purpose.

A part of the justification for the British intervention in Suez was given in Commons on December 3 by Foreign Secretary Lloyd as a response to "Soviet mischief making." "The large supply of Soviet arms to Colonel Nasser," said Mr. Lloyd, "put him very much under Soviet influence. The Baghdad Pact gave a measure of security against direct Soviet penetration from the

North, but the arming of Syria and Egypt, was no doubt intended to turn its flank also." It was this element which rapidly re-emerged from momentary eclipse in American thought as the local crisis became manageable. On January 5, at a time in which the United States was attempting at the United Nations and through direct pressure to bring about a withdrawal of Israeli forces in Egypt, President Eisenhower turned his attention back to the threat of the Soviet Union in the Middle East. In the course of his address to Congress the President said: "All this instability [in the Middle East] has been heightened and, at times, manipulated by International Communism . . . Russia's interest in the Middle East is solely that of power politics. Considering her announced purpose of Communizing the world, it is easy to understand her hope of dominating the Middle East . . . [If this came about] Western Europe would be endangered just as though there had been no Marshall Plan, no North Atlantic Treaty Organization. The free nations of Asia and Africa, too, would be placed in serious jeopardy."

The UN, said President Eisenhower, had shown its abilities when faced by nations with a decent respect for the opinions of mankind, but in Hungary the situation was otherwise. Therefore, "a greater responsibility now devolves upon the United States. We have shown, so that none can doubt, our dedication to the principle that force shall not be used internationally for any aggressive purpose and that the integrity and independence of the nations of the Middle East should be inviolate. Seldom in history has a nation's dedication to principle been tested as severely as ours during recent weeks." The President went on to propose a joint congressional-presidential declaration embodying three features: (1) provision for the United States to cooperate with nations in the area to build up their economic strength; to this end $200 million yearly for the discretionary use of the President was requested; (2) greater flexibility for the President to use funds already allocated to assist any nation or group of nations desiring military assistance and cooperation; and (3) permission to use the "armed forces of the United States to secure and protect the territorial integrity and political independence of such nations, requesting such aid, against overt armed aggression from any nation controlled by International Communism."

Congress passed the Eisenhower Doctrine as a joint resolution on March 9, 1957, and on the same day the President appointed James P. Richards, former chairman of the House Foreign Affairs Committee, as his special assistant to carry the doctrine to the Middle East. Like the doctrine itself, the mission was largely redundant since all that it gained was public endorsement by those states that had already indicated their friendly attitude toward the same policy in a former guise. But upon his return Ambassador Richards spoke glowingly on June 13 to the House Foreign Affairs Committee of his mission. "This new departure, this entirely American line of action, evoked a heart-warming trust from the nations of the area." On his trip, Mr. Richards said, he had managed to give out $120 million of which one half went for economic aid. And his optimism was echoed by other officials. Assistant Secretary Rountree, on May 16, affirmed that American policies were "definitely" achieving their goals. "International Communism," reads the first report of the Richards mission on August 5, 1957, "has been put on notice . . . and the nations of the area are encouraged to help themselves."

The "Syrian crisis" of August and September was a clear test of the assumptions underlying the new doctrine. On August 6 the Soviet government agreed to provide large amounts of economic aid to Syria; on August 15 the Syrian chief of staff was replaced by a man regarded in Washington as pro-Soviet. Then officials of the United States embassy in Damascus were expelled, and in retaliation the Syrian ambassador was asked to leave Washington. United States arms shipments were announced to Jordan (by airlift), Lebanon, Iraq, and Saudi Arabia. These moves were followed by a statement from Secretary Dulles that "Turkey now faces growing military danger from the major build-up of arms in Syria." Nowhere in the Middle East was this taken at face value. Given the facts—the Syrian army contained only about 50,000 men, mostly lacking in battle experience, whose presence on the Israeli frontier was necessary, and whose equipment was new and for which they were poorly trained; the Turkish army of half a million men (the largest field force in NATO) had been armed and trained for a decade by the United States, and, in being able to rely upon NATO guarantees, were able to deploy on the Syrian frontier—it is not surprising that many in the Middle East thought that the United States was looking for an excuse to employ the Eisenhower Doctrine.

It is now clear that the United States was not prepared to take decisive action to block the Soviet Union's offer of aid, but having given the impression that it intended to do so, had both to back down and to be damned for having opposed the good that might result from such aid. As it was, the actions of the United States government were both futile and damaging to its position.

But if the Syrian crisis of the fall showed the shortfalls of the Eisenhower Doctrine, the Lebanese crisis of the spring and summer showed its dangers. On May 8, 1958, the editor of a Beirut newspaper was shot, and this act touched off an already tense and smoldering atmosphere. The contributing causes of the tension were many and deeply rooted in history. A more recent element, of import here, was what many Lebanese regarded as an excessive identification of the government of Lebanon with United States policy to oppose President Nasser of Egypt. The Richards Mission had been interpreted in the Middle East as a demand that the Middle Eastern states leave the neutralist position, which many had found attractive, and "stand up to be counted," a posture for which the United States was prepared to pay cash. Thus, on May 10 the United States Information Service (USIS) library in Tripoli was sacked; on the twelfth Beirut was blockaded. On the fourteenth the United States said it was doubling the marine force with the Sixth Fleet; on the sixteenth announced that it would shortly send further military assistance to Lebanon; and on the seventeenth stated that it was considering sending troops to Lebanon if requested. On the eighteenth the Soviet Union accused the United States of interfering in Lebanese domestic affairs. Great Britain and the United States agreed to joint action if needed and on the twenty-fifth the Royal Air Force delivered arms to Lebanon. By June 3 the last (the fifth) USIS center was closed.

The United States, worried by reports of external espionage activity in Lebanon, maintained its offer to send troops if required but was constantly concerned about the use made of the arms it had supplied for regular military units—these were often given over to partisan forces. On July 3 a United Nations observer group reported "no evidence" of mass infiltration by non-Lebanese agents as charged by the Lebanese government. The situation remained dangerously tense and frightening. Finally, on July 15 some 5000 United States marines landed near the Beirut airport.

The precipitating cause of the American landings had nothing to do with Lebanon directly but was the reflex action following a coup d'etat in Baghdad in the early dawn of July 14.

Like the Lebanese civil war, the coup in Baghdad was the result of many factors. Important also in Iraq was the identification of the Iraqi government with the United States government to such an extent, in the opinion of a large section of the Iraqi population, that the Iraq government was not acting on Iraqi or Arab interests but on behalf of the British and American governments. The attempt to use Iraqi troops outside Iraq to stabilize the Middle Eastern situation was the event which touched off the coup.

In short, the very act of getting the governments in the Middle East to "stand up and be counted" weakened them domestically and so produced results opposite to those expected in Washington.

The coup d'etat in Baghdad clearly caught the United States as much by surprise as it did the senior officials of the Iraq government. Yet, there had been ample warnings from observers both in the United States and in England. The fact that these warnings were not heeded gives rise to the question as to whether or not the assumptions made in the Eisenhower Doctrine prevented it from comprehending Middle Eastern politics. In any event, the United States was clearly left with no reasonable move. It could not seriously maintain that the coup in Iraq was due to Communist subversion, for the Communists initially had almost no part in it. Moreover, having landed a large force in Lebanon with more troops and materials in the "pipe line," and having compromised the Lebanese government by that landing, the United States was faced with the delicate task of extricating itself gently. From the hindsight of Vietnam, we know how much harder is the withdrawal than the intervention. It is fortunate that the Lebanese gift for compromise enabled the United States gracefully, to the tune of heavy spending in the Beirut markets, to withdraw its troops.

No answer had been found to the new situation in Iraq and indeed it is possible that no meaningful action—and perhaps as important—no meaningful inaction within the framework of the Eisenhower Doctrine was possible. The United States was blamed at least as often for what others assumed it might do as for what it did. Baghdad, from being the center post of the Baghdad Pact, rapidly became one of the most anti-American cities in the Middle East, and the United States was forced passively to watch the new government make firmer and closer alliances with the Soviet Bloc. Ironically, this development frightened other Arab nationalists and so proved as awkward in Soviet-Arab politics as the Baghdad Pact had proved in American-Arab relations.

American policy in the last years of the Eisenhower administration might be summarized as embodying a willingness to assist those governments which wanted American help in their development efforts (to this end American mission furnished advice and the American government grants and loans); the firm determination to prevent "another round" in the Arab-Israeli hostilities (to this end the United States reaffirmed the tripartite guarantee of frontiers and gave arms where an imbalance appeared to threaten peace); and a desire to stay out of Arab politics as completely as American commitments and national security interests allow. But the intense preoccupation with the Middle East of the period 1955–58 faded or was eclipsed by other areas of concern from 1959–1961.

XVIII. American Policies in the 1960's

Following the death of John Foster Dulles, it was clear that the United States had been unable to enforce its wishes in the Middle East. Consequently, in the last years of the Eisenhower administration, the American government began to grope toward the re-establishment of friendly ties with the Arab countries; but the last two years of the Eisenhower period were not marked by new approaches. With the advent of the Kennedy administration in 1961, the opportunity naturally arose to reassess and rebuild.

The new administration came into office with the belief that a great deal needed to be changed in policy and personnel. In the appointment of ambassadors in various parts of the world, it sought to show its sympathy with and understanding of other peoples. The appointment of John Badeau as ambassador to Egypt was such a gesture, for he had been President of the American University of Cairo and spoke Arabic. Yet there was more symbolism than reality in the initial approaches of the new administration. The fact was that the Kennedy administration had come to power without any clearly conceived notions of foreign policy in the Middle East and, upon assuming control over the government, was unsure what policies to implement and, more pointedly, which to replace.

The new Secretary of State, Dean Rusk, had been an intimate friend and adviser of John Foster Dulles and shared with him many of the conceptions of America's role in the world arena. As this view affected the Middle East, it became clear in one of his first significant acts as Secretary of State. In April 1961, Secretary Rusk announced that the United States would continue the policies of the previous administration in regard to the CENTO alliance. To emphasize the view he took of this alliance, Rusk himself, that same month, attended the meeting of the CENTO powers. He made this move despite the belief expressed by a number of the President's advisers that the CENTO alliance was not only anachronistic and of little or no value to the United States, but that it was a positive danger in that it emphasized a military role for America in the Middle East, aligned the United States with governments of dubious popular support, and might embroil the United States militarily in a situation similar to the Vietnamese conflict in Southeast Asia.

At the time, the reaffirmation of American policy in regard to CENTO appeared relatively small, even insignificant. Some even suggested that it was not worth the gesture of "disengagement" and contended that Secretary Rusk's trip was a sop to a moribund and irrelevant institution. Moreover, the implications of the move were not fully appreciated. Indeed, the issue of whether or not America should "get out" of CENTO was being debated long after the point of decision had been passed. In foreign affairs, as the Kennedy Administration was to learn, there is a relatively short period in which a new president, without massive resistance from those whose prestige or jobs is dependent upon a continuation of policy, could impose new policies. In those critical early months, much of the energies of the new administration were devoted to what appeared to be far more pressing issues in the Caribbean, Southeast Asia, and Europe. In fact, of course, CENTO played almost no discernible role in ensuing events but it did set the stage for America's posture in the area.

Policies which were inherited from the previous administration —such as attachment to CENTO—grew out of basic military and intelligence requirements. A major inhibition to changes in these policies was the realization that the non-Middle Eastern, essentially Cold War determinants remained the same as in the previous administration. While the U-2 flights no longer set aid and political standards for American policy in Pakistan and Turkey, continuation of other intelligence and military activities and facilities closely hedged in American policy in those areas, in Iran in the East, and in Libya and Morocco in the West. These activities and the commitments on which they were based were to have profound consequences for American policy in the Arab countries.

Moreover, the Department of State—both in the person of the Secretary and the officers at the "working level"—continued to hold the view of the American long-term interests and objectives in the Middle East which underlay the policy of the previous administration. The emphasis on military overflight rights, continuation of the flow of petroleum on acceptable terms to Europe, and, above all, prevention of the real or ostensible incursion of the Soviet Union into the Mediterranean area underlay the policies of both administrations.

It was only gradually and haltingly that the United States determined to try to achieve the same basic objectives through a slight modification of program. Accentuating the trend which had become manifest during Christian Herter's tenure as Secretary of State, the American government began to emphasize the economic aspects of its aid program and to develop a gradual rapprochement with the more radical Arab countries, notably the United Arab Republic.

The theory behind American policy in this period rested on two assumptions: that it might be possible to use American aid to encourage tendencies and people, even where regimes appeared hostile, to create a situation more favorable to American interest; and that the United States could tolerate, with safety to its fundamental objectives, a high level of "static" in Arab political activity. Emphasis was to be placed, planners hoped, on a longer-term strategy. Consequently the United States government was basically undisturbed, however much it might seek to moderate them, by a succession of crises and alarms in 1961.

When the Saudi Arabian government in April 1961, asked the United States to move its military units out of the Dhahran Airfield, the United States was quick to comply; so quick, in fact, as to surprise and apparently to disappoint the Saudi Arabian government. The American government was somewhat more dis-

turbed by the claim advanced by General Qasim of Iraq in June
to hegemony over Kuwait. Since, however, Kuwait was very
much more important to the British than to the Americans, Great
Britain undertook the initial steps to preserve Kuwaiti independence. Kuwait was learning to make itself important to a
number of Arab states, so the British were able to bow out gracefully as their forces were replaced by a mixed Arab contingent.
The breakup of the United Arab Republic in late September 1961,
drew as the American response only the calm assertion that this
was an intra-Arab affair of little concern to the United States.
When the level of "static"—as when the Yemen war threatened
to spill over into Saudi Arabia—grew so high that the United
States government felt impelled to act, it made every effort to
keep its intervention to minimal levels.

The longer term strategy of the United States was based on a
growing appreciation of the fact that the Middle Eastern countries were involved in a basic social transformation and that this
transformation was as evident where regimes were conservative as
where they were radical. At the very heart of the modernization
process was the creation of new capabilities, new forms of social
organization, and "new men." Even before the nature of these
transformations was understood, the United States was committed
to their assistance through the greatly enlarged program of aid
specified in Public Law 480.

Through all of the formulations of policy ran a central theme:
that the United States should do everything in its power to accentuate those tendencies in transformation which appeared likely
to be constructive. The primary assumption behind this policy
was that to the degree that the Middle Eastern Arab countries put
their best efforts toward internal development, they would tend
to de-emphasize those policies which were born of a sense of
frustration, despair, and humiliation. The second assumption was
that as the development process picked up momentum, it would
create higher criteria of success. Central among these would be
the fulfillment of ambitions of human well-being. It was thus anticipated that an ever increasing percentage of the population
would win for itself representation in the civic culture and that

this evolution would make it less possible for governments to act arbitrarily and irresponsibly in external and internal affairs. The third assumption, a much more debatable one, was that as more and more people became aware of their improving standard of living and of a widening horizon toward the future, they would become less prone to the violent, destructive lunges which appear, retrospectively, to typify the last generation of Middle Eastern politics. In short, if not the society as a whole, at least those members of it which were politically effective would develop a stake in peaceful and constructive evolution.

Public Law 480 offered the basic instrumentality of American foreign policy. It disposed of a surplus American commodity, primarily wheat, employed American citizens to process and ship it, enriched American ship-owners who transported it, gave the United States government some apparent "leverage" in foreign policy dealings and, at the recipients' end, was used to generate local currencies which could be committed at the option of the donor. Since the expenditure of monies tied up local currencies, the law had the effect of locking the recipient economy and government into development projects. It appeared that the United States had an almost perfect instrumentality to effect its *strategy* in the Middle East. Unfortunately, what was a perfect tool of strategy was mistakenly assumed to be an adequate tool of *tactics*. Governments could be rewarded or punished in visible ways, by the application or withdrawal of P. L. 480 wheat as their actions pleased or displeased Americans. For the most part they did not respond flexibly or overtly enough. And, as we shall see, both because of the worsening relationship between the United States and the Arab countries in 1966 and the fact that wheat was no longer a surplus commodity in the United States, the P. L. 480 instrumentality was largely given up.

One aspect of the problems of the Middle East was singled out for serious if cautious attention. This was the dilemma of Palestine. In September 1961, the President determined to try a new approach by arranging for the United Nations to send Dr. Joseph Johnson, the President of the Carnegie Foundation and a former

Member of the Policy Planning Staff, to consult with the governments in the area on means to settle the refugee problem. Despite
strenuous efforts by Dr. Johnson, then and in the spring of 1962,
the mission ended in a failure. As was predicted, the refugee problem proved to be both the most complex and intractable aspect of
the Palestine issue.

Dr. Johnson's plan involved giving priority to the wishes of
the refugee, within limited areas of choice, and under the active
supervision of the United Nations. His plan called for the expression of preferences by the refugees on whether to "return" or
not, then, under United Nations auspices, for the processing of
individual refugee families through securities clearances, travel
to Israel, or payment of compensation for settlement outside of
Israel.

As Dr. Johnson pointed out, "neither the Arabs nor Israel would
get what they want. Both would have to give up something."
Israel, he pointed out, "would have to take in some refugees
she did not want, without any prior agreement on the number
(which, parenthetically but most importantly, I am convinced
would, under the procedures I propose, be very small, fewer than
one-tenth of the total of true refugees and their descendants)."
He subsequently pointed out, "if the [American] government—
which of course means the President—decides to pursue such a
course as I have proposed, it must at the same time anticipate and
be prepared to meet a well-organized, efficient, determined, persistent, pervasive effort to alter that course." The American government was not willing to make such an effort, nor did either the
Israeli government or the several Arab governments give the plan
serious consideration as the means of settling the conflict.

Of course, the policies of the United States in the Arab world
were only one part, and not necessarily the leading part, of the
bilateral and multilateral relationships that constituted the United
States' relations with the Arab world. As serious as was the failure
of the new administration to make and utilize sophisticated analy-
ses of the nature of the social transformation in the Middle East,
even more serious was the failure of the leaders of the Arab countries to recognize the true nature of the revolutionary process they

themselves had loosed upon their countries. At the heart of this failure was the incapability of the various Arab rulers, notably President Nasser of Egypt, to recognize the nature of modern power.

As we have noted above, one of the most striking characteristics of the early Egyptian modernizer and reformer, Mehmet Ali, was his perceptive analysis of power in his own time. He knew that it was not the appearance or even the implements of modernization which had made Napoleon capable of defeating France's enemies; rather, the French ability to mobilize and organize themselves to *produce* the implements and cadres of trained men set them apart from their contemporaries. In modern terms, President Nasser, during the 1960's, never appeared to be able to differentiate between the symbols and implements of modern power and the factors which made them employable. Throughout the early and middle years of the 1960's, he and other Arab leaders emphasized the accumulation of military hardware to such an extent as to preempt the skilled personnel and the production capabilities. The growth of military establishments thus tended to sap the energies and to slow down or distort the process of social change. In pursuing the mirage of Arab unity—even in far off Yemen—President Nasser resorted to violent and unsuccessful means. And these factors, the obviously aggressive bent of the government, the extremely hostile pronouncements, and the non-productive appropriation of resources, in turn, tended to operate as a brake on cooperative aspects of American foreign policy.

The Yemen revolution brought the underlying suspicion and hostility to a head. In September 1962, the aged and tyrannical Imam of Yemen died and was succeeded by the Imam Badr. Almost immediately a military revolt broke out, and the Imam's government appeared to have shattered under its impact. However, Yemen, as an isolated, tribal kingdom had virtually no central government, and the modern sector of the society numbered probably less than two hundred or three hundred men. Consequently, it appeared extremely unlikely that the so-called Republican government could survive in the face of almost inevitable tribal hostility. Thus, when the new leader, Abdullah Sallal, requested help from the Egyptians, President Nasser elected to intervene rather than see the modernizing forces crushed. Within a very short period, Egypt put 30,000 troops in Yemen. But, to the surprise of all observers, particularly the Egyptians, these troops proved insufficient to bring the fighting to an end. Indeed, their very presence may have helped to coalesce tribal opposition around the person of the deposed Imam. Yemen then entered into an almost classical military stalemate in which the Egyptians, using air-power, tanks, and other tools of modern warfare—including, on occasion, poison gas—proved unable to defeat the tribal guerrilla forces led by the Imam and assisted by technicians, money, supplies, and material from Saudi Arabia.

After three months' hesitation, the United States recognized the republican regime in December 1962, in circumstances which were rightly criticized as too late to win friends and too early to be safe. To ease the pressure on Saudi Arabia, the United States began a lengthy series of negotiations and demarches designed to effect an Egyptian troop withdrawal. The most visible aspect of this was a mission headed by Ambassador Ellsworth Bunker to Cairo and Riyadh in June and August of 1963. The efforts were ineffectual—mainly because the Egyptian withdrawal appeared certain to cause the collapse of Sallal's government—and more than 70,000 Egyptian troops were still in Yemen in 1967.

Egyptian reliance on Soviet equipment, military training, and, in certain cases, personnel in its Yemen operation, a growing rift with the United States over the Yemen policy, Iraqi and Syrian hostility to the United States, and the ever tense Arab-Israeli situation combined to offer the Soviet Union what appeared to be a tactical advantage. The Soviet Union moved to use it. Employing essentially the same tools used by the United States, the Soviet Union offered massive amounts (estimated to be on the order of $2 billion worth) of military equipment and economic assistance to the various Arab countries. While the amounts of aid appear more or less equally balanced between civilian and military, the overall effect of the Soviet aid programs was to accentuate the militarization of Arab regimes. By catering to demands for the latest and most sophisticated military equipment, the Soviet Union built still further the dream of power which was so humiliatingly shattered in June 1967. What appeared to be an almost endless stream of tanks, self-propelled guns, naval armaments, and jet aircraft poured into Iraq, Syria, and Egypt.

Moreover, in order to increase its bargaining power with the Soviet Union and to accelerate the pace of its own military development, the Egyptian government hired large numbers of extremely expensive German technicians to engage in programs to develop surface-to-surface missiles (essentially a slightly modernized version of the World War II German V-2 missile), a jet-fighter plane, and certain other weapons. The former political affiliations of the technicians, perhaps more than the apparently dangerous nature of the weapons, increased the hostility toward Nasser's regime within the United States and Europe.

In response, despite President Kennedy's strongly stated desire not to add to the burden of weapons in the Middle East but rather to enter into a method of restricting them, the United States began to give certain categories of military equipment, notably the Hawk missile, to Israel, and other items of conventional military equipment to Jordan and Saudi Arabia—two states which sought to remain outside the Egyptian-Syrian-Iraqi "radical" camp. The dynamics of the tactical policy of "balancing" the Soviet arms build-up, however important to the maintenance of peace, did encourage the militarization of these two societies and so undercut the longer-term American strategy. The policy of "balancing" was not, in any event, capable of sustaining the status quo. It merely assured that when the explosion came, it came with a bigger bang.

In the United States, growing tension with the "radical" Arab countries rapidly led to a congressional revolt against the policies of the Kennedy administration. In the debate on the Foreign Assistance Act of 1963, Congress inserted a restriction to withhold aid to any country "engaging in or preparing for aggressive military efforts" against other countries to which the United States also gave aid. President Kennedy opposed inclusion of this restriction but, after his death, it was passed by Congress. Its effect, predictably, was to diminish the already small *tactical* influence of the United States in the Arab countries. However, under the circumstances, it is more remarkable that the administration was given the latitude it had than that it was unable to sustain a sophisticated, long-range policy. In fact, the "static" in the Middle East had proven too loud.

Middle Eastern wars, like old soldiers, never die but merely fade away. One of the bitterest of recent wars in the Middle East was between the government of Iraq and its Kurdish dissident citizens. From their mountain fastnesses in northeastern Iraq, with considerable outside assistance, the Kurds waged a successful guerrilla war against an army armed with late model Soviet equipment. As in Arab wars in the classical period, the fighting in this war was sporadic, occasionally fierce, but more often lulled by negotiations and wary watching. Never really concluded, the war has passed into a phase of inactivity, with only occasional clashes. But it remains an ever present threat to the Iraq Republic.

In Yemen, by contrast, 70,000 Egyptian soldiers, also armed with late model Soviet equipment, fought a sustained, textbook, World War II-type engagement with close air support, strategic bombing, paratroop drops, and armor-formation spearhead sweeps against an elusive, tribal guerrilla force. In Yemen, as in Iraq, the war has not ended but merely petered out. Despite the Jidda Agreement of August 24, 1965, between President Nasser and King Faisal and despite the establishment of a Saudi-Egyptian Peace Commission in Sanaa, Egyptian troops remained. Upon the withdrawal of the troops in the 1967 crisis, observers predicted that the royalist-led guerrilla forces would sack the major cities. To date, this has not happened. With the major target or threat—the Egyptian army—withdrawn, both of the Yemeni "sides" appeared to have split into uncoordinated and mutually hostile clans, factions, and parties. The "war" continues but it is war in the sense of a multiparty feud. The Saudi-Royalist-Egyptian-Republican rectangle now has the appearance of a polygon.

The last major "bastion of imperialism" in the Middle East was the British-controlled area around the town of Aden in South Arabia. Rechristened the South Arabian Federation, Aden was slated for independence but only on a timetable and in ways which could hardly reassure the modernizing nationalists. The area was gerrymandered so that the relatively modern town of Aden was overawed by the backward and tribal interior. Thus, it was relatively easy for the Egyptians and their Yemen allies to touch off and sustain a guerrilla war against the British. This was to lead, ultimately in September 1967, to the withdrawal of British forces in Aden so that at the end of November 1967, when South Arabia became independent, for the first time since Napoleon's invasion of the Middle East in 1798, the Western European powers had no military bases in the area.

Ironically, as the Western withdrawal from the Arab countries was completed, the Soviet Union appeared bent on recreating a situation for itself not dissimilar from that which Secretary Dulles had aimed at in the creation of CENTO, the acquisition of military bases and the build-up of the Sixth Fleet. At the time of the war, June 1967, the Soviet Union had created the equivalent of a Sixth Fleet—a military formation which the more sophisticated military thinkers in the United States had come to realize was obsolescent if not obsolete—and acquired the sort of military facilities which had proven so expensive and of such limited value to America. Thus, as those military strategists most concerned with the Cold War had predicted, the Soviet Union did what it could to enter what had always been thought of by geopolitical planners as a "power vacuum" in the Middle East.

Two of the three great Middle Eastern themes of the 1960's—the internal social revolutionary change with its associated political turbulence, and the ebb and flow of Soviet and Western policy initiative—have been accounted for. The third major trend, intimately associated with but overshadowing these two is the buildup, culmination, and aftermath of the June 1967 war between the Arab states and Israel.

The phases of unfolding are so similar in the major international crises of the twentieth century as to suggest an almost biological pattern. Pronouncements and events, the foreplay of the crisis, create a mood of tension and excitement that impels men and nations seemingly inevitably onward toward a climax. In the growth of the passion of the crisis, strong and rational men are easily swept away by the apparent logic or even necessity of each step in a progression which they neither desire nor can control. It was fortunate that Barbara Tuchman's excellent study, *The Guns of August,* had warned the leaders of the United States of the dangers of such a flow of events and excitement before the onset of the Cuba missile week. No such warning had been read or, if read, appreciated in the Middle East. There, as we shall see, once the events of May 1967, got under way, they, much like the sequence of moves in a passionate love affair, overcame the calculating realism of statesmen and drew them inevitably toward a climactic encounter.

As in all affairs, the beginnings of the crisis were tentative, even unimpressive and fragile. In their early phases, events might have taken a different direction or might have stopped. To understand why they did not, it is as important to know the situation of the participants as it is the individual events.

There was a general propensity on the part of the Arabs and the Israelis to believe the worst about one another. The Arabs were sure that Israel, which they regarded as the last example of imperialism and knew to be a powerful, modernized Western society in their midst, would be impelled by the logic of its situation to attack them if and when it needed more land or concluded that the Arabs were gaining significantly in power. The Israelis, on their side, assumed and were repeatedly warned—by strident public statements of the Arab leaders, by the constant din of the Arab press, and by the bitter invective of the Arab radios—that they were Middle East Public Enemy Number One. At some point in the future, they were constantly told, they would be expelled from the Middle East and their state would be destroyed. The dreary encounters of forty years confirmed the beliefs and assumptions of both parties. It was a fact that the Arabs had lost few opportunities to make the life of the Israelis dangerous or uncomfortable and to arm themselves for what was anticipated to be the final showdown. Conversely, it was a fact that Israel had consorted with Great Britain and France, despite repeated denials of all three powers to attack Egypt in 1956, and based its security policy on massive retaliation and preventive war.

Thus, when in early May the Soviet, the Syrian, and other intelligence forces asserted that Israel appeared to be on the point of launching a massive raid against Syria, the Arabs were quick to credit the reports. Indeed, they had ample reason to believe that such an attack was justified in terms of Israel's stated policy of retaliation, because the Syrian government had for two years sponsored, equipped, and paid the paramilitary force of al-Fattah to raid northern Israel. Beginning in September 1966, the Israeli government continuously warned the Syrian government of retaliatory action. One of these warnings, made by Israeli Prime Minister Levi Eshkol, came on May 13, 1967, and appeared to confirm intelligence warnings that a large-scale Israeli attack was planned on Syria. The Israelis were, within bounds, not unhappy that the Arabs should believe that such an attack was likely unless Syria stopped al-Fattah. However, the pace of events rapidly got beyond that anticipated by either party.

On May 14, the United Arab Republic Chief of Staff flew to Damascus, and, on the following day, the Egyptian army, in an obvious parade of strength, began to deploy through Cairo toward the Sinai Peninsula. Up to this point, all moves by the Syrian, Israeli, and Egyptian armies may be regarded at least in part as designed for domestic consumption—to show their respective populations that each government was doing its duty in preparing to defend its people. But at this point, events began to take control of men: in every Arab city demonstrations broke out in the belief that the moment of vengeance had come. Even distant and sober Kuwait placed its forces under the nominal command of the United Arab Republic. Old enmities, even those as bitter as that between King Faisal and President Nasser, appeared submerged. By May 27, 1967, the Arab League had unanimously declared the solidarity of the Arab world with the United Arab Republic against the expected Israeli attack.

In this situation, President Nasser once again found himself catapulted into a position of leadership and the recipient of almost universal acclaim—a startling contrast to the scorn dealt him by the Syrians and Jordanians only a few weeks before. A rational approach to the situation at this point would have raised such questions as the ability of the Arabs to match the Israeli army in the field—especially with a large part of Egypt's army still in Yemen—or the ability to stop short of "the brink" if war were to be avoided. Skilled and sober planners would have urged the clear definition of goals and objectives short of the brink and of the means of avoiding miscalculation. There is evidence that some Egyptians attempted to make such calculations. However, even with the most sophisticated intelligence and national security apparatus, "brinksmanship" is a dangerous and crude game. When one confronts another "eyeball-to-eyeball", he must run the risk not only of blinking but of getting a finger in his eye. There are limits to the "game," and, the Egyptians, even if they had the will, probably lacked the skill or the power to control events in the required manner. In this circumstance, they seemed hardly to have tried.

The next logical step in the buildup of pressure against Israel was unhindered troop concentration in the Sinai Peninsula. There, the United Nations Emergency Force, UNEF, behind which President Nasser's rivals had constantly accused him of seeking shelter, patrolled the frontier and occupied Sharm ash-Shaikh at the Straits of Tiran. Between May 16 and 18, Egyptian troops forced the withdrawal of UN forces from strategic positions and requested that UN Secretary General Thant withdraw UNEF forces "as soon as possible". The Secretary General complied with the request at a speed which subsequently caused him to be criticized by Israel and the Western countries. In his defense, the Secretary General subsequently said "it is entirely unrealistic to maintain that the conflict would have been solved, or its consequences prevented, if a greater effort had been made to maintain UNEF's presence in the area against the will of the government of the United Arab Republic." Two of the seven governments supplying troops to the contingent, he pointed out, has already notified the United Nations that they were withdrawing their troops. Moreover, he stressed, that when a member government requested the withdrawal, no legal or political base remained for the continued presence of UN troops. Illustrative of this point is the fact that Israel, as late as May 18, refused to allow UNEF to be stationed on Israeli territory in a last-minute attempt to retain their peace-keeping role.

By May 23, UNEF units were withdrawn from the Straits of Tiran and this posed the ultimate question—would Egypt close the Strait to Israeli shipping, an act which Israel had clearly warned would be taken as a cause of war?

"This is the question all Arabs are asking: Will Egypt restore its batteries and guns and close its territorial waters in the Tiran Strait to the enemy? Logic, wisdom, and nationalism make it incumbent upon Egypt to do so . . . if she fails to do so what value would there be in military demonstrations?"

This was the contribution of Amman Radio in those critical days. The answer which President Nasser gave was clear:

"Under no circumstances will we allow the Israeli flag to pass through the Gulf of Aqaba. The Jews threaten war. We tell them you are welcome. We are ready for war, but under no circumstances will we abandon any of our rights. This water is ours."

In retrospect it appears clear that then the die was cast. It would have been almost impossible for Nasser to back down from his public statements although there is some reason to believe that he hoped, even at this stage, that Israel would acquiesce in the "blockade" (which, ironically, was never enforced) and would agree to submit the case to the World Court.

During these hectic days, the United States government was making intensive efforts to calm the Middle Eastern situation and to find some means of compromise. But for the strenuous urging of the United States, the Israelis probably would have attacked almost immediately. In the more public aspects of its diplomatic action, the American government issued a statement emphasizing that "the United States considers the Gulf to be an international waterway and feels that a blockade of Israeli shipping is illegal and potentially disastrous to the cause of peace." The British government took a similar public position and, presumably, as a result of British government initiatives, the Soviet Ambassador dramatically awakened President Nasser in the early hours of the morning of May 26 to deliver a Soviet demarche counseling restraint. In a curious echo from the events of 1956, the British Foreign Secretary called for a "maritime declaration" to marshal multilateral support for an end to the Gulf of Aqaba blockade.

Meanwhile, so long as President Nasser was embarked on a straight and clear anti-Israeli course, no Arab leader could gainsay him. It appeared just barely possible that the last-minute breakdown of Arab unity, the ruptured diplomatic relations between Jordan and Syria on May 23, would serve to divert the forces which had appeared so clearly on a collision course. But, dramatically, on May 30 Jordan's King Husain flew to Cairo to embrace Egypt's President and his policy. The two rulers signed a mutual defense pact and organized a defense council and joint high command under the Chief of Staff of the Egyptian armed forces. Thus, only seven days after the rupture of diplomatic relations between Jordan and Syria the outline of a unified military organization had been drafted. Within a few days, Iraq joined the new military alliance and token units of Egyptian and Iraqi forces moved into Jordan.

In almost continuous behind-the-scenes negotiations, the United States government had used intensive pressure on the Israeli government to forestall immediate military action. It had not, however, been able to devise any peaceful scheme which appeared likely to bring to a halt the Arab military preparations or to reopen the Straits of Tiran. In its last move, the American government had arranged to bring the Egyptian Vice President to Washington for urgent talks. The decision was made on Saturday, June 3, and the Egyptian Vice President was due to arrive on Wednesday, June 7, in what was an almost classic example of "too little and too late."

Two hours after dawn on Monday, June 5, fighter bombers of the Israeli Air Force caught on the ground and largely destroyed the bulk of the Egyptian Air Force.

The events of the six-day war were predicted. They are vividly described in a deluge of books, articles, and press dispatches. Briefly, the Israeli army, having acquired mastery of the air, de-

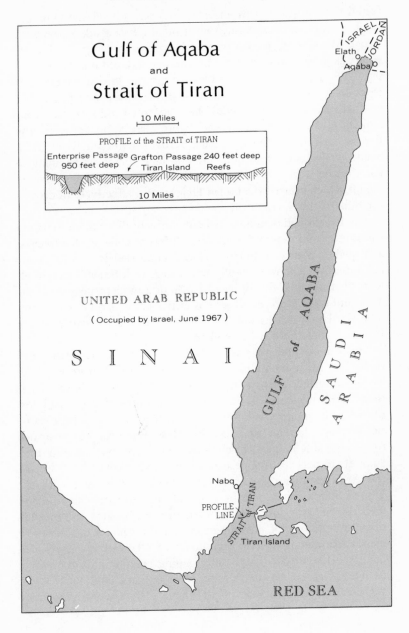

Gulf of Aqaba
and
Strait of Tiran

10 Miles

PROFILE of the STRAIT of TIRAN

Enterprise Passage Grafton Passage 240 feet deep
950 feet deep   Tiran Island   Reefs

10 Miles

ISRAEL
JORDAN
Elath
Aqaba

UNITED ARAB REPUBLIC

(Occupied by Israel, June 1967)

S I N A I

GULF of AQABA

SAUDI ARABIA

Nabq

PROFILE
LINE

STRAIT of TIRAN

Tiran Island

RED SEA

feated the Egyptian army in Sinai, in a series of classic tank and artillery duels, and established itself off the East Bank of the Suez Canal. Meanwhile, Jordan opened hostilities in and around Jerusalem, as presumably required by the five-day-old mutual defense pact. The Israeli government tried to get the Jordan government to cease fighting, offering a sort of informal separate peace; but no Jordanian government could have accepted and survived. Consequently, the Jordanian forces were driven, in some of the fiercest fighting of the war, back across the Jordan River. Iraq, Saudi Arabia, and Lebanon did not take direct or meaningful parts in the war. Lastly, Syria was the object of a furious frontal assault which cleared the Golan Heights and effectively destroyed the bulk of the Syrian army.

The Israelis had demonstrated conclusively that a modern nation can muster and deploy power on a different scale of effectiveness and quality than can underdeveloped countries. Its soldiers were not supermen but were highly motivated, well trained, and excellently led. Against this order of battle of a modern people, all the Migs and tanks were, as all serious critics knew, largely irrelevant. The six-day war was not a replay of Napoleon's Battle of the Pyramids, but there were similarities.

This war of June 1967 was extremely costly to the Arab countries. The full dimensions of the psychological damage have yet to be measured. Perhaps they will not be fully understood for many years to come. The extent of material damage and loss of life in the military is known, but the meaning behind the statistics is more difficult to assess. The loss, for example, of 25,000 to 30,000 able-bodied, disciplined, relatively well-trained men amounts to perhaps five percent of the modernized labor force of the Arab countries. In terms of a rough comparison with the United States, this would be a loss of approximately five million men. In fact, the loss may be even greater, because the proportional expenditure of skilled personnel and resources to train these men were much higher than would be a similar task in a developed country. The extent of the "mortgaging" of the Arab economies to the Soviet Union for the supply of military equipment is not yet determined, but Arab officials have privately and repeatedly indicated that the Soviet Union extracted a considerable price for the military equipment it supplied.

The third aspect of the loss was economic. A recent United Nations survey indicates that Israeli occupation of the West Bank of the Jordan River has deprived Jordan of approximately 38 percent of her productive capacity. In certain sectors the decline has been even more stunning: tourism has declined 85 percent and 80 percent of the olive crop was lost.

Lebanon, which managed to stay out of the war, has lost approximately 26 percent of its tourist revenue, and Saudi Arabia, unaffected directly, has lost 9 percent of its oil revenues and feels obliged to contribute heavily to emergency funds for Jordan and Egypt. The losses in Egypt have not yet been fully reckoned but include oil production in the Sinai Peninsula, and revenues from the Suez Canal and from the oil refineries along the Canal. The large-scale destruction of cities along the canal has made the recovery problem all the more difficult. Additional burdens have been imposed by swarms of refugees pouring into the underdeveloped and damaged Arab economies from the battle zones and occupied areas.

Collectively, these events have severely undercut development programs even in those countries not directly affected by the war. The true cost may be measured, a decade or more hence, in frustration, anxiety, violence, and perhaps in even more radical and embittered governments in the Arab countries. Overcoming these legacies may be the price of peace in the Middle East.

In a perceptive account shortly after the end of the fighting, prepared by the Institute for Strategic Studies, Michael Howard and Robert Hunter prophesied that

the Israelis may well look back with regret to the days when Israel was almost as homogeneous a Jewish state as its Zionist founders intended; for it will never be that again. Two and a half million Jews now control territory containing nearly a million and a half Arabs, and whatever settlement is made on the West Bank, Arabs are likely in future to make up at least a quarter of Israel's population. Israel will be confronted with all the problems of a multi-racial society, in which

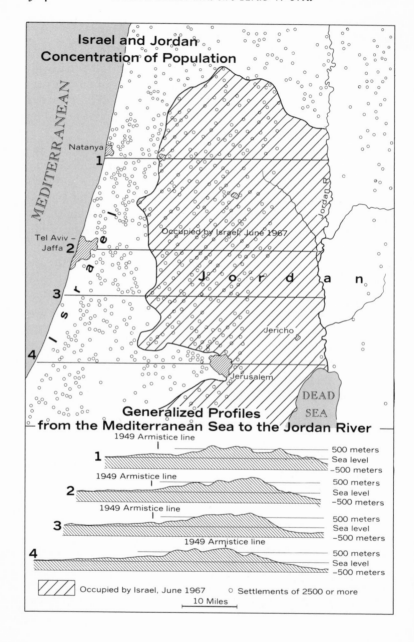

Israel and Jordan
Concentration of Population

MEDITERRANEAN

Natanya
1

Occupied by Israel, June 1967

Tel Aviv –
Jaffa **2**

Israel

Jordan

3

4

Jericho

Jerusalem

DEAD
SEA

Generalized Profiles
from the Mediterranean Sea to the Jordan River

1949 Armistice line
1
500 meters
Sea level
–500 meters

1949 Armistice line
2
500 meters
Sea level
–500 meters

1949 Armistice line
3
500 meters
Sea level
–500 meters

1949 Armistice line
4
500 meters
Sea level
–500 meters

Occupied by Israel, June 1967   ○ Settlements of 2500 or more

10 Miles

the minority group is potentially hostile and sustained by powerful consanguineous supporters beyond the frontier.

On her ability to solve this problem, Israel's future security will depend. If the Arab states have learned anything from their defeat, it should be the folly of challenging Israel to the kind of war which only fully developed societies can effectively fight ... The weapon of revolutionary peoples, as Colonel Boumedienne among others has pointed out, is revolutionary war. There was not much scope for guerrillas in the Sinai Desert; but among a large, discontented Arab population in Israel herself, who knows?

A part of the answer may be found by an almost daily scanning of the newspapers: Arab terrorists have proven effective, as have practically all terrorist movements before them, in carrying out sporadic attacks. While these attacks have as yet been mounted only on a small scale and can hardly be significant in terms of the ostensible aim of disrupting Israeli society, they have, along with past terrorist activities, produced one major result: the polarization of society. Whatever attempts the Israelis would like to make to incorporate Arabs into the Jewish state, it is likely that such events as that reported by the *New York Times* on September 4, 1968, will not allow them to do so. This instance, like dozens which have occurred before and dozens undoubtedly to occur in the future, was a bombing which caused only moderate immediate damage but a predictably ugly mob reaction. Gangs of young men from the Jewish community attacked and severely beat Israeli Arab peddlers, shopkeepers, and other innocent bystanders. The long-term reaction of the beaten and innocent bystanders will probably be one of fear, alienation, and hatred toward those who beat them. Even if they personally feel an antipathy toward those Arabs who carried out the bombing, they will be "polarized." Events, not their thoughts, will determine their relationship to their Jewish fellow citizens of Israel and fellow Arab inhabitants of Israel-occupied areas. Political terror is a standard tactic of guerrilla movements. Algeria, Cyprus, Kenya, Malaya, Angola, Mozambique, the Congo, and the Palestine Mandate bear witness to its effectiveness. The technique was employed by nationalist movements in the Balkans and elsewhere in the nineteenth century to force individuals into national categories by making them pay a price for identifying—or being identified—with their fellows. The Jews themselves used it repeatedly against Arabs and British in the 1940's. And, in all of these instances, no effective counter policy has been found.

Indeed, this issue poses the essence of guerrilla warfare. Usually misunderstood as requiring wild or inhospitable terrain, jungles or mountains, guerrilla warfare, as Mao Tse-tung correctly observed requires only people. Guerrillas, at least in the early stages of a revolutionary war, are, as Mao observed, fish in the sea of the people. Each riposte against the guerrillas themselves has the effect —at least in all known instances—of making the sea, the people, more receptive to the needs of the fish. Each confrontation makes compromise or settlement less likely. It is a tragic lesson of the inhumanity of the twentieth century nationalism that in all of the cases noted above the only effective solution appears to have been in the emigration, either enforced or voluntary, of the bulk of the "sea" or the "land"—the two rivals for occupancy of a part of the earth's surface.

To date, the Israeli ripostes have followed the familiar pattern, with retaliation on those either harboring the guerrillas or ostensibly identified with them. Bombings and shootings have been followed by the destruction of whole villages or individual houses, the hunting down of terrorists, massive reprisal raids against real or imagined safe havens, and, as noted above, the beating of otherwise innocent ethnically identifiable citizens. Large areas have been cleared. At least one village has been completely razed. The Arab population of sensitive areas has been moved and Jews have been placed in their stead. This has been most evident in the Golan Heights, Sinai, and Jerusalem.

In defiance of the United Nations Security Council resolution and despite objections by the United States, Israel has rushed completion of a project to settle what was Arab Jerusalem with Jewish inhabitants. "The object of the settlement," the Israeli Mayor was quoted as saying, in the *New York Times* of July 3, 1968, "is to insure that all of Jerusalem remains forever a part of Israel. If this city is to be our capitol, then we have to make it an integral part of our country and we need Jewish inhabitants to do that." To accomplish this purpose, the Israelis expropriated over 800 acres in the Arab sector.

The most serious obstacle faced by Israel in its attempt to neutralize the Arab community living within Israel—both those Arabs who are Israeli citizens and those living under occupation—is the fact that Israel has always proclaimed itself to be a Jewish state, a state to which Jews all over the world have a special relationship and in which Jewish immigrants can automatically become citizens, a state whose flag is the Star of David and whose national anthem is the Hatikvah. While some Arabs have managed to assimilate, including upwards of a thousand who have married Jewish women, most have the deeply held feeling reported in the Peel Commission Report in 1937: that in a Jewish state they would be little better than the Canaanites of old, "hewers of wood and bearers of water."

It is true that major efforts have been made by the Israeli government and by particular individuals within it to find methods of political compromise. The Mayor of Jerusalem has, for example, made every effort to show his desire to be regarded as the Mayor of all Jerusalem. Even General Moshe Dayan, the leading representative of the Israeli "hawks," has gone out of his way to try to build "bridges" with the Arab community.

Past experience offers us little reason to believe that these efforts will prove successful. The terrible dynamics of guerrilla warfare tend, almost inevitably, to bring out extreme positions in both the guerrillas and the security forces.

Perhaps the real question is whether Arabs make good guerrillas. Do they have the tenacity and the fortitude to match the Israelis in this endeavor? This is a question which is, of course, fraught with racial overtones. The answer is probably, "yes, sooner or later." Not only does Arab culture indicate the ability of its people to retain and direct rancor against a foe over long periods of time, but ample experience in contemporary affairs has shown us that virtually every national group, even that with a reputation as the most humble and submissive of peoples, has remarkable abilities in the field of guerrilla war, if properly motivated. It would be foolish and irresponsible to assume that the Palestinian Arabs lack the warlike qualities shown by their Algerian cousins, and by such diverse peoples as the Greeks, the Cypriots, the Angolese, the Mozambicans, the Kenyians, the Malays, the Chinese, the Philippinos, the Indians, the Kurds, the Yemenis, the Yugoslavs, the Ukrainians, the Italians, and the Congolese.

As the booklet prepared by the Institute for Strategic Studies ends, "Israel thus faces a dilemma to which her military talents provide no solution, and to which even nuclear weapons will be irrelevant. A strategically secure frontier, in the South and the East, will give her a strategically insecure population."

Throughout the Middle East crisis, the American government had organized itself to keep in the closest possible touch with events but had maintained a posture of distant reserve. This was in part enforced upon the government by the fact that the Arab states, charging that the American military units had assisted Israel in the surprise air attack of June 5, 1967, had broken diplomatic relations. More significant, however, was the belief of President Johnson and his close advisers that there was little or nothing that the United States could do under the circumstances and that it was best, perhaps, to let events in the Middle East take their course. This latter contention was based in part upon the belief that the Soviet Union had suffered a serious setback in its Middle Eastern policy because of its unwillingness to intervene on the Arab side but more significantly because Israel, having won the war, had apparently created a new Middle East which was at least not worse than the Middle East with which American policy makers had struggled unsuccessfully for twenty years.

The first major presidential intervention in the Middle East crisis came on June 19, 1967, when President Johnson enunciated five "great principles of peace in the region." These were

(1) "Every nation in the area has a fundamental right to live and to have this right respected by its neighbors."

(2) "Justice for the refugees." "There will be no peace for any party in the Middle East unless this problem is attacked with new energy by all and, certainly, primarily by those who are immediately concerned."

(3) "A third lesson from this last month is that maritime rights must be respected . . . the right of innocent maritime passage must be preserved for all nations."

(4) "Now the waste and futility of the arms race must be apparent to all the peoples of the world. And now there is another moment of choice. The United States of America, for its part, will use every resource of diplomacy and every counsel of reason and prudence to try to find a better course."

(5) "Fifth, the crisis underlines the importance of respect for political independence and territorial integrity of all the states of the area."

Desiring to keep the problems of the Middle East at arm's-length, the United States joined with other nations in a series of debates and resolutions aimed at constituting the United Nations as the focus of diplomatic activity. Finally, on November 22, 1967, the Security Council voted unanimously to adopt a British resolution aimed at bringing peace in the Middle East. After declaring that the acquisition of territory by warfare was inadmissible, the resolution set out a series of principles for the establishment of peace. Included among these were Israeli withdrawal from Arab territory, an end to the state of belligerency, respect for the integrity of each state in the area, freedom from threats or acts of violence, freedom of navigation through international waterways, and reaffirmation of the rights of refugees. The resolution required that the Secretary General designate a representative to arbitrate the dispute in the area. To this end, the Secretary General, on November 23, appointed the Swedish Ambassador to the Soviet Union, Gunnar Jarring, as the Security Council's representative. For nearly a year, as of the writing of this book, Ambassador Jarring has shuttled between the capitals of the great powers and the Arab states and Israel. The fate of his mission still hangs in the balance. Regardless, however, of the apparent success or failure of that mission it is necessary, at this time, to turn to the general principles behind a move toward peace in the Middle East and then to consider the specific determinants of a possible settlement.

XIX. National Interest

   Theorists on international affairs have commonly discussed "national" interest in terms which are abstract from the men and governments which embody them. They have thus afforded themselves a luxury beyond the reach of practitioners. Consequently, a duality of standards has arisen: those who write about and plan foreign policy establish logical systems, sometimes elaborated into "scenarios," so that international relations takes on the cold logic of a chess game. In this disembodied world, domestic politics has little or no part. The sweep of statesmanship is grand. The world is reduced to things, space, and movement. Country A—to amplify an illustration briefly stated in the preface—has an "interest" in Country B because of its location, its power, or its potential use by an enemy, its actual importance to allies, and its material attributes. Since these interests can be "quantified" or "objectified," a sort of science of international affairs could evolve: Country A could arrive at a logical, demonstrable, and measurable analysis of its interest in Country B. This could also—and independently—be ascertained by others. Thus, the real dangers of international affairs are reduced to "miscalculations" when the practitioners, by their stupidity or perverseness, fail to appreciate or to act correctly.

   As a "world view" this theoretical appreciation has had profound influence on a whole generation of statesmen, scholars, and planners. Whole echelons of the government and institutions of governmentally sponsored scholars were dedicated to its measurement and elucidation. From it, followed strategic and military theories, policies and battle plans, training programs, and even academic institutes. Americans, liking traditionally to think of themselves as pragmatic, uncommitted, "loose" in their approach to the world, were only partially aware of how massive was the hold of this new vision of the world on their thoughts and actions. In its own way, this quasi-science of international relations of the 1950's and 1960's is as unrealistic an exaggeration as was the emphasis in the 1930's and 1940's on international "understanding."

In the years before the Cold War, many believed that if the peoples of the world truly *understood* one another the fog of international hostility would lift to reveal a landscape of peaceful agreement. Because of the naïve equation of understanding with agreement, tremendous efforts were made to appreciate the psyche, the culture, the languages, the history of peoples of other lands. The role of scholars and journalists was to achieve and elucidate this understanding. This same impulse created the tremendous outpouring, in the late 1940's, of books on other countries. At its most naïve, the quest for "understanding" resulted in the view of a world populated by happy, dancing, balalaika-playing Russians and charming, poor but proud, agrarian reforming Chinese. At a more sophisticated level, it inspired the establishment of the American Foreign Policy Library, of which this book is a part, and is perhaps most clearly represented by Sumner Wells. It inspired the formation of hundreds of programs in American colleges and universities on the language and cultures of other peoples and gave birth to UNESCO as its institutional personification.

A full understanding between nations, it was believed, would prevent the outbreak of hostilities. International organizations were to perform the role of marriage counselors: they were to act as forums where nations of the world could more clearly enunciate their own goals and objectives while learning those of others, so that workable and livable compromises could evolve.

We have learned at great cost in this century that international understanding does not necessarily, perhaps not even often, constitute a sufficient basis for agreement. If the French had fully understood Germany in 1936, they undoubtedly would have moved even further away from acquiescence or agreement in German policies.

In both of these general approaches to international relations—the "scientific" and the "understanding" schools—there are important elements of truth. No intelligent policy can fail to reckon with the material facts of the world nor with the national characteristics of other peoples. But both leave out important ranges of political reality.

Today, some students of international relations have shifted the focus of their emphasis from "foreign" to "domestic" considerations. Most of the fascinating contemporary political problems are, in reality, multinational not international, domestic but domestic in a number of nations. This is another way of saying that ours is an age characterized by a high degree of politicization. International relations today cannot be carried on without regard to the prejudices, desires, fears, and impulses from the national populations. Thus, while the "interests" of nations are undoubtedly real and compelling in general, in the specific they may prove to be impossible bases for governments to act upon, or possible only if clothed in different apparel. It has been argued, for example, that if the Japanese had not attacked Pearl Harbor, it would have been virtually impossible for the American government to have led the American people to war irrespective of what factors of national interest were involved. When governments seek to thwart or neglect popular impulses—even if for higher national purposes—they often do so at the price of political suicide. Premier Mendes-France, in liquidating the disastrous Indochinese War, was undoubtedly acting in the French national interest. But he brought about the collapse of his own government. Few statesmen can or will pay this ultimate political price.

Even in totalitarian regimes, governments are subjected to political pressures and find that their field of action is confined, or, on certain issues, their hands are forced. It is worth repeating that while Egypt today probably has a national interest in making peace with Israel, one of the great imponderables of Middle Eastern politics is whether or not any Egyptian government is strong enough to be guided by a perception of this national interest, for fear of the consequences to its survival as a government. Clearly no Jordanian or Syrian government could, in current circumstances, survive as a "Vichy" regime.

How much more strong are such impulses in a democracy? The answer of course varies from one specific democracy to the next. Great Britain has had a remarkable degree of "bi-partisanship" or more strictly, non-partisanship in the foreign affairs field. By tradition, politics stops at the English Channel. Yet, even in Great Britain, the domestic political element is strong and clear in the message it conveys to the political leadership. The British adventure at Suez in 1956 was a disaster in many ways, one of the clearest of which was the failure of the government to understand its own people.

In the United States, the popular involvement in foreign affairs has always been strong. Possibly this attitude is a partial result of our background of Revolutionary War and westward expansion. In large part, no doubt, it is a result of our immigrant origins. It used to be said, for example, that the mayor of every American city had to have his own foreign policy to enlist the support of his Italian, German, Irish, and Polish constituencies. These are all, undoubtedly, real political factors. But a further factor is at least as important. It is that the American political system has developed a high susceptibility to informal political pressures. The American system is, among other things, a government of pressures continuously applied by special interest groups. These affect everything: the appointment of petty officials, the placement of vast industrial complexes, and all other facets of American life from the farm to foreign policy. Whether or not one chooses to regard them as selfish and immoral, they are a fact of American political life, and the politicians who neglect them are seldom effective.

More esoteric, but no less important a factor in the dynamics of foreign policy is intra-governmental conflict which surfaces as a struggle for power or ascendency by factors or individuals. "Hawks" and "doves"—as well as birds of other plumage—exist in all governments. And, with a rapidity that often confounds the bird watchers, the quest for power leads individual hawks to transmute themselves into doves and vice versa.

An even more subtle but no less real factor in foreign policy dynamics is the non-ideological and non-political rivalry of individuals and bureaucracies within governments. The self-interest of a president is not necessarily that of a Secretary of State, while the Secretary of State, representing an organization with its own vested interests, is often in conflict with those of his colleagues in other government departments. What is good for the Navy, whether or not it is in the national "interest", may be bad for the Air Force. It is rare indeed that a senior representative can disregard the pride and prejudice of his colleagues to follow a different drummer, even if that drummer be the President and the drum beat be national interest.

In short, while it is useful, indeed even necessary, to discuss in broad and crisp terms grand conceptions of international politics, these are merely the starting points of discussion and will be shaped, modified, and rendered effective or ineffective by other forces. The concept of national interest may be a road map, but the choice of the vehicle, the speed of the movement, the safety or danger of the drive will be dependent upon forces which they neither describe nor generate nor control.

The basic question about the United States interest in the Middle East is "why should we be interested at all?" Like all simple questions, this has extraordinarily complex and diverse answers. Underneath the various governmental syntheses of answers—in terms of national interest—are at least four reasons for the continuous American concern with the modern Middle East.

The first of these has to do with the geographical location of the Middle East, which has throughout history been called the "crossroads" of the world. The second reason results from the Middle East's reputation as a rich area. The flow of petroleum to Europe has been a critical factor in the postwar recovery of the European economy, and the dominant British and American petroleum interests along with certain governments in that area have, as a consequence, waxed rich. The third reason is the contrary of the second reason: it is because the Middle East is an extraordinarily poor area and is susceptible to great power manipulation, or apparent manipulation, to violence, and to rapid transformation in ways which appear likely to upset the vested interests of outsiders. The fourth reason is a corollary of the third: that the United States, in large part because of the Cold War, has conceived an interest in areas, whatever their resources, whatever their modes of life, which are in rapid transformation.

With these general considerations in mind, let us turn to a more specific discussion of the interests and objectives of recent American policy in the Arab countries of the Middle East.

In the first edition of this book written in 1964, and reflecting an official assessment of primary American interests in the Middle East, the following outline of basic American interests was set forth:

The first American interest—one shared with all of the states in the area—is the prevention of an outbreak of hostilities. Hostilities, with their inherent danger of escalation to area-wide or even world war are simply too dangerous for the United States passively to tolerate. The ultimate goal is of course the establishment of a just and lasting peace in the area. But as a practical matter, in the short term, a level of tension *short* of overt, large-scale hostilities can be and is tolerated.

The second objective is to prevent the areas from falling under the control of a great power hostile to the United States. The United States, does not, of course, seek such control for itself.

The third interest is in the maintenance of air and sea transit rights for the United States and her allies. The Suez Canal is one of the world's great arteries of commerce and communications, and the Arab countries are athwart the international air routes from Europe to South Asia and Africa. Closure of this area to air and sea traffic would present the United States and the Atlantic Community with serious economic and military problems which, while solvable by sea traffic diversion around the Horn of Africa and air transit through the center of Africa, would be a serious blow to Western interests.

The fourth interest is the maintenance of the flow of oil from the Middle Eastern oil fields to Western markets. United States companies that have profitable investments in Middle Eastern oil production would like to maintain their ownership of these investments; the United States government, responsive to the wishes of its citizens and corporations and aware of the value of these investments to its balance of payments, would like to maintain the present situation. However, it cannot be argued that maintenance of ownership is on the same order of priority as maintenance of the flow of oil, which is vital to the security of the European component of the Atlantic Community. Again, the flow of oil can be and, if prices rise considerably, will be replaced by oil from other sources, and ultimately in part by nuclear power. Middle Eastern oil, indeed, is a declining interest. It is not nearly so vital as it appeared to be a decade ago; a decade hence its importance may be lowered to a secondary level of American interest.

The second level of United States interests in the Middle East area is, of course, wider. It includes at least the following items. The United States would like to secure for its citizens access to Middle Eastern markets; free and safe entry into the area; progress toward the eventual solution of the Palestine problem, including settlement of the refugees now under the care of the United Nations Relief and Works Agency; a greater concentration on the problems of social growth and improvement; and a lesser concern with arms and military establishments.

The third level of United States interest includes the growth of democratic institutions, popularity of the West, and understanding and sympathy for the American way of life.

In 1968, it is obvious that we have failed to achieve or maintain any of these interests. As we have seen, hostilities did break out on a massive scale in June 1967, but in this instance, the overriding American worldwide objective of avoidance of a direct confronta-·tion with the Soviet Union was achieved by the agreement of the two super-powers and by the speed and course of events in the area itself. The second American objective, prevention of control of the area by a great power hostile to the United States, is still intact, although there can be little doubt that the rupure of diplomatic relations between the United States and the Arab countries, the increased polarization of the area along Soviet-Arab and Israeli-Western lines, and the overt Soviet entry into direct Great Power rivalry for position and base rights in the Middle East give the appearance of a relative decline in American performance. More ominously, for the long run, the peaceful and constructive development programs of the area have, in most of the Arab countries, come to a virtual standstill, while the social and political pressures, the so-called "revolution of rising expectations", continue to grow.

This suggests a period of increased turbulence, perhaps of revolutionary proportions, some years hence, when the failures of the late 1960's will be accounted for.

The third American interest has been largely lost: the Suez Canal is today closed and appears likely to remain closed for some considerable period into the future. Ironically, those primarily harmed by this closure are the Egyptians, who have lost the revenue, (although it has been temporarily made up by grants by other Arab governments) and the Mediterranean countries. Thus, while the Suez canal was previously a basic "national interest," its closing has cost us little.

The fourth interest, the flow of petroleum to Europe, has proven largely impermeable to the level of crisis so far attained.

The second and third levels of the United States interest in the Middle East, as previously defined, have undoubtedly received far larger setbacks, but they are difficult to quantify or otherwise measure and their full effect may not be visible for nearly a generation.

Quite apart from the "national interest," the United States has set for itself certain other objectives in the Middle East. The most basic of these is the continuation of the state of Israel as an independent, friendly, and viable state. The writers who continuously point to the fact that there are practically no American "national interests" in the survival of Israel along lines presently constituted have a point. They neglect, however, two facets of foreign affairs: one is the ideological commitment, however vaguely expressed, of the bulk of the American population for open, democratic societies. Thus, quite apart from other issues, it is likely that the American population would have conceived toward Israel, as it has conceived toward a number of other countries, an emotional commitment which however abstract in terms of realpolitik is quite compelling in terms of political practice.

Much more real, sustained, and influential is the projection of American identification with Israel as a sanctuary for world Jewry. This is an intense and emotionally held commitment on the part of the vast majority of the American Jewish community. However, it quite transcends the American Jewish community in political impact: American Jewry has been able to identify with the cause of Israel the overwhelming bulk of opinion in liberal American politics. The complex skein of emotions which lie beyond this political position falls outside of the purview of the present book. Suffice it to say, as a practical matter, that since 1920, when the American Congress unanimously expressed its approval of the Balfour Declaration as embodied in the proposed League of Nations mandate, American governments of both parties and American politicians aspiring to national office over the whole spectrum of American politics, have found it politically impelling that they express their support for the growth and prosperity of a Jewish national home. In the electoral campaigns of 1968, not only the two major candidates but their principal rivals vied in expressing support for Israel without serious reference to issues of national interest.

Over the years, it has been possible to plot geographically the division of emphasis on national and governmental interests in Washington. "National interest" has been the preserve of the Department of State, the Pentagon and other executive agencies, while governmental interest has been identified with the White House and the Congress. There are those who lament this bifurcation in perception of American world role. But lamentable or not, the biplay and the conflict of world view are the twin origins of American over-seas activity. Those who would neglect the one are generally regarded as mere self-serving politicians, while those who neglect the political realities of domestic American politics are apt to find themselves theorists whose works are respected but whose effect on American action is negligible.

Do American objectives clash with those of the Arabs?

The basic Arab objective as we have seen is to build a more modern, richer, healthier, stronger, independent Arab society which the world will respect. If the Arabs are to do this, they must undertake big development programs. To finance development, all of the Arab countries must rent their transport and communications facilities, sell their oil and cotton, and secure loans and aid from abroad. These can only be done in a reasonably peaceful and constructive atmosphere. Denial of the flow of oil, for example, would hurt Arab interests at least as much as American interests. Even nationalization of the oil fields might hurt Arab interests significantly since the thing which gives value to these fields in the current circumstances of a glut of oil is control of markets. The Russians, who are oil exporters, cannot buy this oil. Denial of air and sea routes would, similarly, lose the Arabs significant income not only from the facilities themselves but from the growing tourist trade.

As we have seen, in the outbreak of hostilities in June 1967, and in the ensuing pulsations between hot and cold war, Arab interests have been hurt far more than American. Development programs have come largely to a standstill, Arab pride has been even more humiliated, and the finances of the Arab countries have been strained virtually to the breaking point. The Soviet Union, willing to supply large amounts of manufacturers' credits for industrial and military equipment, has proven itself unable or unwilling to equate its interests with those of the Arabs so that in the showdown of June 1967, the Arabs were left to take the full brunt of the Israeli attack, essentially unaided by the Soviet Union. Lastly, in an outbreak of hostilities or in the increased diversion of resources to unproductive military expenditure, Arab interests will surely be hurt far more than American. Thus, while the United States government and the several Arab governments will not always put the same priority on each of these various interests, or agree on means to safeguard or enhance them, at base the major interests of both sides coincide to an impressive degree.

However, in the specific instance the Arab governments have been unwilling or unable to act upon an "objective", or nonpolitical, appreciation of their national interest. As we have seen above, the Middle Eastern Arab governments, immediately after their assumption of national sovereignty, accepted as the first challenge to their effectiveness as national organizations, the "challenge" of Zionism. The startling failure of their attempt to prevent the creation of Israel in 1948–1949 led to a deeper and stronger commitment to that end, at least in public pronouncement, by each Arab government. Even those governments which never attempted or planned to attempt serious opposition to the growth and prosperity of Israel loudly and repeatedly proclaimed their opposition to it. In Lebanon, this was taken as useful hyperbole but in Egypt it became a standard by which outsiders and potential rulers judged insiders and actual rules. Thus, it was a potent mainspring of the 1952 coup d'etat which brought, ultimately, Gamal Abdul Nasser to power.

Meanwhile, in Jordan the attempt of the then ruler, King Abdullah, to act in what he perceived to be the national interest by effecting a compromise with Israel led to his assassination. The message in the assassination was read loud and clear by other Arab governments and one after another each sought to proclaim in ever more strident terms, his commitment to the grand national crusade. In Egypt, at first, this was of far less consequence than in Syria or Jordan. It was not until the outbreak in 1955 of the serious frontier trouble between Israel and Egypt and, particularly, the massive Israeli raid against Gaza in April of that year that the Egyptian government began to build a political constituency for an anti-Israeli program among the Egyptian people. In the first instance, the build-up of the Suez crisis was not so much anti-Israeli as anti-British. These events, the French invasion, the British invasion, and the Israeli invasion created a synthesis in the Egyptian popular mind: the equation of the colonialism of the French in Algeria, the imperialism of the British in Egypt, and the aggressiveness of the Israelis with the encouragement of the great European powers. The apparent "victory" of Nasser in Suez allowed him to turn his attention to interior social and economic reform but also encouraged him to emphasize military preparedness and anti-Israeli policies. As we shall see in the concluding chapter, it is the contention of the author that Nasser was the only Arab ruler capable in this period of making peace. However, his willingness and ability to do so declined progressively as the sentiment for pan-Arabism and anti-Israeli feelings grew among his population. Thus, the clash of differing governmental interests has drowned out the appreciation of basic national interests shared by the United States, the Arab countries and, in many areas, Israel.

Is the American position now better or worse than formerly? As we have seen, the United States had no real position in the Middle East, as a great power, prior to 1947. America, as the land of the movie cowboy, a place of universal wealth, the source of the colleges, hospitals, and relief efforts that dot the Middle Eastern scene, and the author of ringing pronouncements on the imperative of freedom and morality, occupied a warm spot in the hearts of the Arabs. But it is only realistic to say that the golden respect for America was little tarnished by political contact. When, after 1947, as a world power the United States came to act on the Middle Eastern stage, it naturally disappointed many who had never considered it as a world power.

Since 1947 United States diplomatic relations have undergone a series of changes. America came under severe Arab criticism for her stand on the Palestine partition issue at the United Nations, but efforts to assist the Arab countries were appreciated and welcomed in some. Following the 1952 coup d'etat in Egypt the United States enjoyed very close relations with the new government and, at the same time, with Nuri Said's government in Iraq, as well as with the Saudi Arabian, Lebanese, and Jordanian governments. But then efforts to induce the Egyptians to join the Middle East Defense Organization failed, and the United States shifted her emphasis to Iraq which joined in the formation of the Baghdad Pact. Nasser regarded this as an attempt to split the Arabs and as a blow to his leadership, so that American relations with those Arabs under Nasser's influence suffered. The United States regarded it as a serious blow to her position in the Middle East when the Egyptians turned to the Soviet Bloc for arms. American refusal to assist in the construction of the Aswan High Dam and Egyptian nationalization of the Suez Canal were the most publicized episodes of this period. There were many others. But this period was ended when the United States acted to halt the invasion of Egypt by Great Britain, France, and Israel in 1956.

The era of the Eisenhower Doctrine was one of cool relations with Egypt and those countries influenced by it and increasingly close ties with Iraq. Then, following the coup d'etat in Baghdad in July 1958, the United States dramatically placed troops in

Lebanon and showed that she had the determination and ability to intervene decisively when she thought American interests were in grave jeopardy. The period of 1959–61 was one of relative inactivity in which the United States took no major initiatives and the Middle East was relatively calm.

Following the advent of the new administration in 1961 the United States reassessed its policies in the Middle East and decided to assist more actively in the growth process of the several countries and, diplomatically, to establish much closer contacts with the Arab governments; in some instances, notably in Yemen, the United States attempted to work out a formula to end inter-Arab quarrels and has tried to foster a slow-down of the arms race between the Arab states and Israel.

By 1964, as we have seen in the preceding chapter, the vigor and sense of purpose in the new approach to Middle Eastern affairs had largely run out. This was true not only because it was not sufficiently well understood in the United States, but because it was not sufficiently accepted in the Arab countries themselves. The United States misjudged how difficult the job of assisting in the development process was (this was not only true of the Middle Eastern area but of Latin America and South and Southeast Asia as well) but the Arab countries misjudged many aspects of the force of direction of their own change and of the scale of investment necessary to achieve their national objectives. Many governments, notably that of President Nasser in Egypt, failed to distinguish between the apparent and the real. They judged themselves to be far stronger, more modern, and more determined than their nations proved to be. Placing their emphasis on the ephemeral and short range trappings of national power, on tanks, jet fighter planes, and radio stations, they failed to meet their own goals in terms of schools, farms, and factories. Thus, in important instances, they thwarted the very processes of assistance coming to them from the outside.

It is in this sphere, and not alone in the Middle East, that the real price of the Cold War was paid: the poorer developing nations have sought for themselves the trappings of great power and, more significantly, have learned from the great powers the conspiratorial notion of history. It is this which encouraged the Arab governments to shift their emphasis from long-term development and peaceful modernization toward an emphasis on military power and subversion. For their own purposes both the United States and the Soviet Union encouraged aspects of this shift. But as the total picture became evident, the ability of American government to pursue a long-term strategy to foster the growth of a peacefully growing and evolving Middle Eastern society declined. How could the American government justify to its people the expenditure of money for wheat in an Egypt whose government noisily announced its intention of destroying Israel, of subverting its more conservative Arab neighbors, and of facilitating the ambitions of the Soviet Union? The fact was here that the arguments behind the American policy were too abstract and too sophisticated to be politically viable. Consequently, the policy of seeking to accentuate those aspects of Arab political, social, and economic development which led toward peaceful evolution were first muted and finally abandoned.

The events of 1967 proved that the Arab governments are still far from being able to act, in pursuit of their most important objective, upon the most sophisticated interpretation of their information. But there is ample evidence that they were well informed. However, as indicated in the previous chapter, it is evident that they were impelled forward on a self-destructive course by events and emotions over which they lost control. These emotions are no less strong today and it appears obvious that there is in the making a public mood, which, if properly ideologized and directed, could convert a significant proportion of the Arabs into proto-revolutionary war societies. In this sense, when the interests of both sides clash, they are in far greater danger today than in any time in the past. Where they coincide, it may be still extraordinarily difficult for governments to act in a perception of true national interest.

It is clearly true today that the Middle East is no longer a Western preserve in which Western countries can set the rules of the game. The Soviet Union offers alternatives which, short of war, invasion, and occupation, cannot now be denied to the Arabs.

Relations are thus more complex and fluid than were those of Britain and France to the Arab World in the 1920's and 1930's. Relative to the Soviet Union, however, the Western position in the Middle East is still strong. As the Arab governments have become more sophisticated and have witnessed naked and ruthless power grabs by the local supporters of the Soviet Union, such as the Iraqi Communists in 1959, they have taken steps, often with Western help, to guard against Communist subversion.

The danger here is that in their fear of Israel, their inability successfully to accomplish their national objectives and the internal failure of their development programs, the Arab governments may find an increased reliance upon the Soviet Union, even to a degree unacceptable to the United States, to be the lesser evil of their alternatives. Left to themselves, the Arabs would find in their nationalism a force antithetical to Soviet inspired or controlled Communism. However, the Arabs are not today and probably will not be in the coming years left to themselves. They find significant proportions of their territory under Israeli occupation and live with the realization that Israeli armies are within a short taxi ride—with virtually nothing to stop them—of Cairo, Amman, Damascus, and Beirut. However we outsiders view it, most Arabs will see this as the immediate danger and will act accordingly.

And, finally, as they have set about reorganizing their economies the Arabs have picked organizational methods which are often not to American taste. As we have seen, the role of the state is large and the sanctity of private property is not deeply rooted in Arab culture or in Middle Eastern history. Popular involvement in government, similarly, is far from the Western conception of democracy. Yet, as a growing proportion of the Arabs become more educated, healthier, and better fed, they can afford to aspire to the "good life." Even today, it is evident that public pressures are exercising a greater influence on governments. As the "new men" of today's schools come forward, power will be diffused amongst them, and some acceptable version of popular participation in governments, within an Arab culture context, will evolve.

The danger is that this cultural context may be adversely conditioned by hostility toward Israel. If this hostility grows in bitterness among the Arab societies, and governments fail either to satisfy or suppress it, there is a strong possibility that the eastern Arab societies will be politicized and revolutionized along the Algerian if not along the Vietnamese or Cuban models.

It must be admitted that the future relationship between the United States and the Arab world or between the Arabs and the rest of the world is very much more in question today than it has been at any time in the recent past. The dynamic of Middle Eastern events would appear to emphasize an evolution toward increased guerrilla warfare with the social homogenation familiar in this process. If this is to be prevented, a conscious effort will be required on the part of the Arabs, the Israelis, and, to a lesser degree, the outside powers. What will make it very much more difficult than before is the obvious disparity between national interest and the interests of governments and political leaders. It will take extraordinary acts of statesmanship to avoid the short course to war.

American interests are always in danger and require vigil, care, energy, commitment, and sophistication on the part of the government and the public to be safe-guarded. No one else has evolved a policy which will be self-protecting and self-correcting, and Americans are unlikely to do so. Policies depend upon people, and must be constantly reassessed. Failure to do so results in a policy out of touch with the real—and changing—world. Following such policies can result in losing genuine interests in pursuit of mirages or secondary objectives. Americans have a right to demand the best from their policy-makers but will get it only in proportion to a national standard of commitment and knowledge.

Tensions between the Arab states and Israel, setbacks in development programs, and the tragic cost of the war in June 1967, have led to further disruptions in Arab society, chaos and despair. In the tremendous dislocation which has been the aftermath of the war, small problems can quickly grow into big crises. It seems at least possible, if not likely, that there will be an accentuation of violence along the Israeli frontiers amongst the Arab population resident in Israel. This, undoubtedly, will lead to frequent and repeated clashes between the Arab governments and Israel.

Americans cannot afford to settle for national policies or for practitioners of policies which aim merely at muddling through. It is possible to project from what is now known of the factors in the Middle East a very much more violent future, a future fraught with potentialities far beyond those of the unpleasant present. A policy which blinds our eyes to the future and seeks merely to get through the present is a recipe for disaster.

How can the United States accomplish its objectives? Actions —and inactions—available to the United States as a great power cover a tremendous range from the supplying of technical advice on planting wheat to interdiction of an invasion by nuclear weapons, from the granting of massive economic assistance to economic boycott, from acquiescence to ultimatum. The tools in the kit are impressive, but they can turn out a product only as good as the skill and discrimination of those who use them. It is the carpenter, not the hammer and saw, that builds the house. But the "house" in international relations is a community project—the Americans, the Arabs, and others will build it—and, consequently, both the design and the materials that go into it must be reasonably acceptable to all. Moreover, over the long run the instruments of any foreign policy must be respected and accepted by those with whom the nation deals in order for the policy to be effective.

A wise policy will, therefore, attempt to accentuate areas of agreement and narrow areas of disagreement, using such instruments as are appropriate to each task.

The principal contingencies against which the United States must guard and the principal opportunities which lie ahead are two sides of the same coin.

The principal danger now discernible is a renewed outbreak of the Arab-Israel war, and the principal opportunity is a settlement of the Arab-Israel hostility.

Failure of development programs and growing population pressure could result in the growth of more radical governments, desperately seeking short cuts and trying to suppress internal urges for a better life. In this circumstance American interests would be threatened. Conversely, with reasonable success development programs will contain pressures for violent and extreme solutions, will achieve a satisfactory rate of improvement in the life of the people, and, gradually, will so broaden the base of public participation as to evolve something like representative government in societies having a vested interest in peace.

XX. Epilogue: Toward an Uncertain Future

A familiar metaphor in Arabic poetry pictures the camel-borne traveler attempting to make his way across a desert as devoid of guidance as "the back of a shield." Before him loom terrors both real and psychological—murderous blasts of heat and sand and the psychological bewilderment brought on by fear of the unknown. But at the end of his course is an upland meadow with cool shade and plentiful water.

Americans, Arabs, Israelis, and others, as travelers on the Middle Eastern scene, are similarly beset by real and imagined dangers in our quest for a better way of life with peace in the Middle East. However, as seen in the foregoing chapters, our way is not without its markers. In these concluding pages Americans face three questions: Where would we like to go? What are the factors that will condition whether or not we get there? And, what is the best route of march?

The goal of Arabs, Israelis, and Americans is basic, and in its general sense, shared; all would like to see an independent, peaceful, and increasingly prosperous Middle East. The Israelis see this goal, obviously, as the context in which their state can exist. The Arabs, perhaps less obviously to outsiders, see it as a part of their drive to achieve a sense of dignity.

In their assessment of their respective capabilities to achieve desired nuances within this basic goal, the Arabs and Israelis must face stubborn facts. Israel must exist in the Middle East and, therefore, over the longer run, must find a way of accommodating herself to the political culture of that area or of so altering the area as to make the Israeli political culture acceptable to it. The Arabs, at great pain and cost, have learned that they cannot now and are unlikely in the near future to be able to expel Israel from the Middle East. Their attempts to do so have deformed their drive toward modernization and betterment of the welfare of their own peoples and have held them up to ridicule throughout the world. Thus, they face the choice between development and growth on the one hand and, on the other hand, self-destructive military confrontations with a country that promises to remain stronger and more advanced than their own. The unpleasant history of the past twenty years may be summarized, simply, as the inability of the Arabs and Israelis to accommodate themselves to these basic facts: the Israelis can defeat the Arabs in the field but cannot achieve peace; the Arabs can prevent the coming of peace but cannot expel Israel.

As this is being written (October 1968), the fate of Ambassador Jarring's mission still hangs in balance. Three new peace plans—by the Soviet Union, Israel, and Egypt—have been added to the dozens of formal and informal plans of the past. There are more "signals"—more contrary indications of intent to go to war or to make peace—than at any time in Middle Eastern history. What the future will hold, of course, is now impossible to predict, but a few general considerations can be set out which may be of use as guides toward the future.

The basic elements in the dispute between the Arabs and the Israelis arise from a clash of nationalisms. Nationalism came late to both the Arabs and the Jews. In both cases, it resulted from the failure of their attempts at assimilation.

For the Jews it was the failure of a half-century of moves to achieve full membership in West European society. On their side, the Arabs were the last of the peoples of the Ottoman Empire to achieve the self-realization of their distinction as a national community. And this came about only after the ruling Turks rebuffed various attempts by the Arabs to move toward political partnership.

The effects of the "pre-national" experience on the two communities were markedly different.

From the European experience, the Jews had a heightened sense of separateness and, having been persecuted, indeed decimated, they brought to Israel not only a sense of national identity but also a sense of national desperation. In their almost religious commitment to the new state, the Zionists shared a basic belief that if Israel failed, the whole of world Jewry would be in mortal danger. This gave to Zionism a transcendent justification and sense of urgency, while the nineteenth-century European experience enabled the Jewish community to achieve an extraordinary level of capability in virtually every field of modern learning. The sense of purpose, the sense of moral rightness, the sense of urgency, the unity of goal, and the basic capability are among the most striking features of Israel today.

As we have seen, their experiences mark the Arabs quite differently. Although they were rejected in their attempt at partnership within the Ottoman Empire, the Arabs were not dispossessed from their land. Their first sense of national purpose was negative: directed at expelling foreign rule. Heirs to a rich cultural tradition, they were insulated by this tradition from a rapid absorption of the ideas and ways of Europe. Marked by their Middle Eastern experience, they had missed the main impulses of modern history—the Renaissance, the Enlightenment, and the Industrial Revolution. Heirs to centuries of neglect, they had sunk to an appallingly low level of health, education, wealth, and political participation. Blindness, poverty, illiteracy, tuberculosis, bilharziasis, cholera, and the plague were the calvary of their apocalypse. In short, they had all of the problems we summarize as underdevelopment.

Ottoman rule was replaced by British and French rule. The Arabs, as an Asian people, were relegated by their European conquerors to a subject status. Taunted by the notion that they were merely, in the words of the Balfour Declaration, the "existing non-Jewish communities in Palestine," infuriated by their own incapacity to act and their inability to coalesce into an effective national unit in the face of the European or Zionist challenge, and ever trying to prove that theirs was not the "empty land" depicted in early Zionist literature, the Arabs retreated from reality into a world of myth, posture, and pretense.

It is difficult for Westerners to recognize the deep well-springs of often self-destructive energies that result from humiliation and a sense of inferiority. The Egyptian, as perhaps the most extreme example, feels as acutely the European taunt summed up in the word "wog" as the American Negro does the term "nigger."

A single action, even a relatively simple and straightforward one, is so differently viewed by the participants that it becomes not a single act but rather a multiplicity of acts, impelled by a bewildering variety of motives and causing not a single effect but a multiplicity of effects.

The Arabs have ever seen in the creation of Israel an attempt to extend the period of Western domination of the Middle East. They regarded the Western unwillingness to take seriously the Arab claims—or to honor pledges repeatedly made—as an indication of the basic contempt of the West for the benighted peoples of Africa and Asia. Ineffective in dealing in the forums of the West, feeling themselves wronged, and constantly looking back to argue about past actions, the more cynical of the Arabs inveigh against the West as immoral and shamelessly hypocritical, as Perfidious Albion writ large.

Our approach to the problems of Arab-Israeli peace is colored by the attitudes we transpose from our own experiences in the West.

Those toward the Israelis are the more simple and obvious. One of these is the transferred guilt of anti-Semitism. Although the initial shock of horror at the bestiality of Nazism is distant in memory for many of us, its impact on Western attitudes toward the foundation of the state of Israel was obviously immense. Reeling before the enormity of the crime of anti-Semitism in the Western world, Westerners of good will sought the means of atonement. Many saw in Palestine a solution—at least in atonement. At the same time, a painful fact is that others saw in Israel a new Liberia, a sort of nationwide ghetto to which Jews, unwelcome in many parts of the West, could be relegated.

Whichever way Westerners approached the question of Jews in the West and Israel in the Middle East, they were apt to see the Jews as European, intelligent, vigorous, and clean. In contrast, the Arabs are seen as an alien folk, incomprehensible, devious, caricatures of Western civilization at best, primitive or even savage at worst. Like the American Negroes, the Arabs are caught in the midst of revolution, are heirs to a miserable past and are both the victims and perpetrators of hatred, insecurity, and frustration. In our inattention to and ignorance of the causes of the unpleasant present, we are revolted by the spectacle, amused by the incongruities or incoherencies of vain boastfulness and colossal ineptitude. Thus, we tend to transpose feelings we hold toward American Negroes to the Arabs and attitudes we hold toward American and European Jews to the Israelis.

One of the basic notions of imperialism has been that the unenlightened peoples of the world, by their incapability of using the resources of the lands on which they live, have forfeited at least some of their rights over the lands. The Arabs failed to exploit Palestine fully whereas the Zionists have made the desert bloom. Consequently, the Zionists have created for themselves a higher claim to the land.

A more politically oriented version of the same basic notion is that because Arabs were largely illiterate, inarticulate, and often grievously exploited by their own gentry, they had no legitimate spokesman, indeed, no real public opinion. Those "leaders" who arrogated to themselves the role of spokesmen were, like the exponents of black power in the America of a later day, merely trouble-makers and agitators without whose baneful intervention there would have been no disturbance.

But more fundamental, indeed cutting to the nerve of white European and American racial concepts, is the evaluation, constantly recurring in the press, in literature and in political jokes, that beneath the thin veneer of his borrowed clothing, the Arab is not truly a civilized man but merely a savage or an animal.

An example of this kind of judgment is seen in the story, widely circulated after the recent fighting, that the Arab soldiers, in order to run away more rapidly, took off their shoes in the Sinai Desert. Of course, no national human being would elect to walk barefoot on scorching sand with mid-day temperatures of 130°. The facts —that captured Arab forces were immobilized by having their equipment and uniforms removed—are less significant than our receptivity and interpretation of the story. Echoing dimly in the subconscious of many of us must have been a description often made of the Southern Negro. Curiously, he too was always said to "take off his shoes to run away faster." Behind both statements is the obvious implication that this creature is not a man but a monkey.

As we all know from our domestic experience, such attitudes and predictions are often self-confirming. The more successful of the Arab politicians have learned our vices but failed to comprehend our virtues. Avid students of our techniques of espionage, for example, they have devoted themselves wholeheartedly to its practice. Having seen that the major actors on the world scene believe in conspiratorial notions of history, they have spent inordinate sums of money subverting one another. Having witnessed propaganda as a major British, French, Russian, and American activity, they have adopted propaganda as a major tool of statecraft.

Lest any of us assume a position of moral grandeur, we should all know that there is hardly a "dirty trick" in the grab bag of covert activity that the West has not exploited to the full in the Middle East. In this school, the Arabs were apt and willing students but hardly the teachers.

Even in their most constructive efforts, the Arabs have often sought out merely the gimmicks of Western activity since they have been unable to duplicate the context of Western development. They have desperately sought shortcuts when confronted with the enormity of the problems of modernization. Unable to convert a backward peasantry into modern farmers quickly enough, they sought, in the high dam or in the use of fertilizer, a modern agriculture. Unable to convert peasants rapidly enough into an industrial society, they sought, in supersonic jet fighter planes and late model tanks, a modern army. And, unable to coalesce as one dedicated, enlightened, and effective nation, the

Arabs have sought, in the trappings of statecraft, elements of dignity.

Tragically, and ironically, the underlying psychological thrust of all these movements has been the same for the Arabs as for the Zionists: a means of creating for themselves a parallel status to other men. If the efforts of either or both are frustrated and come to naught, we can expect nothing but a spiral of violence, frustration, and hate in the period ahead.

Many Arabs have adopted what I call the "phoenix complex." The phoenix, an Arabian bird which burned itself every five hundred years in order to arise renewed from the ashes, was what many Arabs saw in the bitter, long, and destructive Algerian War. From the ashes of its war, Algeria, in the eyes of these Arabs, arose renewed, cleaned, beautified, ennobled. And many Arabs see in a recurring series of fights between the Arab states and Israel the same process by which ultimately—whether a decade, a generation, or a century hence—an Arab nation will emerge from the ashes. Only if this process can be stopped and, indeed, reversed, is there hope of achieving the ultimate aims of both the Arabs and the Israelis.

Starting from a condition of poverty, backwardness, division and divisiveness, foreign occupation, and isolation from one another, the Arabs have performed feats of development which, in comparison to their starting point, are extraordinary. But they have fallen woefully short of their own goals.

In their sense of failure they have compounded their problems by seeking rapid and often violent means to a better future, by striking out negatively at real or presumed enemies and by retreating into an illusory quest for dignity. Even to admit defeat is far beyond the capability of most of their leaders. The admission of defeat in national terms, like the admission of a mistake in individual terms, requires a sense of security which the Arabs have not as yet achieved.

On the surface, the Arabs' refusal to admit their defeat is the major obstacle to peace. It follows, logically, from the Israeli point of view, that the Arabs must recognize the facts of the world as they are and adjust their attitude to accord with them.

Yet, behind this apparently simple analysis looms a maze of political, military, psychological, and other factors. As America came to recognize in the Vietnamese War, the complex juxtaposition of Europe and Asia is a new dimension in world politics. Deeply imbedded in the clash of nationalism are the problems of transforming an antique culture while still preserving its roots, creating or maintaining a sense of dignity, and fostering the formation of strong national value judgments. These factors affect the Arabs, and through them the Israelis, the Russians, and ourselves in markedly different ways.

In the past, statesmen have brushed aside the intangible factors to get at the "practical" aspects of the Arab-Israeli problem. They have tended to view international affairs in terms of national interest abstracted from the interests of the governments and individuals which embody them. In approaching the Arab-Israeli issue, Americans have sought continuously to find the single key which would unlock the door to peace. The door may have been open all the time. Our problem has been to find the means of encouraging men to pass through it. Thus far, attempts have been unsuccessful.

Our first endeavor, stemming naturally from the American experience in the depression years and in Europe after World War II, was an attempt to get the economic "machine" going. Peace, we reasoned, could never be attained in the Middle East so long as its people were desperate, miserable, hungry, uneducated, unhealthy, and fearful. The technical assistance and aid programs of the 1950's had aims and purposes that were generous, far-sighted, intelligent, and deserving not only of the gratitude but of the cooperation of the peoples of the area. Unfortunately, the lens through which the efforts were seen made them appear quite different from what they had appeared to us.

The Arabs were still smarting from the miserable showing of their armies in the 1948–49 war and were humiliated by the presence in their midst of accusing, complaining remnants of the Palestine population that they had failed to defend. They saw

American efforts only as attempts to buy their political acquiescence. In this view, the American aid programs were morally and
politically repugnant. The programs were the more sinister because they were so terribly tempting to a people who desperately
needed help in developing.

In the compromise accommodation, governments and individuals accepted the benefit of the American aid programs but gave
no thanks in return. Still, opponents accused them of having
gained aid at the price of political integrity and attacked them
continuously, forcibly, and often violently.

In Israel, by contrast, there was no such moral or political
dilemma. Sophisticated Israelis, reckoning with the realities of
world power, were prepared to accept aid even from a German
government attempting to atone for the sins of the past regime
and present people. Assistance from the United States and other
countries was actively courted, joyously received, and used with
great effect.

Israel, in the Western European pattern, had a population that
was oriented toward technological or industrial modernity, had
great internal capabilities and, perhaps most important of all, was
geared toward a relatively high standard of living. Thus it was
to be expected that foreign assistance would produce in Israel a
pattern similar to that produced by the Marshall Plan in Europe—
essentially one of *re*development.

In the surrounding Arab countries, the bulk of the population
was not accustomed to a high standard of living, was not oriented
toward modern technological society, and was not possessed by
the skills required for such organization.

The introduction of aid in the Arab countries created new
hopes. The population at large, seeing that change was indeed
possible, could only assume that it had always been possible. Existing regimes were, by implication, guilty for past miseries. And
since change was possible, it must be possible rapidly, if not pain-
lessly.

The group most affected by the new impulses was the small
elite, by and large educated in the West, possessed of the skills
critical in the development process, but unable peacefully to

achieve full political participation. Throughout the Arab countries, politics entered a violent stage of transition in which the older nationalism gave way to attempts, sometimes crude attempts, at social revolution.

American aid to the Arab countries, in the early years at least, thus tended to bring about a heightened political sensitivity and a demand for action on, among other issues, what the Arabs saw as the preeminent national challenge to themselves, the threat of Israel. In the short run, at least, and in an atmosphere of hostility, aid was not the key.

The second American intervention, the second quest for a key to the problems of the area, lay in the distribution of the waters of the Jordan River Valley. The plan devised in 1952 and 1953 assumed that the distribution and development of the Jordan waters was so vital that the Arab and Jewish governments could be led to adjust their politics to allow for cooperation. Through the development and management of the scheme, the four surrounding states—Israel, Lebanon, Syria, and Jordan—would gradually evolve a peaceful relationship which, though initially limited, would gradually influence activities in other spheres as well.

A formula to divide the waters appeared possible, although there were some Arab misgivings about the future adequacy of the distribution once Arab development projects gathered momentum. More fundamental, the leaders of the several countries recognized the ulterior political purpose behind the development scheme.

Thus, while accepting American aid offered within the context of the plan, both the Arabs and the Israelis eventually set about creating a capability to subvert its main elements. On their side, the Israelis constructed a vast pipeline, almost ten feet in diameter, capable of draining the whole of the Sea of Galilee. The Arabs, alarmed at this apparent threat, forced Israel to place its diversionary pumping station in an awkward and expensive position and talked menacingly about diverting the Syrian tributary waters.

Unfortunately, the distribution and development of the Jordan River Valley did not prove to be the absolutely vital component of Middle Eastern life that had been predicted. For Syria and

Lebanon, the plan was obviously marginal from the beginning. In Jordan, the harmful aspects of the plan had at least as much political reality as the beneficial aspects. In the words of an Israeli hydrological engineer, "Implementation of the plan would convert the Jordan River into 'a saline ditch.'"

So the old mutual fears and antagonisms were pinpointed on the issue of water itself, and the very scheme which had appeared to raise the possibility of bypassing politics became itself a central focus of political and occasional military activity. As a way of creating peace, the plan to divide the Jordan waters was a failure.

The third major United States quest for a "key" was an American-backed UN mission in 1962 to evolve a plan for disposing of the Arab refugee problem. Approximately 750,000 Arabs had been turned into refugees by the fighting in 1948 and 1949, and they had multiplied to well over 1,000,000 by the time the fighting broke out in June 1967.

This UN effort of 1962 was probably hopeless from the start. There is no aspect of Arab-Israeli conflict which is politically more explosive or laden with emotion than that of the refugees. Neither the Arab states nor Israel proved to be willing to give even the limited cooperation they had given to the Jordan River plan a decade previously. The refugees' lack of skills added to their plight. For the most part, the refugees remained in their camps, dependent on meager United Nations relief funds for a marginal existence.

The fourth quest has come in arms control. From time to time, worried by the sheer weight of arms flowing into the Middle East and the likelihood that these would be used, the United States, Great Britain, and France have attempted to work out programs of arms embargo, frontier guarantees, or moves aimed at "balancing" the capabilities of the two sides. But cold war rivalries as well as regional rivalries have led to an escalation of the quantity and quality of arms until, in the June 1967 war, both the Arab states and Israel had equipment on a par with the best available to the major powers. Obviously, the point had come at which there was a real cost—in the billions of dollars—to the major powers in supplying armaments.

Much more important, of course, was the burden on the economies of the Middle East from the cost of armaments. Israel, for example, may have spent close to ten percent of her gross national product on its military, and Egypt only slightly less. In this sense, despite massive outside assistance, the arms race directly undercut efforts at economic and social reform.

More serious yet, the growth in size and capability of the military institutions, particularly in the Arab societies, created a serious political disequilibrium. In the Arab countries, the military stood out as the only highly organized, modern institution and, quite naturally, it came to play a predominant role in politics. Even in Israel, where other institutions of society are more highly developed, fears have been expressed about the militarization of the society. But, in the context of hatred and fear, a recognizable pause or an acceptable parity is almost inconceivable. If the American military feels insecure with its massive superiority in nuclear weapons over all other world powers, why should either Israel or the Arabs feel secure today?

Though Israel enjoys an enormous current superiority, it faces a very real danger of guerrilla warfare and of periodic military clashes which, at some future time, may cause it severe harm. The Arabs, as every serious student has long realized, are no match for the Israelis at this time or at any time in the last generation. They are virtually defenseless against a determined Israeli push forward in Egypt, Jordan, or Syria. However, many of the more radical Arabs appear to want a series of clashes with Israel from which, they hope, a new Arab phoenix will arise. Then, they hope, the battle will go differently.

So arms control, in itself, is not a likely panacea for the problems of the Middle East.

The last approach toward solving the Arab-Israeli problem is that of redrawing the frontiers. Few countries in the world have had their frontiers more frequently redrawn or replanned than Palestine. Even if one overlooks the long past in which Palestine quite literally moved across the map, disappeared, was recreated, was amalgamated, was subdivided, was enlarged, and then diminished innumerable times, one still must recognize that in this century it has been a lump of clay in the hands of many sculptors.

In the course of the June fighting, Israel enormously magnified the territory under her control. In doing so, however, she again raised the dilemma which faced earlier partitioners: she has greatly enlarged her Arab population. If the territory now under Israeli control were retained and the Arab inhabitants given Israeli citizenship, the population would contain three Arabs for every five Jews. Given the high Arab birth rate, not many years would pass before Israel would have an Arab majority. At or before that time Israel would be faced with the unpleasant alternatives of continuing to administer a politically dispossessed Arab population as a "white settler" society—a position from which her early Zionist leaders would have recoiled in horror—or of subverting the very idea of Zionism by creating a binational state. The two horns of this dilemma can be avoided for a time, but only for a time, by holding to the understanding that the Arab population of Gaza and the West Bank will eventually be turned back to some Arab state—either to Egypt and Jordan or to a reconstituted "Arab Palestine."

Throughout the years of discussion of peace proposals the Israelis have shown an adamant refusal to discuss "frontier rectification," claiming, quite logically, that they could barely create a viable state in their already small, and almost incredibly misdrawn territory. On their part, the Arabs have been prepared to listen to schemes of frontier "rectification" but have never been moved by the notion that some readjustment of frontiers would bring peace. The truth, looming behind the failures of the past years, is that the "practical" problems of the Middle East will not yield to "rational" answers until progress is made on the desperate, underlying psychological dimensions.

In the uneasy months since the ending of the war of June 1967, both the Suez Canal area and the Jordan River area have been scenes of intense and almost continuous clashes between the Arabs and the Israelis. Within Israel itself, guerrilla activity has been sufficiently serious to split still further the Israeli Jewish and Arab communities and to make the prospect of incorporating the almost 40 percent Arab sector of the population a most uninviting line of policy to the Israeli government. Indeed, it is not an exaggeration to say that as difficult as Arab-Israeli relations have been in the past, as painful as they are in the present, they loom much more dangerous in the future. The intangibles are the most operative aspects of the whole problem. It is not so much the matters of boundaries, of distribution of water, or of arms which lie at the heart of the Palestine problem, nor is it the refugee issue, which embodies some of its most painful psychological aspects; at the core is the sense of dignity. The thrust of nationalism is, fundamentally, the almost desperate attempt to preserve dignity—even at the cost or forfeit of basic national values.

The Arabs have what appears to us an extraordinary appetite for dignity. Arabic literature, like Greek literature, is filled with examples of this passion—and its often tragic consequences. This literature, and the cultural message it imparts, has been passed from generation to generation of Arabs and forms the core of their culture. Its imperative has been enforced, not diminished, by centuries of subjugation to alien rulers. In the colonial period, the alienness of rulers was intensified by religious difference and this made their presence all the more galling and painful. In the period of national independence, the dream of dignity and progress assumed proportions which were mocked by the realities of political experience. The humiliation of each of the three wars between the Arabs and the Israelis further embittered and inflamed the Arab passion for revenge.

It is unfortunately true that dignity is not a present which one individual or nation can give to another. By complex processes, it is won by or accrues to the individual or nation. The loss of the self-esteem and self-confidence which are the preconditions to dignity results in a tragic and pervasive undermining of the whole personality. The Arabs share this loss with certain other peoples in the modern world, notably the American Black community. The repercussions of the problem are so complex and cut so deeply to the core of human experience that practical statesmen prefer to ignore the entire issue in peace-making. However, we can ignore the issue of dignity in the Middle East only at the price of failure to bring about peace.

It is well to remember that one of the most critical aspects of President Charles de Gaulle's successful campaign to bring to a close the costly and destructive Algerian War was his emphasis on honor. This war, he said, was to end neither in defeat nor in victory but in "a peace of the braves," a peace of honorable men who, having fought well, hard, and long, could honorably make peace. This strategy worked when all the guns, all the soldiers, and all the "practical" solutions had failed.

If we sincerely wish peace in the Middle East, we must face the fact that peace cannot be imposed on a humiliated, beaten, and degraded people any more than people can be bombed to the peace table. Two general approaches are apparent. We must undertake activities and promote conditions which will help to restore self-esteem and self-confidence. These conditions are not difficult to imagine nor, for the most part, to effect, but they do require time and thoughtfulness. Very often, they require smallness of dimension. A major aid program, for example, on the scale that we are now undertaking in Vietnam, while contributing enormously to economic impulses, may undermine or even destroy the basic acceptance of responsibility of the people.

On the other hand, at least as important is the *avoidance* of actions which will denigrate the self-esteem of those we are attempting to help toward peace. In contrast to de Gaulle's successful program to compliment the Algerians toward peace, the Israelis and their friends have constantly deprecated their Arab enemies. Such deprecation may prove to be one of the most serious inhibitions to the moves toward peace. History is filled with examples of individuals and nations which have been driven even to a self-destructive vengeance because of their basic insecurity.

If we recognize dignity as the crux of the Palestine problem, it will not be impossible to design ways of coping with it.

The next aspect of the problem of peace is to recognize as stressed above, that peace, like other forms of international relations, is made between men rather than between abstract entities called nation-states. As Thomas Brady wrote in the *New York Times* on April 4, 1968, "the Israelis seem oblivious of new imperatives that King Hussein faces when they insist he should take measures against terrorists that might shake the loyalty of his army and even cost him his throne." The ability of all governments to act is severely limited. Consequently, a prime task of peace-makers is to expand the scope of the principal actors and to help them avoid conditions which they cannot control.

However strong the Israeli government may be vis-a-vis the Arabs, it faces, domestically, a dangerous situation parallel to that of the Arabs. For personal political reasons, Israeli "doves" cannot afford to give Israeli "hawks" opportunities to unseat them.

One of the significant political factors facing any Israeli government in the return to peace is the fact that the Israeli population, for the first time, has tasted the delights of tourism. As Ammon Rubinstein pointed out in the *New York Times Magazine* on June 2, 1968,

the craving for travel may be discounted by outsiders as a marginal factor in the over-all issues facing Israel. In reality, this need for breathing space is of major importance to Israelis. Only those who have lived for twenty years sealed within a state the size of New Jersey can appreciate the power behind this need, not for domination, but for freedom of movement. A return to pre-war Israel would be a return to claustrophobia—more suffocating than before after the taste of spaciousness.

What Israeli politician would risk telling his backers that they must make that return? Regardless of the form of the major elements in negotiations, it is manifest that no peace treaty will stick which is extracted from a government regarded by its people as weak or traitorous. It is not inconceivable that the effect on politics, a generation hence—or perhaps even sooner—would be similar in the

Middle East to that resulting from the humiliating Versailles Treaty and its legacy in the Weimar Republic in Germany: revanchism.

Achievement of peace requires at least one strong and responsible Arab government, accepted as genuinely nationalist, sufficiently influential to insure compliance, and willing to lead. If this statement is valid, then many things must follow. First of all, it is evident that one cannot simultaneously negotiate with and attempt to destroy such a government. Almost all Arabs today believe this is a course upon which Israel is bent; many ascribe a similar policy to the United States. In these circumstances, no peace plan, no matter how brilliantly conceived and negotiated, is more than ephemeral. Thus, the *form* of negotiations becomes one of key importance.

To the Israelis form could be useful, particularly if the substance of the negotiation failed. If the Israelis could bring about a confrontation between senior officials, perhaps between the leaders of Israel and of at least one Arab state, they would have created something tantamount to recognition. More important, they would have also forced the negotiating Arab government into a position from which it could be effectively blackmailed.

The Arabs have long been aware of these risks. The Arab governments, already smarting from their humiliating defeats, criticized and attacked by the more violent of their constituents, are aware of the mortal danger in which they as individuals, and collectively as governments, would be placed by such negotiations. Obviously, they will do everything in their power to avoid negotiating until such time as they are certain the negotiations will be successful. Realistically, therefore, we can hardly expect the Arabs to negotiate face to face with the Israelis. They have adamantly refused to undertake such negotiations and will, I predict, continue to do so.

Despite the superficial validity of the Israeli contention that, if the Arabs really want peace, they must sit down and talk, man to man, with the Israelis, this contention leads to a blind alley. To understand the force of this political imperative, we should ask ourselves whether, in the far less inflamed atmosphere of Chinese Communist–American relations, an American President would be willing or even able to sit and negotiate with Mao Tse-tung when he believed both that Mao and he could not achieve a viable solution and that he would either be assassinated or viciously attacked by his enemies at home. Put in this context, understandable to us, the actions of some Arab leaders do not appear quite so irresponsible or unwise as we are wont to believe.

There are, however, a number of relatively simple and indirect ways to settle some of the major elements of contention in the Arab-Israeli conflict. For example, the issue of a blockade over the Strait of Tiran could be ended without Egypt's seeming to back down in the face of Israeli pressure. This could be accomplished simply by the U.A.R. signing the 1959 Convention on the Law of the Sea to which the United States, the Soviet Union, Israel, and other powers are signatories.

At the opening of the United Nations session in October 1968, the Soviet Union and Israel put forward several stipulations to be considered in a possible solution to the Middle East problem. In private conversations, the Arabs had put forward others. There are common elements in all of these and past private American initiatives.

The specific proposals which I will outline below suggest an order of approach; each must be regarded not only on the basis of its own merits or demerits but in juxtaposition to the other elements of a total package. It must be clear in the negotiations in the Middle East, as in all negotiations, that no one side or party can be the total "winner" with the other the total "loser," if a lasting agreement is to be made. The separate elements of a peace settlement are less important than the atmosphere which the whole creates and projects. For that reason, the following proposals are meant to be suggestive rather than definitive.

1. Israel should return to the pre-1967 armistice boundaries. Following the withdrawal of Israel troops and with the prior agreement of all participants, a United Nations frontier commission

should be established, with permanent members, perhaps including such neutrals as India, Ghana, and Argentina. The commission would suggest rectifications for a more peaceful frontier to be maintained with minimum troop concentrations.

By no means to be thought of as exclusive, but included among these would probably be changes in the Syrian Heights, the Gaza Strip, and the area affected by the so-called Shuna Agreement. These frontiers, approved by the UN, would be guaranteed and, where necessary, patrolled multilaterally by the United Nations.

2. Ideally, Jerusalem should be constituted as an international city, with frontiers open both to Jordan and to Israel and with right of access through the port of Haifa to the Mediterranean. Both Jordanians and Israelis would have free access to the city and every effort should be made to constitute it as a sort of sanctuary—an old Semitic arrangement—to serve as a meeting place between Arabs and Jews.

The government of the city of Jerusalem should be controlled by the United Nations, which might act through an agency administered by Japan. The Japanese as a power that is neutral in terms of religion would be asked, additionally, to strive for the maintenance of an impartial regime over the holy places of the Jews, Moslems, and Christians.

Practically, the government of Israel has gone too far in its reconstitution of Jerusalem as an Israeli city to back away now. Consequently, a "practical" compromise would leave the city in Israeli hands. It should be recognized, however, that what is practical today may turn out to be the seed of hostility in the future; statesmen should, therefore, ponder this issue long and hard.

3. Admitting the costly and dangerous aspects of the previous arms race, Israel, the United Arab Republic, Jordan, and Syria should accept a limitation on the size of their military forces. Granting the overwhelming mobilization capability of the modern Israeli society, every effort should be made to keep the number of standing military forces as low as possible in order to prevent the wastage of scarce foreign currencies on military hardware.

I would suggest that a figure of approximately 50,000 soldiers be the maximum standing force allowed Israel, 40,000 for the United Arab Republic, 20,000 for Jordan, and 30,000 for Syria. No other Arab forces would be stationed in those countries.

Certain categories of weapons, including nuclear and surface-to-surface rockets, would be declared illegal and possession or manufacture of them would be banned. An international inspection force to carry out this provision would be constituted and could comprise West Germany, Canada, and Burma, with a staff assembled from the permanent United Nations civil service.

4. The Arab states party to the agreement would also agree to recognize, *de jure,* the existence of the state of Israel within the frontiers to be approved by the United Nations frontier commission. This is the *sine qua non* of peace in the Middle East. A state of war and/or belligerency would be declared ended.

Additionally, certain particularly sensitive areas could be and should be declared closed to military formations. These might include the Sinai Peninsula, the Golan Heights, and the West Bank of Jordan.

5. No hostile acts or impediments would bar Israel from peaceful concourse in the area. Specifically, the U.A.R. would agree to Israeli passage through the Suez Canal (to the clearance of which Israel would contribute along with the other user nations) and the Strait of Tiran, linking the Gulf of Aqaba and the Red Sea.

The Arab boycott office would be ended and, in stages, over a 15-year period, tariffs and other controls over Israeli goods would be reduced from an initial figure set in the course of negotiations to a level that would facilitate the growth of area trade without overwhelming Arab industry.

6. Every attempt would be made to satisfy the aspirations and needs of the refugee population. A quota system would be worked out to enhance resettlement. Assuming that there are approximately 1,300,000 refugees today, Israel would agree to accept 200,000, the United States 200,000, Canada 100,000, New Zealand and Australia each 75,000, with the rest to be divided among the Arab countries. An international fund would be created to assist

each refugee family with repatriation in whatever country he chose.

Additionally, the current expenditures of the United Nations relief organization on technical training would be increased to a figure which would make possible the rapid growth of capability within the refugee community so that the refugees could become attractive candidates for citizenship. As a rough estimate, I would suggest that the figure devoted to education should be increased between ten and twenty-fold. Each country which agreed in principal to accept refugees would be encouraged to augment this total by individual technical training programs administered either in the Middle East or at home.

A temporary international labor agency would be established to ascertain the choices of the refugee community within the framework of this system and, in so far as possible, to honor those choices in allocating visas and travel papers to refugee families. This agency could also help to find employment opportunities.

7. Both the Arabs and the Israelis would undertake in all official pronouncements to avoid derogatory or taunting propaganda against the opposite side. Every effort would be made to encourage the notion that those who cooperate for peace are the most praiseworthy of the nationalists in each state.

8. The outside powers, and those powers within the Middle East who could contribute, would constitute a fund, to be administered by the World Bank under the soft loan provisions of the International Development Association, to assist in raising the economic level of the Arab countries to a position in which longterm peace becomes feasible. Israel can no more find tranquility in an area whose people live in misery, poverty, disease, and wretchedness than we in America live safely in a neighborhood on whose boundaries live people whose lives are blighted by wretchedness, insecurity, and envy. Day-to-day dissatisfaction, frustrations, and terrors constitute a breeding ground of violence.

Minimum goals of economic growth should be set for each country and monies allocated according to their willingness and abilities to constitute the preconditions for economic growth as well as to the objective need of each country. But essential though it be, aid cannot and must not appear to be a payoff for political compliance; it must be offered toward the end rather than at the beginning of the process.

What hope does lie at the end of a settlement in the Middle East? As we have seen, the Arab Middle East is an essentially poor area, with a rapidly growing population, with its few resources widely scattered and unequally distributed, and its major products of probably declining importance. Suffering from the legacies of backwardness, it requires an enormous capital investment to build the infrastructure of development and to educate and improve the health of its population. This is a grim and gloomy picture, one to lend credence to those who seek desperate shortcuts. But there are important elements of hope, as have been discussed in chapters XIV and XV above. They rank on a level of complexity and costliness with the problems of the Negro community in the American cities. But it is well to remember that both of these great social problems of the times are not problems beyond the ability and knowledge of mankind. The only question is whether they are beyond our will.

Progress will not be easy and the means will often be obscure, but the alternatives are quite literally terrifying. In the Arab countries of the Middle East, contemporary anger and frustration will become tomorrow's violence and frenzy. Populations which are already desperately poor will grow rapidly more numerous. Even if halfhearted developmental efforts succeed in slightly raising their standards of living, the people's ambitions—their threshold of political tolerance—will be rapidly raised to the hopes of tomorrow. Israel is, and will continue to be, blamed as the major source of this misery. Israel in the Middle East, like the white community in America, cannot live securely, happily, richly, and contentedly in an area of slums. Even if the dictates of national security can be satisfied, the conscience of men cannot.

Thus, though it is difficult and frustrating, the fact must be faced that some acceptable degree of accommodation is necessary for the achievement of the minimum goals of the Arabs, the Israelis, and the Americans.

In human affairs there are no crystal balls. But the future grows out of the past and is shaped by men. Knowing the past, and devoting ourselves with energy and wisdom to the present, we can create a better future.

SUGGESTED READING

The purpose of the following list is to suggest further reading on the various subjects treated in broad brush strokes in this book. Obviously it cannot be exhaustive in any section. Only reasonably accessible works in European languages are included.

GENERAL WORKS on the Arabs or on the whole Middle Eastern area abound; unfortunately, generality often masks ignorance of the specific. One of several books which may be highly recommended is M. Berger, *The Arab World Today* (New York, 1962). Another is J. Berque: *Les Arabes d'Hier a Demain* (Paris, 1960). An overall view of the modern Arab scene is given in W. R. Polk (ed.), *Perspective of the Arab World*, an *Atlantic Monthly* Supplement, which was also separately published by Intercultural Publications, Inc. (New York, 1956). Included are articles on Arabic culture, social reform, Arabic literature, and Islam, and translations of Arabic short stories, plays, and poetry. Another delightful collection of Arabic literature is H. Howarth and I. Shakrullah, *Images from the Arab World* (London, 1944).

Beginning students will profit by reading J. Sauvaget, *Introduction à l'histoire de l'Orient Musulman*, Eléments de Bibliographie (Paris, 1946) which, although now somewhat out of date, is a valuable guide. The second edition of this book has been recast by Claude Cahen and appears as *Introduction to a History of the Muslim East: A Bibliographical Guide* (Berkeley, 1965). More detail is usually to be found in the *Encyclopaedia of Islam*, now being issued in a new edition, in Leiden.

Among the periodicals which deal with Middle Eastern affairs the *Middle East Journal* is probably the most accessible and useful. Published in Washington, D.C., quarterly since 1947, it includes articles, book reviews, surveys of other periodicals, and a chronology which make it particularly valuable to students of the modern period. The *Middle East Forum*, published at the American University of Beirut, and *Middle Eastern Affairs* both often contain useful materials. The *Mid-East Mirror*, published weekly since 1947, is a digest of the Arabic press. The Italian magazine *Oriente Moderno* is most valuable for the period of the 1920's and 1930's as is the English *Journal of the Royal Central Asian Society*. The French journal *Orient*, published three times yearly since 1957, contains, among other useful features, frequent translations of significant treaties and pronouncements from the Arab countries. *Studia Islamica*, dealing less with the modern period, contains many significant articles on the history and culture of the Arabs; it is published in Paris, roughly every six months.

Most of the general studies contain bibliographies. None, obviously, can be kept up to date. Perhaps the best ways to keep reasonably up to date is through the reviews in the *Middle East Journal* and *International Affairs*. The Middle East Institute is revising its bibliography and this should be published in 1965. A. R. C. Bolton, *Soviet Middle East Studies, An Analysis and Bibliography* (London, 1959), is so arranged as to show the evolution of Soviet attitudes at different stages of Soviet policies.

THE PEOPLE ON THE LAND are covered in a wide assortment of works. On the bedouin, Alois Musil, *The Manners and Customs of the Rwala Bedouins* (New York, 1928), G. W. Murray, *Sons of Ishmael* (London, 1935), H. Charles, *La Sédentarisation entre Euphrate et Balik* (Beirut, 1942), H. R. P. Dickson, *The Arab of the Desert* (London, 1949), H. Charles, *Tribus moutonnières du Moyen-Euphrate* (Damascus, n.d.), and J. L. Burckhardt, *Notes on Bedouins and Wahabys* (London, 1831), are all classics of description. Important information is also to be found in J. C. Glubb, "The Bedouin of North Arabia" in the *Journal of the Royal Central Asian Society*, 1935, and, in the same journal in 1938, E. Epstein, "The Bedouin of Transjordan." All considered the most masterful survey of bedouin life is R. Montagne, *La Civilisation du desert* (Paris, 1947).

On the nonbedouin rural Arabs, perhaps the best overall studies are A. Latron, *La Vie rurale en Syrie et au Liban* (Beirut, 1936), and J. Weulersse, *Paysans* (Paris, 1941). The Egyptian peasant is treated in H. Ayrout, *The Egyptian Peasant* (new edition, Boston, 1963), J. Berque, *Histoire sociale d'une village Egyptienne au XXème siècle*, and Hamed Ammar, *Growing up in an Egyptian Village* (New York, 1954). The "marsh Arabs" of Iraq are the subject of S. M. Salim, *Marsh Dwellers of the Euphrates Delta* (London, 1962), and Fulanain (pseud.), *Haji Rikkan, Marsh Arab* (London, 1927). Studies of urban life and the relations of the city to the countryside include three excellent Arabic novels, now available in English, Tawfiq el-Hakim, *The Maze of Justice* (London, 1947), and Taha Hussein, *An Egyptian Childhood* (London, 1932) and *The Stream of Days* (London, 1948). C. Hurgronje, *Mekka* (London, 1931), and J. L. Burckhardt, *Travels in Arabia* (London, 1829), give fascinating pictures of Arabia at the beginning and end of the nineteenth century. E. W. Lane, *The Manners and Customs of the Modern Egyptians* (London, 1836 and many subsequent editions), is one of the great classics of description of all times. It was a by-product of the half a lifetime which Lane spent in Cairo translating a huge lexicon of Arabic. Albert de Boucheman: *Une Petite cité caravanière: Suhné* (Damascus, n.d.) shows a typical desert outpost.

Special areas are treated in A. Hourani, *Minorities in the Arab World* (London, 1947), H. St. J. Philby, *The Empty Quarter* (London, 1933), H. Ingrams, *Arabia and the Isles* (London, 1942), D. Ingrams, *A Survey of Social and Economic Conditions in the Aden Protectorate* (Eritrea, 1949), and H. Scott, *In the High Yemen* (London, 1942).

Aspects of the geography of the Arab Middle East are discussed in W. Fisher, *The Middle East* (New York, 1950), and the particular importance of water is brought out in N. Moussly, *Le Problem de l'eau en Syrie* (Lyon, 1951).

Emrys Peters, "Aspects of Rank and Status among Muslims in a Lebanese village" in J. Pitt-Rivers, *Mediterranean Countrymen* (Paris, 1936), is the product of one of the most detailed studies ever made of Arab village life. Finally, G. Baer, *Population and Society in the Arab East* (New York, 1964), is a major synthesis of current knowledge.

THE ANCIENT ARABS are best shown in their own literature. Obviously, this is best understood in Arabic, but the non-Arabist will profit from C. J. Lyall, *Ancient Arabian Poetry* (London, 1930), which contains not only a wide sample of translations but a superb introduction. Two other surveys which put the classical literature in perspective are H. A. R. Gibb, *Arabic Literature* (London, 1926), and R. Nicholson, *Literary History of the Arabs* (Cambridge, Eng., 1953). The heart of pre-Islamic literature is translated in *The Seven Golden Odes of Pagan Arabia, Known Also as the Moallakat* by Lady Anne Blunt and Wilfrid Scrawen Blunt (London, 1903). The scene in Arabia of that period is sketched in H. Lammens, *Le Berceau de l'Islam* (Rome, 1914), *La Mecque à la veille de l'Hégire* (Beirut, 1924), and *La Cité Arabe de Taif à la veille de l'Hégire* (Beirut, 1922).

ISLAM is, of course, the subject of a vast literature in many languages. To understand it, however, it is probably unwise to begin with the *Koran*. Even the Arab Muslims read the *Koran* with the help of a teacher and a commentary. The best translation, however, is very good. It is M. Pickthall, *The Glorious Koran* (London, 1930). To begin, one should read one or more of the following, R. Bell, *Introduction to the Qur'ān* (Edinburgh, 1953), H. A. R. Gibb, *Mohammedanism* (New York, 1955), which is possibly the best general introduction to the whole religious system, A. S. Tritton, *Muslim Theology* (London, 1947) and *Islam, Belief and Practices* (London, 1951), and R. Roberts, *The Social Laws of the Qorân* (London, 1925). A more detailed account of the *Koran* itself is given in A. Jeffry, *The Qur'an* as *Scripture* (New York, 1952). The life of Muhammad is treated in detail by M. Watt in his two volumes *Muhammad at Mecca* (Oxford, 1953) and *Muhammad at Medina* (Oxford, 1956). The older study of W. Muir, the *Life of Mahomet* (London, 1894), is still delightful and valuable, but perhaps the best all-round introduction is T. Andrae, *Mohammed, the Man and his Faith* (London, 1936).

M. Gaudefroy-Demombynes, *Muslim Institutions* (London, 1950), is the best introduction to the social elaboration of Islam. G. von Grunebaum, *Islam, Essays in the Nature and Growth of a*

Cultural Tradition (London, 1955) and *Medieval Islam* (Chicago, second ed., 1953), and L. Gardet, *La Cité Musulmane*, Vie sociale et politique (Paris, 1954), are significant contributions to the subject. N. J. Coulson, *A History of Islamic Law* (Edinburgh, 1964), and N. J. Coulson, *The Development of Islamic Law* (forthcoming), give an excellent account of the development of Islamic law. The "world view" of the great medieval Muslim scholars is given in Seyyed Hossein Nasr, *An Introduction to Islamic Cosmological Doctrines* (Cambridge, 1964).

Special topics in Islam are treated in R. A. Nicholson, *The Mystics of Islam* (London, 1914), A. J. Arberry, *Sufism* (London, 1950), and D. Donaldson, *The Shi'ite Religion* (London, 1933). Detailed coverage on virtually every conceivable aspect of Islam is given in the *Encyclopaedia of Islam,* and those articles of particular interest on the religion have been separately published in H. A. R. Gibb and J. H. Kramers, *Shorter Encyclopaedia of Islam* (Leiden, 1953). Lastly, G. von Grunebaum, *Muhammadan Festivals* (New York, 1951), is a good companion to have if one is living in a Muslim country.

THE CONQUESTS AND CALIPHATE are introduced concisely in B. Lewis, *The Arabs in History* (London, 1950), which is one of the best books ever written on the Arab Middle East. The conquests are the subject of an excellent essay by C. H. Becker in the *Cambridge Medieval History* (Cambridge, Eng., vol. II, 1936) and of M. J. de Goeje, *Mémoire sur la conquête de la Syrie* (Leiden, 1900). S. Lane-Poole, *A History of Egypt in the Middle Ages* (London, 1914), deals with the Arab invasion and subsequent history; H. A. R. Gibb, *The Arab Conquests in Central Asia* (London, 1923), deals with the invasions in the East. Various articles by Gibb on other aspects of the caliphate are reprinted in S. J. Shaw and W. R. Polk (ed.), *Studies on the Civilization of Islam by Hamilton A. R. Gibb* (Boston, 1962). The cultural aspects of medieval Arabic civilization as they affected medieval Europe are covered in T. Arnold and A. Guillaume, *The Legacy of Islam* (Oxford, 1931). Other general histories of note are C. Brockelmann, *History of the Islamic Peoples* (New York, 1947), which has a somewhat wider scope than B. Lewis (above) and P. Hitti, *History of the Arabs* (London, 1951), which is much more detailed but less critical and a series of accounts by General Sir John B. Glubb (Pasha), beginning with *The Great Arab Conquests* (London, 1961), and including *The Empire of the Arabs* (London, 1963), which are primarily of interest in that they are written by a soldier-statesman who asked a different order of questions than did the scholarly Orientalists of established repute. The caliphate is the subject of a virtually undiscriminating reading of the Arabic chronicles in W. Muir, *The Caliphate, Its Rise, Decline and Fall* (Edinburgh, 1915). The Umayyad caliphate is the subject of a number of excellent works including H. Lammens, *Etudes sur le règne du Calife Omaiyade Mo'awia Iᵉʳ* (Leipzig, 1907) and *Etudes sur le siècle des Omayyades* (Beirut, 1930), and, above all, J. Wellhausen, *The Arab Kingdom and Its Fall* (Calcutta, 1927).

The Abbasid caliphate of Baghdad is dealt with in the general studies and in a series of fascinating essays in T. Nöldeke, *Sketches from Eastern History* (Edinburgh, 1892). The bureaucratic breakdown of the empire is the subject of H. Bowen, *Life and Times of 'Ali ibn 'Isa* (Cambridge, 1928). The cultural recovery of Islam in an age of political decline is described in A. Mez, *The Renaissance of Islam* (London, 1937).

The Period of the Alien Empires is covered in some of the general studies noted above. S. Runciman, *History of the Crusades* (Cambridge, Eng., 1952–54), is a masterful and well-written account; other articles on the Crusades of relevance are contained in Marshall W. Baldwin (ed.), *The First Hundred Years*, volume I of *A History of the Crusades* (Philadelphia, 1955). H. A. R. Gibb (trans.), *The Damascus Chronicle of the Crusades* (London, 1932), and P. K. Hitti (trans.), *Memoires of an Arab-Syrian Gentleman* (New York, 1929), present Arab views of the Crusades. C. Cahen, *La Syrie Nord à l'époque des Croisades* (Paris, 1940), is one of the best studies available. The Mongols are treated in G. Vernadsky, *The Mongols and Russia* (New Haven, 1953), better though with less detail on the Middle East than elsewhere. H. Lammens, *La Syrie, précis historique* (Beirut, 1921), deals with the whole sweep of Syrian history; the Mamluk period is covered in Gaudefroy-Demombynes, *La Syrie à l'epoque des Mamelouks*

(Paris, 1923) and Ira Lapidus, *Muslim Cities in the Later Middle Ages* (Cambridge, 1967), is an excellent study of life in Damascus and Aleppo under the Mamluks; and Lebanon is being treated in a series of volumes by Adel Ismail, *Histoire du Liban du XVIIe siècle à nos jours* of which volume I, *Le Liban au temps de Fakhr-ed-Din II*, was published in Paris in 1955. H. A. R. Gibb and H. Bowen, *Islamic Society and the West* (Oxford, 1950, 1957), is a major study of the Arab areas under the Turks. G. Stripling, *The Ottoman Turks and the Arabs* (Urbana, Ill., 1942); S. Longrigg, *Four Centuries of Modern Iraq* (Oxford, 1925); Henri Dehérain, *L'Egypte Turque* (Paris, n.d.); A. N. Poliak, *Feudalism in Egypt, Syria, Palestine and the Lebanon, 1250–1900* (London, 1939); Kamal S. Salibi, *The Modern History of Lebanon* (New York, 1965); Iliya F. Harik, *Politics and Change in a Traditional Society, Lebanon, 1711–1845* (Princeton, 1968); and W. R. Polk, *The Opening of South Lebanon* (Cambridge, Mass., 1963), deal with Arab affairs under Turkish rule. Life in Cairo is the subject of a separate study in Marcel Colombe, "La Vie au Caire au 18ème siècle," Conferences de l'Institut Français d'Archéologie Orientale (Cairo, 1951), and more detailed is S. J. Shaw, *Ottoman Egypt in the Age of the French Revolution* (Cambridge, Mass., 1964).

THE IMPACT OF THE WEST is the subject of a large number of studies. Perhaps the most comprehensive and recent is William R. Polk and Richard Chambers (eds.), *The Beginnings of Modernization in the Middle East* (Chicago, 1968), which collects studies by the most distinguished students of the period, and Charles Issawi, (ed.), *The Economic History of the Middle East, 1800–1914* (Chicago, 1966), which collects the source materials, with comments by the editor. My own *Opening of South Lebanon, A Study of the Impact of the West on the Middle East* (Cambridge, Mass., 1963) is directly addressed to this topic and centers on the Levant. H. A. Rivlin, *The Agricultural Policy of Muhammad 'Ali in Egypt* (Cambridge, Mass., 1961), and G. Baer, *History of Landownership in Modern Egypt, 1800–1950* (London, 1963), deal with rural problems; Moustafa Fahmy, *La Révolution de l'industrie en Egypte et ses conséquences sociales au 19e siècle, 1800–1850* (Leiden, 1954), treats urban changes. J. Heyworth-

Dunne, *Introduction to the History of Education in Modern Egypt* (London, 1938), treats cultural affairs, and J. Bowring, *Report on the Commercial Statistics of Egypt and Syria* (London, 1840) is a mine of information on economic affairs. Egypt under the impact of the West is wonderfully described in E. W. Lane, *Manners and Customs of the Modern Egyptians* (above), and A.-B. Clot, *Aperçu général sur l'Egypte* (Paris, 1840). Gabriel Baer, *A Social and Economic History of Egypt* (Chicago, 1969), gives a new dimension of nineteenth-century history and can now be followed by Robert L. Tignor, *Modernization and British Colonial Rule in Egypt, 1882–1914* (Princeton, 1966), while an overall view is contained in P. M. Holt, *Political and Social Change in Modern Egypt* (London, 1968). The best general treatment of Egypt is F. Charles-Roux, *L'Egypte de 1801–1882* (Paris, n.d.). On the Persian Gulf see A. T. Wilson, *The Persian Gulf* (London, 1928).

ON THE COMING OF THE WEST to the Arab Middle East, David S. Landes, *Bankers and Pashas* (Cambridge, Mass., 1958), is fascinating and can be put in a wider Middle Eastern context with H. Feis, *Europe, the World's Banker* (New Haven, 1930), M. S. Anderson, *The Eastern Question, 1774–1923* (New York, 1966), is a very good synthesis of the European view, and W. L. Langer, *The Diplomacy of Imperialism* (New York, 1935). Zaki Saleh, *Mesopotamia, 1600–1914* (Baghdad, 1957), gives a good account of Iraq in tandem to the spirit of W. S. Blunt, *The Secret History of the English Occupation of Egypt* (New York, 1922). The Crimean War is dealt with, in its Near Eastern aspects, in H. W. V. Temperley, *The Crimea* (London, 1934). John Marlow, *World Ditch: The Making of the Suez Canal* (New York, 1964), is a good account of the great engineering feat. The English view of imperialism is best set out in Lord Cromer, *Modern Egypt* (London, 1908) and *Abbas II* (London, 1915). The political impact and Egyptian reaction is the subject of N. Safran, *Egypt in Search of Political Community* (Cambridge, Mass., 1961), J. Landau, *Parliaments and Parties in Egypt* (New York, 1954), Jamal Ahmad, *The Intellectual Origins of Egyptian Nationalism* (London, 1960), C. C. Adams, *Islam and Modernism in Egypt* (London, 1933),

Malcolm H. Kerr, *Islamic Reform* (Berkeley and Los Angeles, 1966), and A. H. Hourani, *Arabic Thought in the Liberal Age, 1798–1939* (London, 1962). The Egyptian view of the history of the period is in M. Rifaat, *The Awakening of Modern Egypt* (London, 1947).

WORLD WAR I is dealt with in a number of studies and collections of memoirs as well as in official dispatches. On Iraq, the most important work, written by the chief political officer of the British forces, is A. T. Wilson, *Loyalties, Mesopotamia, 1914–1917* and *A Clash of Loyalties, 1917–1920* (London, 1930 and 1931). Edouard Brémond, *Le Hédjaz dans la guerre mondiale* (Paris, 1931), gives a French view of the "reality" behind the Lawrence of Arabia legend. Lawrence's own account, T. E. Lawrence, *Seven Pillars of Wisdom* (New York, 1926), should be read with the critics not far away. Richard Aldington, *Lawrence of Arabia* (London, 1955), is devastating if picky. The diary of the chief political officer of the British forces in the theater, R. Meinertzhagen, *Middle East Diary* (London, 1959), is conclusive. Sir R. Storrs, *Orientations* (London, 1937), is one of the most fascinating views of the period. Lady Bell (ed.), *The Letters of Gertrude Bell* (London, 1927), gives a view of happenings in Baghdad similar to that of Storrs in Cairo and Jerusalem.

Among the official documents, E. L. Woodward and R. Butler (eds.), *Documents on British Foreign Policy, 1919–1939*, first series, vol. IV, 1919 (London, 1952), is essential for the critical year. The terms on which the Arabs entered the war are set out and discussed in Cmd 5957: *Correspondence between Sir Henry McMahon and the Sharif Hussein of Mecca, July 1915–March 1916* (London, 1939); Cmd 5964: *Statements Made on Behalf of His Majesty's Government during the Year 1918 in Regard to the Future Status of Certain Parts of the Ottoman Empire* (London, 1939); and Cmd 6974: *Report of a Committee Set Up to Consider Certain Correspondence between Sir Henry McMahon and the Sharif of Mecca in 1915 and 1916* (London, 1939). *The Balfour Declaration* is the subject and title of a masterly work by Leonard Stein (London, 1961). A fascinating insight into the critical work of Sir Mark Sykes both on the Balfour Declaration and on the Sykes-Picot Agreement is given in Christopher Sykes, *Two Studies in Virtue* (New York, 1953).

E. Kedourie, *England and the Middle East, The Destruction of the Ottoman Empire, 1914–1921* (London, 1956), is well written but somewhat forced. Perhaps the best work on the English role for this as for later periods is E. Monroe, *Britain's Moment in the Middle East* (Baltimore, 1963), although Sir R. Bullard, *Britain and the Middle East* (London, 1951), is a good introduction. American efforts are the subject of H. N. Howard, *The King-Crane Commission* (Beirut, 1963), and the work at the Peace Conference is ably covered in H. W. V. Temperley, *The Peace Conference of Paris* (vol. VI, London, 1921). The Arabs' efforts are described best in Zeine N. Zeine, *The Struggle for Arab Independence* (Beirut, 1960). A fascinating comment on Arab-Zionist negotiations should be read in M. Perlmann, "Chapters of Arab-Jewish Diplomacy, 1918–1922" in *Jewish Social Studies*, 6 (1944): 123 f. Misunderstandings between the British and the French are sketched in H. H. Cumming, *Franco-British Rivalry in the Post-War Near East* (London, 1938). The immediate postwar period is summed up in A. J. Toynbee, *The Islamic World since the Peace Settlement, Survey of International Affairs, 1925*, vol. I (London, 1927).

THE MANDATES PERIOD is the subject of an ever-growing volume of literature. The yearly reports to the League of Nations on the mandates are a treasure house of information. But a number of first-rate studies on one or more of the mandate countries exist. On Syria and Lebanon, S. H. Longrigg, *Syria and Lebanon under French Mandate* (London, 1958), is exhaustive, but older works by A. H. Hourani, *Syria and Lebanon* (London, 1946), and N. A. Ziadeh, *Syria and Lebanon* (London, 1957), are easier to digest and more pointed. In addition to Z. N. Zeine, *The Struggle for Arab Independence* (Beirut, 1960), R. de Bontant-Biron, *Comment la France s'est installée en Syrie* (Paris, 1923), sets out the beginnings of French power. E. Rabbath, *L'Evolution politique de la Syrie sous mandat* (Paris, 1928), and P. Rondot, *Les Institutions politiques du Liban* (Paris, 1947), are very important for an understanding of domestic affairs. An independent view is given in D. Censoni, *Siria e Libano dal Mandato all'indipendenza, 1919–1946* (Bologna, 1948), and the difficulty the French had with the Druze (and others) is described in Général Andréa, *La Révolte Druze et l'Insurrection de Damas, 1925–1926* (Paris, 1937). An overall view, but at something of a distance, from the mandates is given in Quincy Wright, *Mandates under the League of Nations* (Chicago, 1930).

Iraq is the subject of many studies by Englishmen. A basic book is S. H. Longrigg, *'Iraq, 1900–1950, A Political, Social and Economic History* (London, 1953). Still valuable on earlier periods are P. Ireland, *'Iraq* (London, 1937), and M. Khadduri, *Independent Iraq* (London, 1950).

Egypt is dealt with competently in M. Colombe, *L'Evolution de l'Egypte, 1924–1950* (Paris, 1951). However, following the 1952 coup, much of the overt political history of that period seemed to many writers of less consequence than underlying social and economic changes, of which more below. Anglo-Egyptian relations are soberly described in the Royal Institute of International Affairs, *Great Britain and Egypt, 1914–1951* (London, 1952), and, somewhat more vigorously and impartially, in John Marlow, *Anglo-Egyptian Relations, 1800–1953* (London, 1954). The sort of biting satire of Egyptians in the 1930's referred to in the text is C. S. Jarvis, *The Back-Garden of Allah* (London, 1939), which went through nine printings although banned in Egypt, and his *Oriental Spotlight* (London, 1937).

Arabia is the subject of very few books as yet. Among those of recent date are M. W. Wenner, *Modern Yemen* (Baltimore, 1967); Ahmad Mustafa Abu Hakima, *History of Eastern Arabia, 1750–1800* (Beirut, 1965); R. Bayly Winder, *Saudi Arabia in the Nineteenth Century* (New York, 1965); Robert G. Gandau, *Oman since 1856* (Princeton, 1967) and Ragei E. L. Mallakh, *Kuwait* (Chicago, 1968). Additionally, a number of accounts by travelers and articles in the *Encyclopedia of Islam* and in current journals (particularly oil), must suffice.

Neither is there a first-rate book on Jordan. F. G. Peake, *History and Tribes of Jordan* (Miami, 1958), and J. B. Glubb, *The Story of the Arab Legion* (London, 1948), are the product of the two creators of the military force of Jordan. A more current book is Aqil Hyder Hasan Abidi, *Jordan, A Political Study, 1948–1957* (New York, 1965).

THE PALESTINE PROBLEM has received several times the deluge of printer's ink as all the rest of the topics of this book combined. This author has contributed in W. R. Polk, D. Stamler and E. Asfour, *Backdrop to Tragedy, The Struggle for Palestine* (Boston, 1957). For the beginner, the book contains a comprehensive bibliography, a complete set of maps, a concise history, and the assembled viewpoints of an American, an English Zionist, and a Palestine Arab. Perhaps the best study of the political aspects of the Palestine problem is J. C. Hurewitz, *The Struggle for Palestine* (New York, 1950). R. Montagne, "Pour la paix en Palestine," *Politique etrangère,* 1938, is important for the Arab mood of the 1930's, and A. Grannot, *The Land System in Palestine* (London, 1949), is a valuable account of the basis of the problem in the mandate. The many official studies must be read and can be said to be about the best in academic standard and readability of any published. Cmd 5479: *Palestine Royal Commission Report* (London, 1937) and *A Survey of Palestine, Prepared in December 1945 and January 1946 for the Information of the Anglo-American Committee of Inquiry* (Jerusalem, 1946) are extremely valuable. They are followed by the *United Nations Special Committee on Palestine Report* (Lake Success, N.Y., 1947) in utility. G. Kirk, *The Middle East in the War* (London, 1952) and *The Middle East, 1945–1950* (London, 1954), are of great value not only for Palestine but for the whole Middle East.

German policies in the Middle East is the subject of Lukaz Hirszowicz, *The Third Reich and the Arab East* (London, 1966).

THE PERIOD OF TURBULENCE FOLLOWING WORLD WAR II, of *formal independence* and *coups,* is covered in a number of works. G. Kirk, just mentioned, is a good beginning. J. Kimche, *Seven Fallen Pillars* (New York, 1953), is a harsh but accurate description, and M. Alami, "The Lesson of Palestine," *Middle East Journal,* 1949, is an Arab indictment of Arab affairs. A. Hourani, "The Decline of the West in the Middle East," *International Affairs,* 1953–54, is a sensitive and deep study of Arab-European relations.

E. O'Ballance, *The Arab-Israeli War* (London, 1952), sets out the events of the Arab defeat in Palestine.

The Egyptian coup of 1952 and its aftermath is dealt with in a number of books. One of the best is Jean and Simon Lacouture, *Egypt in Transition* (New York, 1958). Nasser and his "team" are described in W. Wynn, *Nasser of Egypt, the Search for Dignity* (Cambridge, Mass., 1959), K. Wheelock, *Nasser's New Egypt* (New York, 1960), P. J. Vatikiotis, *The Egyptian Army in Politics* (Bloomington, Ind., 1961), and T. Little, *Egypt* (New York, 1958). The view from the inside is given in Gamal Abdul Nasser, *The Philosophy of the Revolution* (Washington, 1955), Mohammed Naguib, *Egypt's Destiny* (New York, 1955), and Anwar Sadat, *Revolt on the Nile* (London, 1957). A highly critical view of Nasser's Egypt is Hassan Riad, *L'Égypte Nassérienne* (Paris, 1964).

The situation in Syria is well described in G. Torrey, *Syrian Politics and the Military, 1945-1958* (Columbus, Ohio, 1964) and Patrick Seale, *The Struggle for Syria, 1945-1958* (London, 1965). Iraq has yet to receive comparable treatment. M. Ionides, *Divide and Lose* (London, 1960), and "Caractacus" (pseud.), *Revolution in Iraq* (London, 1959), give the best book-length accounts. Also see W. R. Polk, "The Lesson of Iraq," *Atlantic Monthly*, 1958, for the immediate aftermath of the July coup in Baghdad. King Hussein of Jordan, *Uneasy Lies the Head* (New York, 1962), describes this era of turbulence from another angle. Finally, W. R. Brown, "The Yemeni Dilemma," *Middle East Journal*, 1963, is the best account yet available on Yemen. Lebanon is the subject of Leonard Binder (ed.), *Politics in Lebanon* (New York, 1966) and the intra-Arab consequences are the subject of Malcolm Kerr, *The Arab Cold War* (New York, 1965).

The Suez crisis of 1956-1957 has been the subject of a number of books of which the most useful are Anthony Nutting, *No End of a Lesson* (London, 1967), which benefits from the author's inside knowledge at the British Cabinet; Anthony Moncrieff (ed.), *Suez: Ten Years After* (London, 1967), which synthesized the memories and views of many of the key participants; and Hugh Thomas, *Suez* (New York, 1967), which drew heavily upon the

BBC series by Moncrieff and upon Israeli sources. G. Wint and P. Calvocoressi, *Middle East Crisis* (London, 1957), gives a good account of the events leading up to the crisis while M. Adams, *Suez and After* (Boston, 1958), shows its effects. The U.S. Department of State publication *The Suez Canal Problem* (Washington 1956) gives many of the documents.

SOCIAL CHANGE is a newer subject than any other. The best book in the field is M. Halpern, *The Politics of Social Change* (Princeton, 1963). Gabriel S. Saab, *The Egyptian Agrarian Reform, 1952–1962* (New York, 1967), discusses the rural aspects of social change. One approach to analyzing social change is William R. Polk, "Analyzing Social Change: The Middle East," *Bulletin of the Atomic Scientists*, January 1967, and another is Manfred Halpern, *The Dialectics of Modernization* (forthcoming). H. el-Saaty, "The Middle Classes in Egypt" (Cairo, 1957), and S. Fisher (ed.), *The Role of the Military in the Middle East* (Columbus, Ohio, 1963) are also valuable. C. Issawi, "Economic and Social Foundations of Democracy in the Middle East," *International Affairs*, 1956, is a sobering account of the lack of a basis in the current scene for democratic institutions.

THE ECONOMY of the Arab countries is a relatively new subject. Though much useful work was done by the Middle East Supply Centre during World War II, the first comprehensive study was the Clapp Commission Report, United Nations Conciliation Commission for Palestine, *U.N. Economic Survey Mission for the Middle East* (Lake Success, N.Y., 1949). The rural base of the economy is the subject of D. Warriner's shocking and powerful books, *Land and Poverty in the Middle East* (London, 1948) and *Land Reform and Development in the Middle East* (London, 1957). On industry see A. A. I. El-Gritly, *The Structure of Modern Industry in Egypt* (Cairo, 1948), K. M. Langley, *The Industrialization of Iraq* (Cambridge, Mass., 1961), and A. D. Little, Inc., *A Plan for Industrial Development in Iraq* (Cambridge, Mass., 1956). On development efforts see W. R. Polk (ed.), *The Developmental Revolution* (Washington, 1963). The International Bank studies on *Iraq* (Baltimore, 1952), *Syria* (Baltimore, 1955), and *Jordan* (Baltimore, 1957) are comprehensive. E. Asfour, *Syria,*

Development and Monetary Policy (Cambridge, Mass., 1959) is about the best on Syria. C. Issawi, *Egypt in Revolution* (London, 1963), the third edition of a book first published in 1947, is in a class by itself. New and excellent studies are Donald Mead, *Growth and Structural Change in the Egyptian Economy* (Homewood, Illinois, 1967); Bent Hansen and Girgis A. Marzouk, *Development and Economic Policy in the UAR (Egypt)* (Amsterdam, 1965); C. Issawi and M. Yaganeh, *The Economics of Middle Eastern Oil* (New York, 1962); Ragaei el Mallakh, *Kuwait* (Chicago, 1968). Oil is the subject of a number of studies of which perhaps the best is S. H. Longrigg, *Oil in the Middle East* (London, 1954), and labor is studied in F. Harbison and I. Ibrahim, *Human Resources for Egyptian Enterprize* (New York, 1958). Surveys are available from the United Nations Department of Economic and Social Affairs, *Economic Development of the Middle East, 1945–54* (New York, 1955), with supplements in later years. Finally, the economic research center at the American University of Beirut publishes occasional papers on the economy of the Middle East.

ON THE ARABS IN THE WORLD one should be able to consult the Arabic literature. The American Council of Learned Societies started to make that possible, some years ago, when it began to publish a series of translations of significant Arabic political studies, in its Near Eastern translation program, Washington, 1953 and subsequently. N. Ziadeh, "Recent Arabic Literature on Arabism," *Middle East Journal*, 1952, provides a now-dated but useful survey. H. Z. Nuseibeh, *The Ideas of Arab Nationalism* (Ithaca, N.Y., 1956), is disappointing. W. R. Polk, *What the Arabs Think* (New York, 1952), is based on the thought of the "new men" of Iraq. A. Hourani, *Arabic Thought in the Liberal Age* (London, 1962), G. Antonius, *The Arab Awakening* (London, 1938), C. C. Adams, *Islam and Modernism in Egypt* (London, 1933), H. A. R. Gibb, *Modern Trends in Islam* (Chicago, 1947), and S. G. Haim (ed.), *Arab Nationalism* (Los Angeles, 1962), all deal with aspects of the background to contemporary developments. W. Z. Laqueur, *Communism and Nationalism in the Middle East* (London, 1956), and Laqueur (ed.), *The Middle East in Transition* (New York,

1958), bring the account more up to date. L. Binder, "Radical Reform Nationalism in Syria and Egypt," *Muslim World*, 1959, pushes an analysis of ideology about as far as it can go. The best account of the foreign policy of the Arabs is C. D. Cremeans, *The Arabs and the World* (New York, 1963).

UNITED STATES INTERESTS IN THE MIDDLE EAST are the subject of a large number of works. John C. Campbell, *Defense of the Middle East* (New York, 1960), and G. Stevens (ed.), *The United States and the Middle East* (Englewood Cliffs, N.J., 1964), are good beginnings. J. C. Hurewitz, *Middle East Dilemmas* (New York, 1953), discusses problems that are still with us. Official publications on United States policy include a series by H. N. Howard, *Development of U.S. Policy in the Near East, 1945–51* (Washington, 1952), *U.S. Policy in the Near East, South Asia and Africa, 1951–1952* (Washington, 1953), *U.S. Policy in the Near East during 1953* (Washington, 1954), *U.S. Policy in the Near East during 1954* (Washington, 1955), and *U.S. Policy in the Near East during 1955* (Washington, 1956). An essay by R. H. Nolte and W. R. Polk, "Toward a Policy for the Middle East," *Foreign Affairs Quarterly*, July 1958, may still have interest. John Badeau: *The American Approach to the Arab World* (New York, 1968) attempts to analyze the nature of American policy toward the Arabs in light of the experiences of the Kennedy administration.

Periodic collections of documents, as in *United States Policy in the Middle East, September 1956–June 1957* (Washington, 1957), hearings before congressional committees, and speeches printed in the State Department *Bulletin* provide source materials.

Attempts to influence American policy in the Middle East are detailed in *Activities of Non-Diplomatic Representatives of Foreign Principals in the United States*, Hearings Before the Committee on Foreign Relations, United States Senate, 88th Congress, 1st Session, U.S. Government Printing Office, 1963.

THE SOVIET ROLE IN THE MIDDLE EAST is described, historically, by Ivar Spector, *The Soviet Union and the Muslim World, 1917–1958* (Seattle, 1959), and W. Z. Laqueur, *The Soviet Union and the Middle East* (New York, 1959).

BRITISH INTERESTS are set out in The Royal Institute of International Affairs, *British Interests in the Mediterranean and the Middle East* (London, 1958).

A very good overview is Bernard Lewis, *The Middle East and the West* (New York, 1964).

The June 1967 war has already begun to spawn a motley array of memories, eye-witness accounts, and instant histories. It has not, as of the end of 1968, produced a single first rate full-scale study. The best by far, to date, is Michael Howard and Robert Hunter, *Israel and the Arab World: The Crisis of 1967* (London, 1967).

Index